Grade 4

Themes

- Making a Difference
- Science Fair
- Our Heritage, Our History
- Adaptations in Action
- National Treasures
- Literature Meets Art

McGraw Hill

mheducation.com/prek-12

Send all inquiries to:
McGraw Hill
8787 Orion Place
Columbus, OH 43240

ISBN: 978-1-26-558369-9
MHID: 1-26-558369-2

Printed in the United States of America

3 4 5 6 7 8 9 LWI 27 26 25 24 23 22

Program Authors

Carl Bereiter, Ph.D.
Professor Emeritus at the Ontario Institute for Studies in Education, University of Toronto

Andrew Biemiller, Ph.D.
Professor Emeritus at the Institute of Child Study, University of Toronto

Joe Campione, Ph.D.
Professor Emeritus in the Graduate School of Education at the University of California, Berkeley

Doug Fuchs, Ph.D.
Nicholas Hobbs Professor of Special Education and Human Development at Vanderbilt University

Lynn Fuchs, Ph.D.
Nicholas Hobbs Professor of Special Education and Human Development at Vanderbilt University

Steve Graham, Ph.D.
Mary Emily Warner Professor in the Mary Lou Fulton Teachers College at Arizona State University

Karen Harris, Ph.D.
Mary Emily Warner Professor in the Mary Lou Fulton Teachers College at Arizona State University

Jan Hirshberg, Ed.D.
Reading and writing consultant in Alexandria, Virginia

Anne McKeough, Ph.D.
Professor Emeritus in the Division of Applied Psychology at the University of Calgary

Marsha Roit, Ed.D.
Reading curricula expert and professional development consultant

Marlene Scardamalia, Ph.D.
Presidents' Chair in Education and Knowledge Technologies at the University of Toronto

Marcy Stein, Ph.D.
Professor and founding member of the Education Program at the University of Washington, Tacoma

Gerald H. Treadway Jr, Ph.D.
Professor Emeritus, School of Education at San Diego State University

UNIT 3 | Our Heritage, Our History

UNIT 5 National Treasures

Alice's Adventures in *Wonderland*

by Lewis Carroll
illustrated by John Joven

There was a table set out under a tree in front of the house, and the March Hare and the Hatter were having tea at it. A Dormouse was sitting between them, fast asleep, and the other two were using it as a cushion, resting their elbows on it, and talking over its head. Very uncomfortable for the Dormouse, thought Alice, only, as it's asleep, I suppose it doesn't mind.

The table was a large one, but the three were all crowded together at one corner of it: "No room! No room!" they cried out when they saw Alice coming.

"There's *plenty* of room!" said Alice indignantly, and she sat down in a large armchair at one end of the table.

"Have some punch," the March Hare said in an encouraging tone.

Alice looked all round the table, but there was nothing on it but tea and lemonade. "I don't see any punch," she remarked.

"There isn't any," said the March Hare.

"Then it wasn't very civil of you to offer it," said Alice angrily.

"It wasn't very civil of you to sit down without being invited," said the March Hare.

"I didn't know it was *your* table," said Alice. "It's laid for a great many more than three."

"Your hair wants cutting," said the Hatter. He had been looking at Alice for some time with great curiosity, and this was his first speech.

"You should learn not to make personal remarks," Alice said with some severity. "It's very rude."

The Hatter opened his eyes very wide on hearing this; but all he said was, "Why is a raven like a writing desk?"

Come, we shall have some fun now! thought Alice. I'm glad they've begun asking riddles. "I believe I can guess that," she added aloud.

"Do you mean that you think you can find out the answer to it?" said the March Hare.

"Exactly so," said Alice.

"Then you should say what you mean," the March Hare went on.

"I do," Alice hastily replied. "At least—at least I mean what I say—that's the same thing, you know."

"Not the same thing a bit!" said the Hatter. "You might just as well say that 'I see what I eat' is the same thing as 'I eat what I see'!"

"You might just as well say," added the March Hare, "that 'I like what I get' is the same thing as 'I get what I like'!"

"You might just as well say," added the Dormouse, which seemed to be talking in its sleep, "that 'I breathe when I sleep' is the same thing as 'I sleep when I breathe'!"

"It *is* the same thing with you," said the Hatter, and here the conversation dropped, and the party sat silent for a minute, while Alice thought over all she could remember about ravens and writing desks, which wasn't much.

The Hatter was the first to break the silence. "What day of the month is it?" he said, turning to Alice. He had taken his watch out of his pocket, and was looking at it uneasily, shaking it every now and then, and holding it to his ear.

Alice considered a little, and then said, "The fourth."

"Two days wrong!" sighed the Hatter. "I told you butter would not suit the works!" he added, looking angrily at the March Hare.

"It was the *best* butter," the March Hare meekly replied.

"Yes, but some crumbs must have got in as well," the Hatter grumbled. "You shouldn't have put it in with the bread knife."

The March Hare took the watch and looked at it gloomily, then he dipped it into his cup of tea, and looked at it again. But he could think of nothing better to say than his first remark: "It was the *best* butter, you know."

Alice had been looking over his shoulder with some curiosity. "What a funny watch!" she remarked. "It tells the day of the month, and doesn't tell what o'clock it is!"

"Why should it?" muttered the Hatter. "Does *your* watch tell you what year it is?"

"Of course not," Alice replied very readily, "but that's because it stays the same year for such a long time together."

"Which is just the case with *mine*," said the Hatter.

Alice felt dreadfully puzzled. The Hatter's remark seemed to have no meaning in it, and yet it was certainly English. "I don't quite understand you," she said, as politely as she could.

"The Dormouse is asleep again," said the Hatter, and he poured a little hot tea upon its nose.

The Dormouse shook its head impatiently, and said, without opening its eyes, "Of course, of course; just what I was going to remark myself."

"Have you guessed the riddle yet?" the Hatter said, turning to Alice again.

"No, I give it up," Alice replied. "What's the answer?"

"I haven't the slightest idea," said the Hatter.

"Nor I," said the March Hare.

Alice sighed wearily. "I think you might do something better with the time," she said, "than wasting it asking riddles that have no answers."

"If you knew Time as well as I do," said the Hatter, "you wouldn't talk about wasting *it*. It's *him*."

"I don't know what you mean," said Alice.

"Of course you don't!" the Hatter said, tossing his head contemptuously. "I daresay you never even spoke to Time!"

"Perhaps not," Alice cautiously replied, "but I know I have to beat time when I learn music."

"Ah! that accounts for it," said the Hatter. "He won't stand beating. Now, if you only kept on good terms with him, he'd do almost anything you liked with the clock. For instance, suppose it were nine o'clock in the morning, just time to begin lessons: you'd only have to whisper a hint to Time, and round goes the clock in a twinkling! Half past one, time for dinner!"

("I only wish it was," the March Hare said to itself in a whisper.)

"That would be grand, certainly," said Alice thoughtfully, "but then—I shouldn't be hungry for it, you know."

"Not at first, perhaps," said the Hatter, "but you could keep it to half past one as long as you liked."

"Is that the way *you* manage?" Alice asked.

The Hatter shook his head mournfully. "Not I!" he replied. "We quarreled last March—just before *he* went mad, you know"—pointing with his teaspoon at the March Hare—"it was at the great concert given by the Queen of Hearts, and I had to sing

'Twinkle, twinkle, little bat!
How I wonder what you're at'

You know the song, perhaps?"

"I've heard something like it," said Alice.

"It goes on, you know," the Hatter continued, "in this way: —

'Up above the world you fly,
Like a tea tray in the sky.
Twinkle, twinkle—'

Here the Dormouse shook itself, and began singing in its sleep, *"Twinkle, twinkle, twinkle, twinkle—"* and went on so long that they had to pinch it to make it stop.

"Well, I'd hardly finished the first verse," said the Hatter, "when the Queen jumped up and bawled out, 'He's murdering the time! Off with his head!'"

"How dreadfully savage!" exclaimed Alice.

"And ever since that," the Hatter went on in a mournful tone, "he won't do a thing I ask! It's always six o'clock now."

A bright idea came into Alice's head. "Is that the reason so many tea things are put out here?" she asked.

"Yes, that's it," said the Hatter with a sigh. "It's always teatime, and we've no time to wash the things between whiles."

"Then you keep moving round, I suppose?" said Alice.

"Exactly so," said the Hatter, "as the things get used up."

"But what happens when you come to the beginning again?" Alice ventured to ask.

"Suppose we change the subject," the March Hare interrupted, yawning. "I'm getting tired of this. I vote the young lady tells us a story."

"I'm afraid I don't know one," said Alice, rather alarmed at the proposal.

"Then the Dormouse shall!" they both cried. "Wake up, Dormouse!" And they pinched it on both sides at once.

The Dormouse slowly opened its eyes. "I wasn't asleep," it said in a hoarse, feeble voice. "I heard every word you fellows were saying."

"Tell us a story!" said the March Hare.

"Yes, please do!" pleaded Alice.

"And be quick about it," added the Hatter, "or you'll be asleep again before it's done."

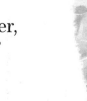

"Once upon a time there were three little sisters," the Dormouse began in a great hurry, "and their names were Elsie, Lacie, and Tillie; and they lived at the bottom of a well—"

"What did they live on?" said Alice, who always took a great interest in questions of eating and drinking.

"They lived on treacle," said the Dormouse, after thinking a minute or two.

"They couldn't have done that, you know," Alice gently remarked, "they'd have been ill."

"So they were," said the Dormouse. "*Very* ill."

Alice tried to fancy to herself what such an extraordinary way of living would be like, but it puzzled her too much, so she went on: "But why did they live at the bottom of a well?"

"Take some more tea," the March Hare said to Alice, very earnestly.

"I've had nothing yet," Alice replied in an offended tone, "so I can't take more."

"You mean you can't take *less*," said the Hatter. "It's very easy to take *more* than nothing."

"Nobody asked *your* opinion," said Alice.

"Who's making personal remarks now?" the Hatter asked triumphantly.

Alice did not quite know what to say to this, so she helped herself to some tea and bread and butter, and then turned to the Dormouse, and repeated her question. "Why did they live at the bottom of a well?"

The Dormouse again took a minute or two to think about it, and then said, "It was a treacle well."

"There's no such thing!" Alice was beginning very angrily, but the Hatter and the March Hare went "Sh! sh!" and the Dormouse sulkily remarked, "If you can't be civil, you'd better finish the story for yourself."

"No, please go on!" Alice said very humbly. "I won't interrupt again. I daresay there may be *one*."

"One, indeed!" said the Dormouse indignantly. However, it consented to go on. "And so these three little sisters—they were learning to draw, you know—"

"What did they draw?" said Alice, quite forgetting her promise.

"Treacle," said the Dormouse, without considering at all this time.

"I want a clean cup," interrupted the Hatter. "Let's all move one place on."

He moved on as he spoke, and the Dormouse followed him:
The March Hare moved into the Dormouse's place, and Alice
rather unwillingly took the place of the March Hare. The Hatter
was the only one who got any advantage from the change, and
Alice was a good deal worse off than before, as the March Hare
had just upset the milk jug into his plate.

Alice did not wish to offend the Dormouse again, so she began
very cautiously: "But I don't understand. Where did they draw the
treacle from?"

"You can draw water out of a water well," said the Hatter, "so I
should think you could draw treacle out of a treacle well—
eh, stupid!"

"But they were *in* the well," Alice said to the Dormouse, not
choosing to notice this last remark.

"Of course they were," said the Dormouse, "—well in."

This answer so confused poor Alice that she let the Dormouse go on for some time without interrupting it.

"They were learning to draw," the Dormouse went on, yawning and rubbing its eyes, for it was getting very sleepy, "and they drew all manner of things—everything that begins with an *M*—"

"Why with an *M*?" said Alice.

"Why not?" said the March Hare.

Alice was silent.

The Dormouse had closed its eyes by this time, and was going off into a doze; but, on being pinched by the Hatter, it woke up again with a little shriek, and went on: "—that begins with an M such as mousetraps, and the moon, and memory, and muchness— you know you say things are 'much of a muchness'—did you ever see such a thing as a drawing of a muchness?"

"Really, now you ask me," said Alice, very much confused, "I don't think—"

"Then you shouldn't talk," said the Hatter.

This piece of rudeness was more than Alice could bear: she got up in great disgust, and walked off; the Dormouse fell asleep instantly, and neither of the others took the least notice of her going, though she looked back once or twice, half hoping that they would call after her. The last time she saw them, they were trying to put the Dormouse into the teapot.

Write the answers to the questions on these pages in your notebook. Use evidence and details from the text to support your answers.

Did You Know?

Dormice are in a different scientific family from other mice, so they're not "true" mice. Dormice spend much of their time hibernating when the weather is cold. They are known for sleeping as much as six months out of the year. The Dormouse in "Alice's Adventures in Wonderland" is most likely a hazel dormouse, the only species native to England, where Louis Carroll lived.

Text Connections

1. The rules of time in Wonderland are different than in reality. Describe the effects these different rules seem to have on the characters, using details from the text.

2. Do you think the characters enjoy having tea all the time? Cite reasons from the text to support your answer.

3. Why do you think Dormouse is so sleepy?

4. Describe a time you had a disagreement with a friend, and compare how you worked it out with how the Hatter and Time have disagreed.

5. Compare and contrast the roles of powerful characters in the Read Aloud "Where the Mountain Meets the Moon" and "Alice's Adventures in Wonderland."

6. At the end of the selection, Alice leaves the party. Describe Alice's reasons for leaving and whether or not you would have left too and why.

Look Closer

Keys to Comprehension

1. Describe details related to how Alice is greeted when she first arrives at the tea party. Infer why the characters behaved the way they did toward each other.

2. Summarize the selection from "Alice's Adventures in Wonderland," and identify a theme of the selection.

Writer's Craft

3. Describe in depth one example of figurative language from this selection, or come up with or recall one from your own experience.

4. Describe details of the structure of "Alice's Adventures in Wonderland" that show it is prose and not a poem or play.

5. Reread the passage in which the characters change places at the table. What do you think the phrase "upset the milk jug" means, based on the context?

Concept Development

6. Describe how one of the illustrations helps you better understand the text.

Write

When the Hatter describes how Time came to be angry with him, he sings "Twinkle, Twinkle, Little Bat." This is a parody, or silly imitation, of the nursery rhyme, "Twinkle, Twinkle, Little Star." Reread this rhyme on page 7. Think of a song you know, and write your own parody of it. Use the same rhyming structure as Hatter's made-up rhyme.

Read this Social Studies Connection. You will answer the questions as a class.

Text Feature

A **bulleted list** calls out items that do not need to go in a particular order.

Essential Etiquette

Have you ever wondered why society values good behavior? The answer is to avoid conflict. Human beings live and work together in groups. If everyone thought only about themselves, humans would always fight. People live better when there is less conflict.

How does society decide what behavior is good? The answer lies in our systems of etiquette, or unspoken rules. These rules of civility are decided upon little by little over time throughout history. The following are descriptions of two basic systems of etiquette:

- **Formal Etiquette.** These are rules of social behavior used by governments, by businesses, and at formal parties. Following formal etiquette is complicated and important. It is so complicated that governments, businesses, and formal party planners may hire experts in etiquette. These experts make sure that guests are treated the way they expect to be treated. Such care can help make peace, lead to new business, and make happy memories.
- **Common Manners.** These are the rules of behavior used in everyday life by people in all areas of society. As with formal etiquette, having good manners shows other people that one cares about them. Such care leads to valuable friendships and happy, healthy families.

These two systems of good behavior do not tell the whole story. Human societies have had many different codes of conduct. All well-organized societies run smoothly because of systems that govern, or decide, good behavior. It's how they stay afloat!

These photos show different ways of "shaking" hands. Shaking hands has been a polite way of greeting one another throughout history.

1. Compare and contrast formal etiquette and common manners.

2. Why and how do societies develop systems of manners?

3. What other codes of conduct or systems of manners can you think of?

 Go Digital

Research systems of etiquette that exist around the world. How do people greet each other? How do they say good-bye? What behaviors are considered polite or impolite?

BIG Idea

What can we do to make a difference?

Theme Connections

How are these people making a difference?

 Background Builder Video
connected.mcgraw-hill.com

Genre Realistic Fiction

Essential Question
How can making a difference start at home?

Ava and Pip

by Carol Weston
illustrated by Olga and Aleksy Ivanov

*The party plans of painfully shy Pip are ruined by a
new, popular girl at school. Her younger sister, Ava, feels
determined to help Pip feel better. Ava pens a story about
Pip's snub and Bea, the girl who caused it, for a school
assignment. Ava titles her story "Sting of the Queen Bee." To
Ava's surprise, it captures the attention of her school. It also
attracts the wrath of Bea. However, after confronting Ava
about her story and learning why she penned it,
Bea decides to help. Bea and Ava work together
to make a difference in Pip's life.*

11/4
Afternoon

Dear Diary,

At 4, Pip and I were in the living room. I was having big problems doing decimals, and she was having no problems doing fractions. I casually said, "Bea's coming over."

"Bea?" Pip said. "Did you say *Bea*?"

"Remember 'Sting of the Queen Bee'?"

"Uh, *yeah*."

"Well, Bea thought it was mean that I thought she was mean."

"Wait, wait, wait! You *talked* to her? To Bea Bates?"

I told Pip that Bea called and said she hadn't known Pip was having a party.

Pip stared at me, and I wondered if I'd been a total traitor.

"And you believed that little phony?" Pip said.

"I did. I do." I looked at her. "I know I called her a thief, but now I think she's the opposite. She's a very giving person."

"Oh, Ava! *You're* a very gullible person!" Pip threw her book down and started stomping around the room.

Since Aesop says honesty is the best policy, I told Pip the truth. "Bea said she helped her brother 'come out of his shell' and now she wants to try her method on you."

"Are you kidding?! I don't need her help! Or her *method*!" Pip said "method" as if she were saying "poison" or "booger" or "throw up." I didn't say anything, and Pip said, "Seriously, Ava, thanks a lot! I bet she's just looking for a new way to humiliate me!"

"I don't think so."

"What's she planning to do anyway? Sprinkle me with popularity powder?" I could tell that Pip was mad, but also a tiny bit curious.

"She isn't planning to *do* anything. She has tips for *you* to do. Pointers." I didn't mention all our meetings or our five-week master plan.

"Thanks, but no thanks. I do not need a personality transplant."

I wanted to shout, "Yes, you do!" But I just sat there and didn't say another word.

At 4:05, I started wondering if Bea was even coming. "Where's Dad, anyway?" I asked.

"Upstairs, putting new wallpaper in the bathroom. He said he had to repaper it and then he looked all happy, because, you know, R-E-P-A-P-E-R. You know what? I'm going to go help him." She started walking upstairs.

The doorbell rang.

Pip stood frozen in place like a statue. It rang again. I waited. Pip waited. It rang one more time. "Well," Pip finally said, "aren't you planning on opening the door for Bossy Bea, your new best friend?"

I did, and Bea burst in holding a bike helmet. "Hi!" *Bea* was *bea*ming. "How's it going?" she said, walking right in. "Pip, I hope Ava told you I'm sorry about your birthday. I had no clue we were both giving a party on the same day."

Pip didn't say anything, but since she usually doesn't, I couldn't tell what she was thinking.

"Want some gum?" Bea said and offered us some pieces.

"What flavor?" I asked.

"Lemon lime," she said. I took a piece, but Pip didn't.

"Pip," Bea began, "Ava says you're a good student and good artist, but that you're a little shy."

Pip glared at me, and I basically died.

"I was thinking," Bea continued, "that you should take another look at the other kids at school. They're not Olympic athletes or famous musicians or anything. Most are just regular." Now Bea turned to me. "So that's why Ava and I think you could put yourself out there a little more."

When Bea said my name again, I could feel Pip's eyes burning a hole in my head.

I didn't want to upset her, and I felt bad that she was being even more speechless than usual, if that's possible.

Finally Pip started talking. "Listen, Bea, thanks for the apology but—"

"My brother used to be shy," Bea jumped in. "Pip, I think I can help you too. Just give it a try?"

Pip looked cornered. She had obviously not been expecting this pep (P-E-P) talk. Should I have prepared her? Warned her?

"Give *what* a try?" she said.

"Your first assignment."

Pip frowned. "I have enough homework."

"C'mon. Just let me explain?"

Pip shrugged, but it was obvious that she was listening.

"Okay, every day this week," Bea began, "all you have to do is smile at one person you don't usually smile at. It can be a teacher. Or a cashier. Or someone's mom or dad."

Pip didn't say anything, so Bea kept going.

"It can be someone next to you in line, or someone you'll never see again. Or even someone who looks like he or she could use a smile. I'll stop by next week, and you can tell me how it went."

"That's it?" Pip said.

"That's it."

"Just smile?"

"Well, you could try to make a little eye contact too."

Pip looked at me, and our eyes made a little contact. Hers were saying, "Ava, I might have to chop you up into tiny pieces."

"You don't have to be someone you're not," Bea reassured Pip. "Just seven little smiles is all we're asking."

She handed Pip the strip of paper. Pip looked at it suspiciously, as if it really had been dipped in poison or boogers or throw up. I knew she recognized the handwriting—and besides, the turquoise was a dead giveaway. I hoped Pip wouldn't be too mad that I'd opened our home to a girl whose guts, one month ago, we'd both decided we hated.

"Mind if I get a glass of water?" Bea asked. We went to the kitchen, and she got herself a glass. "Thanks," she said and put it in the sink. "I'll be back in a week."

After she left, Pip said, "Who does she think she is, anyway?"

"I don't know," I said, hoping Pip felt at least a teensy bit flattered. It wasn't every day that a popular seventh-grader dropped by.

Ava with Hope

11/7
Afternoon

Dear Diary,

After reading (and rereading) a bunch of fables, I decided to write about "The North Wind and the Sun." It's about a competition between the wind and the sun on who can make a traveler take off his coat first. The wind blows and blows as hard as it can, but the more it blows, the more tightly the traveler holds on to his coat. Then the sun takes a turn, and instead of using all its might, it just shines and shines warmly and normally. Next thing you know, the traveler removes his coat. The moral? "Kindness wins where force fails."

Here's what I think: when I wrote that Queen Bee story, I thought I was being *kind*, but I was really being *blind*.

Here's what else I think: you can't force people to change, but you can help them try. Like, Bea and I aren't *forcing* Pip out of her shell, but if she does the assignments, maybe she'll inch out on her own, step by step.

Speaking of Pip, this morning I saw her smile! Our postman rang the doorbell and handed her a bunch of letters. Instead of just taking them silently, she smiled and even said, "Thank you." The postman's eyes got big, and he said, "You're welcome." Then he shot *me* a look that said, "I didn't know your sister could talk."

That may not sound like much to you, Diary, but to me it felt like a mini miracle.

Ava the Amazed

11/11 (a palindrome date)

After School

Dear Diary,

The doorbell rang. I put down *Charlotte's Web* (which is short), and Pip put down *A Tree Grows in Brooklyn* (which is long), and we let Bea in.

"Hi, Ava! Hi, Pip! How'd it go this week?" she said.

Pip stared at Bea as if she were deciding whether or not to smile at her. But Bea just started taking off her gloves, scarf, jacket, and bike helmet.

"It's ccccold out!" she said, and for some reason, that seemed to warm Pip up.

We talked a little about the wind and rain, and then Bea plunked herself on the sofa. "Want some gum?" she asked, and Pip and I each took a piece. It was raspberry mint, which is my favorite after bubblemint.

"So who'd you smile at?" Bea asked Pip with a smile.

"A few people."

"A few? Or seven?"

"Five."

"Well, spit it out. . ."

I imagined Pip spitting (yuck!), but Pip started to answer. "Let's see, on Thursday, I smiled at Ava's friend Maybelle. On Friday, I smiled at the gym teacher, but I don't think she noticed. On Saturday, I smiled at our postman. And on Monday, I smiled at my mom's boss, and he actually told our mom."

"Positive reinforcement!" Bea said, and I wondered how positive she was going to feel once she found out that our stories had gotten posted online.

"On Tuesday," Pip continued, "I smiled at a girl, Nadifa, who just moved here from Somalia. She smiled back and sat by me at lunch. But it was a little awkward because neither of us knew what to say."

"No one ever died of awkwardness," Bea said. "Overall, how did it feel?"

"Overall, pretty good," Pip admitted.

"You think you can keep smiling this week and do a whole new assignment?"

"Depends on the assignment," Pip said.

"Here it is. When you see your reflection in a mirror, I want you to say, 'You are totally awesome!'"

"No way!" Pip said.

"Yes way. But don't worry, not loudly! Mostly just say it to yourself. Or say it in your head. It'll boost your confidence."

"My confidence?" Pip repeated. "No. Sorry. I can't. I really can't."

"Yes, you can! You can do anything!"

"I'd feel too stupid." Pip looked at me for backup, but I stared straight down at my shoelaces.

"Never question your life coach," Bea said. "It may sound weird, but it works. Instead of letting shyness conquer you, you have to conquer it!" She handed Pip the second strip of yellow paper.

Pip looked at me and read the words aloud:

Week Two:
Every time you see your reflection, tell yourself,
"You are totally awesome!"

She rolled her eyes, so Bea added, "If you'd rather give yourself a specific compliment, like 'I draw well,' or 'I'm good in school,' that would be okay too."

Pip shrugged, and Bea shrugged back, so I shrugged too.

"I'll try," Pip said softly, and I wanted to jump up and down shouting, "Y-A-Y!"

"Great," Bea said. "Okay, same time next week!" She started putting back on her gloves, scarf, jacket, and bike helmet, and then got on her bike and rode off.

When she was out of sight, Pip said, "Seriously, Ava, why couldn't you have just minded your own business?"

I didn't know whether to say, "I don't have a business," or "C'mon, it's kind of working," or "Can't you see I have worries of my own?"

So I pulled a Pip—I kept quiet.

Ava,
Agitated

Middle-of-the-Night

Dear Diary,

I just got out of bed and turned on my lamp. I hope Mom and Dad don't notice and tell me to turn it off and go to sleep, but there's something else I want to tell you.

In gym we combined classes and this lady came to teach us yoga. She talked about "breathing" and "balance," and it was actually pretty calming. Then she said to pretend we were trees.

First, we stood on our right leg and lifted our left foot in the air and raised our arm-branches and wriggled our finger-leaves and tried not to fall. Then we switched and stood on our left leg and lifted our right foot in the air and raised our arm-branches and wriggled our finger-leaves and tried not to fall.

It was hard!

Most of us couldn't help wriggling and jiggling, and some of us (including me) kept putting our feet down so we wouldn't keel over. A few of us did fall!

Only Chuck had no problem standing perfectly still. I bet he could have stood there like a tree all day long. He's either extra coordinated . . . or part egret?

Well, the yoga instructor told us to form a circle, stand on one leg, hold hands, and make a "group tree." (She should have said "forest.") I was in between Maybelle and Alex, and as I reached for their hands, I started to giggle, but the instructor said, "No giggling, and please close your eyes."

Next thing you know, we were all in a circle with our eyes shut.

"Some of you are still swaying, like trees in a breeze," the instructor said. "But notice how you are holding each other up and supporting one another. Be aware that you can trust each other, and know that you will not let each other fall."

The amazing thing was: she was right! All of us (except Chuck) kept wobbling, but not one kid fell! Not one! Alex and I almost fell, but we both "supported" each other and even shared a teeny tiny half-smile.

Right now, under my covers, I'm thinking that even though my plate is chock-full of worries, and even though Pip can sometimes be annoying, I'm glad that Bea and I are helping her.

She's my sister, after all, and I'm not going to let her fall.

Ava Wren, Yoga Tree

Write the answers to the questions on these pages in your notebook. Use evidence and details from the text to support your answers.

Text Connections

1. Contrast Pip's and Ava's opinions about Bea at the beginning of the selection.

2. Why do you think Bea's saying, "It's ccccold out!" makes Pip feel friendlier toward her?

3. Describe a time when you encouraged someone else. Compare how you felt with the way that Ava feels at the end of the selection.

4. Ava tells Pip the truth about Bea's plan because "honesty is the best policy." Do you think Pip's reaction proves Ava's belief is correct? Why or why not?

5. Bea's first assignment for Pip is just to try smiling at people. What effect does smiling have on other people? Give a real-world example.

6. Compare and contrast an act of bravery from the Read Aloud "Saving the City Below the Sea" to one from "Ava and Pip." Why do you think these are brave actions?

Did You Know?

Bea called herself Pip's "life coach." This is a career some adults choose. Life coaches ask people questions and challenge them. By working with life coaches, people get help with solving job problems, choosing life goals, and better understanding themselves.

Look Closer

Keys to Comprehension

1. Describe Ava's personality in depth, using examples from the text.

2. Infer how Pip's attitude toward Bea is different when Bea comes back a second time. Give a specific example from the text to support your answer.

3. Summarize the steps Bea takes to help Pip, and explain why Bea thinks they will work.

Writer's Craft

4. Explain what Ava means when she says that Bea helped her brother "come out of his shell."

5. This story is written as a series of diary entries. What point of view is this, and how does it help you better understand Ava?

Concept Development

6. Explain the similarity between "The North Wind and the Sun," as described by Ava, and Bea's method of encouraging Pip, as Ava sees it.

Read this Social Studies Connection. You will answer the questions as a class.

Text Feature

A **caption** tells about a photograph and adds information to an article or story.

A Diary that Lives On

In "Ava and Pip," the author tells Ava's story through her diary entries. Although this diary is fictional, real-life diaries have also been published. They give us a peek into the private thoughts of people from different time periods. These diaries have evolved into irreplaceable sources of knowledge about those time periods.

The earliest known diaries date to the Roman Empire. Early diaries were primarily used to document events and daily chores. In the seventeenth century, diaries became more popular as books became more accessible and more people learned to read and write. As a result, people began using diaries not only to write about their daily observations, but also about their personal thoughts and feelings.

This more personal use for a diary has given scholars a reliable and intimate view of people's experiences from various time periods. Though most diaries are never seen by the public, museums have elected to publish and display the diaries and journals of some historical figures. These important texts provide a window into the private lives and experiences of people who came before us.

Diaries are often made of paper and bound in leather for reinforcement. However, a physical diary is not always necessary in today's world. People have turned to the Internet to record their everyday thoughts and feelings. Such online publications are sometimes known as web logs, or blogs. Some authors of blogs choose to share their writing, making it possible for us to read about people's experiences from all over the world.

People have traditionally kept diaries in blank books like this one, and many people now keep online or electronic diaries.

1. Why do people read diaries from long ago?

2. Why is the past important to us today?

3. Think about some of your own writings that you have saved. How are they part of human history?

 Go Digital

Archives are collections of historical documents like diaries and letters. Research the types of documents that are saved in state and national historical archives. Why do you think those types of documents are worth saving?

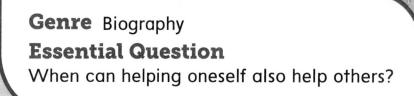

Genre Biography
Essential Question
When can helping oneself also help others?

LOUIS BRAILLE'S GIFT TO THE BLIND

by Tanya Anderson
illustrated by Juan Manuel Moreno

On January 4, 1809, a boy was born in the rural town of Coupvray, France, not far from Paris. He was the youngest child of Simon-René and Monique Braille. They named the child Louis. He was tiny and frail, and in those days, babies like Louis often died, but Louis grew stronger and delighted his parents. He was curious and bright and loved investigating his father's workshop.

Louis's father was a harness maker. He used leather and sharp tools to make straps, bridles, and collars for horses. One day while his father was busy with a customer, three-year-old Louis went into the workshop and began playing. He tried to do what he had seen his father do. Louis picked up an awl, a sharp tool that pokes holes in leather, and pushed it into a piece of tough leather. The awl slipped. Louis screamed, and his parents ran to him.

His right eye was bleeding badly, and Louis cried out from the pain. His parents did their best to clean the wound, but infection set in and then spread to Louis's left eye. Over the next two years, his vision gradually became completely dark.

In those days, blind people had no hope of an education or a way to make a good living. Most of them became beggars. Louis's parents were happy when the local school allowed Louis to attend. A sighted boy took Louis to and from school every day.

The teacher could tell Louis was an intelligent child. However, when the other children were reading and writing, Louis had no way to take part.

A local priest and official told Louis's parents about a boarding school in Paris that educated poor, blind children, the Royal Institute for Blind Youth. Paris was a four-hour carriage ride away. If Louis were accepted, he would have to live at the school most of the year. He was only ten years old. Louis's parents were certain the school was best for their son, so they decided to send him there. On February 15, 1819, Louis and his father boarded a carriage for Paris.

The city was so different from Louis's country home. Paris was noisy and smelled terrible. The school building was old, damp, and cold. At one time, it had been a prison! The students had to climb long, winding staircases to their classes and dormitory rooms. The unsanitary water they used was piped in from the nearby Seine River. Many of the students, including Louis, became ill while they lived there.

Even so, Louis did well at the school. The students learned to read by using books with raised, or embossed, letters they could feel with their fingers. The books were heavy and expensive, and this method of reading was difficult. Writing was not easy to learn, either, because the students could not see the words they were creating.

The school focused on other studies, though. Louis learned geography by touching embossed maps. He could feel mountains, boundaries, rivers, and oceans. Students learned music, too, and practiced on many different instruments. Many students became quite good, including Louis, who excelled at playing the piano and organ. The school also provided training in trades that could help students someday earn a living. These trades included basket weaving, slipper making, knitting, running a printing press, and weaving cane strips to make chair seats.

When Louis was twelve years old, a man came to his school. Captain Charles Barbier had invented a code, called night writing, for the French military to use to pass messages in the dark. The code was based on sets of up to twelve dots and dashes that were punched into cardboard. Certain sets of the dots and dashes represented different sounds. The sounds formed words. Barbier hoped his invention would help the blind learn to read and write. When Louis touched the raised symbols, he grew excited. Other students found the system difficult, but for him, this method worked! Louis practiced reading and writing sentences with his roommate and lifelong friend, Gabriel Gauthier. They used the tools Barbier had introduced: a board with metal strips that lay over thick paper and a stylus, or a pointed stick.

Louis was thrilled with Barbier's code, but he knew it was not perfect. It was too complicated for most blind people to use, mainly because it was based on sounds, not letters. It worked with French but would not work well in other languages. In addition, Barbier's code did not include numbers, punctuation, or musical symbols.

Other students gave up on Barbier's invention. Louis would not give up. He was fascinated by the idea of using dots instead of letters to form words. The young boy began to think of ways he could improve the captain's system and started to work on his own design. Soon he was ready to share his ideas and experiments with the school's director, Dr. André Pignier.

Pignier was impressed with Louis's efforts. He decided to tell Barbier about this young student who was working on his code. Of course, Barbier wanted to find out more, so he came to the school to meet twelve-year-old Louis Braille.

Louis was prepared for the meeting. He understood that Barbier was a powerful man who thought he was helping the blind with his invention. Louis was polite and praised the man for creating such a useful code. Then he humbly suggested it could be improved. Barbier was not used to having someone, especially a child, question him. Still, he listened to Louis's ideas but remained certain his own method of dots and dashes should not be changed.

For a while, Louis kept working on the project, hoping to create a technique that worked better than Barbier's system. At night, Gabriel often awoke to the sound of Louis pushing his stylus through paper. Some nights, Louis never slept at all.

When Louis returned to his home in Coupvray, he took his work with him. On warm summer days, he used a cane to walk the familiar paths around town. Sometimes he sat on a grassy hill, his head bent over a writing board. People passing by remembered the boy and shouted greetings to him. Louis was a town favorite.

At school, Louis persevered with his studies, excelling at almost everything he did. But nothing satisfied his need to keep trying to improve Barbier's code. Louis was driven to perfect a method that would allow the blind to read and write, to become as literate as people with sight.

Louis began to grow frustrated with his efforts. Perhaps the methods the school already used were the best ways to teach the blind. When he was losing hope, Louis found inspiration in another visitor.

Long before Louis was born, a man named Valentin Haüy had founded Louis's school. When Haüy had grown older and become blind himself, the school honored him with a concert. The choir sang, and the musicians played. Haüy spoke to them all. He reminded them that, despite some successes, much more needed to be done to help the blind live better lives. The day of the concert Louis met Haüy, who took Louis's hands into his own. At that moment, Louis felt it was his calling to give the gift of reading and writing to the blind.

Over the next few years, Louis worked on his new code. In the end, the only similarity between his code and Barbier's was the use of dots. Louis eliminated the dashes, because they could be mistaken as two dots. Another difference was that Louis's code used dots to represent letters, not sounds. He was also able to create codes for numbers, punctuation, and even musical notes.

The new code Louis devised consisted of two columns of three vertical dots—six dots, not twelve. One braille cell looks like this:

:. .:
:. .:
:. .:

Finally, Louis was ready to share his invention with Pignier. Louis wanted to show the director how his code worked, so he prepared an exercise.

He asked Pignier to read from any book he wanted— to read slowly and distinctly. As the director read aloud, Louis used his board and stylus to write what he heard.

When Pignier finished reading, Louis turned over the paper and ran his fingers across the dots he had made. He read, word for word, the exact text from Pignier's book. Impressed, but not convinced, Pignier repeated the exercise. Once again, Louis wrote and read precisely what Pignier had read aloud. The director stood up and hugged Louis. He had done it!

The entire school learned Louis's new code. Students murmured with excitement as they quickly learned to read and write using only six little dots. Louis even invented a new board to make writing easier. It had a slide rule with cut out sections. Students positioned the stylus in the sections to punch dots in the correct places on the paper beneath. Blind people now could write as quickly as sighted people.

At seventeen, Louis began teaching at the school. He perfected what came to be known as the braille system, and when he issued a public piece about his method, Louis thanked everyone who had helped him. He especially named Charles Barbier, saying that his invention gave Louis the idea to begin working on his system.

Today the braille system is used throughout the world, in many languages. Louis Braille gave the blind exactly what they needed: a way to learn and communicate using the written word.

Write the answers to the questions on these pages in your notebook. Use evidence and details from the text to support your answers.

Text Connections

1. Why did Louis Braille move to Paris as a child?

2. Describe three problems with Captain Barbier's writing system.

3. Biographers have noted Louis Braille had a stubborn personality. Give examples from Braille's life to support the benefits of this character trait.

4. Valentin Haüy's life of service inspired Braille to work to help others. Describe a time someone else inspired you to do something difficult.

5. Recall "Ava and Pip" from Lesson 1. Do you think Ava or Louis Braille made the bigger sacrifice in order to help other people? Explain your answer, using examples from the selections.

6. Consider how Braille's achievement led to improved access to learning for blind people. Do you think braille writing is still as important today as it was in his time? Why or why not?

Did You Know?

People use braille writing worldwide, but getting books published in braille has sometimes been tough. In 2016, the Marrakesh Treaty was put into effect. A treaty is a kind of agreement. This one lets countries easily publish and share books in formats like braille.

Look Closer

Keys to Comprehension

1. Describe two drawbacks of Captain Barbier's system, and infer why they were a problem.

2. Explain the idea that came to Louis Braille, and how it led him to finally invent the braille writing system.

Writer's Craft

3. "Pass the torch" is a common idiom to describe working toward a goal where another has left off. Describe how this idiom might be used to describe Braille's experience in regard to Haüy.

4. Explain whether "Louis Braille's Gift to the Blind" has a compare-and-contrast structure or a chronological order structure, and how you know.

Concept Development

5. Did the Royal Institute for Blind Youth teach only boys? How do you know?

6. How does the author of "Louis Braille's Gift to the Blind" give evidence that "Louis would not give up"?

Write

Think of an invention that could make life easier for others. Write a description of your idea. Then, look at page 44. There is a simple graphic showing how one Braille cell looks. Add a small graphic or illustration to show your invention.

Text Feature

A **figure** in informational text is an illustration, a table, or a photograph that gives more information about the text.

How to Use a Braille Slate and Stylus

A braille letter is made using a rectangular cell. A cell has two columns of three raised dots. The dots in a braille cell represent each letter (see figure 1).

So how do people write using braille? A slate and stylus is the oldest writing tool. A braille slate has a hinge on one side. It has rows of openings, or braille cells. A stylus has a metal point for punching dots (see figure 2).

Today there are also certain kinds of braille-writing machines. However, a slate is easy to take places. People can use it in places where there is no electricity.

To make a braille letter *a*, follow these steps:

1. Place the slate with the hinge on the left.
2. Open the slate like a book. Put a piece of braille paper inside. Close the slate.
3. When you write in braille, you write from right to left. This means you should start with your stylus in the top right braille cell.
4. Each cell has ridges on its edge. They help you find the six dot positions. When writing, dots 1 through 3 are in the right column. Dots 4 through 6 are in the left column.
5. Put the stylus at the top of the right column. Punch to form dot 1.
6. Open the slate and flip the paper over. Feel the braille letter *a* with your fingertips.

Figure 1. Lowercase braille alphabet

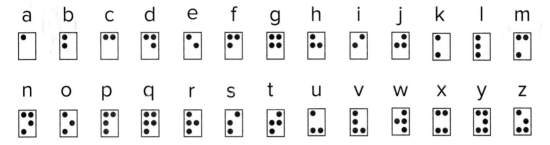

Figure 2. Braille slate and stylus

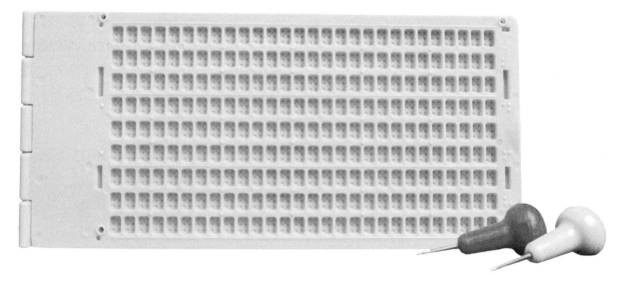

1. How are braille letters formed?

2. Braille-writing machines are newer technology. Are these machines always more useful than a braille slate and stylus? Why or why not?

3. Pretend you are in charge of the braille-writing equipment for a school. How might you manage both of these writing technologies so that the greatest number of students benefit?

 Go Digital

Basic braille spells out every letter. Because books in basic braille are very long, people came up with other braille forms. Research contracted braille and Nemeth Braille Code. When do people use these types of braille?

Genre Fantasy

Essential Question
What can friends do to help each other?

Charlotte's Web

by E. B. White
illustrated by Garth Williams

A young pig, Wilbur, raised up from being the runt of his litter by a kind girl named Fern Arable, has just settled into a new life at a new home. After suffering a period of awful loneliness, he has become acquainted with the other animals on the Zuckerman farm. Templeton the rat, a small flock of sheep, and a small family of geese live together with Wilbur in the cellar of a barn. Wilbur has even found a special friend in Charlotte, a common gray spider who spins her web in the barn doorway.

Wilbur grows and grows, as young pigs do, until one day an old sheep informs him of his fate. Wilbur is to be fattened up and eaten at a feast! Distraught, Wilbur cries and cries over this news, but kind Charlotte is wise. She calms Wilbur and promises to think of a way to save him.

Day after day the spider waited, head-down, for an idea to come to her. Hour by hour she sat motionless, deep in thought. Having promised Wilbur that she would save his life, she was determined to keep her promise.

Charlotte was naturally patient. She knew from experience that if she waited long enough, a fly would come to her web; and she felt sure that if she thought long enough about Wilbur's problem, an idea would come to her mind.

Finally, one morning toward the middle of July, the idea came. "Why, how perfectly simple!" she said to herself. "The way to save Wilbur's life is to play a trick on Zuckerman. If I can fool a bug," thought Charlotte, "I can surely fool a man. People are not as smart as bugs."

Wilbur walked into his yard just at that moment.

"What are you thinking about, Charlotte?" he asked.

"I was just thinking," said the spider, "that people are very gullible."

"What does 'gullible' mean?"

"Easy to fool," said Charlotte.

"That's a mercy," replied Wilbur, and he lay down in the shade of his fence and went fast asleep. The spider, however, stayed wide awake, gazing affectionately at him and making plans for his future. Summer was half gone. She knew she didn't have much time.

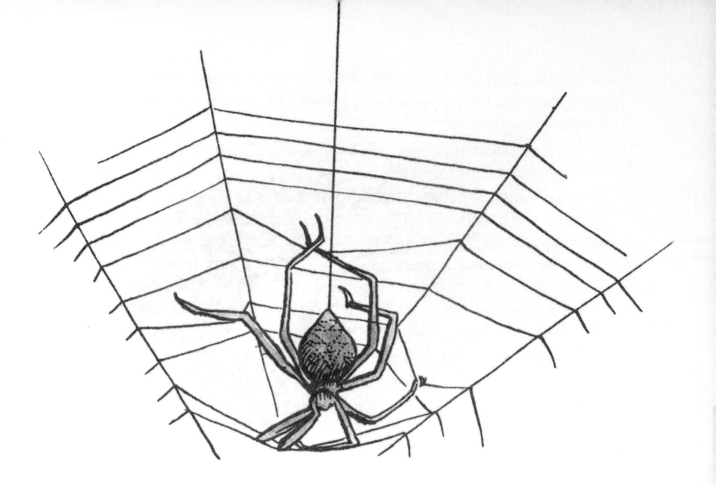

The afternoon passed, and evening came. Shadows lengthened. The cool and kindly breath of evening entered through doors and windows. Astride her web, Charlotte sat moodily eating a horsefly and thinking about the future. After a while she bestirred herself.

She descended to the center of the web and there she began to cut some of her lines. She worked slowly but steadily while the other creatures drowsed. None of the others, not even the goose, noticed that she was at work. Deep in his soft bed, Wilbur snoozed. Over in their favorite corner, the goslings whistled a night song.

Charlotte tore quite a section out of her web, leaving an open space in the middle. Then she started weaving something to take the place of the threads she had removed. When Templeton got back from the dump, around midnight, the spider was still at work.

The next day was foggy. Everything on the farm was dripping wet. The grass looked like a magic carpet. The asparagus patch looked like a silver forest.

On foggy mornings, Charlotte's web was truly a thing of beauty. This morning each thin strand was decorated with dozens of tiny beads of water. The web glistened in the light and made a pattern of loveliness and mystery, like a delicate veil. Even Lurvy, who wasn't particularly interested in beauty, noticed the web when he came with the pig's breakfast. He noted how clearly it showed up and he noted how big and carefully built it was. And then he took another look and he saw something that made him set his pail down. There, in the center of the web, neatly woven in block letters, was a message. It said:

SOME PIG!

Lurvy felt weak. He brushed his hand across his eyes and stared harder at Charlotte's web.

"I'm seeing things," he whispered. He dropped to his knees and uttered a short prayer. Then, forgetting all about Wilbur's breakfast, he walked back to the house and called Mr. Zuckerman.

"I think you'd better come down to the pigpen," he said.

"What's the trouble?" asked Mr. Zuckerman. "Anything wrong with the pig?"

"N-not exactly," said Lurvy. "Come and see for yourself."

The two men walked silently down to Wilbur's yard. Lurvy pointed to the spider's web. "Do you see what I see?" he asked.

Zuckerman stared at the writing on the web. Then he murmured the words "Some Pig." Then he looked at Lurvy. Then they both began to tremble. Charlotte, sleepy after her night's exertions, smiled as she watched. Wilbur came and stood directly under the web.

"Some pig!" muttered Lurvy in a low voice.

"Some pig!" whispered Mr. Zuckerman. They stared and stared for a long time at Wilbur. Then they stared at Charlotte.

"You don't suppose that that spider . . ." began Mr. Zuckerman— but he shook his head and didn't finish the sentence. Instead, he walked solemnly back up to the house and spoke to his wife. "Edith, something has happened," he said, in a weak voice. He went into the living room and sat down, and Mrs. Zuckerman followed.

"I've got something to tell you, Edith," he said. "You better sit down."

Mrs. Zuckerman sank into a chair. She looked pale and frightened.

"Edith," he said, trying to keep his voice steady, "I think you had best be told that we have a very unusual pig."

A look of complete bewilderment came over Mrs. Zuckerman's face. "Homer Zuckerman, what in the world are you talking about?" she said.

"This is a very serious thing, Edith," he replied. "Our pig is completely out of the ordinary."

"What's unusual about the pig?" asked Mrs. Zuckerman, who was beginning to recover from her scare.

"Well, I don't really know yet," said Mr. Zuckerman. "But we have received a sign, Edith—a mysterious sign. A miracle has happened on this farm. There is a large spider's web in the doorway of the barn cellar, right over the pigpen, and when Lurvy went to feed the pig this morning, he noticed the web because it was foggy, and you know how a spider's web looks very distinct in a fog. And right spang in the middle of the web there were the words 'Some Pig.' The words were woven right into the web. They were actually part of the web, Edith. I know, because I have been down there and seen them. It says, 'Some Pig,' just as clear as clear can be. There can be no mistake about it. A miracle has happened and a sign has occurred here on earth, right on our farm, and we have no ordinary pig."

"Well," said Mrs. Zuckerman, "it seems to me you're a little off. It seems to me we have no ordinary *spider*."

"Oh, no," said Zuckerman. "It's the pig that's unusual. It says so, right there in the middle of the web."

"Maybe so," said Mrs. Zuckerman. "Just the same, I intend to have a look at that spider."

"It's just a common grey spider," said Zuckerman.

They got up, and together they walked down to Wilbur's yard. "You see, Edith? It's just a common grey spider."

Wilbur was pleased to receive so much attention. Lurvy was still standing there, and Mr. and Mrs. Zuckerman, all three, stood for about an hour, reading the words on the web over and over, and watching Wilbur.

Charlotte was delighted with the way her trick was working. She sat without moving a muscle, and listened to the conversation of the people. When a small fly blundered into the web, just beyond the word "pig," Charlotte dropped quickly down, rolled the fly up, and carried it out of the way.

After a while the fog lifted. The web dried off and the words didn't show up so plainly. The Zuckermans and Lurvy walked back to the house. Just before they left the pigpen, Mr. Zuckerman took one last look at Wilbur.

"You know," he said, in an important voice, "I've thought all along that that pig of ours was an extra good one. He's a solid pig. That pig is as solid as they come. You notice how solid he is around the shoulders, Lurvy?"

"Sure. Sure I do," said Lurvy. "I've always noticed that pig. He's quite a pig."

"He's long, and he's smooth," said Zuckerman.

"That's right," agreed Lurvy. "He's as smooth as they come. He's some pig."

The news spread all over the county. Everybody knew that a sign had appeared in a spider's web on the Zuckerman place. Everybody knew that the Zuckermans had a wondrous pig. People came from miles around to look at Wilbur and to read the words on Charlotte's web. The Zuckermans' driveway was full of cars and trucks from morning till night. The news of the wonderful pig spread clear up into the hills, and farmers came rattling down in buggies and buckboards, to stand hour after hour at Wilbur's pen admiring the miraculous animal. All said they had never seen such a pig before in their lives.

In the days that followed, Mr. Zuckerman was so busy entertaining visitors that he neglected his farm work. He wore his good clothes all the time now— got right into them when he got up in the morning. Mrs. Zuckerman prepared special meals for Wilbur. Lurvy shaved and got a haircut; and his principal farm duty was to feed the pig while people looked on.

Mr. Zuckerman ordered Lurvy to increase Wilbur's feedings from three meals a day to four meals a day. The Zuckermans were so busy with visitors they forgot about other things on the farm. The blackberries got ripe, and Mrs. Zuckerman failed to put up any blackberry jam. The corn needed hoeing, and Lurvy didn't find time to hoe it.

All in all, the Zuckermans' pigpen was the center of attraction. Fern was happy, for she felt that Charlotte's trick was working and that Wilbur's life would be saved. But she found that the barn was not nearly as pleasant—too many people. She liked it better when she could be all alone with her friends the animals.

Write the answers to the questions on these pages in your notebook. Use evidence and details from the text to support your answers.

Text Connections

1. Charlotte writes "Some Pig" in her web. Interpret how that is a trick on Zuckerman.

2. Charlotte decides it will be possible to trick Zuckerman because "People are not as smart as bugs." Are all of the human characters easily tricked? Do any of them doubt the trick or seem to be in on it? Explain your reasoning.

3. Why did people travel from miles around to see Wilbur?

4. Why do you think people tend to believe something once it is written down? Give an example from your experience.

5. Describe Charlotte's thinking behind making a sign for Wilbur. Why does she think doing so will save his life?

6. "Charlotte's Web" is a fantasy, but it has elements of realism. Give an example of something in the story that seems realistic, based on what you know about farms in the real world.

Did You Know?

In 1948, E.B. White noticed a busy spider in his barn in Maine and decided to save her egg sac. White took it with him to New York City in a box. A few weeks later, baby spiders hatched and scurried out, surprising him. The experience enchanted White, and a year later he was researching what would become "Charlotte's Web."

Look Closer

Keys to Comprehension

1. Infer how Charlotte feels about Wilbur, using examples from the selection.

2. Describe the setting of "Charlotte's Web" in depth, using details in the text.

Writer's Craft

3. Charlotte describes people as "gullible." What did she mean by that, and how do you know?

4. How is the point of view of "Charlotte's Web" different from the point of view of another selection you have read? Explain how these points of view illustrate the major differences between the types of narrators found in literature.

Concept Development

5. With a partner, read aloud the conversation that Homer and Edith Zuckerman have with each other in the selection. Pay attention to directions the text gives for how each should speak. In what ways did your oral reading reflect those directions?

6. How do both "Charlotte's Web" and "Louis Braille's Gift to the Blind" involve characters on a long-term quest to help others?

Write

Think about the word *acquainted*, found on page 51. Charlotte's messages help others become acquainted with Wilbur's finer qualities. Write a positive message about a friend, as a way to help others become acquainted with him or her.

Read this Science Connection. You will answer the questions as a class.

Text Feature

A **caption** is a phrase or sentence that tells more about a diagram or photograph.

A Web-Spinning Trick

Barn spiders, like Charlotte, catch insects in the sticky parts of their delicate webs. But have you ever wondered why the insects do not fly around the webs?

Scientists have found an interesting answer to this question. Insect eyes see differently than human eyes. An insect's eye cannot see colors such as red, yellow, or orange very well. However, it can detect some colors humans cannot see. Colors in the ultraviolet part of the spectrum are very attractive to insects.

Ultraviolet light fills the sky because it comes from the sun. When an insect sees ultraviolet light, it assumes there is open space ahead. Some insects are attracted to ultraviolet light when it reflects off of flowers. The light guides each insect to a place where nectar and pollen are. When the insect gathers nectar, it helps the plant reproduce by pollinating it.

Spiders have adapted to take advantage of this. Some years ago scientists found that many spiderwebs reflect ultraviolet light too. Some spiders even weave "decorations" with special silk so parts of the web look like flowers. This means that when an insect sees a web, it thinks it is either open space or a flower. When an insect blunders into a web, it sometimes does it on purpose, mistaking the web for something it is not.

A flower as insects see it

A flower as humans see it

1. Compare and contrast how some spiderwebs and flowers use ultraviolet light to attract insects.

2. Cut two circles out of a patterned piece of paper. Place one circle on a piece of paper with a matching pattern. Place the other circle on a white piece of paper. On which paper is it easier to distinguish the circle?

3. Which paper shows the way insects see some spiderwebs? Explain why this is a good model.

 Go Digital

Many spiders have eight eyes, but how well do they see? Research the eyes of web-spinning spiders. Why do you think these spiders only need this type of vision?

Genre Biography

Essential Question
How can a small idea grow into a big difference?

Seeds of Change
Planting a Path to Peace

by Jen Cullerton Johnson
illustrated by Sonia Lynn Sadler

"Come," Wangari's mother called. She beckoned her young daughter over to a tall tree with a wide, smooth trunk and a crown of green, oval leaves.

"Feel," her mother whispered.

Wangari spread her small hands over the tree's trunk. She smoothed her fingers over the rough bark.

"This is the *mugumo*," her mother said. "It is home to many. It feeds many too."

She snapped off a wild fig from a low branch, and gave it to her daughter. Wangari ate the delicious fruit, just as geckos and elephants did. High in the tree, birds chirped in their nests. The branches bounced with jumping monkeys.

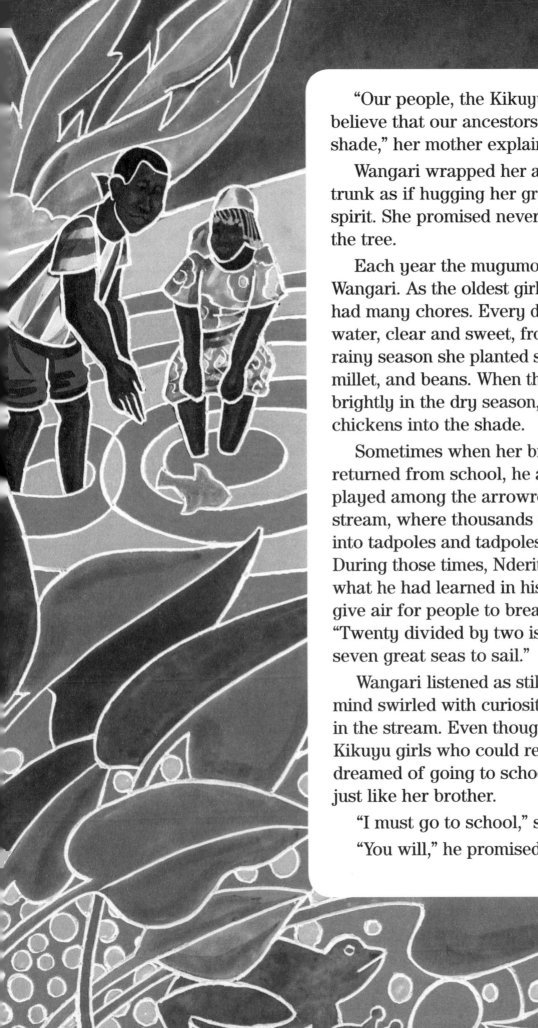

"Our people, the Kikuyu of Kenya, believe that our ancestors rest in the tree's shade," her mother explained.

Wangari wrapped her arms around the trunk as if hugging her great-grandmother's spirit. She promised never to cut down the tree.

Each year the mugumo grew, and so did Wangari. As the oldest girl in her family, she had many chores. Every day she fetched water, clear and sweet, from the river. In the rainy season she planted sweet potatoes, millet, and beans. When the sun shone brightly in the dry season, she shooed the chickens into the shade.

Sometimes when her brother, Nderitu, returned from school, he and Wangari played among the arrowroot plants by the stream, where thousands of eggs hatched into tadpoles and tadpoles turned into frogs. During those times, Nderitu told Wangari what he had learned in his classes. "Plants give air for people to breathe," he said. "Twenty divided by two is ten. There are seven great seas to sail."

Wangari listened as still as a tree, but her mind swirled with curiosity like the currents in the stream. Even though she knew few Kikuyu girls who could read, Wangari dreamed of going to school and learning, just like her brother.

"I must go to school," she told him.

"You will," he promised.

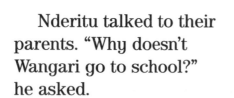

Nderitu talked to their parents. "Why doesn't Wangari go to school?" he asked.

Wangari's parents knew she was smart and a hard worker. Although it was unusual for a girl to be educated, they decided to send her to school. They knew she would not disappoint them. After some time to arrange for fees and supplies, Wangari's mother came to her. "You are going to school," she told her daughter.

Wangari grinned widely and hugged her mother. "Thank you!" she cried. "I will make you proud."

Wangari walked the long road to a one-room schoolhouse with walls made of mud, a floor of dirt, and a roof of tin. In time she learned to copy her letters and trace numbers. Wangari's letters soon made words, and her words made sentences. She learned how numbers could be added and subtracted, multiplied and divided. Animals and plants, she discovered, were like human beings in many ways. They needed air, water, and nourishment too.

When Wangari finished elementary school, she was eleven years old. Her mind was like a seed rooted in rich soil, ready to grow. Wangari wanted to continue her education, but to do so she would have to leave her village and move to the capital city of Nairobi. Wangari had never been farther than her valley's ridge. She was scared.

"Go," her mother said. She picked up a handful of earth and placed it gently into her daughter's hand. "Where you go, we go."

Wangari was sad to leave, but she knew that what her mother said was true. Wherever Wangari went, so went her family, her village, and her Kikuyu ways. She kissed her family and said good-bye to the mugumo tree, remembering her promise always to protect it.

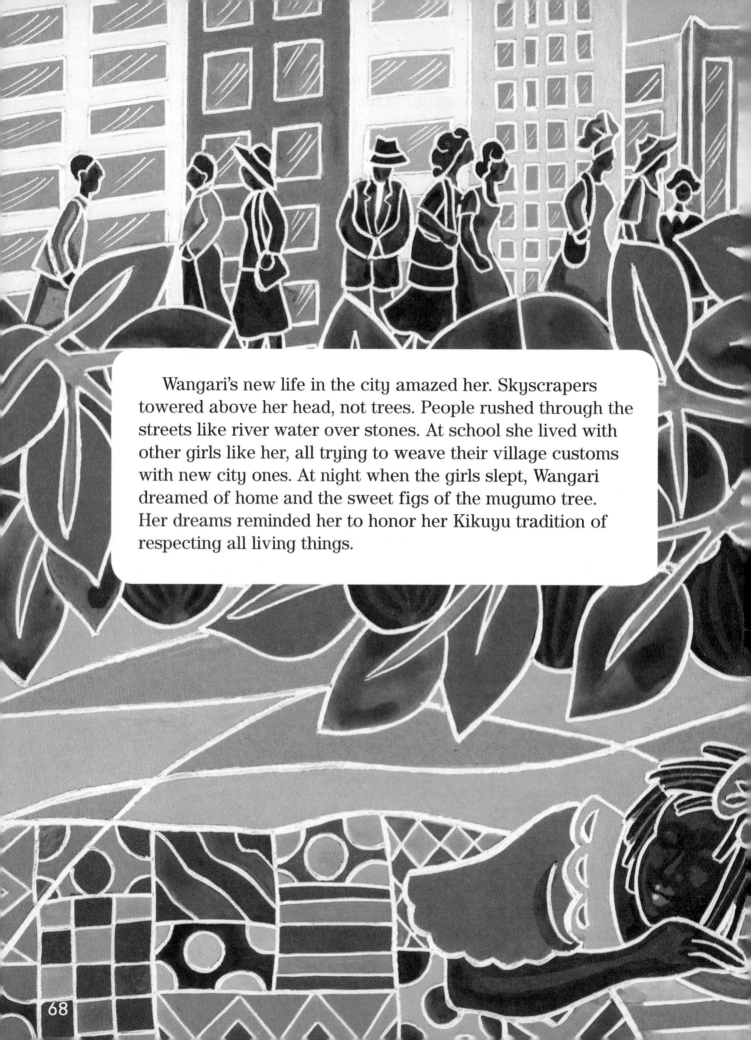

Wangari's new life in the city amazed her. Skyscrapers towered above her head, not trees. People rushed through the streets like river water over stones. At school she lived with other girls like her, all trying to weave their village customs with new city ones. At night when the girls slept, Wangari dreamed of home and the sweet figs of the mugumo tree. Her dreams reminded her to honor her Kikuyu tradition of respecting all living things.

Wangari was an excellent student, and science became her favorite subject. She especially loved studying living things. Air, she learned, was made from two molecules of oxygen bonded together. Bodies were made up of cells. Leaves changed color because of photosynthesis.

As graduation neared, Wangari told her friends she wanted to become a biologist.

"Not many native women become scientists," they told her.

"I will," she said.

Wangari would have to travel halfway around the world to the United States to study biology. She had never left Kenya and had little money. But with her teachers' help, she won a scholarship to a college in Kansas.

America was very different from Kenya. In college, many of Wangari's science professors were women. From them she learned that a woman could do anything she wanted to, even if it hadn't been done before. While Wangari discovered how molecules move under a microscope lens and how cells divide in petri dishes, she also found her strength as a woman scientist.

After she graduated from college, Wangari traveled to Pennsylvania to continue her studies. Letters from home told Wangari about changes in Kenya. The people had elected a Kikuyu president, Jomo Kenyatta. Proud of her country and proud to be Kikuyu, Wangari decided to return home to Kenya to help her people.

America had changed Wangari. She had discovered a spirit of possibility and freedom that she wanted to share with Kenyan women. She accepted a teaching job at the University of Nairobi. Not many women were professors then, and even fewer taught science. Wangari led the way for other women and girls. She worked for equal rights so that female scientists would be treated with the same respect as male scientists.

Wangari watched sadly as her government sold more and more land to big foreign companies that cut down forests for timber and to clear land for coffee plantations. Native trees such as cedar and acacia vanished. Without trees, birds had no place to nest. Monkeys lost their swings. Tired mothers walked miles for firewood.

When Wangari visited her village she saw that the Kikuyu custom of not chopping down the mugumo trees had been lost. No longer held in place by tree roots, the soil streamed into the rivers. The water that had been used to grow maize, bananas, and sweet potatoes turned to mud and dried up. Many families went hungry.

Wangari could not bear to think of the land being destroyed. Now married and the mother of three children, she worried about what would happen to all the mothers and children who depended on the land.

"We must do something," Wangari said.

Wangari had an idea as small as a seed but as tall as a tree that reaches for the sky. "*Harabee!* Let's work together!" she said to her countrywomen—mothers like her. Wangari dug deep into the soil, a seedling by her side. "We must plant trees."

Many women listened. Many planted seedlings. Some men laughed and sneered. Planting trees was women's work, they said. Others complained that Wangari was too outspoken— with too many opinions and too much education for a woman.

Wangari refused to listen to those who criticized her.

Instead she told them, "Those trees [you] are cutting down today were not planted by [you] but by those who came before. You must plant trees that will benefit the community to come, like a seedling with sun, good soil, and abundant rain, the roots of our future will bury themselves in the ground and a canopy of hope will reach the sky."

Wangari traveled to villages, towns, and cities with saplings and seeds, shovels and hoes. At each place she went, women planted rows of trees that looked like green belts across the land. Because of this they started calling themselves the Green Belt Movement.

"We might not change the big world but we can change the landscape of the forest," she said.

One tree turned to ten, ten to one hundred, one hundred to one million, all the way up to thirty million planted trees. Kenya grew green again. Birds nested in new trees. Monkeys swung on branches. Rivers filled with clean water. Wild figs grew heavy in mugumo branches.

Mothers fed their children maize, bananas, and sweet potatoes until they could eat no more.

As the Green Belts moved farther across Kenya, powerful voices rose up against Wangari's movement. Foreign business people, greedy for more land for their coffee plantations and trees for timber, asked, "Who is this woman who can change so many lives with a sapling? Why should we give up our land and profits for trees?"

They made a plan to stop Wangari.

One day while she was out planting a tree, some wealthy businessmen paid corrupt police officers to arrest Wangari.

In her jail cell, Wangari prayed. And like a sturdy tree against a mighty wind, her faith kept her strong. Instead of giving up, she made friends with the other women prisoners. They told her their stories. She taught them about her seeds and saplings. Together, they helped one another.

Wangari knew many people in Kenya and other countries. They banded together to fight for her release. Before she was freed, Wangari promised to help fight for the rights of the other women prisoners too.

Wangari realized that the people who had put her in jail didn't like the changes in the land or in the women. The people in charge of big companies wanted to keep the land for themselves, and the government was frightened of too many advances made by women. If she wanted to help save her country and countrywomen, Wangari would have to go out into the world to spread her message. She would have to leave her home once more.

Wangari began to travel, telling her story to teachers, presidents, farmers, ambassadors, and schoolchildren all over the world. She dug in the dirt, planted seedlings, and spoke about women's rights. With everyone she met, she shared the seeds of change.

In time Kenya changed. More people listened to Wangari's message, calling her the *Mama Miti*, "Mother of Trees." They wanted her to lead them into Kenya's new democracy. Wangari was elected to Kenya's parliament and became minister of the environment.

Still, she did not stop planting trees.

In 2004 Wangari won the most prestigious peace prize in the world, the Nobel Peace Prize. It had never before been awarded to an African woman or an environmentalist.

Standing in front of an audience of people from around the world, far from her village, Wangari remembered her girlhood lesson of the mugumo. She understood that persistence, patience, and commitment—to an idea as small as a seed but as tall as a tree that reaches for the sky—must be planted in every child's heart. "Young people, you are our hope and our future," she said.

And then, as she had done so many times before, Wangari planted a tree.

Write the answers to the questions on these pages in your notebook. Use evidence and details from the text to support your answers.

Text Connections

1. Why did Wangari Maathai move to Nairobi when she was eleven?

2. Explain how Maathai's studies in America changed her view of women.

3. Compare and contrast Maathai's primary schools in her village and in Nairobi with your own school experience.

4. Why were fighting for equal rights for women and planting trees both ways Maathai could "honor her Kikuyu tradition of respecting all living things"?

5. Compare how people in "Louis Braille's Gift to the Blind" and "Seeds of Change" worked for human equality.

6. Do you think the Green Belt Movement still has work to do today? Why or why not?

Did You Know?

Swahili is a language related to the native language of the Kikuyu people of Kenya. People in several African countries, including Tanzania, Kenya, and Uganda, share Swahili as a first or second language.

Look Closer

Keys to Comprehension

1. Make an inference about Wangari Maathai's relationship with her parents, using details from the text.

2. Who helped with Maathai's Green Belt Movement? Use evidence from the text to support why you think they were the people who were most interested in helping.

Writer's Craft

3. Why did people call Maathai's movement "the Green Belt Movement"?

4. Explain two meanings of the phrase "she shared the seeds of change."

Concept Development

5. How does the illustration on page 71 help you better understand Maathai's reaction to the destruction of Kenyan forestland?

6. Describe the evidence the author gives to show the effectiveness of the Green Belt Movement.

Write

Reread page 72. When Maathai first has her idea, she uses the word *Harabee*, which means, "let's work together." Write a poem with the title "*Harabee*," and include details about one or more goals you think people should work together to achieve.

Read this Science Connection. You will answer the questions as a class.

Text Feature

Scientific names in text are set in **italics**.

Survival of the Wild Fig Tree

The mugumo tree, or *Ficus thonningii*, is one of many types of wild ficus, or fig, trees in East Africa. Ficus trees have special adaptations. The adaptations help the trees better survive.

A ficus tree can grow when a seed falls in rich soil or when a person plants a branch cutting. Some types, however, can also begin growing in moss on another tree. How can the seedling's roots reach the ground? Slowly, roots from the seedling grow downward, snaking along the host tree's trunk. Over time, those roots reach the soil. Eventually, that young ficus will grow so strong that it often kills the host tree altogether.

A ficus's roots are a useful adaptation. They spread over a large area. Because East Africa can have very dry weather, this is important for survival. The sturdy root systems can even force their way into the cracks of rocks. Some scientists think these trees might even draw water out of damp night air!

Ficus trees have a special relationship with wasps. Certain wasp species only lay their eggs in ficus flowers. While they work to lay their eggs, the wasps accidentally pollinate the flowers. This allows the ficus to produce seeds. Ficuses near each other produce flowers at staggered times so that wasps will spread the pollen across many trees.

Wild fig trees grow well in East Africa. They are well suited to life in a difficult environment.

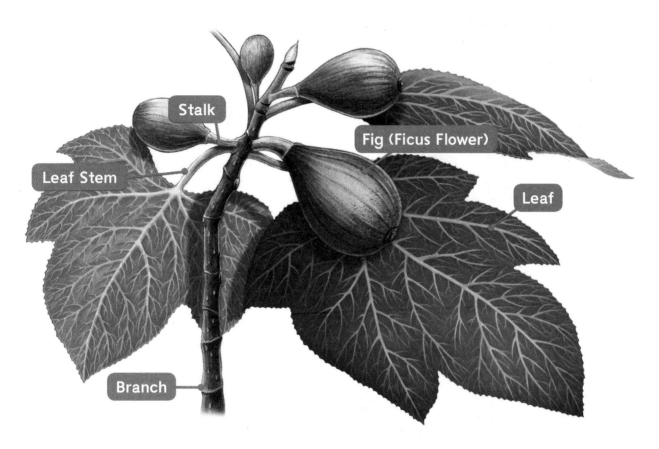

Stalk

Fig (Ficus Flower)

Leaf Stem

Leaf

Branch

1. On the diagram, locate the part of the ficus in which fig wasps lay their eggs. How do fig wasps and ficus trees benefit, or help, each other?

2. Explain how some ficuses can grow even if they do not sprout on the ground.

3. Using what you know about ficus tree adaptations, construct an argument showing that a particular fig tree structure functions in a way that supports survival.

 Go Digital

Although some fig trees can begin life above the ground, most must eventually send roots into the soil. But some plants never need the soil at all! These plants, known as epiphytes, spend their whole lives growing above the ground. Do research to find out about one type of epiphyte. What adaptations does it have that help it survive?

Nelson Mandela

words and paintings by Kadir Nelson

Rolihlahla played barefooted
on the grassy hills of Qunu.
He fought boys with sticks
and shot birds with slingshots.
The smartest Madiba child of thirteen,
he was the only one chosen for school.
His new teacher would not say his Xhosa name.
She called him Nelson instead.

Nelson was nine when his father
joined the ancestors in the sky.
To continue his schooling,
Nelson was sent miles away
to live with a powerful chief.
"Brace yourself, my boy."
His mother held her tears
and said good-bye.

The chief held counsel to warriors,
medicine men, farmers, and laborers.
The elder ones told stories of old Africa.

For centuries
Thembu, Pondo, Xhosa, and Zulu peoples
lived in the mountains and valleys of South Africa.
The land was bountiful, fertile, and rich.
The people hunted, fished, and raised crops, living in relative peace.
But they made war on European settlers
who came in search of land and treasure.
The settlers' weapons were stronger and breathed fire.
Slowly, the people were conquered.
Their land was taken and spirits dimmed.
South Africa belonged to Europe.

The elders grew quiet and Nelson felt sorry.

Nelson grew into a young man
and attended fine schools
in the golden city of Johannesburg,
where Africans were poor
and powerless.
Nelson became a lawyer
and defended those
who could not defend themselves.

The government grew harsh
and created a cruel policy.
It split the people in three—
African. Indian. European.
It was called apartheid.
The people were set apart.
"European Only" beaches.
"European Only" parks.
"European Only" theaters.
And the people protested.

THE DIVISIONAL COUNCIL OF THE CAPE

WHITE AREA
BY ORDER SECRETARY

DIE AFDELINGSRAAD VAN DIE KAAP

BLANKE GEBIED
OP LAS SEKRETARIS

Nelson organized rallies
to fight apartheid.
"We must win back Africa," he told them.
"South Africa is for all South Africans."
"Amandla!" he shouted.
"Ngawethu!" they responded.
Power to the people!
And the people loved him.

Speaking out was against the law
and Nelson was arrested and jailed
for a fortnight with a hundred men.
They danced and sang,
calling the ancestors
to join the fight for freedom.

Amandla!
Ngawethu!

The ancestors sent their daughter Winnie
to stand next to Nelson.
They found love and married
and welcomed children into the world.
Together they stood
and fought apartheid.

The state vowed to put Nelson in jail
and he went underground.
He wore different disguises
and lived in the shadows.
Empty flats, farmhouses, and
bedrooms of friends became Nelson's home
while he organized more rallies and protests.
The police put out a warrant for his arrest
but they could not find him.

Nelson slipped across the border to visit free nations
where black Liberians, Ethiopians, and Moroccans
freely conversed with white Europeans
and brown Egyptians.
They shook hands—
a glimpse of freedom for life at home.
Nelson returned to South Africa
to cleanse his homeland of hate and discrimination.

With a vision for peace and harmony,
Nelson felt renewed and ready
to fight for freedom.
But on a drive to town
he was captured,
arrested, and taken to jail.
The people cried
"Free Mandela,"
"Free Mandela."
Wet paint
and posters
covered South African walls.

On a small island off the coast
of the southern tip of Africa,
Nelson sat in a tiny cell.
Every day
the world passed him by.
Cold mealies, thin blankets, hard labor.
Nelson hammered rocks into dust, and
read, studied, and educated fellow prisoners.
Days turned into weeks, months, and years.

His children grew up.
Relatives passed away.
South Africa began to fall apart.
There were more protests,
more rallies,
and violence.
The people needed a leader.
Nelson snuck a message to the people:
"I will return."

As years passed,
the world pressed South Africa to change.
The new president agreed,
and "European Only" signs came down.
Beaches, parks,
and theaters opened.
Nelson's comrades were set free.
Apartheid was no more.

Nelson was an old man.
After twenty-seven and one-half years,
the prison gates opened
and Nelson was at last
set free.
Thousands surrounded him
and Winnie hugged him.
Nelson looked into the sky
and smiled at the ancestors.
"*Amandla!* Thank you."
The sun sparkled in his gray and white hair.

Nelson stood proudly
with the wind at his back
and spoke to a colorful sea of people.
"We must forget our terrible past
and build a better future for South Africa.
Let us continue to fight for justice
and walk the last mile to freedom."

Millions were given the vote
and elected Nelson Mandela
their new leader.
South Africa was free at last
and finally at peace.
The ancestors,
The people,
The world,
Celebrated.

Amandla!
Ngawethu!

Nelson Mandela

Nelson Mandela was born on July 18, 1918, in the Transkei region of South Africa. Nelson was the youngest son in a family of four boys and nine girls and was born with the name Rolihlahla, which translates as "troublemaker." However, his birth name was changed to Nelson on his first day of school.

When Nelson was nine years old, his father died. To continue his schooling, Nelson was sent miles away to live with a powerful chief named Jongitaba. During his time with the chief, Nelson began to learn about South African tribal history, politics, and diplomacy.

Nelson later studied law and joined the African National Congress (ANC) Youth League, a political organization, to fight against the new discriminatory apartheid laws enforced by the South African government. The laws segregated beaches, parks, and public institutions, making it so that white, Indian, and black Africans were not allowed to enjoy them together. Europeans Only signs were posted all over South Africa, igniting widespread protests and violence.

Nelson Mandela attends his first Conference of the African National Congress in 30 years.

Antelope in South Africa

Nelson traveled the country to organize a resistance campaign to protest the new policy. This soon led to his arrest and brief imprisonment.

Nelson then opened what was to be South Africa's first black law firm in August 1952 in Johannesburg with colleague Oliver Tambo. As Nelson continued to participate in resistance campaigns with the ANC (which was soon declared illegal by the South African government), he was often arrested, banned, and imprisoned.

In the late 1950s, as a result of his involvement with the ANC, Nelson was accused of treason and put on trial with 156 other men. It was during this trial that Nelson met and married Winnie Madikizela. The trial was later dismissed, but Nelson was placed at the top of the government's most wanted list of political agitators. As a result, Nelson decided to go underground to lead the resistance campaign against apartheid. During this time, Nelson secretly left South Africa to visit other African and European countries to garner support for South Africa's resistance movement.

■ ■ ■

However, upon his return to South Africa, Nelson was captured, convicted, and sentenced to life imprisonment for illegally leaving the country and for his involvement in the resistance movement.

While Nelson sat in prison, South Africa became unstable with widespread violence and protests. South Africa, spurred by political pressure from other world nations, yearned for new leadership and ultimately declared apartheid illegal.

Johannesburg, Gauteng, South Africa

Quiver trees in Nieuwoudtville, South Africa

At long last, Nelson and his comrades were released in early 1990 after having spent more than twenty-seven years behind bars as political prisoners. Nelson was soon elected president of the ANC, and three years later he was awarded the Nobel Peace Prize (along with F. W. de Klerk, president of South Africa). One year later Nelson was inaugurated the first black president of South Africa in a landslide election.

–Kadir Nelson

THE STATESMAN

by J. Patrick Lewis

It is as if he's landed on the moon
Five years before the actual event.
At Robben Island Prison, his descent
Into a nightmare world, an outcast dune,
Begins at forty-six. His fate derails.
There are no clocks, his life's defined by bell
And whistle, sisal mats (no beds), his cell
Is seven feet square. But destiny prevails.

He keeps for an eternity of years
His keepers, not the other way around,
Marked by a calm refinement so profound
As to alleviate his captors' fears.
He said, once they had turned the jailhouse key,
No man will rob me of my dignity.

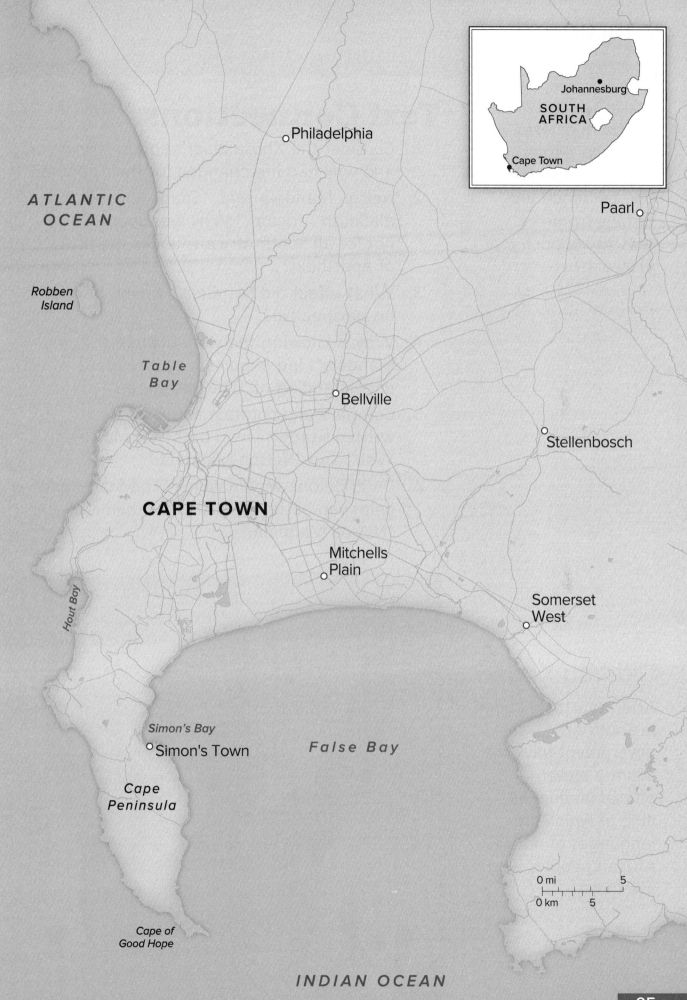

ATLANTIC
OCEAN

Robben
Island

*Table
Bay*

Philadelphia

SOUTH
AFRICA

Johannesburg

Cape Town

Paarl

Bellville

Stellenbosch

CAPE TOWN

Mitchells
Plain

Somerset
West

Hout Bay

Simon's Bay
Simon's Town

False Bay

Cape
Peninsula

Cape of
Good Hope

0 mi   5

0 km   5

INDIAN OCEAN

Write the answers to the questions on these pages in your notebook. Use evidence and details from the text to support your answers.

Text Connections

1. Consider the Xhosa chief's counsel. How and why had life changed for their people?
2. Nelson Mandela said, "South Africa is for all South Africans." Why was South Africa not for all South Africans under the policy of apartheid?
3. What effect did Mandela's travels have on his perspective?
4. Why is knowing the story of Nelson Mandela's life important to a reader's understanding of "The Statesman"?
5. Compare and contrast an effect that written words have in both "Charlotte's Web" and "Nelson Mandela."
6. Describe one way in which "The Statesman" helps you better understand a theme of "Nelson Mandela."

Did You Know?

After apartheid ended in South Africa, the government gave the country eleven official languages, nine of which are languages of native African peoples who live there.

Look Closer

Keys to Comprehension

1. Why did Nelson Mandela use Xhosa words, rather than English words, to cry for "power to the people"? Use what you know about the situation to make an inference.

2. Use information from the text to explain why Mandela was eventually freed.

Writer's Craft

3. The text says apartheid was a "cruel policy." Determine what a government policy is, based on the context.

4. Each stanza in "Nelson Mandela" describes one or more causes and effects. Explain the structure of the stanza about Nelson going "underground." What causes and effects are there? The stanzas of "The Statesman" have a different structure. Is the structure chronological, compare and contrast, problem/solution, or another structure? Why?

Concept Development

5. Compare and contrast the two illustrations of a beach in the text. How do they help to illustrate important events in South Africa?

6. What evidence does the author give to support the idea that many South African people loved Nelson Mandela?

Write

Mandela used the call-and-response phrase *"Amandla!"* *"Ngawethu!"* to gather support at rallies. These words were important to Mandela. Create a phrase you could use to call for something that is important to you. Explain why you chose the words in your phrase.

Read this Social Studies Connection. You will answer the questions as a class.

Text Feature

A **label** is a word, phrase, or sentence that describes a part of a chart, diagram, graph, or time line.

Truth and Reconciliation in South Africa

After Nelson Mandela was freed, the South African government ended apartheid. People began changing the country. Mandela and other leaders of political groups wrote a new constitution. Some years later, Mandela was elected president.

However, big changes in a country are difficult. Apartheid had been a time of pain and fighting, and many people had been hurt in various ways. Who would satisfy cries for justice? How could the peoples of the country reunite?

At other times in history, countries had simply tried to punish perpetrators of great injustice. This time, however, people tried something new. After consulting with leaders from around the world, as well as the victims of apartheid, the government formed the Truth and Reconciliation Commission. Commission leaders worked to find out about past hurts. If people who did wrong would tell the truth, some could escape punishment. The government offered victims money as a way of making amends. The commission worked to tell everyone what had actually happened. They hoped that openness and honesty could cleanse relationships and lead to healing.

The Truth and Reconciliation Commission was not perfect. Some refused to take part in its work. The government did not do everything the commission asked it to. However, this method impressed many people around the world. It was a new way to deal with the difficult problem of injustice.

Truth and Reconciliation Commission Time Line

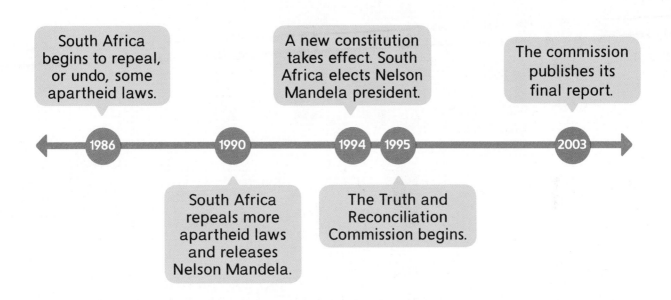

South Africa begins to repeal, or undo, some apartheid laws. — 1986

South Africa repeals more apartheid laws and releases Nelson Mandela. — 1990

A new constitution takes effect. South Africa elects Nelson Mandela president. — 1994

The Truth and Reconciliation Commission begins. — 1995

The commission publishes its final report. — 2003

1. Read the time line and think about what you know about the history of South Africa. What negative and positive roles has the government played in that country?

2. How do government agencies change?

3. How does your country's government influence things in your life?

 Go Digital

Many of Mandela's supporters called him "Madiba," after the name of his Xhosa clan. Research to find out more about the traditional culture of the Xhosa people of South Africa.

MORE THAN A GAME

MAKING A DIFFERENCE THROUGH ATHLETICS

by Dennis Fertig

Great athletes earn respect and admiration with their accomplishments. Days and even years after a game or a sports season has ended, people continue to celebrate athletes who made a difference: those who won championships, broke long-standing records, and inspired onlookers with outstanding performances.

Through sports, athletes capture the attention of an audience. Fans watch an athletic performance and think, *someday I can do that!* Audiences celebrate athletes who have persevered despite obstacles, who have defied skeptics, or who used their positions to help pave the way for others.

The following offers a look at some of those figures, some well-known and others lesser known, who sparked imagination in audiences and made a difference in the world through sports.

Few athletes have performed as well in so many sports as Jim Thorpe. Many consider him the best athlete of the twentieth century. Thorpe, a Native American, was born in Oklahoma. He attended school there, but family tragedies hindered his academic progress. At sixteen, Thorpe went to Carlisle Indian Industrial School in Pennsylvania, where coaches recognized and nurtured his athletic talents.

At Carlisle, Thorpe excelled in football and track and field. In both 1911 and 1912, he was named to All-American football teams. In the 1912 Olympics, he easily won two gold medals in track and field events. From 1913 to 1919, he played for three Major League Baseball teams. After that, he starred in professional football in what became the National Football League. He played his last NFL football game at age forty-one!

However, sadness continued to pervade Thorpe's life. Because Thorpe had earned a small amount of money playing semi-professional baseball years before the Olympics, the Olympic committee stripped him of his gold medals. Playing professional sports was against Olympic amateur rules. After Thorpe died, the rules changed, and the medals were awarded back to his family.

Jesse Owens

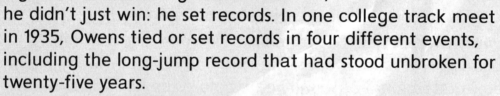

The 1936 Olympics took place in Berlin, Germany. Adolf Hitler, Germany's authoritarian leader, wanted the Olympics to demonstrate what he believed—that people he called Aryans were the most superior people in the world. Jesse Owens would prove Hitler wrong.

Jesse Owens was not Aryan. He was an African American athlete who went to Berlin to win medals. He had good reason to believe he could win, since he had a long history of victories. Throughout his high-school and college athletic career, he didn't just win: he set records. In one college track meet in 1935, Owens tied or set records in four different events, including the long-jump record that had stood unbroken for twenty-five years.

At the Berlin Olympics, Owens dominated his opponents, winning four gold medals. Owens set three world records and tied a fourth.

Hitler did not enjoy Owens's success. The crowd, however, went wild and cheered Owens's victories. Today, people all over the world, including Germans, still honor Owens. Jesse Owens made a huge difference in the world of sports and history, proving that a person's race does not matter, during a time when making that point counted the most.

Larry Snyder

Besides great athletes, great coaches encourage younger people to achieve their full potential. Larry Snyder was such a coach. He guided American Olympic athletes to fifteen medals—ten were gold.

Snyder was a natural teacher. During World War I, he taught Army pilots how to fly. Later, at The Ohio State University, he spent more than thirty years teaching athletes how to win.

During those years, he understood that even the smallest change in an athlete's training could make a big difference in his or her performance.

Jesse Owens was the most successful athlete that Snyder coached. Owens would likely have been a world-class runner no matter who worked with him. With Coach Snyder encouraging him, Owens reached his full potential. Owens became the greatest runner of his time.

Even after they parted ways as coach and athlete, Snyder and Owens remained lifelong friends.

Women in Baseball

Women have been playing baseball since men have been playing baseball. Women's baseball leagues first appeared in the 1860s. It was not, however, until World War II, that women baseball players captured the full attention of the nation.

During the war, the All-American Girls Professional League (AAGPL) was founded. With so many young men being sent overseas to fight, people thought Major League Baseball might be suspended. AAGPL replaced it until the war ended and men returned to play.

Women, not girls, played for the AAGPL, and they were talented athletes. During the war and for almost ten years afterward, AAGPL games drew large crowds. Fans enjoyed watching great athletes play baseball.

The league made a lasting difference by inspiring girls and women to persevere in their love of sports. The league also showed that women could play baseball at a high level. Nonetheless in 1952, Major League Baseball banned women from signing Major League contracts.

Jackie Robinson

Every April 25th, all Major League Baseball players wear uniforms with the number 42. That was Jackie Robinson's number. No other Major League player is honored in that way. Few players have made such a big contribution in baseball.

Until the 1940s, African Americans were denied the opportunity to play Major League Baseball. In 1947, Robinson changed that when he joined the Brooklyn Dodgers.

During his ten years as a player, the Dodgers played in six World Series. Robinson was on six All-Star teams and was the 1947 Rookie of the Year. He was the National League's Most Valuable Player in 1949. These special achievements, however, are not the only reason uniform number 42 is honored.

When Robinson started playing, he received much hatred and abuse from some fans and even fellow players. His ability to endure harsh treatment, and yet play the game so well, helped guarantee that other African Americans would play Major League Baseball. Robinson's courage, strength, determination, and athletic ability made a lasting difference in baseball and our world.

Wally Yonamine

Wally Yonamine was an American citizen born to Japanese parents in Hawaii. In 1947, Yonamine became the first Japanese American professional football player, playing for the San Francisco 49ers. But because the United States had recently fought Japan in World War II, some fans had strong feelings against Japanese Americans.

Injuries ended Yonamine's football career. Then in 1952, he became the first American to play in Japan's professional baseball league since World War II. However, many Japanese fans and players did not welcome Yonamine because he was an American. Many Japanese people also had strong feelings about the war against Americans.

At first, Yonamine faced challenges in Japan similar to challenges Jackie Robinson faced in Major League Baseball. Like Robinson, Yonamine rose above his challenges and proved to be a tough, great player. He was voted into Japan's Baseball Hall of Fame, having led his team to eight championships. Yonamine retired as one of Japan's greatest and most admired baseball players.

Roberto Clemente

A star for the Pittsburgh Pirates, Roberto Clemente was a great baseball player. A team leader, Clemente helped the Pirates win year after year.

Clemente was also one of the first Major League Baseball players from Latin America. Prejudice led some fans and sportswriters to treat him poorly. That angered Clemente. He demanded fair treatment for all ballplayers.

In addition to being outspoken, Clemente showed much generosity to others. He shared the rewards of his success with many people, especially children. As each baseball season ended, he returned to Puerto Rico and involved himself in charities.

In December 1972, an earthquake hit the country of Nicaragua. Clemente arranged to fly supplies to earthquake victims. During takeoff from Puerto Rico, a plane loaded with those supplies as well as Clemente crashed. He died as he lived, trying to make a difference in other people's lives.

In the first half of the twentieth century, Babe Didrikson Zaharias challenged the status quo in three sports! Zaharias first excelled in women's amateur basketball. In the early 1930s, she was named to the women's All-American basketball team for three years in a row. She also became a track-and-field star.

Zaharias excelled in very different track-and-field events: the high jump, hurdles, and javelin toss. In a 1932 national women's track competition, she competed as a one-person team. She took first place in six events and set world records in four of them. She won the *entire* competition, even though the second-place team had twenty-two athletes!

That same year in the Olympics, Zaharias won three medals in track and field. She won gold in the javelin throw and the high hurdles. She won silver in the high jump. She could have won more if she had been allowed to compete in more events.

In 1932, Zaharias learned to play golf. She quickly and amazingly began winning tournaments around the world. At one point, she won seventeen golf tournaments in a row. By the end of her life she had won eighty-two.

In 1950, Zaharias was voted Greatest Female Athlete of the first half of the twentieth century. Her feats inspired young women—and men—to participate and succeed in the sporting world.

Wilma Rudolph

Life did not start easily for Wilma Rudolph. She suffered from many illnesses, including scarlet fever. Her biggest challenge was polio, a disease that weakens muscles. Doctors in her town did not accept African American patients. Her parents drove her long distances each week for medical treatment.

From the age of six to twelve, Rudolph wore a leg brace. She did difficult exercises to build strength. The determined Rudolph overcame her leg brace and polio.

Once healthy, Rudolph turned to sports and became a high-school basketball and track star. At sixteen, just four years after removing her leg brace, Rudolph earned a spot on the 1956 U.S. Olympic team. While other kids were in high school, Rudolph won an Olympic bronze medal.

In the 1960 Olympics in Rome, twenty-year-old Rudolph won three gold medals. No other American woman had ever accomplished that. Over the next years, Rudolph set running records and won numerous athletic awards. When she retired from running, she was voted into three different halls of fame, including the Olympic Hall of Fame.

Don Haskins

Don Haskins coached college basketball at the University of Texas at El Paso for thirty-eight years. He had a reputation as a good, tough coach. In addition to being good athletes, his players were good students.

In 1966, Haskins had a great team that played incredibly well in the end-of-season tournament. The team made it into the championship game against the University of Kentucky. For many years, Kentucky teams had been among the nation's best. In those days, all the Kentucky players were white. In fact, most college teams were all or mostly white.

In the championship game, Coach Haskins did something no coach had ever done before. He started five African American players, and they played most of the game. That upset many fans, but Haskins did not care. He had simply put his best players on the basketball court. Those players won the game and the national championship.

Coach Haskins' decision and the efforts of his team won a championship and changed college basketball forever.

Althea Gibson

In the early 1940s, Althea Gibson loved tennis. She played in tournaments run by the American Tennis Association (ATA), an African American organization.

ATA coaches noticed Gibson's talent. With the ATA's help, she graduated from high school and college. Gibson also became a wonderful tennis player and good enough to play in the world's best tournaments. However, African American players were not allowed to compete.

Then in 1950, Gibson received an invitation to play in the U.S. National Championship (now known as the U.S. Open). No African American had ever played in this tournament. Though Gibson did not win, she played well enough to receive invitations to play in more tournaments.

At first, Gibson was not a star. Then in 1956, she began to win in tournaments around the world. In 1957, she was named Female Athlete of the Year. It was the first time any African American had won that honor.

In 1964, Gibson began to play golf. Again, she made a difference by becoming the first African American to play in the Ladies Professional Golf Association.

Duke Kahanamoku

Native Hawaiian surfer and swimmer Duke Kahanamoku was on U.S. Olympic teams in 1912, 1920, and 1924. He won three gold medals and one silver medal.

At first, some U.S. swimming officials were not sure that Kahanamoku would even make the team. In 1911, he broke the 100-yard world record for swimming by an incredible five seconds. He was the real deal.

In addition to swimming, Kahanamoku also loved surfing. He helped make the ancient Hawaiian practice of surfing popular on distant shores, inspiring youths all over the world to participate.

The efforts of these athletes and coaches paved the way for people of all colors, creeds, and genders to participate in activities they love and to represent their cities, states, and nations with pride. New names and faces continue to step forward to the plate, line, or platform to challenge old records and perceptions about what is possible.

Essential Question
Why do we honor difference makers?

Swim, GIRL, Swim

by J. Patrick Lewis
illustrated by Mark Summers

As Europe woke from sleep,
Young Trudy Ederle
At Cap Gris Nez in France
Dived into a daunting sea.

Many had tried to make
This superhuman swim—
Thirty-five punishing miles.
Chances, at best, were slim.

When Fury found the waves,
Far from the western shore,
Her trainer shouted, "Let's turn back!"
But Trudy cried, "What for?"

Under an English moon,
The celebration began
After the fastest crossing
By woman or by man.

"Swim, Girl, Swim" was the name of a movie based on Gertrude Ederle's achievement. As an eight-year-old visiting her grandmother in Germany, Gertrude tumbled into a pond and nearly drowned. Frightened but indomitable, she practiced swimming relentlessly. In 1925, the nineteen-year-old New Yorker came within seven miles of swimming the English Channel. But in August 1926, fighting rain, twenty-foot waves, jellyfish, and a numb left leg, she became the first woman to swim the Channel, and in a time—14 hours, 31 minutes—that beat the men's mark by nearly two hours and remained the women's record for thirty-five years.

Gertrude Ederle
American swimmer
1906–2003

Text Connections

1. Describe the way one athlete from "More Than a Game" changed sports for athletes that followed him or her.

2. Using details from one of the profiles about a coach, formulate an argument about the impact coaches can have on sports.

3. The background for "Swim, Girl, Swim" states that Gertrude Ederle nearly drowned as a child. How do you think this informed Ederle's response to her trainer's advice to turn back?

4. Think of an athlete and the challenges he or she had to overcome. Compare a time that you overcame a tough situation with how the athlete pushed through his or her challenge.

5. Compare instances of prejudice in "More Than a Game" with the prejudice faced by Nelson Mandela.

6. Think about the section titled "Women in Baseball." Do you think women should be included in today's professional sports leagues? Why, or why not?

Did You Know?

The Paralympic Games exist alongside the Olympics. Competitions for injured veterans of World War II led to the development of the first Paralympic Games in 1960. Today, people with disabilities have the opportunity to compete in many types of sports in both summer and winter Paralympic Games.

Look Closer

Keys to Comprehension

1. Infer why prejudice harms professional sports, citing examples from "More Than a Game" to support your inference.

2. Describe the main idea of "More Than a Game," and explain how the profiles within it support that main idea.

Writer's Craft

3. What is the "status quo"? Use information from the profile of Babe Didrikson Zaharias to determine this term's meaning.

4. How does the author structure information in "More Than a Game"?

Concept Development

5. Explain how the author uses reasons and evidence to support the idea that Roberto Clemente tried "to make a difference in other people's lives."

6. Integrating information from "Swim, Girl, Swim" and "More Than a Game," explain the way women athletes have changed people's perception of women and sports.

Write

Think about the vocabulary word *honor*. Write about a hero of yours, using a format similar to the profiles in "More Than a Game."

Read this Science Connection. You will answer the questions as a class.

Text Feature

Informational text often sets important, domain-specific terms in dark print, or **boldface**.

Swimming Can Be a Drag

When Gertrude Ederle swam the English Channel, she may or may not have been thinking about physics, but physics is a huge part of swimming! Physics is the study of matter and its motion. Energy is also an important concept in physics. To understand swimming, it helps to know a little physics.

A swimmer exerts energy to move through water. When Ederle waited to begin her swim, she had **potential energy**. Potential energy is stored energy. Once she started swimming, her potential energy changed into **kinetic energy**, or the energy of motion. She was using energy to do work.

Several forces affect a swimmer's work. One important force is **drag**. As Ederle swam, her body collided with the water. Drag slows a swimmer down as he or she moves through the water.

To decrease the amount of drag, professional swimmers streamline their bodies. When they swim they try to stay in straight, tight positions. They also compete in close-fitting suits. At the time Ederle swam, women usually swam in wool dresses, but all that fabric caused extra drag. Ederle's bathing suit decreased the drag and allowed her to use less energy to swim.

Since physics explains motion, energy, and forces, it is an important part of sports. Athletes like Ederle succeed when they consider the science of physics.

1. When Ederle was swimming, what objects collided?

2. What happens when one object with kinetic energy collides with another object at rest? Use two coins to design an experiment demonstrating this, and describe it.

3. Think about the force of drag. Write down a related question that you could answer by changing a variable in your experiment, and then write down your prediction about what will happen.

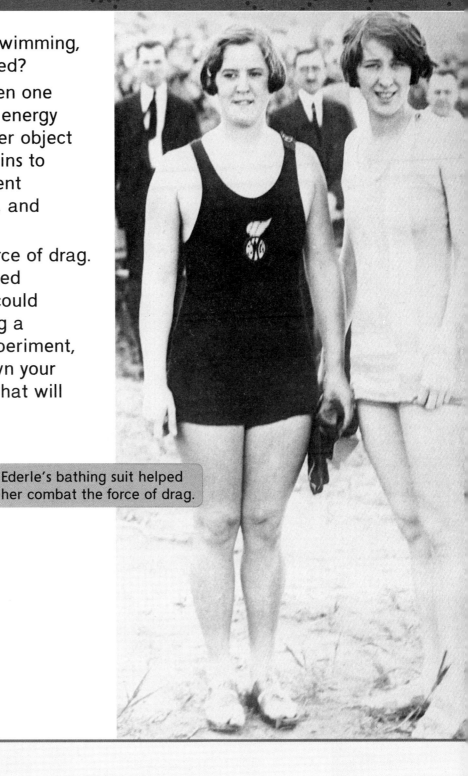

Ederle's bathing suit helped her combat the force of drag.

 Go Digital

Physics is important to all sports. Research the concept of the "sweet spot" on a baseball bat. In what ways does this have to do with collisions and a transfer of energy?

Science Fair

BIG Idea

How is science put into action?

Theme Connections

What can we learn from studying science?

 Background Builder Video
connected.mcgraw-hill.com

Genre Play

Essential Questions

How do scientists collaborate? What do they learn from each other?

THE DISCOVERY FAIR

by Vidas Barzdukas
illustrated by Nancy Lane

Characters

ELIYA

SARAH

GALILEO

WILLIAM HERSCHEL

CAROLINE HERSCHEL

DANIEL HALE WILLIAMS

YNÉS MEXÍA

MARIE CURIE

CHIEN-SHIUNG WU

THOMAS EDISON

LEWIS HOWARD LATIMER

SETTING: *A science fair in a school auditorium. Inventors and scientists dressed in clothes from various time periods converse with each other.*

(ELIYA and SARAH enter in a rush.)

ELIYA. This is the science fair I was telling you about, Sarah.

SARAH. Who are all these people?

ELIYA. I told you. They're some of the greatest inventors and scientists in the world!

SARAH. Is that man wearing a robe?

ELIYA. Quiet, they can hear you. We need to write a biography on a famous inventor or scientist for school. What better way to write a biography than to talk to the person?

(GALILEO enters.)

SARAH. Why is he dressed like Galileo?

ELIYA. Because that *is* Galileo.

SARAH. Oh! Hello.

GALILEO. *Ciao!*

ELIYA. *Ciao,* I'm Eliya. This is my friend, Sarah. We're here because we need to write a biography on a famous inventor or scientist.

GALILEO. *Che bello!* What better person to write about than me, Galileo Galilei?

SARAH. You're the person who invented the telescope, right?

GALILEO. The telescope had already been invented, but I made it *better.* You see, I originally constructed my telescope for sailors to spot other ships on the open seas. But when I pointed my telescope to the night skies . . .

SARAH. What happened?

GALILEO. I saw the wonders of the universe! I discovered that Venus has phases just like our own moon. And that the planets revolve around the sun, not Earth.

ELIYA. Everyone knows that.

GALILEO. They didn't during my time. When I was your age, scholars believed the planets revolved around Earth, not the sun.

SARAH. I remember reading about that. An astronomer named Copernicus was the first to theorize that the planets revolved around the sun.

GALILEO. My observations proved that Copernicus was right, but you see—

(WILLIAM HERSCHEL and CAROLINE HERSCHEL enter.)

WILLIAM HERSCHEL *(interrupting).* The telescope is a wonderful invention, isn't it?

GALILEO *(annoyed). Mamma mia!*

SARAH. Who are you?

CAROLINE HERSCHEL. Caroline Herschel. This is my brother, William.

WILLIAM HERSCHEL. How do you do?

GALILEO. They are writing a biography about a famous person. I am telling them about my telescope.

CAROLINE HERSCHEL. *Your* telescope? The telescopes during your time were fine if you wanted to see nearby objects. But what if you wanted to see even more amazing objects deep in the distant universe?

ELIYA. That would be very exciting!

WILLIAM HERSCHEL. The problem was that these telescopes didn't exist when Galileo was around. That's why I had to construct my own.

GALILEO. Here we go again . . .

WILLIAM HERSCHEL. These weren't your normal run-of-the-mill telescopes, mind you. They had giant lenses and could see farther than any telescopes made before!

CAROLINE HERSCHEL. Tell them about the ladder.

WILLIAM HERSCHEL. Oh yes! I would stand on a ladder to peer through my telescope and describe what I saw to my sister. Then one night, I realized that one star wasn't a star at all, but a planet. I called this new planet . . . Uranus!

CAROLINE HERSCHEL. It was very exciting. Almost as exciting as when I discovered three nebulas.

SARAH. I know what that is! A nebula is a cluster of gas and dust in space where stars form.

CAROLINE HERSCHEL. That's right! And did you know I was also the first woman to discover a comet? In fact, I discovered eight comets in my lifetime. Several of the comets are named after me. *(Whispering)* I don't have the heart to tell my brother, though. He can get a bit jealous.

(DANIEL HALE WILLIAMS enters.)

DANIEL HALE WILLIAMS. Did someone say "heart"?

GALILEO. Have you met Daniel Hale Williams?

DANIEL HALE WILLIAMS. That's *Doctor* Daniel Hale Williams. I remember like it happened yesterday. It was a hot and humid summer night in Chicago. A patient was rushed to the hospital with a severe stab wound to the chest. He was going to perish within a matter of hours. I had to do something!

ELIYA. What did you do?

DANIEL HALE WILLIAMS. Risking my professional reputation, I performed a procedure that had never been attempted before. I performed open-heart surgery. Why do you ask?

SARAH. We're writing a biography.

DANIEL HALE WILLIAMS. Well, then! You should write a biography about me. Most decidedly! In 1893 I was one of the first doctors to perform the procedure successfully. Did I mention that I risked my professional reputation to perform the procedure? It had never been attempted before! That little bit of drama will really make your biography interesting. Yes, yes indeed. You should write about me.

ELIYA. Did the patient survive?

DANIEL HALE WILLIAMS. But of course! With flying colors.

(YNÉS MEXÍA enters carrying a Mexianthus mexicanus.)

YNÉS MEXÍA *(interrupting).* Speaking of colors, have you seen the petals on this *Mexianthus mexicanus?*

DANIEL HALE WILLIAMS. Ynés Mexía! I was telling these girls about my open-heart surgery! Did you know that I risked my professional—

YNÉS MEXÍA. —reputation performing a procedure that had never been attempted before. Yes, we've heard it many times. Let's talk about the beauty of nature, instead! Take these flowers, for example . . .

ELIYA. Let me see!

YNÉS MEXÍA. This plant grows in western Mexico. It's part of the sunflower family.

ELIYA. It's beautiful.

SARAH. Are you an explorer?

YNÉS MEXÍA. I'm a botanist. However, I did explore remote regions of South America and Central America pursuing and collecting new species of plants.

ELIYA. Did you find any?

YNÉS MEXÍA. Yes, I collected more than 150,000 specimens and discovered more than 500 new species. No woman collected more plant specimens or traveled farther to find plants than I.

SARAH. We studied your work during Women's History Month at school last year.

YNÉS MEXÍA. There's only a month? There should definitely be more time spent on the accomplishments of women! There are so many of us in science, the arts, leadership . . . And we really get into the thick of it, too, in all professions! It was only the other day that I was thinking about the time I fell off a cliff while looking for plants in Mexico. I broke many bones—botany can be dangerous work, you know! Never fear, I was not hurt too badly!

(MARIE CURIE enters.)

MARIE CURIE *(interrupting).* I can tell you a thing or two about dangerous work!

SARAH. You're Marie Curie. We studied you during Women's History Month, too.

ELIYA. You won two Nobel Prizes.

MARIE CURIE. Of course you studied me. My work was spectacular. But it wasn't easy. In my day, young women growing up in Poland weren't allowed to acquire university degrees. So my sister and I scrounged up enough money to go to school elsewhere.

WILLIAM HERSCHEL. You studied in France, if I'm not mistaken.

MARIE CURIE. That's right. We spent all our money on school, which left little money for other things. But all that hard work paid off. I received degrees in physics and math. And then I met my husband, Pierre.

GALILEO. It was a match made in a laboratory.

MARIE CURIE. Pierre and I worked together for years. For example, we discovered the elements polonium and radium, for which we won the Nobel Prize in Physics. I won my second Nobel Prize, in Chemistry, for separating radium from the rock in which it was found as a pure metal.

CAROLINE HERSCHEL. Tell them about the dangerous part.

MARIE CURIE. I was just getting there. I also studied the rays of energy given off by uranium. I called this energy radioactivity. At the time, no one knew the dangers of radioactivity. Today, scientists wear special equipment when handling uranium. I wore no special equipment whatsoever.

SARAH. That had to be dangerous! We have to wear heavy lead smocks when getting our teeth x-rayed because of the radiation.

MARIE CURIE. It was very dangerous. I eventually died from radiation poisoning. I certainly wish I'd had a heavy lead smock while inventing x-ray technology. However, the idea that radiation could affect people and other living organisms became the catalyst for research into life-saving medical treatments. I was a key researcher and thought leader, until my work killed me.

(CHIEN-SHIUNG WU enters.)

CHIEN-SHIUNG WU *(interrupting).* Did I hear you say "radioactivity?"

MARIE CURIE. Allow me to introduce Chien-Shiung Wu. Though I won a Nobel Prize, she is known as "the first lady of physics."

ELIYA. Why is that?

CHIEN-SHIUNG WU. Like esteemed Madame, my significant contributions to science also dealt with radiation and physics. For example, I worked on the Manhattan Project during World War II.

MARIE CURIE. The Manhattan Project's roots lay in my work on radioactivity and the work of other physicists on atoms. It produced the first nuclear bomb during World War II, an extremely destructive and very controversial weapon. Nuclear energy and medical advances are more peaceful uses of this technology.

CHIEN-SHIUNG WU. That's correct. I was a member of the Manhattan Project, which wasn't based in New York, by the way. Research sites were scattered all over the country. My site was in Tennessee. Not only was I one of a handful of women working at the Tennessee research facility, I was the only Chinese scientist there. It was lonely and isolating at times, but I'm proud of my legacy as a trailblazer.

ELIYA. Wow!

CHIEN-SHIUNG WU. After the war, I did more experiments involving nuclear energy that disproved theories of the time. However, while my fellow researchers won Nobel Prizes for our work, I did not. Whether I was overlooked because of my contribution or because I was a woman, I will never know.

(THOMAS EDISON enters.)

THOMAS EDISON *(interrupting).* Did someone say "light bulb?"

SCIENTISTS *(in unison).* No!

THOMAS EDISON. Well, that's *one* of the things I invented. I'm known as one of the greatest inventors in the world, you know.

GALILEO *(exasperated).* "He holds more than a thousand patents . . ."

THOMAS EDISON *(pompous).* I hold more than a thousand patents . . .

GALILEO. ". . . for his inventions."

THOMAS EDISON. . . . for my inventions.

GALILEO *(aside to CHIEN-SHIUNG WU).* For about the thousandth time.

THOMAS EDISON *(to GALILEO).* Hey, I heard that. *(to SARAH and ELIYA)* As a patent holder, I'd like to know why you're so interested anyway . . . Not doing competing research, are you? Trying to infringe on my work?

SARAH *(gestures with annoyance).* We're writing a biography!

THOMAS EDISON. I see, I see. Yes, hmm . . . free publicity . . . That could be good. Very good for me. I would make an excellent subject for a biography!

ELIYA. You look like Thomas Edison.

THOMAS EDISON. That's because I *am* Thomas Edison. Why don't you film me with your movie camera? I invented that. Or send a message to your family using a telegraph? I invented that, too. Why don't you ask me where I performed my first experiment?

SARAH. Where did you perform—?

THOMAS EDISON. In the back of a train baggage car; thanks for asking. I set up a little laboratory in one of the cars.

ELIYA. I bet your experiment was a success.

THOMAS EDISON. Actually, I started a small fire and I was kicked off the train. But that's not important! The lesson here is that I didn't give up. I continued experimenting and figuring out not just how to make things, but how to make them better. Why don't you ask me about Menlo Park?

SARAH. What was Menlo—?

THOMAS EDISON. Menlo Park was where my research facility was located. It was there that I invented the phonograph and a way to project a motion picture. I then invented the light bulb, which would bring electric lights to cities all around the world.

(LEWIS HOWARD LATIMER enters.)

LEWIS HOWARD LATIMER *(interrupting)*. Did someone say "light bulb?"

SARAH. Hello. Who are you?

THOMAS EDISON. His name is Lewis Howard Latimer, inventor, draftsman—

LEWIS HOWARD LATIMER. . . .and the person who improved, and wrote the book on, *your* light bulb, Thomas. *(pats THOMAS EDISON on the back)*

THOMAS EDISON. Mr. Edison, if you please, Mr. Latimer!

LEWIS HOWARD LATIMER. Yes, yes, of course, old chap. Not to bore you with the technical jargon, found in my book *Incandescent Electric Lighting,* but Thomas's, er . . . *Mr. Edison's* light bulb contained a carbon wire filament encased in a glass bulb. When this wire filament burned, it became extremely hot and glowed.

THOMAS EDISON *(interjects)*. It was a flash of luminous genius!

LEWIS HOWARD LATIMER. A "flash" is right. Those bulbs burned out quickly and were also wasteful. I discovered that if you placed a cardboard envelope around the carbon wire, it prevented it from breaking so easily. My idea made the bulb more efficient and less expensive.

SARAH. That's pretty cool.

THOMAS EDISON. Actually . . .

LEWIS HOWARD LATIMER. The bulbs became hot!

THOMAS EDISON. Hot enough to bake brownies, under the right conditions.

LEWIS HOWARD LATIMER. All that heat was extra energy going to waste. Very few of your bulbs today use our filaments, but anyway we worked together to bring the electric light into the world.

(A bell rings.)

GALILEO. The science fair is over. You're going to write about me, right? Remember, I used a telescope to observe that the Earth revolved around the sun which gave us—

CHIEN-SHIUNG WU. Radiation! We all know that women scientists have been more appealing to the girls. They are going to write about the power of—

YNÉS MEXÍA. Women botanists! Women who traveled the world to discover new—

WILLIAM HERSCHEL. Planets! Scientists who used telescopes to explore the universe—

CAROLINE HERSCHEL. Of comets. I opened the door for—

DANIEL HALE WILLIAMS. Open-heart surgery! If it hadn't been for me, that patient would have perished by—

MARIE CURIE. Radium! Without my work, the world would still be in the dark about—

THOMAS EDISON. Telegraphs, movie cameras, and light bulbs—

LEWIS HOWARD LATIMER. That I made better.

(The inventors and scientists exit.)

SARAH. We have so many great inventors and scientists to write about!

ELIYA. I'm not sure whom I want to write about, though.

SARAH. I wish we could include all of them somehow . . . What if we wrote a play about the inventors having a conversation that incorporated all of their accomplishments?

ELIYA. And we could have Thomas Edison and Lewis Howard Latimer being competitive about their roles . . .

SARAH. And Daniel Hale Williams could keep repeating the same things over and over and . . .

THE END

Write the answers to the questions on these pages in your notebook. Use evidence and details from the text to support your answers.

Did You Know?

Problems often lead to new inventions. During an energy crisis in the 1970s, researchers began investigating how to make more efficient light bulbs. As a result, the first compact fluorescent light was invented in 1976. Innovation on light bulbs continued. Bulbs that are even more efficient are in use today.

Text Connections

1. What elements help you know "The Discovery Fair" could not happen in the real world?

2. Describe Galileo's personality in "The Discovery Fair," based on his speech and actions.

3. Explain how the playwright uses dialogue to introduce new inventors.

4. Compare and contrast the work of Dr. Mesmer from "Mesmerized" with the work of Doctor Daniel Hale Williams from "The Discovery Fair."

5. In "The Discovery Fair," Ynés Mexía says, "There should definitely be more time spent on the accomplishments of women!" Explain why you think this character feels this way.

6. Think of another famous invention like those described in "The Discovery Fair." Explain why it is as important as inventions like the light bulb.

Look Closer

Keys to Comprehension

1. Why do the other scientists all say "No!" when Edison asks, "Did someone say 'light bulb?'" Use details from the text to support your inference.

2. Based on the choice of inventors in "The Discovery Fair," what is one message of this play?

3. Describe in depth the setting of "The Discovery Fair" and what it possibly implies.

Writer's Craft

4. Contrast the different structures of the Read Aloud "Mesmerized" and "The Discovery Fair."

5. *Ciao* is an Italian word. Using context clues, determine this word's meaning. How do Sarah and Eliya know the correct response if they do not speak Italian?

Concept Development

6. If you were to stage a performance of "The Discovery Fair," how would it be the same as and different from the way the play appears in the text?

Write

Describe a problem you have observed and an imaginary invention that solves that problem. Compare and contrast your invention with one of the inventions described in "The Discovery Fair."

Read this Social Studies Connection. You will answer the questions as a class.

Text Feature

A **caption** is a phrase or sentence that tells more about an illustration or photograph.

Radium and the FDA

When Marie and Pierre Curie discovered the element radium, no one knew much about radioactivity. Radiation was something new and fascinating. People wondered if radium could be good for people's health.

In the early 1900s, the United States government did not have much power over drugs and foods. People were excited about radium, so companies quickly began selling radioactive candies and creams. In the 1920s, one company created Radithor, a kind of bottled radioactive water. Radithor was supposed to make its drinkers healthier, although no one tested Radithor to be sure this was true. People did not immediately observe any bad effects. They believed the company's claims.

However, when Radithor led to the death of a famous millionaire in 1932, the truth about radium's dangers began to come out. People were already pushing Congress to make a new law with standards for foods and drugs. They wanted protection against false promises in advertising. When making the argument for the new law, the federal Food and Drug Administration, or FDA, used Radithor as one of its examples of a product that hurt, rather than helped, its users.

In 1938, President Roosevelt signed the Food, Drug, and Cosmetic Act into law. The FDA was now able to inspect foods and drugs. Before companies could create products like Radithor, they would need to study their effects and make sure they were safe.

President Franklin Roosevelt signs a bill in the East Hall of the White House.

1. How did the Food, Drug, and Cosmetic Act of 1938 change the role of the institution called the FDA?

2. Why was that change important?

3. Infer how you think the FDA influences foods you eat.

 Go Digital

Research how Marie and Pierre Curie chose the names *radium* and *polonium* for the elements they discovered, and research the origin of the unit of measurement called a *curie*.

Ruby Goldberg's Bright Idea

by Anna Humphrey
illustrated by Lauren Gallegos

Some people don't know how to mind their own business. Dominic Robinson is *definitely* one of them.

It started on Friday afternoon at shared reading time. Every kid in Ms. Slate's fifth-grade class was supposed to be taking turns reading from *Sadako and the Thousand Paper Cranes* while everyone else was supposed to be listening and following along with their finger.

And listening was *exactly* what I was doing—minus the finger part. Because my fingers were busy building something, which is a far better use of fingers, if you ask me.

"Why do you think the author included the spider in chapter one?" Ms. Slate asked the class. "Any ideas?"

Homework
Read Ch. 3–4
Answer Q's 7–16

"Because it's lucky?" Supeng ventured.

"That's right," Ms. Slate said. "In Japanese culture spiders are considered lucky."

"Or maybe because it might rain?" Eleni suggested. "My yaya says it rains when you see a spider."

I knew a lot about spiders from the Amazing Arachnids exhibit at the Museum of Science in Boston, where my grandpa takes me every month. I was pretty sure the rain thing was only if you *stepped* on the spider . . . and even then it was only a superstition—*not* a scientific fact. Normally I would have set the record straight, but I was a little preoccupied. In a minute we'd be turning the page to chapter two, and my invention wasn't ready yet.

My best friend, Penny, waved from across the room to get my attention. *What are you doing?* she signed. Penny isn't deaf, but her cousin is, so she goes to sign language class on Tuesdays after school to learn how to communicate with him. As an added bonus, it comes in handy when your teacher sits you and your best friend on opposite ends of the room so you'll stop talking.

Making, I signed back, since I didn't know the American Sign Language sign for "inventing." I tilted my book up to show her the clothespin on a string I'd attached to it, then held up my mini battery-powered pocket fan.

C-A-R-E-F-U-L, she finger-spelled back. Then she started twirling a strand of her shiny black hair around one finger, which is always what she does when she's worried. I nodded. Penny was right. Caution was a must. The day before, during silent reading, I'd shared a really cool fact with the class. It was about the Hangzhou Bay Bridge in China, which is twenty-two miles long and crosses an entire ocean! You'd think everyone would have thanked me for the interesting and educational information, right?

Ms. Slate didn't . . . and because it wasn't the first (or second or third) time I'd shared a fact when we were supposed to be reading silently, and because then everyone got distracted from their books and started talking, she kept the whole class in for part of recess.

Plus there was the time the week before when I'd accidentally broken the candy jar on her desk because I'd wanted to be first in line for the Friday treat, and then *nobody* got to have a chocolate.

"You know, Ruby . . . not everything has to be a contest of who's first," Ally had said, sighing as she'd packed away her notebooks that day. "Now you ruined the greatest part of the week for everyone."

"Yeah . . . ," Colin had agreed. "Just like you ruined the honey field trip last year because you were showing off."

Okay—that hadn't been exactly my fault. When we'd visited a real working beehive last fall, the bee tender had gone on and on about how bees pollinate flowers (which everyone already knew). She hadn't even mentioned the really interesting part—how bees communicate by dancing. So I'd helped her out with a short demonstration. Not that anyone had appreciated it.

"You owe us honey *and* chocolate now," Colin had added. Then he'd stormed off behind Ally.

I didn't mean to ruin things, of course. But didn't everyone want to be first in line? And didn't people want to know interesting things? I knew I definitely did!

All the same, Penny was right to warn me about my invention. I couldn't afford to get in trouble again, or even *she* might get mad at me—not that she did that very often. As best friends went, Penny was amazingly patient, which was a good thing, because sometimes dealing with me took a lot of patience.

"Colin, would you start us off on chapter two?" Ms. Slate asked. The rustling of paper filled the air as everyone turned the page and Colin began. This was it. Ready or not, it was time to test the Ruby Goldberg Page-o-Matic (patent pending).

I could picture the infomercial already: *Why strain yourself turning hundreds of pages? Get the Page-o-Matic today! With one easy motion you can pull the string attached to the clothespin, which opens to release the page and tilts the ruler, which hits the button that turns on the fan that blows the page over for you!*

Or at least in theory it did—unless the clothespin wasn't attached quite right. In which case it might come sproinging off the book and hit someone in the head.

"Ouch!" Brianne glared at me from across the aisle and rubbed her ear. "Ruby!" she said under her breath.

"Sorry," I whispered. Luckily, Colin was having trouble pronouncing a Japanese word from the book, and Ms. Slate was so busy helping him that she hadn't noticed the attack of the flying clothespin.

I pulled on the string to reel the clothespin back to my desk. Then I reattached the clothespin, firmly, to the book.

"Pssst. Ruby!" Dominic Robinson—a.k.a. the nosiest kid I know—leaned across the aisle on my other side. His thick brown hair fell into his eyes, like it always does, and he blinked out from underneath it. I couldn't quite put my finger on it, but there was something about him that always reminded me of a turtle. "Try propping this under the fan." He held out a pencil case with cartoon dogs on it. "It'll give you a better angle."

Now, don't get me wrong. Even though he's a first-class snoop, I won't deny that Dominic Robinson is good at many things . . . multiplying with decimal places, acing every science test, sharpening his pencils to perfect points . . . but whispering in class is *not* one of them. He was talking WAY too loudly. Plus, he was looking right at me. Even the most amateur whisperer knows that the way to avoid getting caught is to look straight ahead!

"At shared reading time we show respect to our classmates by listening," Ms. Slate reminded the whole room, but she was looking right at us when she said it. Dominic was still holding out the pencil case to me. I grabbed it and shoved it under my desk before we could get in any more trouble.

As Colin kept reading, I went back to work, looping the string on the clothespin more tightly so that I could control the tension better.

"Ally, would you read next?" Ms. Slate asked.

As everyone turned the page, I pulled carefully on my string. The clothespin opened. The page was released. The ruler tipped, hitting the button on the fan, which whirred to life, only—ACK! Dominic had been right. The angle of the fan was wrong. Instead of blowing page nine over, the fan rustled page eight uselessly. I didn't have much time. Without thinking, I grabbed Dominic's pencil case and propped it underneath. Only, I shoved just a little too hard, and all of a sudden—*CRASH!*

The entire Ruby Goldberg Page-o-Matic smashed to the floor, along with my book and Dominic's pencil case, which spewed markers everywhere. The pocket fan leapt and vibrated in crazy circles like some kind of deranged beetle, then smacked loudly into the leg of Dominic's desk and went dead.

"Ruby!" Ms. Slate said, walking down the aisle. "What, may I ask, are you doing now?"

"Turning the page," I answered. It was the honest truth. I bent over and picked up the string, ruler, and clothespin, then started to collect the spilled markers.

Ms. Slate sighed. "Next time see if you can turn the page without disrupting the entire class." A bunch of kids at the front laughed. "There's a time and place for experimenting and making inventions," she went on, eyeing the collection of stuff on my desk, "and it isn't during shared reading time . . . or math . . . or language arts . . . or community circle. We've talked about this before."

"I know," I said, tilting my head to one side and making my best, most angelic apology face. It wasn't even that hard to do, because I *was* sorry. I didn't mean to be disruptive. It was just that ideas had a way of rushing into my brain and filling it up so full that there was barely room left to focus on anything else.

"Books away," Ms. Slate said, letting the subject drop. "We'll keep reading on Monday. Before the bell rings, we need to talk about the science fair, anyway."

Now she had my full attention. Along with Nature Week—when we got to take walks and study trees and bugs—the science fair was my favorite thing of the year. Two years ago, I'd taken the bronze medal for making a pinhole camera . . . and last year I'd won silver for my digital clock that ran on lemon juice.

"Here." Dominic picked my pocket fan up off the floor and set it on the edge of my desk. It immediately rolled off again. "Oh. Sorry," he said.

But even though bronze and silver were good, they weren't gold! Dominic had won first prize the past two years—in third grade with a project where he'd taken apart and studied the inside of a digital camera, and then last year with a full-size grandfather clock that had run on the energy from potatoes. Both clear rip-offs of my ideas! Not that the judges had seemed to notice or care.

Dominic bent down, picked the pocket fan up again, and handed it to me this time. "Thanks," I said coldly. After all, if he'd been minding his own business and reading *Sadako,* he wouldn't have noticed me building the Page-o-Matic, or passed me his stupid pencil case. Then I wouldn't have dropped my stuff and gotten in trouble in the first place. And, more important, if it hadn't been for his copycat photography project and potato clock, I would have won the gold medal—or at least the silver—two years running.

Sure, Dominic appeared harmless enough with his blinky eyes, "helpful" suggestions, and cartoon doggy pencil case, but only I knew the truth. Underneath those overgrown bangs lurked a cunning, spying, ruthless science-project-stealer who would stop at nothing to win.

Well, not this year, I thought as I took a science fair sign-up sheet off the top of the pile and passed the others back. This year Ruby Goldberg was going for gold, and nobody—especially not Dominic Robinson—was going to stop me.

Michael Built a
Bicycle

by Jack Prelutsky
illustrated by Roland Garrigue

Michael built a bicycle
unsuitable for speed,
it's crammed with more accessories
than anyone could need,
there's an AM-FM radio,
a deck to play cassettes,
a refrigerator-freezer,
and a pair of TV sets.

There are shelves for shirts and sweaters,
there are hangers for his jeans,
a drawer for socks and underwear,
a rack for magazines,
there's a fishtank and a birdcage
perched upon the handlebars,
a bookcase, and a telescope
to watch the moon and stars.

There's a telephone, a blender,
and a stove to cook his meals,
there's a sink to do the dishes
somehow fastened to the wheels,
there's a portable piano,
and a set of model trains,
an automatic bumbershoot
that opens when it rains.

There's a desk for typing letters
on his fabulous machine,
a stall for taking showers,
and a broom to keep things clean,
but you'll never see him ride it,
for it isn't quite complete,
Michael left no room for pedals,
and there isn't any seat.

Write the answers to the questions on these pages in your notebook. Use evidence and details from the text to support your answers.

Did You Know?

People in the United States held the first national science fair in 1950 in Philadelphia, Pennsylvania.

Text Connections

1. Why does Ruby share "interesting things" with other people?

2. Explain two benefits of Penny knowing sign language, according to Ruby.

3. Why do you think Ruby is annoyed that Dominic doesn't mind his own business?

4. In "Ruby Goldberg's Bright Idea," Ruby laments that ideas have a way of filling up her brain so there is "barely room left to focus on anything else." Describe something in your life that has a similar effect on you. How does this help you understand Ruby's feelings?

5. Both "Michael Built a Bicycle" and "Ruby Goldberg's Bright Idea" describe an invention. How does each invention similarly "miss the mark" in terms of being useful?

6. Describe a situation in which a properly working "Page-o-Matic" would be useful.

Look Closer

Keys to Comprehension

1. Name the major city Ruby either lives near or in, and explain what evidence in "Ruby Goldberg's Bright Idea" led you to make this inference.

2. Give reasons from "Ruby Goldberg's Bright Idea" that support Ruby's claim that dealing with her "took a lot of patience."

3. Compare and contrast the characters Ruby and Dominic, based on details in "Ruby Goldberg's Bright Idea."

Writer's Craft

4. Explain the author's use of the phrase "some kind of deranged beetle" when making a comparison in "Ruby Goldberg's Bright Idea."

5. Explain two structural details that help you know "Michael Built a Bicycle" is a poem and not prose.

Concept Development

6. Compare and contrast how characters in "Ruby Goldberg's Bright Idea" and "The Discovery Fair" handle competitiveness related to scientific work.

Write

Do you think competition helps or hurts scientific investigations? Write a paragraph giving reasons to support your opinion. Use examples from "Ruby Goldberg's Bright Idea," like Ruby's rivalry with Dominic, to back up your opinion.

Read this Science Connection. You will answer the questions as a class.

Text Feature

A **diagram** is a visual that shows the arrangements or parts of something.

Camera Obscura

Ruby Goldberg's science fair projects included a pinhole camera, which is a version of something called a *camera obscura*. This is a Latin phrase meaning "dark chamber." Long ago, people discovered that if they darkened a room with a single small hole in one wall, light coming through the hole would project an upside-down image. When done with caution, it is a safe way to study a solar eclipse. Artists sometimes used small *camerae obscurae*—pinhole cameras—to trace landscape images.

To understand why this works, you have to understand light. Imagine there is a tree near a pinhole camera. As sunlight travels, it goes in a straight line. It hits the tree and reflects off each part. The bumpy tree disrupts the path of light. Rays reflect in many different directions. When that reflected light enters the pinhole, it hits the opposite wall inside. Because the hole is so small, the reflected light from each tree part can only hit one spot. This creates an image of the tree.

The image is upside-down because light travels in a straight line. When light reflects from the tree's top, it shoots down in a straight line, goes through the pinhole, and hits the bottom of the opposite wall. Light reflecting from the bottom of the tree hits the top of the wall. The tree's image is upside down (see diagram 1).

Did you know that light enters your eye in a similar way? Your eye focuses reflected light onto a cell layer. As with the pinhole camera, the image is upside-down. The eyes and brain work together to interpret the information so that we do not see upside-down. Still, light travels in the same way for both.

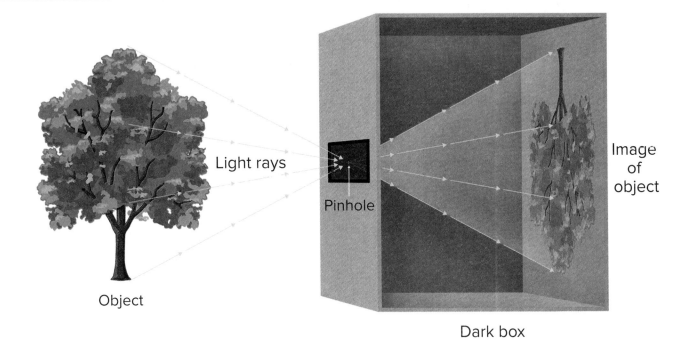

Light rays

Pinhole

Object

Image
of
object

Dark box

Diagram 1. Light reflects off an object to create a flipped image inside a pinhole camera.

1. Why is the image inside a pinhole camera upside-down?
2. Create a pinhole camera. Take a small, lidded cardboard box, and remove the lid. Tape waxed paper over the open end. Punch a pinhole in the bottom of the box. Sit in a dim room and point the pinhole toward a bright window. Cover your head and the container with a towel, but let the pinhole end peek out. Look at the waxed paper end. Move the camera away from you until you see a small upside-down image through the paper. How is this a model of the way light enters the eye?

 **Go Digital**

Ruby Goldberg also created a digital clock that ran on lemon juice. Research how to make a lemon battery and why it works.

My Brothers' Flying Machine

Wilbur, Orville, and Me

by Jane Yolen
paintings by Jim Burke

**"When the world speaks of the Wrights, it must include
our sister. Much of our effort has been inspired by her."**
—Orville Wright

I was four years old when
Papa brought home a little flying machine.
He tossed it into the air
right in front of Orv and Will.
They leaped up to catch it.
"Is it a bat?" Orv asked.
Or maybe it was Will.
When at last the "bat" fell to the floor,
they gathered it up
like some sultan's treasure,
marveling at its paper wings,
admiring the twisted rubber band
that gave it power.

I wanted to touch it, too,
but they would not let me,
saying I was too little,
though I was but three years younger
than Orv, to the very day.
When the "bat" broke, they fixed it together,
Will directing Orv — with his busy hands —
tinkering till the toy worked better
than when Papa first brought it home.

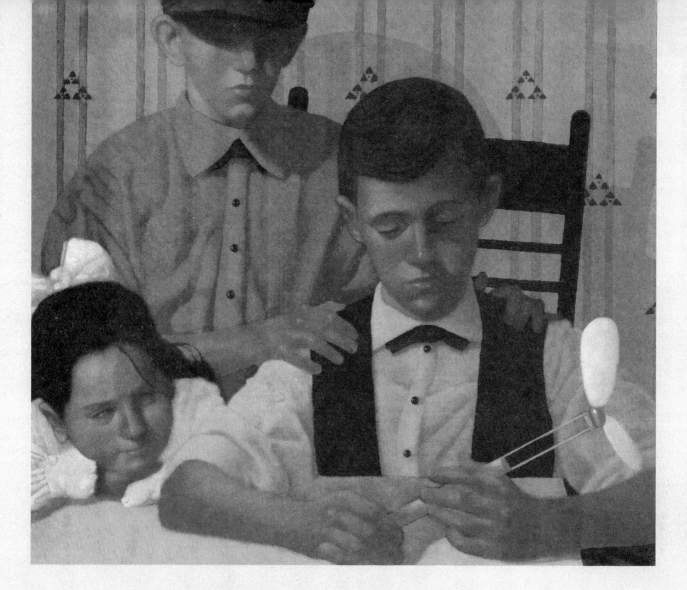

Our older brothers, Reuchlin and Lorin,
looked down on such childish activity,
but Will was not put off.
He made one,
   and two,
     and three more "bats,"
each one bigger than the last.
Orv was his constant helper.
I stood on tiptoe by the table,
watching them work.
Will shook his head.
"On a much larger scale," he said,
"the machine fails to work so well."
They were both puzzled.
They did not know yet
that a machine twice as big
needs eight times the power to fly.

After that, Will built sturdy kites,
which he sold to his pals in school.
Orv made a printing press,
with an old tombstone for a press bed,
wheels and cogs from a junkyard,
and the folding top of my old baby buggy
that he had found out in the barn.
My, it made me smile to see it.
Papa and Mama applauded their efforts.
Orv's press could print a thousand pages an hour.
A printer from the great city of Denver
came to visit and climbed under and over
Orv's baby-buggy press.
At last he laughed, amazed.
"Well, it works," he said,
"but I certainly don't see how."

Orv and Will made many messes,
but Mama never complained.
She'd always been the one
who gave them a hand building things
when they were boys.
Poor Papa. He knew God's word well enough,
but not how to drive a nail.
When dear Mama died of tuberculosis,
I took over her role:
keeping the house, making the meals,
and always giving the boys applause,
even after I graduated from college
and worked as a teacher.
Will and Orv never went on in school.
They ran a print shop, then a bicycle shop,
repairing and making custom-built models
they called the Van Cleve and the St. Clair.
Theirs was not the biggest bicycle shop in Dayton,
but I like to think it was the best.

Will and Orv. Orv and Will.
They worked side by side
in the bicycle shop,
whistling at the same time,
humming the same tune.
They even — so Will said — *thought* together.
Some folks mistook them for twins,
though they looked nothing alike.
Will had a hawk's face,
and Orv a red mustache.
Orv was the neat one.
He wore special cuffs for his sleeves
and a blue-and-white-striped apron
to protect his clothes.
But Will — land's sake, he was a mess.
I had to remind him when his suit needed pressing
and when his socks did not match,
or find him one of Orv's shirts
when he was ready to go off to give a speech.

The newspapers and magazines
were full of stories about people trying to fly.
Lilienthal, Pilcher, Chanute,
MEN INTO BIRDS, the headlines read.
I wondered if such a thing were really possible.
Orv said: "Insects, birds, and mammals
fly every day at pleasure,
it is reasonable to suppose that man might also fly."
Will wrote off to the Smithsonian
for all their books and pamphlets on flight.
He and Orv studied page after page.
The first question they asked was:
How can we control the flight?

They knew that a bicycle is unstable by itself,
yet it can be controlled by a rider.
How much more control would an aeroplane need?
Overhead, buzzards wheeled in the sky,
constantly changing the position of their wings
to catch the flow of air.
"If birds can do it," Orv mused out loud, "so can men."
He seemed so certain,
I began to believe it could be done.
I began to believe it could be done
by Will and Orv.

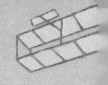

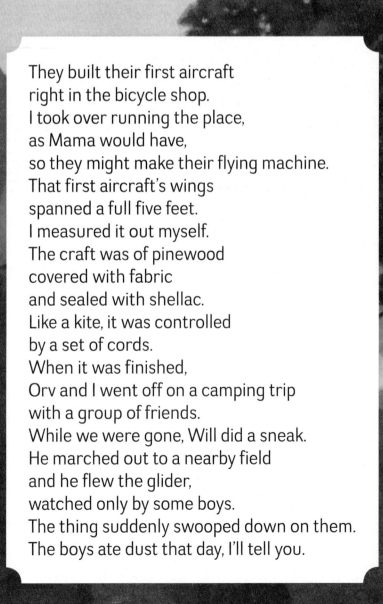

They built their first aircraft
right in the bicycle shop.
I took over running the place,
as Mama would have,
so they might make their flying machine.
That first aircraft's wings
spanned a full five feet.
I measured it out myself.
The craft was of pinewood
covered with fabric
and sealed with shellac.
Like a kite, it was controlled
by a set of cords.
When it was finished,
Orv and I went off on a camping trip
with a group of friends.
While we were gone, Will did a sneak.
He marched out to a nearby field
and he flew the glider,
watched only by some boys.
The thing suddenly swooped down on them.
The boys ate dust that day, I'll tell you.

Their first aircraft was a big kite.
But a kite is not an aeroplane.
So Will and Orv set about to build it bigger —
sixteen or seventeen feet,
large enough to carry a man
but still open to all the elements.
Will lay facedown on the lower wing,
showing me how he planned to fly.
I tried to imagine the wind in his face,
the dirt and grass rushing up to greet him
like an old bore at a party.
"Is it safe?" I whispered.
He winked at me, smiled, and said,
"If you are looking for perfect safety,
sit on the fence and watch the birds."

Dayton, Ohio, where we lived,
was not the place to fly the craft.
Will and Orv needed somewhere
with open spaces and strong, regular breezes.
They thought about San Diego,
about St. James, Florida,
about the coasts of South Carolina and Georgia.
At last they settled on Kitty Hawk
on the Outer Banks,
a two-hundred-mile strip of sand
with the ocean at its face
and North Carolina at its back.
Will called it "a safe place for practice."
Only sand and hearty breezes.
Only sun and a moon so bright
Orv could read his watch all hours.
I kept the store.
Will and Orv kept the sky.

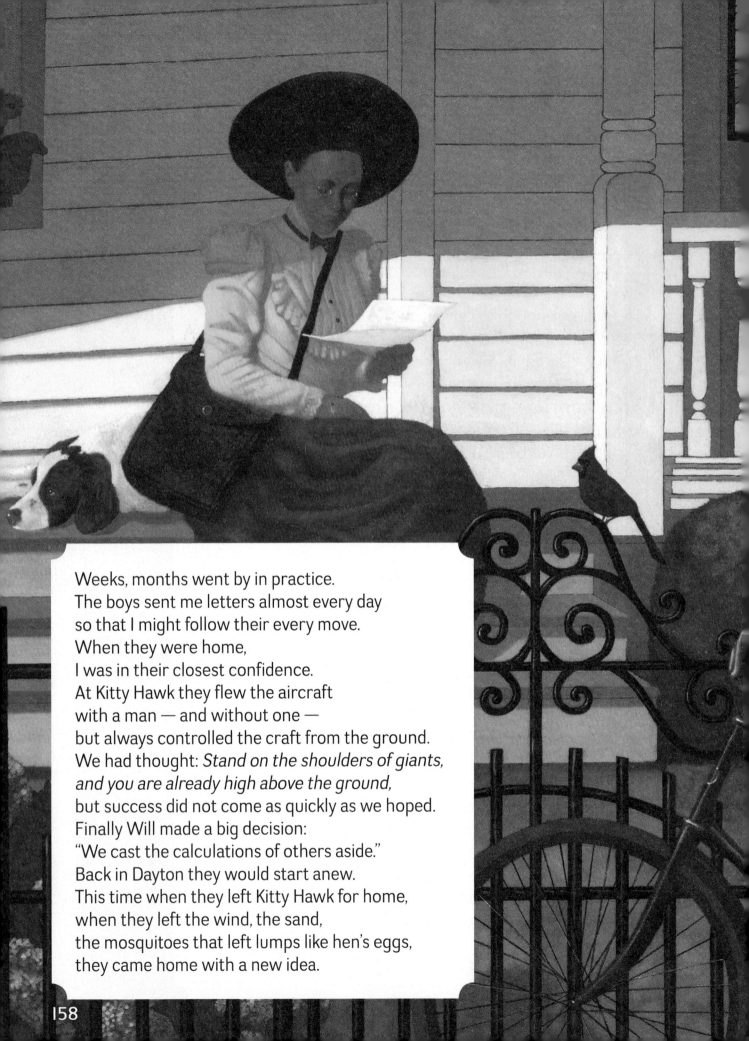

Weeks, months went by in practice.
The boys sent me letters almost every day
so that I might follow their every move.
When they were home,
I was in their closest confidence.
At Kitty Hawk they flew the aircraft
with a man — and without one —
but always controlled the craft from the ground.
We had thought: *Stand on the shoulders of giants,*
and you are already high above the ground,
but success did not come as quickly as we hoped.
Finally Will made a big decision:
"We cast the calculations of others aside."
Back in Dayton they would start anew.
This time when they left Kitty Hawk for home,
when they left the wind, the sand,
the mosquitoes that left lumps like hen's eggs,
they came home with a new idea.

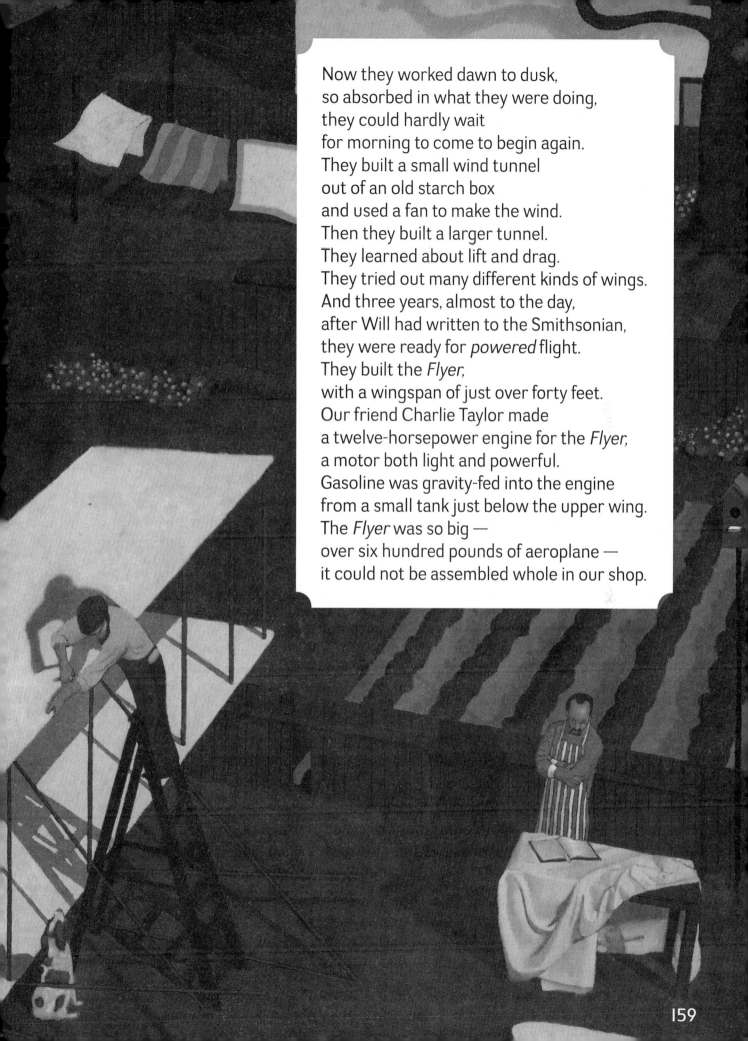

Now they worked dawn to dusk,
so absorbed in what they were doing,
they could hardly wait
for morning to come to begin again.
They built a small wind tunnel
out of an old starch box
and used a fan to make the wind.
Then they built a larger tunnel.
They learned about lift and drag.
They tried out many different kinds of wings.
And three years, almost to the day,
after Will had written to the Smithsonian,
they were ready for *powered* flight.
They built the *Flyer*,
with a wingspan of just over forty feet.
Our friend Charlie Taylor made
a twelve-horsepower engine for the *Flyer*,
a motor both light and powerful.
Gasoline was gravity-fed into the engine
from a small tank just below the upper wing.
The *Flyer* was so big —
over six hundred pounds of aeroplane —
it could not be assembled whole in our shop.

Back to Kitty Hawk they went
at the tag end of September 1903,
carrying crates filled with aircraft parts.
It took weeks to put the *Flyer* together,
weeks more to prepare for the flight.
Winter came blustering in early.
It was cold in camp,
each morning the washbasin was frozen solid,
so they wrote in their letters.
They kept fiddling,
tinkering, changing things.
Finally, on December 14, they were ready.
They flipped a coin to see who would be pilot.
Will won, grinned, climbed into the hip cradle,
and off the *Flyer* went,
rattling down the sixty-foot starting track,
then sailing fifteen feet into the air,
where it stalled,
crashed.
But they were encouraged nonetheless.
The telegram they sent to Papa and me read:
Rudder only injured.
Success assured.
Keep quiet.

On December 17, a cold and windy day,
the *Flyer* repaired and ready,
they decided to try again.
Hoisting a red flag to the top of a pole,
they signaled the lifesaving station for witnesses.
Four men and a teenage boy appeared.
The men helped them get the *Flyer*
onto the starting track.
Orv lay down on the lower wing,
his hips in the padded cradle.
Will shook Orv's hand.
"Now you men," Will called out,
"laugh and holler and clap
and try to cheer my brother."
The motor began:
Cough, cough, chug-a-chug-a-chug.
Orv released the wire
that held the plane to the track.
Then the plane raced forward
into the strong wind
and into history.
The boys sent a telegram home to Papa and me.

After that, the world was never the same.
Many men went into the air.
Women, too.
I was not the first woman to fly.
That honor went to the wife
of one of our sponsors,
Mrs. Hart O. Berg, with a rope around her skirt
to keep it from blowing about
and showing her legs.
She flew for two minutes and seven seconds,
sitting stiffly upright next to Will.
A Parisian dressmaker who watched the flight
invented the hobble skirt,
which for a short time was quite smart.
Such is fashion.
But how I laughed when I had my turn at last,
flying at Pau in France on February 15, 1909.
Will took his seat beside me.
Orv waved from the ground.
The plane took off into the cold blue.
Wind scoured my face
till my cheeks turned bright red.
Then I opened my arms wide,
welcoming all the sky before me.

Genre Primary Source — Diary

Essential Questions
How do scientists record their observations?
Why do they record them?

The Diary of Orville Wright, 1903

from the
Wilbur and Orville Wright Papers
at the Library of Congress

When we got up a wind of between 20 and 25 miles was blowing from the north. We got the machine out early and put out the signal for the men at the station. Before we were quite ready, John T. Daniels, W. S. Dough, A.D. Etheridge, W.C. Brinkley of Manteo, and Jonny Moore, of Nags Head arrived. After running the engine and propellers a few minutes to get them in working order, I got on the machine at 10:35 for the first trial. The wind according to our anemometers at this time was blowing a little over 20 miles (corrected) 27 miles according to the Government anemometer at Kitty Hawk. On slipping the rope the machine started off increasing in speed to probably 7 or 8 miles. The machine lifted from the truck just as it was entering on the fourth rail. Mr. Daniels took a picture just as it left the tracks. I found the control of the front rudder quite difficult on account of its being balanced too near the center and thus had a tendency to turn itself when started so that the rudder was turned too far on one side and then too far on the other. As a result the machine would rise suddenly to about 10 ft and then as suddenly, on turning the rudder, dart for the ground. A sudden dart when out about 100 feet from the end of the tracks ended the flight. Time about 12 seconds (not known exactly as watch was not promptly stopped). The lever for throwing off the engine was broken, and the skid under the rudder cracked. After repairs, at 20 minutes after 11 o'clock Will made the second trial.

The course was about like mine, up and down but a little longer over the ground though about the same in time. Distance not measured but about 175 feet. Wind speed not quite so strong. With the aid of the station men present, we picked the machine up and carried it back to the starting ways. At about 20 minutes till 12 o'clock I made the third trial. While out about the same distance as Will's, I met with a strong gust from the left which raised the left wing and sidled the machine off to the right in a lively manner. I immediately turned the rudder to bring the machine down and then worked the end control. Much to our surprise, on reaching the ground the left wing struck first, showing the lateral control of this machine much more effective than on any of our former ones. At the time of its sidling it had raised to a height of probably 12 to 14 feet. At just 12 o'clock Will started on the fourth and last trip. The machine started off with its ups and downs as it had before, but by the time he had gone three or four hundred feet he had it under much better control, and was traveling on a fairly even course. It proceed in this manner till it reached a small hummock out about 800 feet from the starting ways, when it begun its pitching again and suddenly darted into the ground. The front rudder frame was badly broken up, but the main frame suffered none at all. The distance over the ground was 852 feet in 59 seconds. The engine turns was 1071, but this included several seconds while on the starting ways and probably about a half second after landing. The jar of landing had set the watch on machine back so that we have no exact record for the 1071 turns. Will took a picture of my third flight just before the gust struck the machine. The machine left the ways successfully at every trial, and the track was never caught by the truck as we had feared.

After removing the front rudder, we carried the machine back to camp. We set the machine down a few feet west of the building, and while standing about discussing the last flight, a sudden gust of wind struck the machine and started to turn it over. All rushed to stop it. Will who was near the end ran to the front, but too late to do any good. Mr. Daniels and myself seized spars at the rear, but to no purpose. The machine gradually turned over on us. Mr. Daniels, having had no experience in handling a machine of this kind, hung on to it from the inside, and as a result was knocked down and turned over and over with it as it went. His escape was miraculous, as he was in with the engine and chains. The engine legs were all broken off, the chain guides badly bent, a number of uprights, and nearly all the rear ends of the ribs were broken. One spare only was broken.

After dinner we went to Kitty Hawk to send off telegram to M. W. While there we called on Captain and Mrs. Hobbs, Dr. Cogswell and the station men.

Essential Questions
Why do inventors need courage?
How can having perseverance pay off?

Crazy Boys

by Beverly McLoughland
illustrated by Kailey Whitney

Watching buzzards,
Flying kites,
Lazy, crazy boys
The Wrights.   They

Tried to fly
Just like a bird
Foolish dreamers
Strange.   Absurd.   We

Scoffed and scorned
Their dreams of flight
But we were wrong
And they were Wright.

Write the answers to the questions on these pages in your notebook. Use evidence and details from the text to support your answers.

Text Connections

1. Why do people mistake Wilbur and Orville Wright for twins, even though the brothers do not look alike?

2. How do you know that the Wright brothers are close to their sister?

3. How does Wilbur do "a sneak" when he takes the first aircraft out for a flight, and what is the result?

4. How are the Wright brothers like Ruby Goldberg or any of the inventors from "The Discovery Fair"?

5. Orville describes how a gust of wind badly wrecks their flyer after their flight trials in "The Diary of Orville Wright, 1903." Would this discourage you if you were him? Explain.

6. Explain why "the world was never the same" after the flight of the 1903 flyer.

Did You Know?

The flying toy the Wright brothers' father brought them was an 1871 invention by Alphonse Pénaud. Pénaud is sometimes called the "Father of Flying Models."

Look Closer

Keys to Comprehension

1. Infer why Orville Wright says that the world must include their sister when it speaks of the Wright brothers' achievements, based on evidence from "My Brothers' Flying Machine."

2. Explain the importance of the first event in "My Brothers' Flying Machine," based on the events that follow.

Writer's Craft

3. Explain the origin of the hobble skirt and infer how this skirt looks.

4. Consider "The Diary of Orville Wright, 1903" and "My Brothers' Flying Machine." Compare and contrast the focus of and information in the firsthand and secondhand accounts of December 17, 1903.

Concept Development

5. How does the collage of photographs help you better visualize Orville's experience in "The Diary of Orville Wright, 1903"?

6. Drawing on both "The Diary of Orville Wright, 1903" and "My Brothers' Flying Machine," describe the first successful flight of the Wright flyer.

Write

Write a diary entry about some of the things you did yesterday. Look at "The Diary of Orville Wright, 1903" to see how a diary is normally structured. Use first-person words like "my" and "we" in your diary entry.

Read this Science Connection. You will answer the questions as a class.

Text Feature

An **outline** organizes ideas into larger and smaller groups, using numbers and sometimes letters.

Gliding Toward Powered Flight

On the way to inventing their 1903 Flyer, the Wright brothers created another important invention—the first controllable glider aircraft. Before that, no one had solved the problem of how to safely steer an aircraft.

Certain forces must be balanced or a glider is unstable. The brothers tinkered with their glider design to balance the following:

1. **Weight** The first force on a glider is its weight. The force of gravity, which pulls the glider toward Earth's center, determines weight.

2. **Aerodynamic force** This complex force has to do with air and motion. People often break it into the following two forces to make it easier to understand:

   a. **Lift** This force raises a glider off the ground, overcoming the force of gravity. The glider's wings create lift.

   b. **Drag** Air resistance against the glider creates the force of drag. Drag always pushes against the direction of the glider's motion.

Unlike a glider, an airplane has another force: thrust. An airplane uses engines to create thrust, which overcomes drag. A glider doesn't have an engine, though. The Wrights added a rudder to their 1902 glider, making it the first that could be controlled left and right. However, it still could only glide in a downward direction from a high location to a low one. Still, the glider's invention was important. It was a needed step on the way to controllable powered flight.

The 1902 Wright glider was the first aircraft that could be fully controlled by the pilot.

1. Compare and contrast the forces on a glider and a powered airplane.

2. Create a simple glider. Gather a small binder clip, masking tape, and two 3 × 5 index cards. Place the cards end to end on one 3-inch side and tape them, forming a hinge.

3. You must now figure out a way to add the binder clip so that your glider goes as far as possible and travels in a straight line. Using a clock, give yourself 5 minutes to experiment. Write down the distance your glider achieves with each clip placement. What placement allows your glider to travel both straight and far?

 Go Digital

An airfoil is a curved structure, and is the name for the cross-sectional shape of an airplane's wing. Research airfoil design and how it affects the force of lift.

Godspeed, John Glenn

written and illustrated by Richard Hilliard

When John Glenn was a boy living in Ohio, he and his dad took a ride in an airplane. This was a great thrill for young John, and he never forgot the feeling of flying through the sky. Many nights he lay in bed dreaming of flying planes when he grew up.

JOHN GLENN JR.

BORN: July 18, 1921, in Cambridge, Ohio

EDUCATION: Bachelor of science degree in engineering from Muskingum College; doctor of science degree (honorary) in engineering from Muskingum College.

HONORS AND MEDALS: Awarded the Distinguished Flying Cross on six occasions and holds the Air Medal with 18 Clusters for service during World War II and Korea. Also holds Navy Unit Commendation for Service in Korea, the Asiatic-Pacific Campaign Medal, the American Campaign Medal, the World War II Victory Medal, the China Service Medal, the National Defense Service Medal, the Korean Service Medal, the United Nations Service Medal, the Korean Presidential Unit Citation, the Navy's Astronaut Wings, the Marine Corps' Astronaut Medal, the NASA Distinguished Service Medal, and the Congressional Space Medal of Honor.

In college, John studied aerodynamics and took flight classes. After the bombing of Pearl Harbor, John volunteered in the U.S. Navy. He became a fighter pilot in the Marine Corps and flew during both World War II and the war in Korea. He won many medals, including the Distinguished Flying Cross, the highest honor a pilot can receive.

As peacetime settled in the 1950s, John became a test pilot. Flying experimental aircraft, he went higher and faster with every flight. As America entered the "space age," John volunteered for a new and dangerous duty—becoming an astronaut.

It took a special breed of aviator to be a test pilot. Not only did the test pilot need to be an excellent flyer, but he also needed lightning-fast reflexes and the ability to think clearly under intense physical and emotional pressure. Making a critical decision a half second too late could mean disaster—and possibly death—when flying experimental aircraft. The men chosen for this hazardous duty were said by historians to have "the right stuff." In 1957 John Glenn became the first pilot to fly from New York to Los Angeles at supersonic speed (750 mph or faster). He made the flight in 3 hours and 23 minutes.

Hundreds of men tested for this new service that would ultimately launch Americans into the vacuum of space. In 1959 John Glenn was selected along with six other test pilots to become America's first astronauts—the Mercury Seven. John didn't know where the Astronaut Corps would take him, but he was excited to be one of the first pioneers of this new frontier.

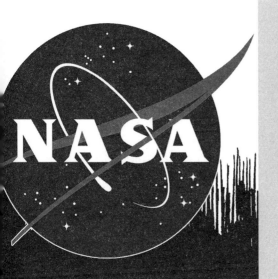

The Mercury Seven Astronauts:

M. Scott Carpenter

L. Gordon Cooper Jr.

John Glenn Jr.

Virgil "Gus" Grissom

Walter "Wally" Schirra Jr.

Alan Shepard Jr.

Donald "Deke" Slayton

Each man was a highly trained aviator, but training to go into space required the toughest physical and mental conditioning they had ever seen. This was partly due to the unknown factors of performing in the weightlessness of space, but also because the whole world would be watching them taking these first steps. The slightest error could spell disaster for not only the astronaut but also the future of America's space program. For the astronauts, perfection was the only option.

As the astronauts spent many months in training, America began to send chimpanzees into space. People started to wonder if the astronauts were up to the difficult challenge of going into orbit. John and the others knew they were ready but needed to make sure the spacecraft was safe enough to take a man into space and bring him back to Earth.

Before men and women ventured into orbit, rockets carried animals into the sky. This tested whether a living creature could withstand the changes in pressure and be brought back to Earth without injury. America's first space celebrity was Ham. This male chimpanzee flew into space on January 31, 1961, blasting off from Cape Canaveral and traveling more than 150 miles in a Mercury capsule before splashing down safely in the ocean. His little pod was strapped into the human-sized seat, providing him with oxygen and keeping him comfortable. Ham became famous after the flight and was featured on many magazine covers.

The first missions to carry astronauts into orbit were called Mercury. The first two human missions went only to the edge of space, proving an astronaut could work in the weightless environment. The third mission would send an astronaut into orbit around Earth, circling the planet many times. John felt very honored when he was selected to take this historic flight.

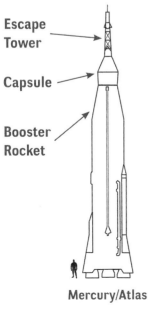

Escape Tower

Capsule

Booster Rocket

Mercury/Atlas

For the first two American space flights, the capsules rode atop small Redstone boosters into suborbital space. The Redstone was not powerful enough to push the Mercury capsule into orbit. To get the needed power for orbit, American rocket scientists turned to the Atlas booster rocket for their next flight. Unfortunately, the Atlas had many failed test launches, which caused the big rocket to explode. Scientists worked night and day to fix the problem. The Atlas was finally ready to fly with the third manned mission that would take John Glenn into space. The rocket consisted of three main parts: the escape tower, which would carry the capsule away from the booster in an emergency; the capsule, which held the astronaut and instrumentation; and the booster, which carried the main fuel and rocket engines.

On February 20, 1962, on a launch platform at Cape Canaveral, Florida, John was strapped into the small Mercury capsule, called *Friendship 7*. As the countdown ended, the giant Atlas rocket engine roared to life, slowly raising the spacecraft off the launch platform. As John's capsule cleared the tower, astronaut Scott Carpenter radioed the world, "Godspeed, John Glenn," wishing him good luck as he rose into the sky.

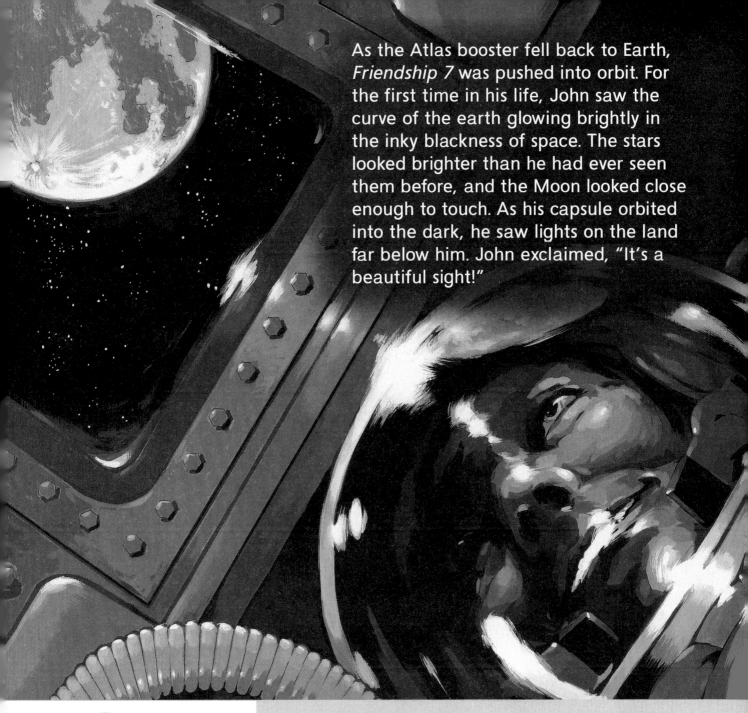

As the Atlas booster fell back to Earth, *Friendship 7* was pushed into orbit. For the first time in his life, John saw the curve of the earth glowing brightly in the inky blackness of space. The stars looked brighter than he had ever seen them before, and the Moon looked close enough to touch. As his capsule orbited into the dark, he saw lights on the land far below him. John exclaimed, "It's a beautiful sight!"

Once the Atlas booster was out of fuel, it separated from the capsule, falling back to Earth. This is called "staging." A booster rocket's fate depends on its size. A booster may fall through the atmosphere, building up heat and burning up before it gets anywhere near the surface. If it is so large that it could not burn up entirely, parachutes would bring it back for a soft ocean landing. The Atlas was not large enough to need an ocean landing, so it burned up once it came back into Earth's atmosphere. Having done its job of putting the capsule into orbit, it was no longer needed.

Everything was going perfectly, and John was told by Mission Control that he could expect at least seven orbits of the globe, each orbit taking only eighty-eight minutes. Although the *Friendship 7* capsule was very cramped, John felt comfortable in the weightless environment as he conducted experiments and piloted the capsule around the world. From every corner of the globe, people tuned in their radios and televisions to hear the updates on John's flight.

Although the Mercury astronauts were in one-man capsules traveling through space, they were never truly alone. Back on Earth, the people of Mission Control constantly monitored them. Linked to the capsule by radio signals, the technicians could keep track of almost every function of the spacecraft in orbit. Doctors were able to watch the astronaut's heartbeat and breathing patterns, while engineers monitored the speed and location of the capsule. If anything went wrong, Mission Control was there to help the astronaut work through the problem.

Back at Mission Control in Florida, things looked good until suddenly a beeping alarm sounded, indicating something was wrong. The heat shield on John's capsule might be loose, and if it came off, John would burn up as the spacecraft reentered Earth's atmosphere. Everyone decided that John would have to be brought back after only three orbits.

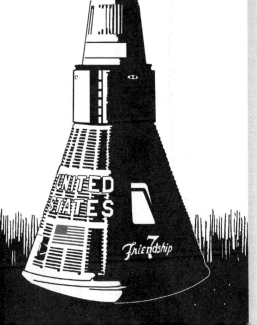

Like a giant bowl covering the bottom of the space capsule, the heat shield protected the spacecraft from burning up during reentry. Made of thick, ceramic material, the heat shield absorbed and deflected the temperature buildup as the capsule plunged through Earth's upper atmosphere. As the capsule fell, air molecules moved against the surface, creating friction. This friction gets so intense that the bottom of the capsule turns into a fireball. Without the heat shield, the capsule could never return safely.

As the capsule plunged back to Earth, John's spacecraft was engulfed in flame. His only protection was the heat shield that might not be working properly, and the retropack, which began to melt and break away from the capsule. Everyone at Mission Control was nervous that John would not return safely. Even John was worried and started humming a tune to himself to stay calm. Hearing John's voice through the crackling radio, Mission Control knew he survived the fiery descent. He radioed to Scott and the others at the Cape, "That was a real fireball there!"

With the possibility of a loose heat shield, Mission Control decided to leave the retropack attached to the bottom of John's capsule. Normally, this small collection of rocket nozzles would be jettisoned, or automatically pushed away before reentry. Mission Control hoped the pack's straps would hold the heat shield in place. As it later turned out, the malfunction was not with the heat shield but with the control panel on Earth. In any event, fast thinking helped maintain the astronaut's safety.

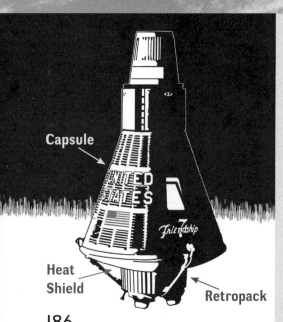

Capsule

Heat
Shield

Retropack

Almost two miles above the waters of the Pacific Ocean, a big parachute shot out of the capsule's nose as the flames died down. *Friendship 7* floated gently into the waves as U.S. Navy ships moved in to pick up John and his capsule. The navy crew cheered wildly for John as he came aboard the large ship.

After the historic flight, John became a hero to millions of people around the world who were inspired by his courage in facing the unknown. Huge crowds lined the streets of Washington, D.C., as a parade took John and his wife, Annie, to meet the president. Later John gave a speech to Congress about the importance of space exploration and the quest to land on the Moon.

John F. Kennedy was the president of the United States during the early days of the space program. After the first successful Mercury mission in 1961, Kennedy became convinced that landing on the Moon could be achieved by American astronauts. He set a goal for NASA and the rest of the country to get a man on the Moon by the end of 1969. Many did not believe this was possible, but President Kennedy, as America's foremost space cheerleader of the day, did everything he could to make this dream a reality. John Glenn's successful mission was a major step in realizing Kennedy's dream.

John left the Astronaut Corps and Marines in 1964 and later became a prominent U.S. senator. In 1998, he surprised the world when he went back into space aboard the space shuttle *Discovery*. John Glenn was living proof that life's adventures never stop.

189

Write the answers to the questions on these pages in your notebook. Use evidence and details from the text to support your answers.

Text Connections

1. If you were to stop reading at the end of page 178 of "Godspeed, John Glenn," what could you infer about the rest of the text? How would you know?

2. Why do you think John Glenn hummed a tune to himself as he returned to Earth?

3. What event inspired John Glenn to become a pilot?

4. Why can we infer that NASA's process of invention in "Godspeed, John Glenn" was more complicated than the Wright brothers' process of invention?

5. John Glenn's fellow astronaut wished him good luck as he lifted off. Have you ever been wished good luck by someone, or wish someone good luck yourself? Describe the situation.

6. The text describes the Atlas rocket as having "many failed test launches." Do you think these failures contributed to the success of the mission, or were they just problems to be solved?

Did You Know?

Seven years after John Glenn's historic orbit, Neil Armstrong became the first person to step foot on the moon. In this century, NASA and other space agencies aspire to send humans back to the moon and to Mars as well.

Look Closer

Keys to Comprehension

1. Summarize "Godspeed, John Glenn" using the main idea and key details from the text.

2. Describe in your own words the concept of having "the right stuff," using details from the text.

Writer's Craft

3. Identify some scientific words or phrases from the selection and explain their meanings. Why do you think the author included these words?

4. Is "Godspeed, John Glenn" organized by time? Does it follow any other organizational patterns? If so, describe how you know.

Concept Development

5. On page 178 the author of "Godspeed, John Glenn" describes becoming an astronaut as "a new and dangerous duty." What reasons and evidence support this idea?

6. Using information from "My Brothers' Flying Machine" and "Godspeed, John Glenn" describe how scientific inspiration and innovation change over time.

Write

Think about a moment in your life that required knowledge, trust, and courage. Describe the moment and how it changed you. Compare that moment to a time John Glenn displayed trust or courage, like when he signed up to be an astronaut.

Read this Science Connection. You will answer the questions as a class.

Text Feature

Diagrams are drawings that show the arrangements or parts of something.

The Art of Scientific Teamwork

When speaking about an invention, one may say who owns it. For instance, "Thomas Edison invented the light bulb." While true, such a statement leaves out the fact that inventors hardly work in a vacuum, or all alone. Each innovator benefits from collaborating with someone else.

Collaboration is sharing information or resources on a quest toward a goal. When Lewis Howard Latimer shared his ideas about filaments with Thomas Edison, they collaborated. When the Smithsonian Institution sent information about flight to the Wright Brothers, that was collaboration too. NASA scientists and test pilots collaborated as they conducted tests of their space crafts.

Scientific collaboration brings together many minds to solve a problem. Think of these proverbs: "Many hands make light work." "Two heads are better than one." Both explain why collaboration works. Scientists share energy and resources. They also share their knowledge and experiences (see Diagram 1). One person may think of part of a solution, while another comes up with another part, and a third thinks of the last part. They ultimately find the best way to solve a complex problem.

The scientific questions being researched today are much more complex than the ones tackled in the past. Hundreds or even thousands of scientists and engineers may work together. Collaboration has been important in the past, and it will remain important in the future.

Scientific Collaboration

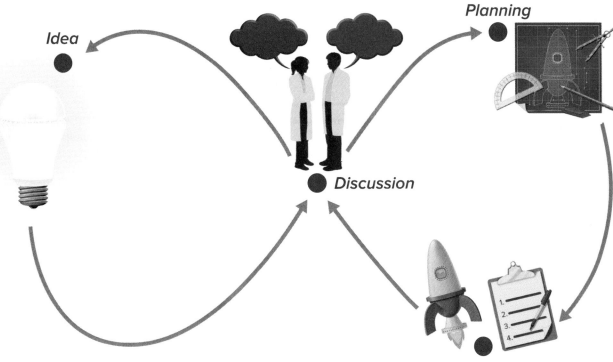

Diagram 1: The process of scientific collaboration

1. What happens when scientists and engineers collaborate?

2. How does information in the diagram help you better understand the main text?

3. Using information from the text, construct an argument about the necessity of collaboration.

 Go Digital

Research the ways in which innovators collaborate. Also research a student-appropriate physics experiment. Consider doing that experiment with your class and note the ways in which you collaborate in the process.

Genre Autobiography

Essential Questions

Why do scientists go to space? What do they hope to learn?

TO SPACE & BACK

by Sally Ride with Susan Okie

"What's it like to be in space?" "Is it scary?" "Is it cold?" "Do you have trouble sleeping?" These are questions that everyone asks astronauts who have been in space.

The experience is hard to describe. The words and pictures in this book will help you imagine what it's like to blast off in a rocket and float effortlessly in midair while circling hundreds of miles above the Earth.

My first space flight was in June 1983, with four other astronauts: Bob Crippen, Rick Hauck, John Fabian, and Norm Thagard. We blasted off from a launch pad in Florida; then we circled the Earth for seven days. As we went around and around the planet, we launched two satellites, studied the Earth, and learned about weightlessness. After a week in orbit we returned to Earth. Our adventure ended as the space shuttle glided back through the atmosphere to a smooth landing in California.

When I was growing up, I was always fascinated by the planets, stars, and galaxies, but I never thought about becoming an astronaut. I studied math and science in high school, and then I spent my years in college learning physics— the study of the laws of nature and the universe. Just as I was finishing my education, NASA, the United States space agency, began looking for scientists who wanted to become astronauts. Suddenly I knew that I wanted a chance to see the Earth and the stars from outer space. I sent my application to NASA, and after a series of tests and interviews, I was chosen to be an astronaut.

I wrote this book because I wanted to answer some of the questions that young people ask of astronauts. Many of the questions are about feelings, and one that now may have added meaning is, "Is it scary?"

All adventures—especially into new territory—are scary, and there has always been an element of danger in space flight. I wanted to be an astronaut because I thought it would be a challenging opportunity. It was; it was also an experience that I shall never forget.

—SALLY RIDE

LAUNCH MORNING.

6 . . . 5 . . . 4 . . .

The alarm clock counts down.

3 . . . 2 . . . 1 . . .

Rrring! 3:15 A.M. *Launch minus four hours.* Time to get up.

It's pitch black outside. In four hours a space shuttle launch will light up the sky.

Nine miles from the launch pad, in the astronaut crew quarters, we put on our flight suits, get some last-minute information, and eat a light breakfast.

Launch minus three hours. It's still dark. We leave the crew quarters, climb into the astronaut van, and head for the launch pad.

The space shuttle stands with its nose pointed toward the sky, attached to the big orange fuel tank and two white rockets that will lift it—and us—into space.

The spotlights shining on the space shuttle light the last part of our route. Although we're alone, we know that thousands of people are watching us now, during the final part of the countdown.

When we step out onto the pad, we're dwarfed by the thirty-story-high space shuttle. Our spaceplane looked peaceful from the road, but now we can hear it hissing and gurgling as though it's alive.

The long elevator ride up the launch tower takes us to a level near the nose of the space shuttle, 195 feet above the ground. Trying hard not to look down at the pad far below, we walk out onto an access arm and into the "white room." The white room, a small white chamber at the end of the movable walkway, fits right next to the space shuttle's hatch. The only other people on the launch pad—in fact, the only other people for miles—are the six technicians waiting for us in the white room. They help us put on our escape harnesses and launch helmets and help us climb through the hatch. Then they strap us into our seats.

Because the space shuttle is standing on its tail, we are lying on our backs as we face the nose. It's awkward to twist around to look out the windows. The commander has a good view of the launch tower, and the pilot has a good view of the Atlantic Ocean, but no one else can see much outside.

Launch minus one hour. We check to make sure that we are strapped in properly, that oxygen will flow into our helmets, that our radio communication with Mission Control is working, and that our pencils and our books—the procedure manuals and checklists we'll need during liftoff—are attached to something to keep them from shaking loose. Then we wait.

The technicians close the hatch and then head for safety three miles away. We're all alone on the launch pad.

Launch minus seven minutes. The walkway with the white room at the end slowly pulls away. Far below us the power units start whirring, sending a shudder through the shuttle. We close the visors on our helmets and begin to breathe from the oxygen supply. Then the space shuttle quivers again as its launch engines slowly move into position for blast-off.

Launch minus 10 seconds . . . 9 . . . 8 . . . 7 . . . The three launch engines light. The shuttle shakes and strains at the bolts holding it to the launch pad. The computers check the engines. It isn't up to us anymore—the computers will decide whether we launch.

3 . . . 2 . . . 1 . . . The rockets light! The shuttle leaps off the launch pad in a cloud of steam and a trail of fire. Inside, the ride is rough and loud. Our heads are rattling around inside our helmets. We can barely hear the voices from Mission Control in our headsets above the thunder of the rockets and engines. For an instant I wonder if everything is working right. But there's no more time to wonder, and no time to be scared.

In only a few seconds we zoom past the clouds. Two minutes later the rockets burn out, and with a brilliant whitish-orange flash, they fall away from the shuttle as it streaks on toward space. Suddenly the ride becomes very, very smooth and quiet. The shuttle is still attached to the big tank, and the launch engines are pushing us out of Earth's atmosphere. The sky is black. All we can see of the trail of fire behind us is a faint, pulsating glow through the top window.

Launch plus six minutes. The force pushing us against the backs of our seats steadily increases. We can barely move because we're being held in place by a force of 3 g's—three times the force of gravity we feel on Earth. At first we don't mind it—we've all felt much more than that when we've done acrobatics in our jet training airplanes. But that lasted only a few seconds, and this seems to go on forever. After a couple of minutes of 3 g's, we're uncomfortable, straining to hold our books on our laps and craning our necks against the force to read the instruments. I find myself wishing we'd hurry up and get into orbit.

Launch plus eight and one-half minutes. The launch engines cut off. Suddenly the force is gone, and we lurch forward in our seats. During the next few minutes the empty fuel tank drops away and falls to Earth, and we are very busy getting the shuttle ready to enter orbit. But we're not too busy to notice that our books and pencils are floating in midair. We're in space!

The atmosphere thins gradually as we travel farther from Earth. At fifty miles up, we're above most of the air, and we're officially "in space." We aren't in orbit yet, though, and without additional push the shuttle would come crashing back to Earth.

We use the shuttle's smaller space engines to get us into our final, safe orbit about two hundred miles above Earth. In that orbit we are much higher than airplanes, which fly about six miles up, but much lower than weather satellites, which circle Earth more than twenty-two thousand miles up.

Once we are in orbit, our ride is very peaceful. The engines have shut down, and the only noise we hear is the hum of the fans that circulate our air. We are traveling at five miles a second, going around the Earth once every ninety minutes, but we don't feel the motion. We can't even tell we're moving unless we look out the window at Earth.

We stay much closer to home than the astronauts who flew space capsules to the moon in 1969. When those astronauts stood on the moon, they described the distant Earth as a big blue-and-white marble suspended in space. We are a long way from the moon, and we never get far enough from Earth to see the whole planet at once.

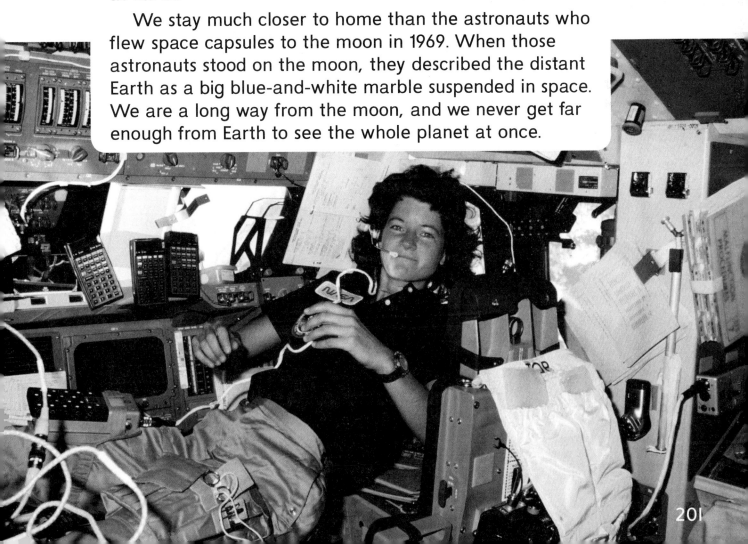

We still have a magnificent view. The sparkling blue oceans and bright orange deserts are glorious against the blackness of space. Even if we can't see the whole planet, we can see quite a distance. When we are over Los Angeles we can see as far as Oregon; when we are over Florida we can see New York.

We see mountain ranges reaching up to us and canyons falling away. We see huge dust storms blowing over deserts in Africa and smoke spewing from the craters of active volcanoes in Hawaii. We see enormous chunks of ice floating in the Antarctic Ocean and electrical storms raging over the Atlantic.

Sunrises and sunsets are spectacular from orbit. Since we see one sunrise and one sunset each time we go around the Earth, we can watch sixteen sunrises and sixteen sunsets every twenty-four hours. Our sightseeing doesn't stop while we are over the dark side of the planet. We can see twinkling city lights, the reflection of the moon in the sea, and flashes of lightning from thunderstorms.

These natural features are not the only things we can see. We can also spot cities, airport runways, bridges, and other signs of civilization. When our orbit takes us over Florida, we are even able to see the launch pad at Cape Canaveral, where we crawled into the space shuttle just hours earlier.

AFTERWORD

In the rest of To Space & Back, astronaut Sally Ride describes daily life and scientific work in orbit around Earth. She also describes the process of reentering Earth's atmosphere and landing the space shuttle. NASA's last space shuttle landed in 2011, but American astronauts continue to travel to space and back. Sally Ride died of cancer in 2012. She is remembered as the first American woman in space.

Write the answers to the questions on these pages in your notebook. Use evidence and details from the text to support your answers.

Did You Know?

Though it was not until the 1980s that U.S. women became astronauts, women have always been an important part of space exploration. Women have worked as NASA computers, engineers, and leaders, just to name a few important roles!

Text Connections

1. How long was Sally Ride's first space flight?

2. Why do you think astronauts practice doing "acrobatics in . . . jet training airplanes" before going into space?

3. Describe and explain the reasons for some changes the astronauts feel and see once they are in space.

4. Describe ways both Sally Ride and Ynés Mexía from "The Discovery Fair" prioritized scientific discovery over worries about danger.

5. Does Sally Ride's account make you aspire to be an astronaut? Why or why not?

6. Infer why astronauts often have backgrounds in science, technology, engineering, and math.

Look Closer

Keys to Comprehension

1. Why did Sally Ride write her book, and how do you know?

2. Summarize the main topic of the selection from "To Space & Back."

3. Describe the procedures Sally Ride and other astronauts went through when preparing for liftoff in the space shuttle.

Writer's Craft

4. Explain what *orbit* means, and why it was important to the space shuttle.

5. Give examples to support the idea that "To Space & Back" is mostly structured using a chronological order of usual events.

Concept Development

6. In "To Space & Back," how does Sally Ride support the idea that space flight is wonderful, despite being scary at times?

Write

In "To Space and Back," Sally Ride described seeing canyons and city lights from space. Imagine you are an astronaut. Describe the places you would most like to see when orbiting Earth in your spacecraft.

Read this Social Studies Connection. You will answer the questions as a class.

Text Feature

A **caption** gives more information about a photograph or other image.

The Women of the FLATs Group

In 1978, NASA chose a group of 35 astronauts that for the first time included women, African Americans, and Asian Americans. Out of that group, four women ended up setting important firsts in space. These were not the first American women, however, to have hopes of becoming astronauts.

Years before, in 1960, a man named Dr. William Randolph Lovelace II began researching this possibility. Lovelace had helped NASA design testing for the Mercury astronauts, and he believed that women could also be astronauts. A woman named Jerrie Cobb underwent some of the same tests as the Mercury astronauts. By 1961, a total of 13 women had passed these tests. They nicknamed themselves the FLATs, which stood for Fellow Lady Astronaut Trainees. However, NASA's leaders did not yet want to consider applications from women. The program suddenly ended.

Some people helped to get a special government subcommittee to consider the matter in 1962. Unfortunately, NASA officials argued against having women become astronauts. As a result, women from the FLATs group watched as the Soviet Union launched cosmonaut Valentina Tereshkova—the first woman—into space in 1963. It wasn't until 1983 that Sally Ride finally became the first American woman in space.

People still remember and honor the women of the FLATs group today. They were important trailblazers on the path to equality in space.

Pilot Jerrie Cobb trains in a NASA facility during the Mercury program.

1. What was the FLATs group?
2. Infer how non-scientific beliefs affected NASA in the 1960s.
3. How did NASA change over time to accommodate new ideas about women? How has this affected the U.S. space program?

 **Go Digital**

Research the other people in Sally Ride's 1978 class of astronaut candidates, and discover other firsts accomplished by these astronauts.

Essential Questions
What has science made possible? What will it make possible in the future?

An
Out-of-This-World
Experience

by Matthew Martinez
illustrated by Peter Bull

What goes faster than the speediest race car? What makes you feel heavier than you've ever felt? What lets you float as if you weigh nothing at all? The answer to all these questions requires a flight into space.

Few people have had this experience. Those who have ridden into space have described the ride. Their words help the rest of us "feel" what it is like. Put on your imaginary space suit and let's go!

This image looks like a photo, but it's actually an illustration of a new rocket design! When humans return to the moon and go to Mars, it may be atop a rocket that looks very similar to this one.

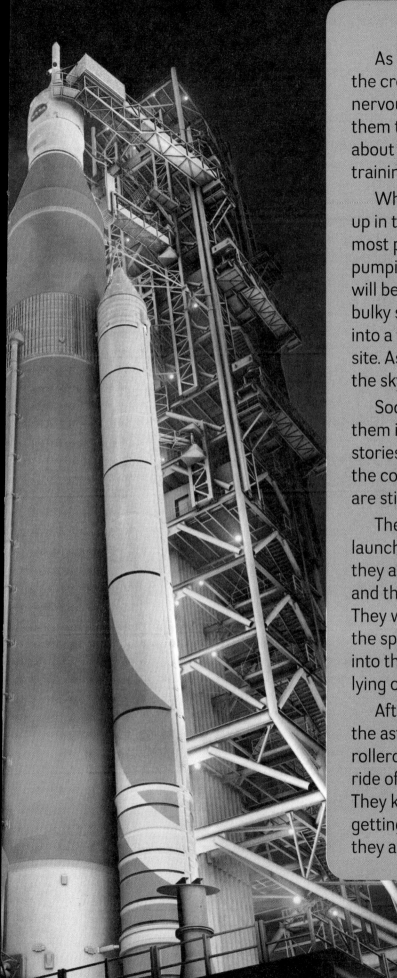

Before the Launch

As the day of liftoff comes closer and closer, the crew of astronauts gets excited—and a bit nervous. The butterflies in their stomachs tell them the ride into space is risky. They all know about the dangers. Even so, they keep busy training for the launch.

When the day arrives, the astronauts wake up in the darkness of the early morning, while most people are still asleep. Their hearts are pumping with anticipation. In a few hours, they will be in space. The astronauts put on their bulky space suits and helmets. They load up into a vehicle that will take them to the launch site. As they ride, they soak in the dark quiet of the sky above. That is where they are headed.

Soon they see the spacecraft that will carry them into space. It towers above them, many stories tall. They get out of the vehicle and feel the cool air on their faces. Their helmet visors are still open, and they breathe in Earth's air.

The team gets into an elevator beside the launch vehicle. It takes them up, up, up until they are near the top. The elevator doors open, and they see the open door of the spacecraft. They walk, one by one, from the platform into the spacecraft. The members of the crew get into their assigned seats, facing upward and lying on their backs.

After they are strapped in tightly, the astronauts wait. It is like sitting in a rollercoaster car waiting for the most exciting ride of their life. This wait lasts for two hours. They know the crew on the ground is busy getting the launch ready for countdown, and they are eager to get their mission started.

The countdown reaches ten, nine, eight, seven, six . . . Then the engines fire, and the whole craft sways because of the power. The noise of the rumbling engines matches the shaking seats. Astronauts focus on their tasks, pushing their minds beyond the thundering sound and strong vibrations.

As it rises, the spacecraft pushes against gravity. The spacecraft keeps going faster and faster, racing to reach 17,500 miles per hour. As the force of the engines, called thrust, pushes the spacecraft toward space, the force of gravity pulls the astronauts down into their seats. The crew members feel as if sand is being poured on their chests. The increasing pressure on their bodies makes it hard to breathe. As they ascend, they must use their muscles to force their lungs to breathe in and breathe out. Raising their hands to flip switches in front of them takes extra effort, as if they were lifting weights.

After eight-and-a-half long minutes, the heaviness is suddenly gone. Now everyone and everything feels weightless. The heavy load they felt is replaced with the freedom of floating.

Microgravity in Space

Gravity still exists in space. In fact, gravity is what holds Earth and other planets in the sun's orbit. Humans in space experience microgravity. This means everything appears to weigh nothing. Anything that is not tied down floats in midair. If an elephant were in microgravity, it would float, too.

Astronauts feel the weightlessness. They feel taller—because they are. Having no gravity pulling down on their skeleton allows the bones in their spine to stretch out. Most people are about two inches taller in space than on Earth. All the body's fluids float around inside too. Blood and water move up into the astronauts' skulls. As a result, astronauts suffer from pounding headaches for a couple of days. Then their bodies adapt and dispose of the extra fluids.

Microgravity also affects the crew's sense of balance. This can cause some of the astronauts to get sick to their stomachs, just like getting dizzy on a theme park ride or from feeling unbalanced on a ship at sea. They all have to learn to ignore their normal sense of "up" and "down." This helps their brains get used to floating around in space.

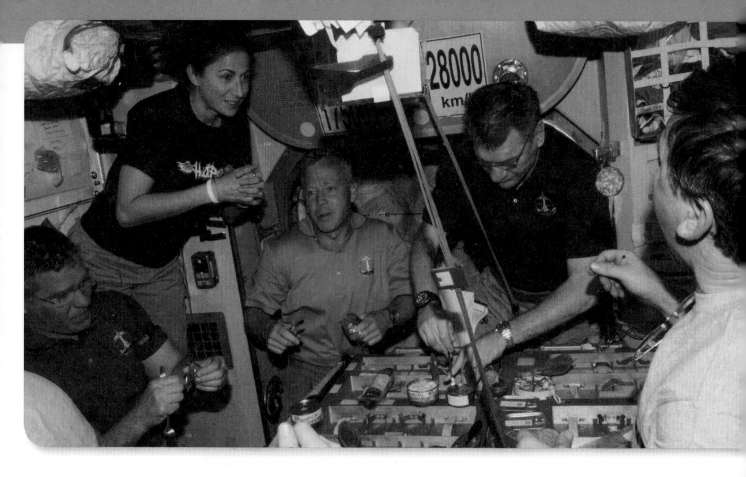

After the nausea dissipates, the astronauts are ready for their first meal in space. Even their taste buds are affected by microgravity. Food tastes bland, if it has any flavor at all. Even chocolate tastes like a piece of wax.

Moving around in microgravity takes practice. At first, the astronauts are clumsy and bump into walls, objects, and each other. After they get used to floating, they learn to zoom along from place to place, gliding like graceful birds.

Sleeping bags for the crew are attached to the walls of the spacecraft. To keep from floating away, the astronauts tighten straps inside the sleeping bags around their bodies. Even their heads are strapped down to foam pillows.

In Orbit

Outside of Earth's atmosphere, a spacecraft docked to the *International Space Station (ISS)* goes around the planet once every ninety minutes. When the astronauts are on the same side of Earth as the sun, it is daylight. On the other side of Earth, it is night. As they orbit the planet from the darkness, the crew sees a bend of colorful light outlining Earth. A sunrise! The crew witnesses sixteen sunrises every Earth day, or 24 hours.

Even though they have jobs to do, the astronauts know this is a special experience. They take time to look outside and see Earth below and the stars beyond. Astronauts who traveled to the moon in the 1960s saw Earth, too, but they traveled much farther away. From the moon, Earth looks like a small, blue marble. The crew members aboard the *ISS* see Earth differently. They are too close to see the whole planet, but far enough away to see the curvature of Earth and its atmosphere. Heavy swirling clouds of dust are visible across the African deserts. Thunderstorms and cyclones are visible during the day, and flashes of lightning can be seen at night. As the *ISS* passes over the nighttime side of Earth, the lights of cities shine brightly, like clusters of earthbound stars. While city dwellers on Earth may see a few stars in the sky at night, and people in rural areas see more, astronauts in space see a dark sky that looks like it is filled with billions of tiny diamonds. In a short while, though, the glittery sky gives way to another sunrise coming into view.

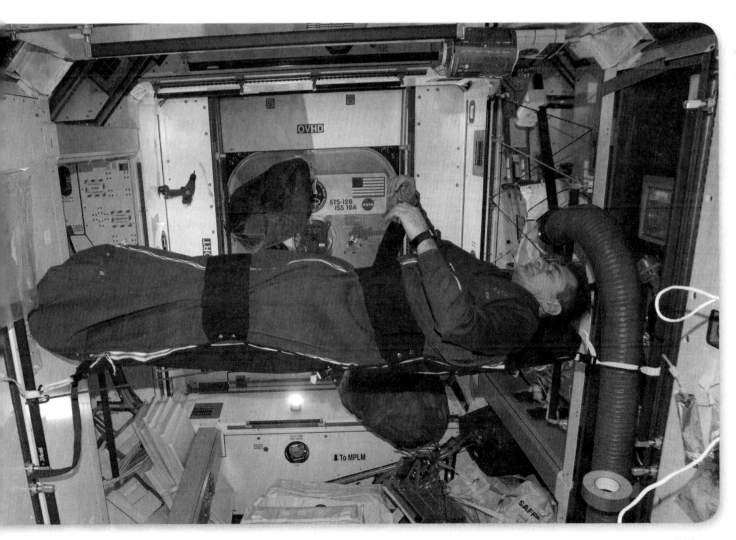

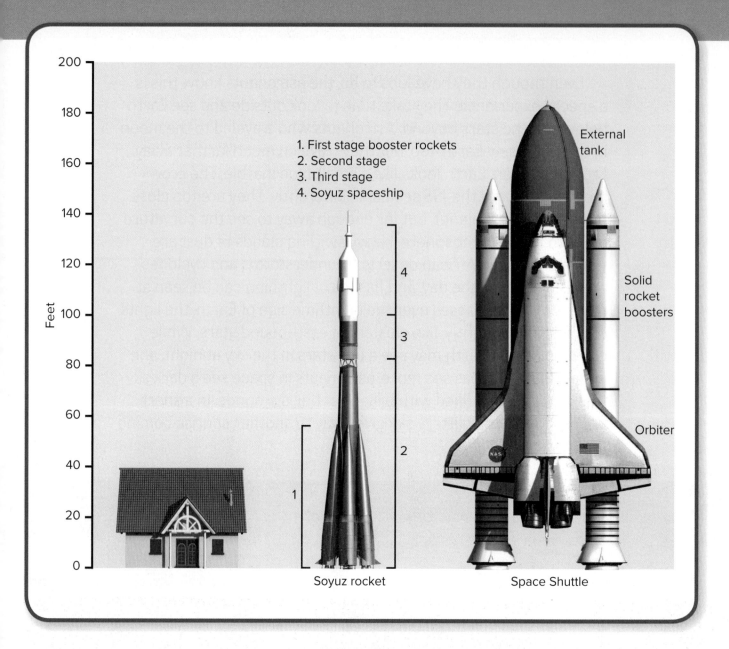

1. First stage booster rockets
2. Second stage
3. Third stage
4. Soyuz spaceship

External tank

Solid rocket boosters

Orbiter

Soyuz rocket

Space Shuttle

Leaving the *ISS*

When their mission is complete, the astronauts prepare for reentry to Earth's atmosphere. They board their spacecraft and strap themselves into their seats. Then, the spacecraft detaches from the space station and thrusters push the spacecraft toward the atmosphere at a high rate of speed. The spacecraft collides with the thick gasses of the atmosphere, causing friction and the light and heat that come with it. The more than 3,000°F heat of reentry makes the outside of the spacecraft glow. The astronauts see bright colors forming. They see a halo of bright orange, red, and hot pink surround them like a beautiful sunset.

Two Ways to Land

Humans have used two types of spacecraft to go to and return from space: a spacecraft with wings and a capsule. They have generally been launched in much the same way: attached to large rockets and launched vertically off the ground. The ways in which they return to Earth's atmosphere and land, however, have been very different.

The space shuttle returns much like a glider or an airplane. The astronauts are strapped into place, as when they took off. The shuttle detaches from the *ISS* and slows down in order to enter Earth's atmosphere safely. As soon as the space shuttle enters the atmosphere, the astronauts again feel Earth's full gravitational force as they slam into their seats, feeling the power of their descent. The shuttle sails toward Earth like a glider at an immense speed. It dips down a bit, going slower and slower as it glides toward a runway. Landing gear descends from the belly of the shuttle and locks into place. It glides along above the ground, just like an airplane coming in for a landing. Then it touches down. Brakes and parachutes work hard to slow the shuttle, and the astronauts are pushed forward against their harnesses by their own inertia as the spacecraft slows and stops. The astronauts are home.

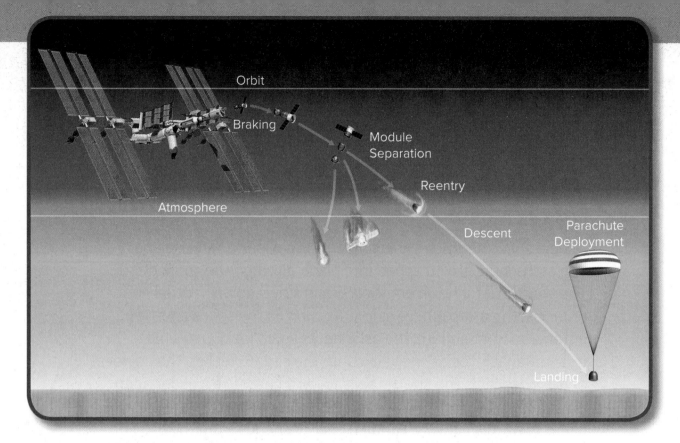

Orbit

Braking

Module
Separation

Reentry

Atmosphere

Descent

Parachute
Deployment

Landing

Astronauts aboard capsules also strap in and detach their spacecraft from the *ISS*. Then the part of the capsule they are in, the landing module, detaches further, leaving the rest of the capsule behind. Thrusters push the landing module toward Earth's atmosphere. As it approaches Earth, the astronauts feel the force of gravity return to their bodies, ever so gently. As gravity increases, the astronauts feel the heaviness in every way. Their heads feel too heavy to hold up. The gloves on their hands feel like weights. Even lifting their checklists is a difficult task.

Once the module is safely inside Earth's atmosphere, it is no longer floating, it is falling rapidly. Astronauts begin to hear the sound of air rushing past them, like a powerful windstorm outside. Then a huge parachute opens. The cords attached to the open parachute pull tight, tugging violently on the module, slowing it abruptly and sending it into a crazy, rocking spin. The crew inside has the wildest ride of their lives. Next, another parachute opens. This part of the ride is gentle, lowering the module more slowly toward Earth. The astronauts prepare to hit the ground in what is called a "soft landing." They pull themselves tightly into their seats, holding their arms against their chests. The module hits the ground hard—like a car crash. The astronaut's seats absorb the impact of the landing. Then everything is still. Silence fills the cabin until one crew member says, "Welcome home!"

After the Experience

Living in space, even for a short time, affects the human body. The astronauts' muscles weaken because of microgravity. Being back on Earth and feeling gravity again makes them feel heavy and slow. It is like they suddenly are carrying a big backpack filled with heavy books. It takes effort just to lift a drink or laptop. Lots of things get dropped or spilled for a while. The astronauts have trouble with balance, too. Just turning their heads too quickly makes them dizzy.

Within a few days, though, the astronauts begin to feel normal again. On the outside, they look like the rest of us. On the inside, however, they are different. They have seen more stars than others. They have floated in space. They are filled with experiences few human beings have had.

Write the answers to the questions on these pages in your notebook. Use evidence and details from the text to support your answers.

Text Connections

1. What are some of the emotions a crew feels aboard a spacecraft? What causes each feeling?

2. Why does the text say that astronauts are different inside after their return to Earth?

3. Why do people in rural areas see more stars than people in cities? Why do *ISS* astronauts see more stars than people on Earth?

4. Using information from both "An Out-of-This-World Experience" and "To Space & Back," describe the view of Earth from an orbiting spacecraft.

5. What do you think would be the most difficult part of being an astronaut?

6. Why do you think people still want to become astronauts, even though it is dangerous?

Did You Know?

Scientific innovation can bring people together. During the Cold War, the United States and Soviet Union were very competitive with each other. Nevertheless, in 1975 the two nations worked together on a special mission. Their spacecraft met in orbit for the first time. This was the very first step toward building an international space station.

Look Closer

Keys to Comprehension

1. Infer why astronauts "pull themselves tightly into their seats, holding their arms against their chests" when landing in a capsule's landing module.

2. Explain reasons for the effects of weightlessness on astronauts' bodies, both before and after spaceflight.

Writer's Craft

3. Define *microgravity*.

4. Compare and contrast the focus of and information in "To Space & Back" and "An Out-of-This-World Experience."

Concept Development

5. Compare and contrast the two types of crafts astronauts use to return to Earth, based on the images in "An Out-of-This-World Experience."

6. Using information from both "To Space & Back" and "An Out-of-This-World Experience," describe the physical experience of blasting off in a spacecraft.

Write

Do you think it would be fun to experience microgravity? Use examples from the text, like how astronauts have to sleep, to explain why or why not.

Read this Science Connection. You will answer the questions as a class.

Text Feature

Important terms are often **boldfaced** in a text so that they stand out.

What Makes a Rocket Move?

Have you ever wondered how a spacecraft moves through airless space? To understand the answer, you need to know a little about observations made by Isaac Newton.

Isaac Newton was a scientist who discovered and explained some important ideas related to physics, or the science of matter, motion, and energy. One thing he noticed was the idea that, for every action, there is an equal and opposite reaction. This is now called **Newton's Third Law of Motion.**

To make something move, one object has to exert force on another in a way that causes thrust. Thrust is a kind of **reaction force**. If you push on a wall while wearing roller skates, your action will cause you to roll in the opposite direction, or away from the wall. The more energy you put into your push, the greater the reaction force, and the faster you will roll.

So how does this apply to the rocket in a spacecraft? Well, a rocket's fuel has a lot of **potential energy.** This becomes **kinetic energy,** or energy in motion, when the fuel burns. Burning fuel creates gas that quickly expands. Some gas slams into the back of the rocket. The rocket pushes back against the gas. The impact causes the rocket to move forward, while the gas is pushed backward. The spacecraft moves through space because of this forward thrust.

The fuel in the spacecraft creates a reaction force as it burns.

1. Explain what causes thrust in a rocket.

2. Create a balloon rocket to model reaction forces. Thread a nylon string through a drinking straw, and tie the string between two chairs, pulling it taut. Blow up a balloon as much as possible. Hold it shut—do not tie it. Hold the blown-up balloon to the straw and have a friend tape the balloon to the straw. Pull the straw and balloon back to one end of the string. Let go of the balloon and see what happens. Test this again, but do not blow the balloon up as much. Describe both tests.

3. In which test did the balloon rocket exert the most energy, and how do you know?

 Go Digital

Research planned future missions in space. Which of them do or do not involve astronauts, and why?

Our Heritage, Our History

BIG Idea

Where do the people in our country come from?

Theme Connections

What themes of heritage do you see here?

 Background Builder Video
connected.mcgraw-hill.com

The Unbreakable Code

by Sara Hoagland Hunter
illustrated by Julia Miner

John raced up the trail, sending pebbles skidding behind him. When he reached his favorite hiding place, he fell to the ground out of breath. Here between the old piñon tree and the towering walls of the canyon, he felt safe. The river full of late-summer rain looked like a silver thread winding through his grandfather's farm land. They would be looking for him now, but he was never coming down.

His mother had married the man from Minnesota. There was nothing he could do about that. But he was not going with them. He closed his eyes and rested in the stillness. The faint bleat of a mountain goat echoed off the canyon walls.

Suddenly a voice boomed above him: "Shouldn't you be packing?"

John's eyes flew open. It was his grandfather on horseback.

"Your stepfather's coming with the pickup in an hour."

"I'm not going," John said.

"You have to go. School's starting soon," said Grandfather, stepping down from his horse. "You'll be back next summer."

John dug his toe deeper into the dirt. "I want to stay with you," he said.

Grandfather's soft, brown eyes disappeared in the wrinkles of a smile. John thought they were the kindest eyes he had ever seen.

"You're going to be all right," Grandfather said. "You have an unbreakable code."

"What's that?" asked John.

Grandfather sat down and began to speak gently in Navajo. The sounds wove up and down, in and out, as warm and familiar as the patterns of one of Grandmother's Navajo blankets. John leaned his head against his grandfather's knee.

"The unbreakable code is what saved my life in World War II," he said. "It's the Navajo language."

John's shoulders sagged. Navajo couldn't help him. Nobody in his new school spoke Navajo.

"I'll probably forget how to speak Navajo," he whispered.

"Navajo is your language," said his grandfather sternly. "Navajo you must never forget."

The lump in John's throat was close to a sob. "You don't know what it's like there!" he said.

His grandfather continued quietly in Navajo. "I had to go to a government boarding school when I was five. It was the law.

"They gave me an English name and cut my hair off. I wasn't allowed to speak my language. Anyone who spoke Navajo had to chew on squares of soap. Believe me, I chewed a lot of soap during those years. 'Speak English,' they said. But Navajo was my language and Navajo I would never forget.

"Every summer I went home to herd the sheep and help with the crops. I cried when the cottonwoods turned gold and it was time to go back. Finally, one night in the tenth grade, I was working in the kitchen when I heard a bulletin on the school radio:

"'Navajos needed for special duty to the Marines. Must be between the ages of seventeen and thirty-two, fluent in English and Navajo, and in excellent physical condition.'

"Just before lights out, I snuck past the bunks and out the door towards the open plain. I felt like a wild horse with the lasso finally off its neck. Out in the open, the stars danced above me and the tumbleweeds blew by my feet as I ran. The next day, I enlisted."

"But you weren't seventeen," said John.

"The reservation had no birth records," Grandfather said with a grin. "Two weeks later I was on a bus headed for boot camp with twenty-eight other Navajos. I stared out the window into the darkness. I was going outside of the Four Sacred Mountains for the first time in my life."

"Were you scared?" asked John.

"Of course," said his grandfather. "I didn't know where I was going or what our special mission was. Most of all, I didn't know how I would measure up to the people out there I had heard so much about."

"How did you?" asked John, chewing his fingernail.

His grandfather began to laugh. "We were known as the toughest platoon at boot camp. We had done so much marching at boarding school that the drills were no problem. Hiking in the desert of California with a heavy pack was no worse than hauling water in the canyon in midsummer. And I'd done that since I was four years old.

"As for the survival exercises, we had all gone without food for a few days. A Navajo learns to survive.

"One weekend they bused us to a new camp in San Diego. On Monday we were marched to a building with bars on every window. They locked us in a classroom at the end of a long, narrow corridor. An officer told us our mission was top secret. We would not even be allowed to tell our families. We were desperately needed for a successful invasion of the Pacific Islands. So far the Japanese had been able to intercept and decode all American radio messages in only minutes. This meant that no information could be passed between American ships, planes, and land forces.

"The government thought the Navajo language might be the secret weapon. Only a few outsiders had ever learned it. Most importantly, the language had never been written down, so there was no alphabet for the Japanese to discover and decode.

"He gave us a list of more than two hundred military terms to code. Everything had to be memorized. No trace of the code could ever be found in writing. It would live or die with us in battle.

"When the officer walked out of the room, I looked at the Navajo next to me and began to laugh. 'All those years they told us to forget Navajo, and now the government needs it to save the country!'

"We were marched every day to that classroom. We were never allowed to leave the building. We couldn't even use the bathroom by ourselves. Each night, an officer locked our notes in a safe.

"The code had to be simple and fast. We would have only one chance to send each message. After that, the Japanese would be tracing our location to bomb us or trying to record the code.

"We chose words from nature that would be easy to remember under fire. Since Navajo has no alphabet, we made up our own.

"'A' became *wollachee.*"

"Ant?" asked John in English.

Grandfather nodded.

"'B' was *shush.*"

"Bear," said John.

"'C' was *moasi.* 'D' *be.* 'E', *dzeh.*" His grandfather continued through the alphabet. Each time he named the Navajo word, John answered with the English.

"We named the aircraft after birds. The dive-bomber was a chicken hawk. The observation plane was an owl. A patrol plane was a crow. Bomber was buzzard.

"At night we would lie in our bunks and test each other. Pretty soon I was dreaming in code.

"Since we would be radiomen, we had to learn all kinds of radio operations. We were taught how to take a radio apart and put it together blindfolded. The Japanese fought at night, so we would have to do most of our work in complete darkness. Even the tiniest match flame could be a target.

"When the day came for the code to be tested in front of the top Marine officers, I was terrified. I knelt at one end of a field with our radio ground set. The officers marched towards me. Behind a building at the other end of the field, another code talker sat under military guard waiting for my transmission. One officer handed me a written message:

"'Receiving steady machine gun fire. Request reinforcements.'

"It took only seconds for me to speak into the microphone in Navajo code. The officer sent a runner to the end of the field to check the speed and accuracy of the message. The Navajo at the other end handed him the exact message written in English before he even came around the corner of the building! They tested us over and over. Each time, we were successful. The government requested two hundred Navajo recruits immediately. Two of our group stayed behind to train them. The rest of us were on our way."

"Tell me about the fighting!" said John.

Suddenly Grandfather's face looked as creased and battered as the canyon walls behind him. After a long pause he said, "What I saw is better left back there. I would not want to touch my home or my family with those pictures.

"Before we invaded, I looked out at that island. It had been flattened and burned. 'Let this never happen to a beautiful island again,' I thought. I just stayed on the deck of the ship thinking about the ceremonies they were doing for me at home. We invaded at dawn.

"I almost drowned in a bomb crater before I even got to shore. I was trying to run through the water and the bullets when I felt myself sinking into a bottomless hole. My eighty-pound radio pack pulled me straight down. I lost my rifle paddling to the surface.

"I had to move through the jungle at night, broadcasting in code from different locations. One unit needed medical supplies. Another needed machine-gun support. I had just begun broadcasting to another code talker. 'Arizona! New Mexico!' I called. The next thing I knew, an American soldier behind me was yelling, 'Do you know what we do to spies?'

"'Don't shoot!' I said. 'I'm an American. Look at my uniform.' He didn't believe me. He had heard the foreign language. He had seen my hair and eyes. Japanese spies had been known to steal uniforms from fallen American soldiers.

"One of my buddies jumped out of the bushes right at that moment and saved my life."

"How did you stay alive the rest of the time?" asked John.

"My belief was my shield," Grandfather answered.

He drew a ragged wallet from deep inside of his shirt pocket. "Inside of this, I carried corn pollen from the medicine man. 'Never be afraid,' he said. 'Nothing's going to touch you.' And nothing ever did. More than four hundred code talkers fought in some of the bloodiest battles of World War II. All but a few of us survived.

"The Japanese never did crack the code. When they finally discovered what language it was, they captured and tortured one poor Navajo. He wasn't a code talker and couldn't understand the message they had intercepted. He told them we were talking about what we ate for breakfast. Our code word for bombs was 'eggs'.

"Six months before the war ended, Navajo code talkers passed more than eight hundred messages in two days during the invasion of Iwo Jima.

"When the American flag was raised on top of Iwo Jima's mountain, the victory was announced in code to the American fleet. 'Sheep-Uncle-Ram-Ice-Bear-Ant-Cat-Horse-Itch' came the code."

John tried to spell out the letters. "Suribachi?" asked John.

"Yes," said Grandfather. "Mount Suribachi.

"When I came home, I walked the twelve miles from the bus station to this spot. There weren't any parades or parties.

"I knew I wasn't allowed to tell anyone about the code. I looked down at that beautiful canyon floor and thought, 'I'm never leaving again.'"

"But why did you leave in the first place?" asked John.

His grandfather lifted him gently onto the horse. "The answer to that is in the code," he said. "The code name for America was 'Our Mother.' You fight for what you love. You fight for what is yours."

He swung his leg behind John and reached around him to hold the reins. "Keep my wallet," he said. "It will remind you of the unbreakable code that once saved your country."

John clutched the wallet with one hand and held the horse's mane with the other. He wasn't as scared of going to a new place any more. His grandfather had taught him who he was and what he would always have with him. He was the grandson of a Navajo code talker and he had a language that had once helped save his country.

235

Write the answers to the questions on these pages in your notebook. Use evidence and details from the text to support your answers.

Text Connections

1. Why is John hiding in the beginning of "The Unbreakable Code"?

2. How does Grandfather's experience at boarding school connect to his choice to enlist in the Marines?

3. How do the code talkers structure their code, and why?

4. How does prejudice affect Grandfather when he is a part of the fighting?

5. Based on information from the Read Aloud "Listen" and "The Unbreakable Code," are all Americans descended from immigrants? Why or why not?

6. Why do you think a strong sense of heritage can help people be brave? Give an example.

Did You Know?

The Navajo language is part of the Athabaskan language family. Native peoples who speak these languages live in Alaska, western Canada, and the north- and southwestern United States. People who study languages are called linguists. Linguists think that, as Navajo ancestors journeyed south, their language remained linked to the peoples of the Arctic.

Look Closer

Keys to Comprehension

1. Why were the code talker recruits locked inside a building? Give details to support your answer.

2. What is the main idea of "The Unbreakable Code," and how do details support it?

3. How does the author use reasons to support Grandfather's claim that the Navajo platoon was "the toughest platoon at boot camp"?

Writer's Craft

4. What is the meaning of the word *bulletin* on page 226? How do you know?

5. Is "The Unbreakable Code" a poem, prose, or play? How does it structure information about the Navajo code talkers?

Concept Development

6. How did the illustrations on page 231 help you better understand how the code talkers sent messages?

Write

Create a simple word substitution cipher, where you substitute a word for each letter of the alphabet. Look at page 230 for an example of a word substitution cipher. Explain with whom you would use your cipher and why.

Read this Social Studies Connection. You will answer the questions as a class.

Text Feature

Captions are sentences or phrases that tell more about figures such as photographs and diagrams.

The First Code Talkers

Today, many people have heard of the World War II Navajo Code Talkers. These brave men, however, were not the first Native Americans to help the military with their language. The first were soldiers during World War I.

Thousands of Native Americans, including some from the Choctaw tribe, joined the U.S. armed forces during World War I. They chose to fight for the United States even though, at that time, they were not considered U.S. citizens. In France, 1918, the United States and Allied forces had a problem. No matter what, it seemed, their German opponents would break their codes.

At some point, a division captain in France overheard Choctaw soldiers chatting in their native language. He had an idea. What if they sent messages coded in Choctaw? After all, very few people knew the Choctaw language. The soldiers tried it, and the transmission was a huge success.

During World War II, a man named Philip Johnston had a similar idea. Johnston was not Navajo, but had grown up among the Navajo people. When he read about the military again considering languages for code, he thought Navajo might be the perfect option. He shared his idea with the military. The Marines decided to try it. They created the first all-Navajo platoon in the spring of 1942.

This story is not limited to the Choctaw and Navajo languages. Native American servicemen used many different indigenous languages to send coded messages in battle. In all cases, they offered the United States a great service. They bravely served a country that had not always supported their indigenous ways of life.

Code Talker Languages

World War I	Both Wars	World War II
Osage, Yankton Sioux	Cherokee, Choctaw, Comanche	Assiniboine, Chippewa/Oneida, Hopi, Kiowa, Menominee, Muscogee/Creek and Seminole, Navajo, Pawnee, Sac and Fox/Meskwaki, Sioux – Lakota and Dakota

Source: National Museum of the American Indian

This Venn diagram shows the Native American languages spoken by code talkers during both World Wars.

In 2008, Congress honored the contributions of the code talkers with gold medals. A different design honors each tribe or nation whose members served in World War I or II. This design honors the Choctaw Nation.

1. The Choctaw chose to fight for the United States, despite not being full citizens. Why might they have done this?

2. How might the experiences of Native Americans in the military have shaped their personal identities?

3. How might the interactions between Native and non-Native members of the military have shaped how members of each group viewed the other?

 Go Digital

Research to learn more about Native American code talkers who have served in the United States military.

Genre Narrative Nonfiction

Essential Questions
What struggles did our ancestors face? How does
telling stories of our ancestors' struggles honor them?

Ben
and the
Emancipation
Proclamation

by Pat Sherman
illustrated by Floyd Cooper

"Excuse me, sir." Ben tugged on the sleeve of a passing gentleman. "Does that say Broad Street?" He pointed to the wooden sign on the corner.

"Yes." The man pulled away impatiently.

"And that other one, please. That's King Street, right?"

"Right."

Ben studied the signs, trying to remember the letters. Broad. B-R-O-A-D. King. K-I . . .

"Boy?" The man had turned to stare at him. "Shouldn't you be getting along?"

"Yes, sir." Ben threw his carrying sack over his shoulder and hurried away. *Don't let them know you can read.* That's what his father had told him. Slaves weren't allowed to read.

Ben's father had known how to read a little — just enough to teach Ben the alphabet. But then his father had been sold and now no one knew where he was. Ben's mother had wanted him to keep learning, but she couldn't read, and Ben was so busy helping in the kitchen. He had no time for alphabet letters.

A few months ago, though, the master had apprenticed him to Mr. Bleeker, a tailor in Charleston. Ben was still a slave, but he could learn a trade and live in the city.

Learning the tailor trade wasn't easy. Mr. Bleeker was always barking orders. Not just "Dust the shelves!" or "Sweep the floor!" but "Get me the extra-fine silk thread!" or "Where did I put my ledger again?" Ben wondered how Mr. Bleeker had ever found anything before he came along. Ben spent so much time searching and fetching, he felt dizzy by the end of the day.

Then he discovered something wonderful. There were all kinds of secret ways to learn how to read. Almost without thinking, Ben had begun to recognize the names Mr. Bleeker wrote in the ledger. He could even tell what was inside the boxes on the shelves by the words on the outside.

"I don't know what it is about Ben," he heard Mr. Bleeker boast to a customer. "He just seems to know so much."

Now Mr. Bleeker was sending Ben on errands all over the city.

M-A-R-K-E-T. He turned onto Market Street. He loved walking around Charleston. There were words everywhere, on the sides of wagons and in store windows: Ice and Coal, Fresh Eggs and Cream, Hats and Gloves, China Teas.

S-T-A-T-I-O-N-E-R-Y. He studied the window. The stationery store sold paper, ink, and pens of all sorts.

Simon's Dry Goods Store, his next stop, was always busy. Ben studied the words on the shelves and barrels while he waited in line.

When his turn came, he handed Mrs. Bleeker's list to the girl behind the counter. Ben watched as she took things from the shelves.

"Uh, excuse me," Ben said pointing to the soap. "Mrs. Bleeker wants Pear's Soap, not Pearl's."

"That's Pear's." The girl slapped the box down hard.

"I mean, she said the kind that comes in the yellow box, not the blue one," Ben added quickly.

The clerk replaced the soap. Her face was sour.

"Well, you tell Miz Bleeker Pearl's Soap is as good as Pear's any day. See?"

"Yes, Ma'am." Ben piled everything into his sack, making sure it was all there. Mrs. Bleeker trusted him. Nothing was ever missing from her list.

Outside the store, Ben spied a copy of the *Charleston Mercury* that someone had tossed into the gutter. He snatched up the newspaper, glad to see that it wasn't too torn and dirty. He began to fold it into a hat as he walked along. Lots of boys and men, white and black, wore paper hats to keep off the sun. No one would wonder why he had a newspaper as long as he kept it on his head.

Before Ben got back to the tailor shop, he stopped beneath a big beech tree. The dense, low branches hid him from prying eyes as he unfolded the newspaper and spread it on the ground. He began searching for the names and words he had heard people talking about. Henry Clay . . . Daniel Webster . . . Abolition. A-B-O-L-I-T-I-O-N. Ben spelled it out. That word meant the end of slavery. Emancipation. E-M-A-N-C-I-P-A-T-I-O-N. That meant freedom. The *Charleston Mercury* didn't like those two words at all.

It was getting late. Ben rolled up the rest of the paper and stuffed it into his shirt.

After Ben had worked as an apprentice for a year,
Mr. Bleeker gave him permission to visit his mother. He was
allowed to spend a Sunday on the plantation, as long as he
was back before sunset.

Ben was so excited he couldn't sleep. He got dressed in
the dark, tucked a copy of the *Mercury* inside his shirt, and
started the twelve-mile hike well before sunrise. If he hurried,
Ben figured he'd be there by breakfast. The road wound past
the tobacco fields where the field hands were already out
working. No Sunday rest for them.

Word that Ben was coming got to the house before he did.
His mother was waiting for him at the door. And everybody
on the plantation who had family in Charleston wanted to
see Ben. All morning, they asked him questions about their
families and gave him messages to take back.

Finally, Ben and his mother had some time alone. First, Ben read her a passage from an old, worn Bible she had hidden in her room. Then he read her the newspaper, every word. She made him repeat the name "Abraham Lincoln" twice. "That's the new fellow that's running the country," Ben explained.

"I know," she said quietly. Ben noticed the tiredness in her voice. She had taken extra jobs, she told him, mending and sewing for ladies on nearby plantations, often working late into the night after her own chores were done. Slaves could earn money that way, penny by penny.

She reached into her apron pocket and took out a gold coin. She held it up. "This is a dollar." Ben had never seen a gold dollar before, not even in the tailor shop.

"When you learn to write, it will be yours," she said.

Ben began to study harder than ever. He wouldn't disappoint his mother.

When he swept the shop in the early morning, Ben wrote letters with his finger in the dust. When he washed the windows, he wrote letters with soap and quickly wiped them clean. He saved every scrap of paper Mr. Bleeker threw out and filled an empty inkwell with water to make pale ink. Then he whittled a twig to a sharp point and began to make letters on the back of the used paper.

The one thing he couldn't do was keep his reading and writing a secret from the other slaves. Word got around.

When he made deliveries, people pulled him into the kitchen or the little back rooms where they slept. "Teach us," they whispered.

"Teach me." The little girl scrubbing the steps asked him to write her name in water on the stones.

"Teach me." The boy shoveling coal wanted to write his name with soot.

"Teach me." Every place he went.

At Christmas, Ben's mother gave him the gold coin.

He never saw his mother again.

In the spring, war broke out between the states, and you didn't need a newspaper to know it. Overnight, the streets filled with soldiers in gray uniforms. A dozen times a day someone would stop Ben to ask where he was going. Over and over he repeated that he was Mr. Bleeker's boy, Ben, just running errands. He kept his eyes down. He didn't look at signs anymore.

But he still picked up a newspaper every chance he got.

As the Union Army pushed closer to the city, white people began to flee. The Bleekers boarded up their tailor shop. They had to go, Mr. Bleeker said. He was sorry they couldn't take Ben with them.

Ben was sent to a slave prison, the place where slaves had to stay until they were sold. The prison was a single large shed on the waterfront, so packed with men and boys that there was hardly any place to sit.

Weeks went by. No one knew what was going to happen. Some men insisted they were all going to be sold inland. Others claimed there was a whole regiment of black soldiers fighting for the Union up at Fort Wagner. They said they'd join up the minute they got the chance to run away.

Somebody even said that Lincoln had issued a Proclamation of Emancipation — that he had freed the slaves. Could Lincoln really do that? everyone asked.

Even though Ben wanted a newspaper more than anything, he kept quiet. He would just forget about reading. It could only lead to trouble.

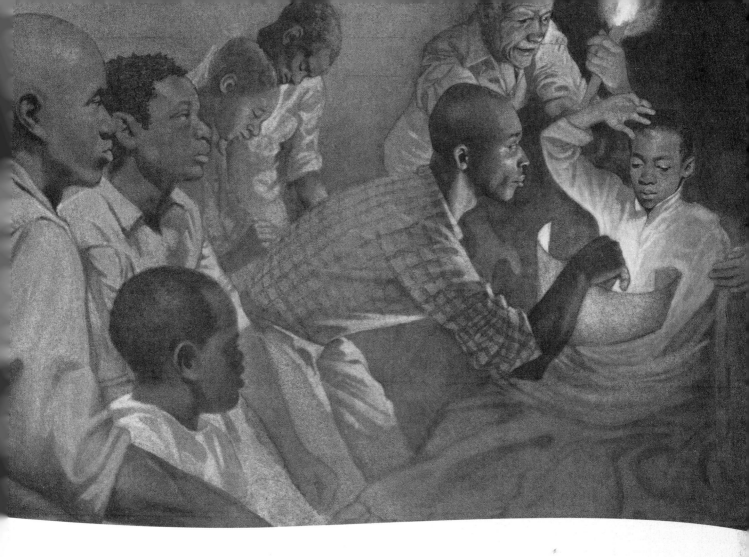

One night someone jostled him awake. A voice whispered that the men had the latest copy of the *Mercury*.

They lit a torch so he could see. Ben squinted at the paper.

"Go on," someone murmured. "Read it. We all know you can read."

Ben hesitated.

"Read." Voices rose from the darkness. "Read!"

"The Message of Abraham Lincoln is to be found in this journal this morning . . ." Ben read softly.

"Louder," someone called out. "Stand up."

Slowly Ben stood up. Every man in the prison was awake, every face turned towards him. He drew a deep breath.

"On the first day of January, in the year of our Lord one thousand eight hundred and sixty-three . . ." His voice became stronger and clearer. "All persons held as slaves within any State or designated part of a State, the people whereof shall then be in rebellion against the United States, shall be then, thenceforward, and forever free. . . ."

Everyone broke into cheers. They stomped and clapped and didn't care who heard. After a moment, Ben realized they weren't just cheering for Abraham Lincoln; they were cheering for him too. For the first time in their lives, these men had heard a black man read out loud. Hands reached out to shake his. Talk swirled around him. What did this new freedom mean?

Ben reached into his pocket and touched his mother's gold coin. He knew she would have been proud of the way he read tonight.

Daylight was coming now. Ben peered through a chink between the slats of the shed. Whatever this new freedom looked like, he wanted to be the first to see it. Carefully, he folded up the newspaper and tucked it in his shirt, ready to read it again whenever he could.

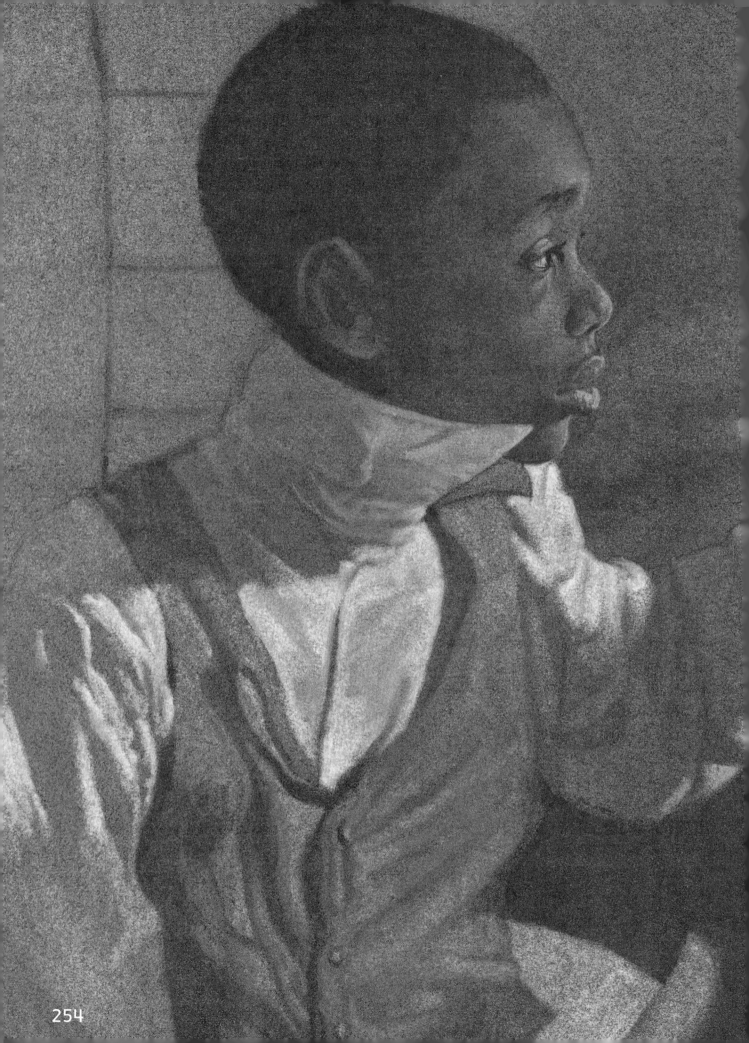

AUTHOR'S NOTE

Benjamin C. Holmes was born a slave in South Carolina in 1846 or 1848. His father, who had a little education, taught him a few letters of the alphabet. While still a child, Holmes was apprenticed to a tailor in Charleston. There, he taught himself to read by studying the signs on streets and in shop windows.

After the Civil War broke out, his master sent him to the slave prison in Charleston to await sale. While there, a copy of the *Charleston Mercury* was smuggled in and Holmes read the Emancipation Proclamation to the applause of his fellow inmates — certainly one of the most remarkable readings of that document ever recorded.

Like most slaves, he did not immediately gain his freedom. He was sent to Chattanooga, Tennessee, where he worked in a general store, eventually running the business when his new master was drafted into the Confederate Army. After the war he worked in several other businesses, but his main ambition in life remained education. In 1868 he enrolled in Nashville's newly founded Fisk University. An excellent singer, he was soon invited to join the school's chorus, which later became known as the Jubilee Singers. He toured with the Singers throughout America and Europe. He also taught in a rural school in Tennessee, a task he considered even more important than singing.

He died, probably of tuberculosis, in the early 1870s. The exact date of his death, like that of his birth, remains unknown.

Genre Historical Document

Essential Questions

Why do we read historical documents? What can we learn from them?

The National Archives houses and preserves the original Emancipation Proclamation.

THE EMANCIPATION PROCLAMATION

1863

by the President of the United States of America:

A Proclamation.

Whereas, on the twenty-second day of September, in the year of our Lord one thousand eight hundred and sixty-two, a proclamation was issued by the President of the United States, containing, among other things, the following, to wit:

"That on the first day of January, in the year of our Lord one thousand eight hundred and sixty-three, all persons held as slaves within any State or designated part of a State, the people whereof shall then be in rebellion against the United States, shall be then, thenceforward, and forever free; and the Executive Government of the United States, including the military and naval authority thereof, will recognize and maintain the freedom of such persons, and will do no act or acts to repress such persons, or any of them, in any efforts they may make for their actual freedom.

"That the Executive will, on the first day of January aforesaid, by proclamation, designate the States and parts of States, if any, in which the people thereof, respectively, shall then be in rebellion against the United States; and the fact that any State, or the people thereof, shall on that day be, in good faith, represented in the Congress of the United States by members chosen thereto at elections wherein a majority of the qualified voters of such State shall have participated, shall, in the absence of strong countervailing testimony, be deemed conclusive evidence that such State, and the people thereof, are not then in rebellion against the United States."

Now, therefore I, Abraham Lincoln, President of the United States, by virtue of the power in me vested as Commander-in-Chief, of the Army and Navy of the United States in time of actual armed rebellion against the authority and government of the United States, and as a fit and necessary war measure for suppressing said rebellion, do, on this first day of January, in the year of our Lord one thousand eight hundred and sixty-three, and in accordance with my purpose so to do publicly proclaimed for the full period of one hundred days, from the day first above mentioned, order and designate as the States and parts of States wherein the people thereof respectively, are this day in rebellion against the United States, the following, to wit:

Arkansas, Texas, Louisiana, (except the Parishes of St. Bernard, Plaquemines, Jefferson, St. John, St. Charles, St. James Ascension, Assumption, Terrebonne, Lafourche, St. Mary, St. Martin, and Orleans, including the City of New Orleans) Mississippi, Alabama, Florida, Georgia, South Carolina, North Carolina, and Virginia, (except the forty-eight counties designated as West Virginia, and also the counties of Berkley, Accomac, Northampton, Elizabeth City, York, Princess Ann, and Norfolk, including the cities of Norfolk and Portsmouth[)], and which excepted parts, are for the present, left precisely as if this proclamation were not issued.

Antietam National Battlefield, Maryland

And by virtue of the power, and for the purpose aforesaid, I do order and declare that all persons held as slaves within said designated States, and parts of States, are, and henceforward shall be free; and that the Executive government of the United States, including the military and naval authorities thereof, will recognize and maintain the freedom of said persons.

And I hereby enjoin upon the people so declared to be free to abstain from all violence, unless in necessary self-defence; and I recommend to them that, in all cases when allowed, they labor faithfully for reasonable wages.

And I further declare and make known, that such persons of suitable condition, will be received into the armed service of the United States to garrison forts, positions, stations, and other places, and to man vessels of all sorts in said service.

And upon this act, sincerely believed to be an act of justice, warranted by the Constitution, upon military necessity, I invoke the considerate judgment of mankind, and the gracious favor of Almighty God.

In witness whereof, I have hereunto set my hand and caused the seal of the United States to be affixed.

Done at the City of Washington, this first day of January, in the year of our Lord one thousand eight hundred and sixty three, and of the Independence of the United States of America the eighty-seventh.

By the President:
ABRAHAM LINCOLN

WILLIAM H. SEWARD,
Secretary of State.

President Lincoln signs the proclamation.

A woman views the Emancipation Proclamation on display.

Did You Know?

Abraham Lincoln considered the Emancipation Proclamation to be the act he should most be remembered for. He said, "If my name ever goes into history it will be for this act, and my whole soul is in it."

Text Connections

1. When Ben asks the man about the street signs for Broad and King Streets, how is this an example of him secretly learning to read?

2. Why does Ben pretend that Mrs. Bleeker had told him to ask for soap in "the yellow box, not the blue one," when the clerk tries to give him the wrong soap?

3. When Abraham Lincoln says the government "will recognize and maintain the freedom" to what is he referring and why?

4. How do child characters in "Ben and the Emancipation Proclamation" and "The Unbreakable Code" both experience prejudice?

5. Why do you think grown-up Ben considered teaching a task "even more important than singing"?

6. How did the Emancipation Proclamation pave the way toward a fight for equal rights for all people in the United States?

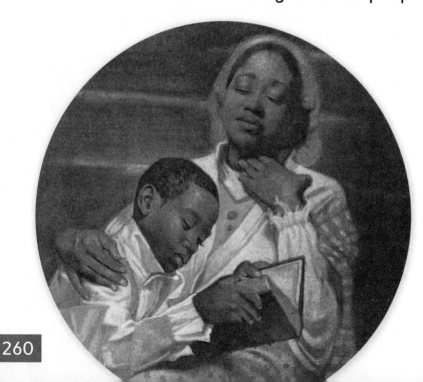

Look Closer

Keys to Comprehension

1. Why is it that Ben "just seems to know so much" when helping Mr. Bleeker? Refer to details in the text that support your answer.

2. Explain what happens to Ben after Mr. Bleeker and his family flee Charleston, and why this happens, based on the text's information.

Writer's Craft

3. Infer what a *tailor* does, based on the context and illustrations in "Ben and the Emancipation Proclamation."

4. How do you know the Emancipation Proclamation is a primary source document and not written recently?

5. How does the structure of "Ben and the Emancipation Proclamation" change during the Author's Note at the end?

Concept Development

6. How does the author use evidence in the text to support the idea that Ben loves his mother and wants to please her?

Write

Write an imaginary letter Ben might have written to his own children, explaining why education is important. Use examples from "Ben and the Emancipation Proclamation" to show why Ben believes education is so important.

Read this Social Studies Connection. You will answer the questions as a class.

Text Feature

Longer quotations in informational text are often indented and set in **italics**.

Songs of Freedom

From the end of the 1700s on, an organized system in the North for helping enslaved African Americans flee to freedom grew. By the 1840s, some people called this system "the Underground Railroad." Brave abolitionists, people who wanted to end slavery, acted as "conductors" or "stationmasters." Their designated "stations" gave rest along secret routes to freedom.

People planning to escape could not openly talk about it. At some point, songs became a way to share coded messages. Enslaved people sang as they worked on Southern plantations. Certain songs passed along information.

Accounts of the songs vary because they were not written down at first. Former fugitives from slavery recalled and passed on the songs years later. Historians began documenting the songs well after slavery ended. This verse from "Follow the Drinking Gourd" is one example:

Where the great big river meets the little river, follow the Drinking Gourd.
For the Old Man is a-waiting for to carry you to freedom
if you follow the Drinking Gourd.

Here, the "Drinking Gourd" was the Big Dipper star group, which points to the North Star. By finding the North Star, fugitives from slavery could be sure they were traveling north. This verse also told people to look for the place where the small Tennessee River joined the larger Ohio River. There, a conductor would meet them.

To people outside the Underground Railroad, songs like "Follow the Drinking Gourd" were just work songs. To enslaved people, however, they were clues on the road to freedom.

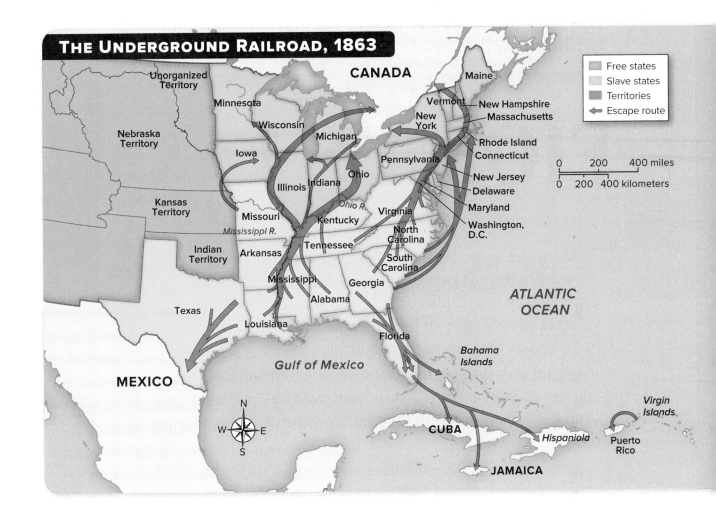

THE UNDERGROUND RAILROAD, 1863

Legend:
- Free states
- Slave states
- Territories
- ← Escape route

1. Why did fugitives from slavery take the risk of running away?

2. Why is the Underground Railroad usually described as running south-to-north?

3. How could studying songs such as "Follow the Drinking Gourd" help you better understand the experiences of enslaved people and fugitives from slavery?

 Go Digital

Research Harriet Tubman, a famous conductor on the Underground Railroad. What songs did Tubman use to communicate paths to freedom?

Genre Historical Fiction

Essential Questions
How is art a part of heritage? How can art contribute
to traditions?

FIONA'S LACE

by Patricia Polacco

Many years ago my father's family lived in a small, poor village a few miles from Limerick in Ireland. Everyone in the village depended on the textile mill that was soon to close. Most of the villagers were unsure of their futures. But Glen Kerry was their home and all that any of them had ever known.

My father's great-grandmother Fiona told him later that she and her younger sister, Ailish, used to wait by their front gate almost every day to greet their father as he came home from the mill.

Their mother, Annie, was known far and wide for her hearty soups and lovely bread. Supper in the Hughes household was a celebration of good food! But the best part of supper for Fiona and Ailish was to hear their father, Mick, tell grand stories.

"Da, tell us about how you got Muther to marry you," Fiona whispered.

"Oh yes, Da. Tell us!" Ailish chirped.

Their father's eyes blazed as he began. "Now, ye can believe this, or ye can believe it not," he started. The girls and their mother leaned in.

"Back when your muther and I worked at the textile mill in Limerick, I used to walk by the lace parlor on me way to lunch." He paused. Fiona smiled broadly at Ailish. They knew this story by heart.

"That is when I saw the most beautiful little lass I ever laid eyes on."

"Such talk, Mick. . . . You've been kissin' the Blarney." Their mother blushed.

"So I asked all of the other girls in her parlor where she lived so's I could come a-callin' and spark her. But not one of them would tell me. One day as I left the mill I noticed a lovely little bunch of lace tied to a bush just down the lane. I could see other little bits of lace tied to trees, bushes, front stoops, and lampposts further on. I recognized her lace, so I followed it down the paths and lanes until they stopped just in front of a darlin' little cottage. I looked further on and saw no more of 'em . . . so I knew this was your muther's house."

Fiona and Ailish tittered.

"'Twasn't more than a fortnight that I started courtin' your mum. We were married right here at Saint Timothy's and I brought me bride home to this very house. Carried her over that threshold just there," he said with a sweeping gesture.

"Both you girls were born right here next to the hearth," their mother added.

"To think a trail of lace brought you to our mum," Fiona said dreamily.

Then, just as she did every evening, Fiona ran to get her day's handiwork to show her father. Her mother was teaching her to be a fine lace maker. "Mum showed me her secret runnin' stitch today," Fiona said proudly as she held a small pillow covered with lace in front of her father's face.

"Aye, Fiona, your muther was one of the finest makers of lace in all of Limerick," Father said wistfully as he smiled at her mother.

"Sure the arthritis stopped all that, Mick," Annie said quietly. She tried to smile, but it was heartbreaking to them all that Annie's fingers were swollen from the pain.

"Fiona will be grander than I ever hoped to be. And as soon as she is old enough, we'll take her to the parlor in Limerick and she'll be their best!" Annie crowed proudly as she inspected her daughter's lace.

Times were already hard in all of Ireland, but harder still in Glen Kerry. The mill closed as rumored. It broke many a man and forced families to leave all they knew and seek work elsewhere.

"Where will we go, Mick?" Annie said one day. Her heart was deeply troubled.

One day their neighbor Mrs. O'Flarity spoke to Annie over their back fence.

"My Jocko and I have signed a contract. That's all we had to do to get passage to America!" she said as she hung up her wash.

"A contract to do what?" Annie asked.

"To serve a wealthy family in America. We are going to be in domestic service for them."

"You mean you'll be their maid?" Annie asked.

"Of course, and Jocko will help on the grounds. The wealthy family will pay our way there on a ship. All we have to do is promise to work for them until the passage is paid off!" Mrs. O'Flarity answered.

When Annie told Mick that evening, they stayed up into the wee hours of the night talking about it. Within a week they too went to an agency and signed a contract to work for a family in Chicago, America!

"Chicago, America!" Fiona yelped. Part of her was excited because she'd heard so much about America, but part of her was very sad for she loved her little village.

For the next weeks it was hard for all of them. They had to decide what to take with them and what to leave behind.

The last night they were home Fiona and Ailish put out a bowl of milk for the leprechauns and the wee people, the fairies, as they had done all their lives.

"Fiona, in America servants have servants of their own. The streets are paved with gold and we shall live in a fancy house. If only we could take the wee people to America with us. Do you think we could?" Ailish asked her sister.

"No, Ailish. I think the only place that the wee ones can be happy is here where the woodbine twineth, near the forest . . . here in Glen Kerry," Fiona whispered.

The next morning Fiona's mother and father bade tearful farewells to lifelong friends. After old Mr. Fitzgerald helped them load the last bundle on the wagon, the family climbed aboard.

As they left their homestead and village they all looked back as long as they could. When they crested the hill, their beloved village disappeared behind a grove of trees. Ailish and Fiona cried for miles. So did their mother. Their father just stared off into the distance.

They traveled most of that night and part of the next day. When they arrived in Belfast, they made their way directly to the shipyard to board the steamer that was bound for America.

As the ship pulled away from the docks they took one last longing look at their beloved Ireland. Crossing the Atlantic was long and hard. Almost everyone aboard was seasick and miserable. To pass the time, Fiona made lace—yards and yards of lace.

Finally they neared the harbor in New York. They could hardly wait to set foot on dry land.

When they did, they barely had time to be processed and then make their way directly to the train station to catch the train to Chicago.

On the train there were no bunks or cots to sleep in. They had to take turns sleeping on the hard seats of the coach car.

"At least on the ship we had bunks to sleep in," Annie said wearily.

Days passed. Fiona busied herself making more and more lace. The journey was bumpy, hot, and dusty. They stopped at many towns and cities. Every so many stops they bought bread and cheese.

Finally, one day, the conductor announced that they were approaching Chicago!

"We're here! We're here!" Ailish crowed happily.

The train pulled through what seemed like miles and miles of stockyards full of cattle. They could see a big city, tall buildings off in the distance.

"I'm guessin' the cattle are waitin' to be slaughtered. The Americans eat well. I'll be bound—there must be a joint of beef on every table!" their father sang out.

"Look, Muther, the sea is right next to Chicago. I wonder why the ship didn't bring us right here?" Fiona said.

"That there is Lake Michigan, folks. And it sure does look big enough to be the ocean, don't it?" the conductor said.

At the depot in Chicago there were drivers for hire with wagons to take travelers home. Fiona's father had the address of the rooming house that their employers had arranged.

As they drove through the city Fiona couldn't believe her eyes. Every building was grander than the last—row upon row of them. Elegant people were strolling with arms full of packages.

"Look at those lovely frocks." Annie sighed.

"Made with fine Irish lace, I'll wager," Father added.

"Is this where we are going to be livin'?" Ailish chirped excitedly.

"Our flat is on Dekonen Street. Is that near here?" their father asked the driver.

The driver smiled. "No, sir, we have quite a ways to go," he answered.

The farther they drove, the clearer it became that they were coming into to a part of Chicago that wasn't so grand. The streets were crowded with sprookers selling their wares from wagons. The buildings and houses were shabby and run-down.

"This is it—120 Dekonen Street," the driver sang out. Then he helped them unload and lug their belongings up rickety stairs.

"Yoo-hoo, Annie!" It was Mrs. O'Flarity, their neighbor from Glen Kerry. "We work for the same family. They told us you were comin'. I tidied up your flat and made your beds," she called out.

"This must be a mistake, Muther. If you and Da are workin' for fine rich folks, why would they be putting us up in a place like this?" Fiona whispered to her mother.

Annie and the girls cleaned and swept while Father went for supplies. After a good scrubbing, and after they covered the shabby old furniture with throws and quilts they'd brought, the two-room flat was almost livable. They had never seen a place like it. The sink and dry kitchen were in one room, and the other room was crowded with three beds.

Annie and Mrs. O'Flarity worked as kitchen maids for the same family. It took them three trolley rides to get there each day.

"I can't wait for our first pay packet. The girls will be needin' new shoes when they start school," Annie whispered as she scrubbed the floor.

"Pay packet!" Mrs. O'Flarity scoffed. "Don't you know that you won't be getting pay for servin' them? They paid your way here, so every penny that you would earn belongs to them until you repay them!"

"Remember, they are chargin' us rent for the rattrap we live in—they own it! And they'll be levying for your uniform as well," Pert Haggerty, another maid, added.

"But how will we live, then?" Annie muttered.

"You'll have to take second jobs and work in the evenings, darlin'. We all do, you know."

The other maids were quite right. Both Annie and Mick took second jobs—Mick at the slaughterhouse and Annie scrubbing laundry at a downtown hotel. But it wasn't long before Mrs. O'Flarity told Annie about a posh dressmaker in the city. "They are lookin' for to find Irish lace, and your Fiona makes the finest that I've ever seen!" Mrs. O'Flarity crowed.

Annie made an appointment and took Fiona to show her lace to the store's buyers.

Sure enough, they were heartily impressed. They made an offer on the spot to pay a pretty penny for Fiona's lace.

"We'll buy as much as the girl can make!"

When Annie and Fiona got home and told Ailish and Father the news, they decided right then and there to have a party.

"Now we'll be able to save money and buy our own home right here in America!" Annie called out as she danced around the room.

"I know just the place, too. We'll be crossin' that great sea they call Michigan Lake, and we're goin' to buy land . . . ," Father sang out.

"We'll have a sweet farm and maybe some sheep," Ailish cooed.

"What is this place called where we'll be goin', Da?" Fiona asked.

"Michigan!" he crowed as he reached for his tin whistle.

That evening all of their neighbors gathered and sang and danced—some of them even while holding pieces of Fiona's lace.

"To Fiona!" they sang out as they whirled around the room.

"This lass and her lace has saved the Hughes family!" Mrs. O'Flarity called out.

As the months passed it wasn't long before the Hughes family had put away money in a tea tin on the high shelf in the kitchen. It was the month of October, and All Hallows' Eve would be coming. One night before their father and mother left for their night jobs, Father sat down to tell them a story.

"This is about the Pooka, the ghostly black horse that is harnessed to the Costa Bower, the carriage of death. The Banshee screeches and pounds on the door to collect souls that have passed from this life," Father said as he pretended to shiver.

"I don't want this story, Da. I want to hear about the trail of lace that you took to Mum again!" Ailish insisted.

"Darlin', you know that one by heart!"

"I want to hear it too, Da. I want to hear about Glen Kerry. I miss Ireland!"

Their father obliged them and then he and their mother hugged Fiona and Ailish in for the night.

While Ailish slept, Fiona made lace for what seemed like hours. As she looked up to rest her eyes she noticed a light glowing through the window. It was late. What could the light be?

She heard shouting and people running about. Then there was a pounding on the door.

"It's the Banshee . . . comin' for us!" Ailish screamed, waking from a deep sleep.

Then they heard a voice call out, "Fire . . . there's fire . . . run for your lives!"

With that, Fiona dressed Ailish, pulled on their shawls, grabbed the tea tin and her bolt of lace, and ran for the door, pulling her crying sister.

They all but tumbled down the rickety stairs and made for the alley.

There were people everywhere running and screaming. As Fiona looked back down the alley she could see nothing but flames lapping at the sky. It was dark and smoky. Just then a clanging bell, neighing horses, and thundering hoofs rushed by them.

"It's the Pooka and the Costa Bower!" Ailish shrieked.

"No, Ailish, that's the fire wagon. They're comin' to put down the fire," Fiona called out as she pulled her sister along.

"Where are Mum and Da? Where are they? If our house burns down, how will they ever find us?" Ailish sobbed.

Fiona didn't answer. They ran and ran until they tasted blood in the backs of their throats.

"Where are we going, Fiona—where?" Ailish panted.

"We're doublin' back to our house. The fire has already been there and won't be back," Fiona answered urgently.

"How will Mum and Da ever find us?" Ailish sobbed again.

Fiona took out her bolt of lace. Her scissors were still around her neck. She pulled off some lace and started cutting it.

"No, Fiona. Your beautiful lace . . . your lovely lace!" Ailish screamed as she became hysterical.

"Ailish, this is the only way. We'll leave a trail of my lace. That's how Mum and Da will find us!" Fiona said softly, trying to comfort her sister.

Just as Fiona tied her last piece of lace to the doorway of a basement, she and Ailish crawled in.

They huddled there together for hours, through the darkness of the night.

From time to time Fiona thought she heard voices, but then they'd get faint and disappear.

At morning's light, Ailish started to cry again.

"Mum and Da should have found us by now ... they should have!" she insisted through her sobs.

"The trail of lace will bring them right here to us. I know it, Ailish. I know it!" Fiona tried to comfort her.

"What if they perished in this awful fire? There's nothin' left of Chicago—nothin'!" Ailish sobbed even harder.

It was exactly at that moment they heard a familiar voice ...

"My lambs ... my wee little lambs!"

It was their mother. She and their father were both clutching pieces of sooty lace.

"We've been lookin' for hours. We'd almost given up hope," their mother said as she held them close.

"That's when we saw it—the first little glimmer of hope—your lace, Fiona. . . . YOUR LACE TIED TO A LAMPPOST!" their father cried.

"So we followed it. We followed each and every little bundle of it," their mother added.

"And it brought us right to you, my darlings . . . right here to you!" Father said as tears rolled down his cheeks.

"But, Muther, Fiona's lace is ruined. It's covered with smoke and soot," Ailish whispered.

"No, darlin', this is her most beautiful creation—soot and all—for it saved you both . . . and us as well." Their mother cried as she held them close.

"We and generations after us will cherish this lace, Fiona. Always. Always!" their father exclaimed.

Write the answers to the questions on these pages in your notebook. Use evidence and details from the text to support your answers.

Did You Know?

Although people argue about the origins of lace, it is certain that Venice, Italy, was one of the first lace-making centers in Europe. By 1600, popular Venetian lace was called *punto in aria* or "points in the air," because of its fine details.

Text Connections

1. Fiona and Ailish know the story of their father and mother's courtship by heart. What can you infer about that story?

2. Why can't Fiona's mother make fine lace anymore?

3. How do the wealthy people who bring Fiona's family over to America treat them?

4. Think about a personal story that is very important to you. Why would you want future generations in your family to know that story?

5. How do characters improve their lives by using elements of their heritage in both "The Unbreakable Code" and "Fiona's Lace"?

6. How can hardships like those of Fiona's family bring people closer together?

Look Closer

Keys to Comprehension

1. What is one theme of "Fiona's Lace," based on the role lace plays in the story?

2. Describe the character of Fiona using details from the text.

Write

Describe a memory you have that makes you feel *wistful,* like Father's memory of Mother on page 266. Why is that memory important to you?

Writer's Craft

3. Explain what the Pooka and Banshee are in Irish mythology.

4. How would "Fiona's Lace" be different if it were written like the play "The Discovery Fair"? How might the portrayal of events change if this story were performed onstage?

5. Identify the points of view in "My Brothers' Flying Machine" and "Fiona's Lace," and compare and contrast the effect each has on the story.

Concept Development

6. What information can you get from the illustrations on pages 271 and 272 that is not specifically described in the text of "Fiona's Lace"?

Text Feature

Captions are sentences or phrases that tell more about photographs.

The History of Crochet Lace in Ireland

Beginning in 1845, a terrible disease, called blight, infected Ireland's potatoes. Potatoes were an important Irish crop at that time. The blight caused the potato crop to fail several years in a row. A great famine overtook the land.

Around the same time, a woman named Mademoiselle Riego de la Blanchardiere invented a technique for crocheting lace. Her crocheted lace looked similar to more time-consuming needlepoint lace, but could be made much more quickly. People were looking for ways to help the Irish people. Crochet lace seemed like a good option. Soon religious groups and societies dedicated to helping people were teaching Irish women how to crochet lace.

Crocheted lace was based around shapes or symbols, called motifs. They were connected by a web or net. Individual women could work on the motifs, often in their homes, and others could join them together later. As the art form grew, different areas of the country became known for particular motifs.

Irish crocheted lace became popular in posh circles. People around the world bought it. Unfortunately, some people took advantage of these women, creating industrial mills that did not pay these skilled women the money they deserved. After World War I, machine-made lace became cheap enough that few wanted to pay for Irish crochet lace. Today, however, many people have started teaching this technique again — keeping the craft alive and honoring the past.

This 1800s photograph of Irish crochet lace (presumed) was preserved by the National Gallery of Art.

1. Explain the connection between the Great Famine in Ireland and the supply of crochet lace.

2. What factors influenced Irish decision making about producing goods such as lace?

3. How did global interdependence impact the women who made crochet lace in the 1800s?

 Go Digital

Research other elements of Irish culture that spread to the United States with the mass immigration of Irish people in the 1800s.

Genre Informational Text

Essential Question
Why is the United States sometimes referred to as a nation of immigrants?

HOPE and TEARS

Ellis Island Voices

by Gwenyth Swain

Nearing the island:
Ellis — place of hope and tears —
and meetings with joy

When the door opens
to this new land, watch me race
right in, barefooted

Wear your best hat for
the never-ending waiting . . .
this is history!

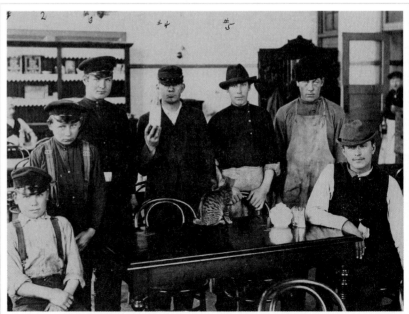

Ellis Island processed its first immigrant, fifteen-year-old Annie Moore from Ireland, on January 1, 1892. Millions of immigrants followed, with nearly twelve thousand arriving in a single day in 1907. In many ways, Annie Moore wasn't typical of the immigrants who passed through Ellis Island. By then, even though many Irish still came to America, they were no longer the largest group arriving from Europe.

Ellis Island's immigrants arrived from many countries, including Russia, Italy, Germany, Hungary, Czechoslovakia, Denmark, and Armenia, just to name a few. For nearly all, the journey to America was an anxious time. Depending on the ship's age and condition, crossing the Atlantic Ocean from a European port might take five days . . . or five weeks. Once travelers arrived in New York Harbor; the waiting game continued. "[W]e glided up the still waters of the harbor," one man remembered. "The whole prow was a black mass of passengers staring at the ferry-boats, the distant factories, and sky-scrapers."

Doctors from the Public Health Service, based on Ellis Island, boarded immigrant ships in New York Harbor to check for contagious diseases. They examined first- and second-class passengers for any additional medical conditions that might make them poor bets as immigrants. After healthy first- and second-class passengers got off the ship, third-class, or steerage, passengers were led to barges. These barges would take them away from New York City's docks to Ellis Island, where their true arrival as Americans would begin.

Annie Moore, Irish Immigrant (1892)

Would you warrant it?

So far, I've waited two whole years.

Not until this November could our parents pay the passage.

That's two years of living with Auntie.

Two years of being a sort of mother to Phillip and Anthony,

but not near so good a mother as our own.

Two years to wonder: will my parents know me, with all I've grown?

Now, after twelve days on this ship, crossing from Ireland,

I'm waiting for the end of waiting.

It's daybreak, sun spilling over the harbor.

I hear we're to be heaved onto smaller boats.

Pulling Phillip and Anthony behind, I make for the first one.

I'm running toward the end of waiting.

At last our barge bumps the dock by a tall building—

like a grand hotel, but all of wood and glass and smelling

   of fresh paint and sap.

"Ladies first!" someone calls.

And *hop*! All of a hurry, here I am, at the head of the line.

I trip over a gangplank that rocks against the shore.

There are cheers, and a crowd presses in.

A hundred tin whistles sound.

A priest gives me a blessing, bless my soul!

Someone thrusts a gold piece into my hands.

A man with a large mustache hands me a certificate.

All this just because I'm the first person through this place!

Lovely gifts, I'm sure.

But I know what waits within.

Our parents . . . the best present of all.

Annie Moore, whose statue can be seen today at Ellis Island, was officially the island's first immigrant. She came from Ireland with her brothers Phillip and Anthony on January 1, 1892—her fifteenth birthday.

Arriving at Ellis Island, immigrants had already passed through a number of inspections. The steamship companies were supposed to do their best to sort out any "undesirable" immigrants before they got to America. Until the 1920s, immigrants did not need passports to board a ship, but they did have to show that they were healthy. Doctors inspected them before they left ports in Europe as well as on shipboard, making notes on inspection cards. Immigrants carried these cards with them to show the doctors on Ellis Island. Pinned to their clothing before arrival was another card, called a boarding tag, which was given to immigration officials.

Once their feet touched the ground on Ellis Island, immigrants were sorted into groups of about thirty. Women and children were grouped separately from men, but all group members were passengers of the same ship. Each immigrant—often carrying a large bundle or bag—stood in a line that made its way to the ground floor of the main building on Island One.

Upon entering the building, immigrants stood before a United States Public Health Service doctor. Any immigrant made breathless by the short walk from the dock was suspected of hiding illness. Those who limped also were pulled aside. Immigrants removed their hats so doctors could inspect for lice or scalp diseases, such as favus. Farther along the inspection line, still more doctors turned up the eyelids of each immigrant, looking for trachoma, a contagious eye disease. Some of the doctors used their fingers. Others used small metal hooks more commonly used to button boots.

If an immigrant showed signs of disease (either mental or physical), the doctor took a piece of chalk and made a mark on the immigrant's clothing. The mark was meant to tell other doctors in nearby examination rooms what was wrong. *H* stood for "heart"; *L* for "lameness"; *X* for "suspected mental illness."

Those who passed "line" inspections by doctors were then directed up the stairs and into lines stretching across the Registry Room floor. At the far end of the room, the immigrant could see a row of inspectors sitting at high wooden desks. These inspectors first checked off the immigrant's name and number (from the boarding tag) against a long list called a ship's manifest.

Then inspectors questioned immigrants, looking for any legal reason not to admit them. For example, immigrants were required to have a certain amount of money (about twenty dollars) in order to enter the country. Beginning in 1917, immigrants had to pass a test to prove that they could read. They might have been turned away if they claimed to have a job already lined up in their new home. Such arrangements could have stopped current American citizens from finding work.

For those who passed inspection, Ellis Island was a short stop (three to five hours on average) on the long journey toward becoming American. But being short didn't make the Ellis Island experience any less frightening.

Emigrants from Europe on board a ship headed to America around the early 1900s.

Margaret, English Immigrant (early 1900s)

Dear Diary,

We pushed up broad stairs to a brick and stone building,

red and cream, like London's Albert Hall.

A tall man in uniform stood ahead.

He looked like a soldier, but a woman called him "doctor" and he answered.

Soon he was leaning over the girl in front of me.

She's a baker's helper from Bristol.

We'd talked, you know, about this and that.

The doctor didn't want to get to know her, though.

He pulled a hook from his pocket, and I nearly cried out.

I know that kind of hook well, I do.

It's meant for boots with buttons, not Bristol bakers.

In a flash, the doctor used it to pry up her eyelids.

He sighed, he frowned, and that girl sank to the ground.

I heard him say "trachoma" and knew the worst.

It's a contagious disease, can make you blind sometimes.

Always, it keeps you out of America, no matter how you want in.

Back to Bristol she'll be going.

Sure, that doctor tried to catch me with his ugly metal hook.

But when I passed inspection,

I slipped through his net.

All the same, Diary dear,

I'll be buying boots with laces from this day on.

After inspection, most immigrants left the Registry Room, going downstairs to meet relatives, find baggage, exchange foreign money for U.S. dollars, or buy train tickets for longer journeys. But not all immigrants passed inspections. Those who were pulled out of line for any reason, legal or medical, had to wait in detention.

Immigrants have their eyes examined by doctors on Ellis Island. Those who had trachoma, a contagious eye disease, were turned away.

Even those who passed inspections might have to wait. Women and girls traveling alone were not allowed to leave the island until a male relative came to claim them. Families with members who were ill (and staying at the island's hospitals) often stayed in detention until everyone was healthy and ready to travel together.

Some found the waiting easy. Others found it painfully hard. Most were mystified by Ellis Island—its food, its rules, and its hard beds. Perhaps those who were sick with contagious diseases suffered most. Beginning in 1912, they were treated on Island Three, and the sickest among them could not have any visitors.

Some arrivals were labeled "likely to become public charges," an official term covering a wide range of people and circumstances. These included young women traveling alone or traveling with children born outside of marriage; people arriving without money or with no clear means of support; people who were mentally ill; and those with disabilities (such as blindness or lameness) or with infectious diseases (such as trachoma or tuberculosis). Immigrants who were likely to require help from the government in order to survive were often brought before the Board of Special Inquiry. When the final decision came, some repacked their bundles and waited for the next ship home.

Pearl Libow, Russian Immigrant (1922)

The sickness starts on the boat.

Doctors wrap me in sheets,

Cold sheets, they tell me, straight from the icebox.

But I burn hotter than the ship's coal fire.

Then, suddenly, I feel jolts and bumps.

Voices, so many voices.

A wall of sound I can't break through,

so little makes sense to my ears.

Then, just as suddenly, all's quiet

Sleep finally quenches the fire inside.

When I wake again, I'm thirsty.

My eyes drink in sights.

My ears drink in sounds.

Where am I?

A man in white comes to my side.

Silver whiskers poke out from behind a mask when he talks.

I smile at those wiggling whiskers

and wonder, *Does he imagine I know what he's saying?*

Slowly, I understand:

I am on an island, far from home.

I'm on *that* island.

Ellis Island. Island of Hope, Island of Tears.

No one will say when I can leave.

Outside the window, the Liberty Lady stands tall.

I can't see her face yet, not from here.

But I promise you this:

I won't stay in bed.

Soon enough, I'll leave this island and take my place in this new land.

I won't let Lady Liberty turn her back on me.

More than 650 people worked on Ellis Island in 1913, at the height of immigration. Groupers kept immigrants organized. Doctors inspected immigrants and cared for them in the island's hospitals. Immigrant inspectors decided who would be allowed into the United States and who would be kept out.

Other people filled jobs as cooks, maids, dock workers, special inquiry judges, nurses, administrators, social workers, teachers, and interpreters. Many doctors and nurses lived on the island, since their services were needed at any time. Sometimes the children of these employees were also island residents.

There were frequent visitors as well, such as volunteers from church groups and other charitable organizations that helped immigrants. Sometimes film crews visited for a day or two, shooting scenes for movies set on the island. All of these people, both young and old, formed an ever-changing community, part of the fabric of Ellis Island life.

Like the immigrants they served, most workers at Ellis Island traveled to the island by ferry. But, unlike the immigrants, they could leave when they pleased.

Augustus Sherman, Clerk and Photographer
(early 1900s)

Busy day today.

Such a lot of interesting faces and Old World costumes.

When I could, I made pictures of the immigrants,

right before they shed their old skins.

"Tell her to face a little more to the left, please."

As usual, I direct the scene from behind my camera,

and the interpreter speaks.

I watch through the lens.

A flash of understanding lights the woman's tired eyes,

and she turns, shifting her children along with her.

She asks, "Will this hurt?"

I try to explain.

I will, of course, have to use a sulfur flash.

The natural lighting in the Registry Room is good, but not so bright.

The blinding flash frightens her and her children.

But it is a small fright in a day that, with luck, has ended in joy.

I collect their faces, caught between fear and joy.

I keep things in focus.

And for good focus, I need all the light I can get.

One of more than two hundred photographs taken by Augustus Sherman, a clerk on Ellis Island, in the early 1900s.

Lucia, Cook (early 1900s)

It's not like cooking for family.

It's not like cooking at a restaurant.

I should know.

I've raised seven *bambini*.

I've piled plates with *pasta e fagioli* at a *trattoria*.

They always say the north of Italy is different from the boot,

where I'm from.

And they're right.

But the people who crowd my tables are more different than I can say.

They are the new ingredients of this country, all strange to me.

Serve rice, and some love it while others spit it out.

Roast tender pork, and at the first sniff,

some won't even enter my dining hall.

Boil pasta, top it with my mother's simplest sauce,

and don't be surprised if they act scared.

Would you believe?

They think I'm serving white worms!

There's almost no pleasing this crowd,

except in little things . . .

like bread.

A yeasty smell escapes my kitchen.

They sniff the air and know I've been baking.

So they crowd the doorway, well in advance of the dinner bell.

They stuff their cheeks and then their pockets.

Don't imagine I don't know.

I make extra so they can take the little roll that comforts them later,

in the dark, when the babies and the wild winds moan.

Mangia! I say, wiping the flour from my hands.

Eat well.

Many immigrants continued to pour into Ellis Island until the 1920s, when the United States Congress put limits on the numbers allowed in. By the end of the decade, the great waves of new immigrants had slowed to a gentle lapping on the island's shores.

From the late 1920s until 1954, the main work of Ellis Island was deportation, sending undesirable immigrants back home. During World War II, the island also housed people thought to be a threat to the United States. Some of these "enemy aliens" were children who actually were American citizens. Their only crime was being born to parents suspected of spying for countries at war with America.

During the restoration of Ellis Island, much graffiti left by immigrants was uncovered.

After 1954, Ellis Island stood silent and empty. The great hall breathed in wet sea air. Walls became soggy. Paint peeled, tiles cracked, and windowpanes shattered.

Then, as the nation prepared to celebrate its bicentennial in 1976, things changed. Researchers sought out people who passed through or worked on Ellis Island, and recorded their memories in oral history interviews. Tours were given during the late 1970s to raise awareness about the island and the need for restoration work. That work began in the 1980s, with efforts focusing on Island One.

To dry out buildings, temporary furnaces piped in warm air. And as walls dried, layers of paint and plaster began to crumble. In some places, graffiti left behind by immigrants was revealed, such as this portion of a poem in Chinese:

Lucky just to arrive in flowery flag country.
I expected peace with no worries.
Who knew immigration guards would detain us?
Left locked up without a reason.
How can we change these harsh laws?

Ellis Island reopened to the public in 1990 as an immigration museum. Although the floods of immigrants are a thing of the past, the island bustles again.

Write the answers to the questions on these pages in your notebook. Use evidence and details from the text to support your answers.

Text Connections

1. Infer what Annie Moore's situation was when coming to the United States.

2. Why do you think immigrants had to have about twenty dollars in order to enter the United States?

3. What food did immigrants unfamiliar with Italian cooking think was "white worms"?

4. What do you think would be the hardest part about going through Ellis Island?

5. In "The Unbreakable Code," Grandfather experienced prejudice while fighting in World War II. How was his experience similar to that of people kept at Ellis Island during that war, based on the information in "Hope and Tears"?

6. Why is Ellis Island worth preserving?

Did You Know?

Some immigrants and visitors that came through Ellis Island are now very well known. For example, Albert Einstein, the German-born physicist, first entered the United States through Ellis Island.

Look Closer

Keys to Comprehension

1. Explain how first-, second-, and third-class passengers were treated when they arrived in New York Harbor. Make an inference about the reason for these differences.

2. Explain the basic procedure immigrants followed once they stepped off the barge at Ellis Island.

Writer's Craft

3. Explain what a ship's manifest is. Why was it important to the inspectors?

4. Compare and contrast the description of an Ellis Island medical inspection found in Margaret's poem with the informational description that appears on pages 288 and 289.

Concept Development

5. Choose a photograph from "Hope and Tears." Explain how it helps you better understand a detail related to the text.

6. Integrate information from "Fiona's Lace" and "Hope and Tears" in order to describe what might have been the route and experience of Irish immigrants coming to the United States in the late 1800s.

Write

Based on what you read in "Hope and Tears," write an opinion paragraph explaining one thing you think should have been done differently during the immigration years of Ellis Island.

Text Feature

Informational texts often **boldface** important terms.

Science and Hospital Design at Ellis Island

When immigrants arrived at Ellis Island, they underwent a medical inspection. If they had certain illnesses, they were not allowed in the United States. They were instead taken to the hospital complex on the south side of the island.

By the time the Ellis Island hospital was built, hospital designs were changing. Before the mid-1800s, most hospitals had large rooms called **wards.** These wards sometimes had 100 beds. People did not understand germs. Patients with different illnesses might be put close together.

The Ellis Island hospital was an example of a new kind of design. Thanks to Florence Nightingale, a British nursing pioneer, people were building hospitals in the **pavilion style.** Instead of large rooms, the hospital had one central hall. Fingerlike pavilions, or long narrow wards, pointed out from it. On Ellis Island, the beds were near windows. Nightingale had argued that fresh air was important to patient recovery.

Another influence on the hospital was **germ theory.** Scientists like Louis Pasteur and Robert Koch made discoveries about germs during the 1850s through the 1870s. Germ theory says that specific germs cause specific diseases. It says that germs transfer disease from one body to others. Because of this, the Ellis Island pavilions did not face each other. People with contagious diseases were kept away from others.

Some details of the medical care on Ellis Island are now outdated. Everyone was not always diagnosed fairly or correctly. However, no disease outbreaks ever came from an Ellis Island immigrant. For its time, the Ellis Island hospital was mostly a success.

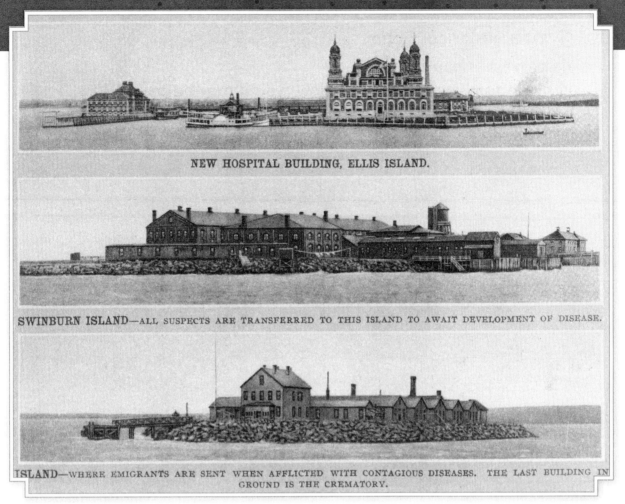

NEW HOSPITAL BUILDING, ELLIS ISLAND.

SWINBURN ISLAND—ALL SUSPECTS ARE TRANSFERRED TO THIS ISLAND TO AWAIT DEVELOPMENT OF DISEASE.

ISLAND—WHERE EMIGRANTS ARE SENT WHEN AFFLICTED WITH CONTAGIOUS DISEASES. THE LAST BUILDING IN GROUND IS THE CREMATORY.

The hospital and quarantine facilities of Ellis Island

1. What scientific advances affected the design of the Ellis Island hospital complex?

2. Do you think change based on scientific advances is always better than what it replaces? Why or why not?

3. Modern hospital rooms in the United States usually house one or two patients and also have windows. Compare this with the multi-bed wards on Ellis Island. Why do you think our modern hospitals are designed the way they are?

 Go Digital

Ellis Island became part of the Statue of Liberty National Monument in 1965 and was restored beginning in the 1980s. Research to find out how the restored buildings look today, and what work is still being done on them.

Genre Historical Fiction

Essential Questions
Why do families immigrate? How would moving to a different country change your life?

302

My Diary from Here to There

by Amada Irma Pérez
illustrated by Maya Christina Gonzalez

Dear Diary, I know I should be asleep already, but I just can't sleep. If I don't write this all down, I'll burst! Tonight after my brothers—Mario, Víctor, Héctor, Raúl, and Sergio—and I all climbed into bed, I overheard Mamá and Papá whispering. They were talking about leaving our little house in Juárez, Mexico, where we've lived our whole lives, and moving to Los Angeles in the United States. But why? How can I sleep knowing we might leave Mexico forever? I'll have to get to the bottom of this tomorrow.

Today at breakfast, Mamá explained everything. She said, "Papá lost his job. There's no work here, no jobs at all. We know moving will be hard, but we want the best for all of you. Try to understand." I thought the boys would be upset, but instead they got really excited about moving to the States.

"The big stores in El Paso sell all kinds of toys!"

"And they have escalators to ride!"

"And the air smells like popcorn, yum!"

Am I the only one who is scared of leaving our home, our beautiful country, and all the people we might never see again?

My best friend Michi and I walked to the park today. We passed Don Nacho's corner store and the women at the *tortilla* shop, their hands blurring like hummingbird wings as they worked the dough over the griddle.

At the park we braided each other's hair and promised never to forget each other. We each picked out a smooth, heart-shaped stone to remind us always of our friendship, of the little park, of Don Nacho and the *tortilla* shop. I've known Michi since we were little, and I don't think I'll ever find a friend like her in California.

"You're lucky your family will be together over there," Michi said. Her sisters and father work in the U.S. I can't imagine leaving anyone in our family behind.

305

Today while we were packing, Papá pulled me aside. He said, "Amada, *m'ija*, I can see how worried you've been. Don't be scared. Everything will be all right."

"But how do you know? What will happen to us?" I said.

He smiled. "*M'ija*, I was born in Arizona, in the States. When I was six — not a big kid like you — my Papá and Mamá moved our family back to Mexico. It was a big change, but we got through it. I know you can, too. You are stronger than you think." I hope he's right. I still need to pack my special rock (and you, Diary!). We leave tomorrow!

Our trip was long and hard. At night the desert was so cold we had to huddle together to keep warm. We drove right along the border, across from New Mexico and Arizona. Mexico and the U.S. are two different countries, but they look exactly the same on both sides of the border, with giant saguaros pointing up at the pink-orange sky and enormous clouds. I made a wish on the first star I saw. Soon there were too many stars in the sky to count. Our little house in Juárez already seems so far away.

We arrived in Mexicali late at night and my grandparents Nana and Tata, and all our aunts, uncles and cousins (there must be fifty of them!) welcomed us with a feast of *tamales*, beans, *pan dulce*, and hot chocolate with cinnamon sticks. It's so good to see them all! Everyone gathered around us and told stories late into the night. We played so much that the boys fell asleep before the last blanket was rolled out onto the floor. But, Diary, I can't sleep. I keep thinking about Papá leaving tomorrow.

Papá left for Los Angeles this morning. Nana comforted Mamá, saying that Papá is a U.S. citizen, so he won't have a problem getting our "green cards" from the U.S. government. Papá told us that we each need a green card to live in the States, because we weren't born there.

I can't believe Papá's gone. Tío Tito keeps trying to make us laugh instead of cry. Tío Raúl let me wear his special *medalla*. And Tío Chato even pulled a silver coin out of my ear. The boys try to copy his tricks but coins just end up flying everywhere. They drive me nuts sometimes, but today it feels good to laugh.

We got a letter from Papá today! I'm pasting it into your pages, Diary.

My dear family,

I have been picking grapes and strawberries in the fields of Delano, 140 miles north of Los Angeles, saving money and always thinking of you. It is hard, tiring work. There is a man here in the fields named César Chávez, who speaks of unions, strikes, and boycotts. These new words hold the hope of better conditions for us farmworkers.

So far, getting your green cards has been difficult, for we are not the only family trying to start a new life here. Please be patient. It won't be long before we are all together again.

Hugs and kisses, Papá

I miss Papá so much — it feels like he left ages ago. It's been tough to stay hopeful. So far we've had to live in three different houses with some of Mamá's sisters. First, the boys broke Tía Tuca's jewelry box and were so noisy she kicked us out. Then, at Nana's house, they kept trying on Tía Nena's high heels and purses. Even Nana herself got mad when they used her pots and pans to make "music." And they keep trying to read what I've written here, and to hide my special rock. Tía Lupe finally took us in, but where will we go if she decides she's had enough of us?

FINALLY! Papá sent our green cards—we're going to cross the border at last! He can't come for us but will meet us in Los Angeles.

The whole family is making a big farewell dinner for us tonight. Even after all the trouble the boys have caused, I think everyone is sad to see us go. Nana even gave me a new journal to write in for when I finish this one. She said, "Never forget who you are and where you are from. Keep your language and culture alive in your diary and in your heart."

We leave this weekend. I'm so excited I can hardly write!

My first time writing in the U.S.A.! We're in San Ysidro, California, waiting for the bus to Los Angeles. Crossing the border in Tijuana was crazy. Everyone was pushing and shoving. There were babies crying, and people fighting to be first in line. We held hands the whole way. When we finally got across, Mario had only one shoe on and his hat had fallen off. I counted everyone and I still had five brothers. Whew!

Papá is meeting us at the bus station in Los Angeles. It's been so long—I hope he recognizes us!

What a long ride! One woman and her children got kicked off the bus when the immigration patrol boarded to check everyone's papers. Mamá held Mario and our green cards close to her heart.

Papá was waiting at the station, just like he promised. We all jumped into his arms and laughed, and Mamá even cried a little. Papá's hugs felt so much better than when he left us in Mexicali!

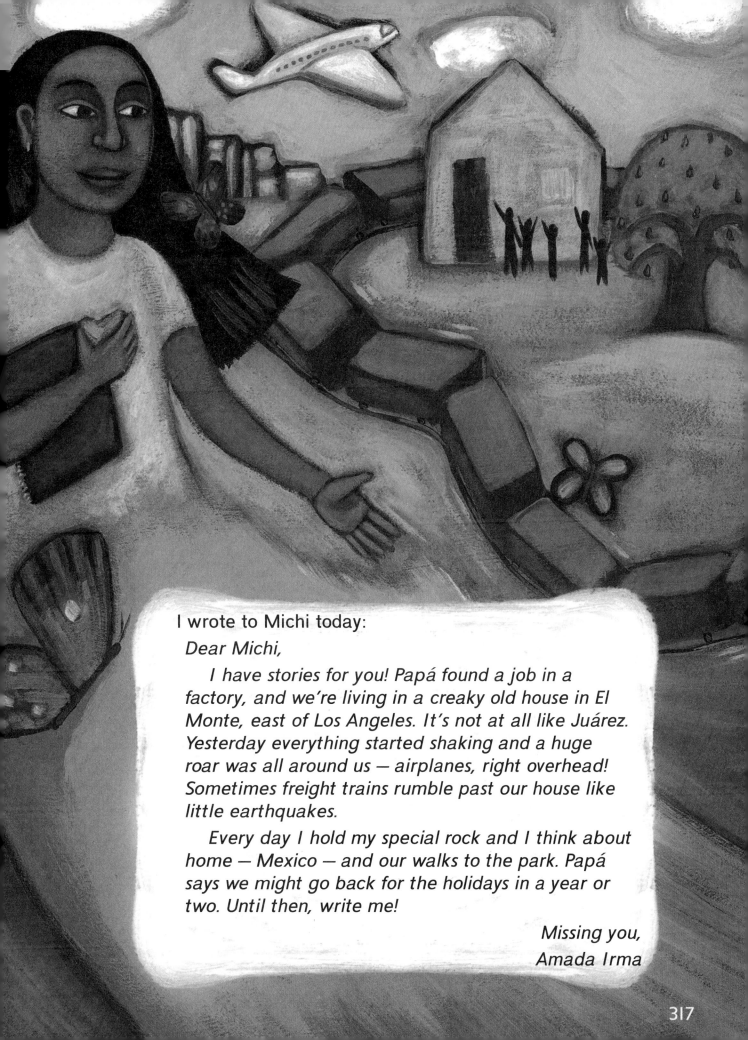

I wrote to Michi today:

Dear Michi,

I have stories for you! Papá found a job in a factory, and we're living in a creaky old house in El Monte, east of Los Angeles. It's not at all like Juárez. Yesterday everything started shaking and a huge roar was all around us — airplanes, right overhead! Sometimes freight trains rumble past our house like little earthquakes.

Every day I hold my special rock and I think about home — Mexico — and our walks to the park. Papá says we might go back for the holidays in a year or two. Until then, write me!

Missing you,
Amada Irma

Well, Diary, I finally found a place where I can sit and think and write. It may not be the little park in Juárez, but it's pretty. You know, just because I'm far away from Juárez and Michi and my family in Mexicali, it doesn't mean they're not here with me. They're inside my little rock; they're here in your pages and in the language that I speak; and they're in my memories and my heart. Papá was right. I AM stronger than I think — in Mexico, in the States, anywhere.

P. S. I've almost filled this whole journal and can't wait to start my new one. Maybe someday I'll even write a book about our journey!

318

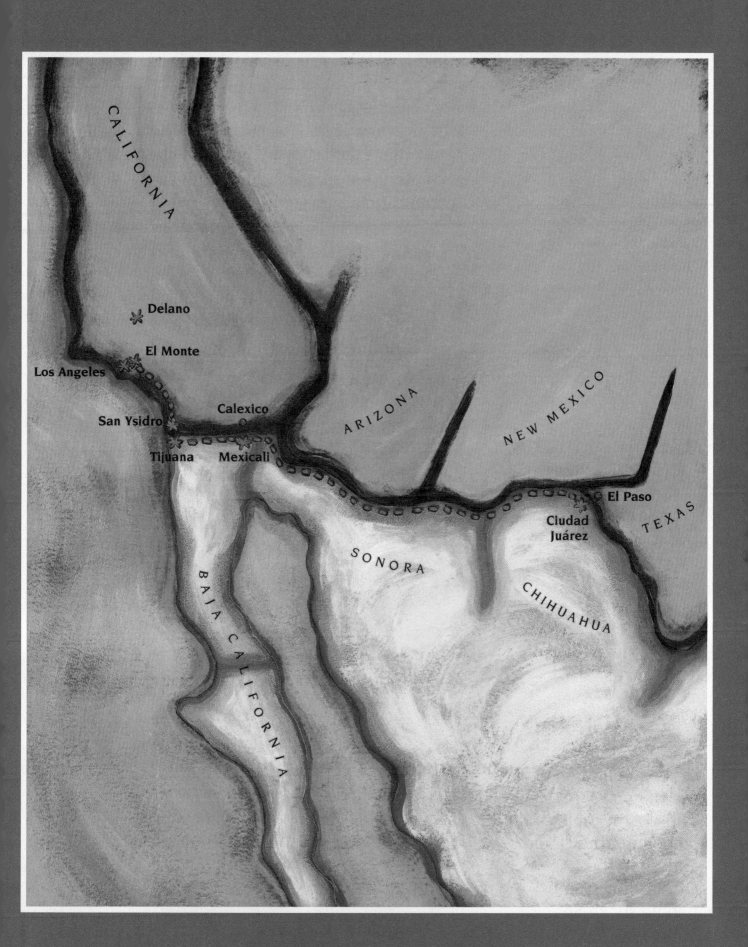

CALIFORNIA

Delano

El Monte

Los Angeles

Calexico

San Ysidro

ARIZONA

NEW MEXICO

Tijuana   Mexicali

El Paso

Ciudad
Juárez

TEXAS

BAJA CALIFORNIA

SONORA

CHIHUAHUA

319

Write the answers to the questions on these pages in your notebook. Use evidence and details from the text to support your answers.

Text Connections

1. Why do you think Amada's brothers are excited about moving, while Amada isn't?

2. How does Amada's papá understand what she is going through?

3. Why does Amada's family have trouble finding places to stay while waiting for Papá to send for them?

4. In what ways is language important in both "The Unbreakable Code" and "My Diary from Here to There"?

5. How do you stay connected to people that are far away from you?

6. Do you agree with Amada and her father that people have to be strong in order to move from one country to another? Explain.

Did You Know?

In 2015, 21 percent of the population of the United States said they spoke a language other than English in their home. Of that group, most people spoke Spanish in their homes.

Look Closer

Keys to Comprehension

1. Using details from the text, explain how Amada says good-bye to her home in Mexico.

2. Contrast details of the settings of Amada's homes in Mexico and in the United States.

Writer's Craft

3. Explain what green cards are and why they are important to Amada's family.

4. Describe the points of view from which "Fiona's Lace" and "My Diary from Here to There" are told, and contrast how each affects the story.

Concept Development

5. Study the text and illustration on page 304. What information can you gather about how the characters are reacting to moving?

6. Compare and contrast the experiences of immigrants in both "My Diary from Here to There" and "Fiona's Lace."

Write

Imagine you and your family moved away from your current town. Write a diary entry, like Amada did in "My Diary from Here to There," about what you would miss most about your town.

Read this Social Studies Connection. You will answer the questions as a class.

Text Feature

Acronyms are abbreviations formed from the first letters of the words in an organization's name.

The Delano Grape Strike and Boycott

Over fifty years ago, workers who harvested grapes in California faced terrible conditions and extremely low pay. At that time, most farm workers were paid less than one dollar an hour. Children often worked alongside their mothers and fathers. Workers toiled from dawn to dusk.

Farm workers had tried to organize strikes in the past. These attempts, however, had failed. By the mid-1960s, two groups had organized. One was called the Agricultural Workers Organizing Committee (AWOC). Another was called the National Farm Workers Association (NFWA). A man named César Chávez started this group. He hoped it could become a union for farm workers.

In the fall of 1965, workers were to pick grapes near the town of Delano, California. Chávez and the NFWA joined forces with the AWOC, and workers began to strike. People who were striking would walk near the farms, carrying signs and convincing others to stop picking and join them. Chávez led strikers on a well-publicized march from Delano to Sacramento. The NFWA and AWOC combined to become the United Farm Workers (UFW). UFW volunteers carried the message of the strike to big cities. Consumers across the United States and around the world were sympathetic. They began boycotting non-union California table grapes.

It was a long fight, but by 1970, the grape growers accepted union contracts and gave in to the UFW's demands. Chávez became a hero to many. Like his role models Mahatma Gandhi and Dr. Martin Luther King, Jr., Chávez was a voice calling for nonviolence as a way to bring about change.

César Chávez gives an interview in 1979.

1. How did workers become involved in the Delano Grape Strike and Boycott?

2. How do strikes and boycotts like these bring about change?

3. What do you think the role of the citizen is in the community?

 Go Digital

Conduct research on the boycotts during the civil rights movement, which was going on at the same time as the UFW strike. How might the actions of people involved in each have influenced each other?

Genre Historical Fiction

Essential Questions

What challenges can groups of people face? How can people work together to overcome challenges set before them?

Fish for Jimmy

Inspired by One Family's Experience in a Japanese American Internment Camp

by Katie Yamasaki

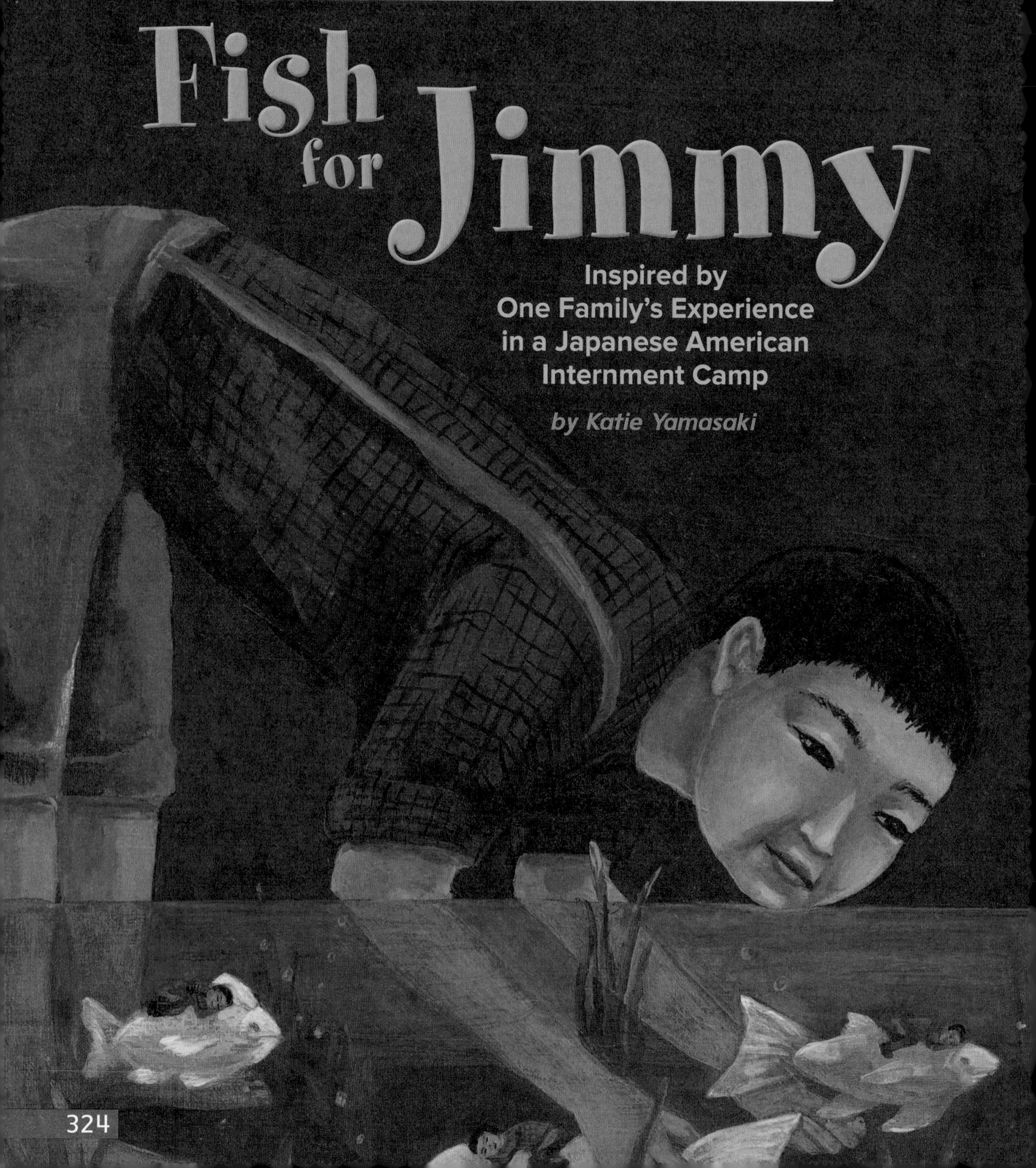

When Taro and Jimmy went to the ocean, Taro would tell Jimmy about the fish. The fish had taught Taro how to swim, he said. Jimmy hoped that one day he would be as strong and smart as Taro, that he too would learn the ways of the fish and the water.

Then Taro would point across the great Pacific Ocean and tell his brother stories about Japan, the land Mother and Father had left long ago in search of a better life.

The life they found in California was good indeed. Father and two other men opened a vegetable market. Farmers brought their vegetables to Father's market, and he would sell them to owners of small vegetable stands.

Some days, Mother helped by keeping track of the stock and greeting the vegetable stand owners as they searched for the ripest tomatoes and the leafiest lettuce.

But one night early in December 1941, Mother and Father frowned deeply at what they heard on the radio. Japan had bombed Pearl Harbor, in Hawaii.

Taro and Jimmy wondered why their parents were so worried. Hawaii was far away, and Japan was even farther.

Bang! Bang! Bang! Mother answered the door to three men whose badges read FBI. The men told Father that, because he was Japanese, he posed a threat to America. Father tried to explain that he loved living in America. He had a home and a vegetable market and a family here. But the men said he had to go with them.

As Father left, he said to Taro, "You are the man of the house now." You must help your mother and take care of Jimmy until I return." But Father would not return soon.

One day signs went up all across California with orders for people of Japanese descent.

Japan and America were at war, and Japanese people were forced to leave their homes and schools and jobs. Taking only what they could carry, they boarded crowded buses with covered windows.

The buses carried Mother, Jimmy, Taro, and others to a desolate land where they were forced to live in tiny barracks surrounded by guarded fences.

In the dusty internment camp, Jimmy lost his appetite.

"Whose child is that?" the cooks whispered, glancing at Jimmy. "He hasn't eaten since we've been here."

Mother bowed her head in shame and desperation.

Meal after meal, day after day, Mother tried to get Jimmy to eat. "It's delicious today, Jimmy, I promise. Now open wide."

Then Taro tried. Jimmy refused Taro too.

Jimmy didn't understand why his family couldn't be together at home near the Pacific Ocean, at home where they could eat in their own kitchen. Why couldn't his mother cook the good rice and noodles, fresh vegetables and fish that he was used to?

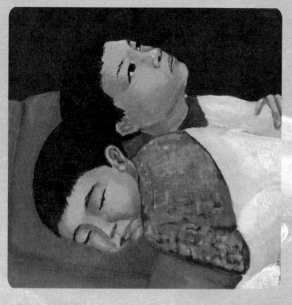

Soon Jimmy stopped asking about the Pacific fish and could no longer remember how the ocean looked and smelled. He stopped running with the other children. Mother and Taro feared that Jimmy was becoming ill.

Taro could not sleep, as his mind filled with troubling thoughts. He worried about Jimmy. He worried about their father and remembered the night in December when the men took him away.

"You must help your mother and take care of Jimmy until I return," his father had said.

Quiet as a breeze, Taro wrapped the shears he had secretly borrowed from the camp garden in his mother's scarf and slid them into his pocket. He slipped out the front door.

Taro crept from shadow to shadow until he arrived at the fence. He glanced at the guards in the distance. Impossible as it was, he feared they could hear his heart pounding in his chest.

He clipped the fence and slipped into the darkness.

Taro ran fast and far until, breathing heavily, he arrived at a mountain. A trickle of water led to a quiet pool, where still, black water reflected in the night sky.

Standing in the pool, Taro felt fish bump against his legs. He slowly lowered his hands into the water and let his fingers sway like reeds. He silently asked the river fish to help his brother.

A fish swam to the swaying fingers, and Taro caught it. He caught another and another until he had seven fish for Jimmy.

With the fish wrapped in his mother's scarf, Taro retraced his steps. He felt the fresh air of freedom. The cool mountain air was so different from what he breathed in the barracks.

Back at camp, he slipped through the hole in the fence and once again crept from shadow to shadow back to his prison home.

In the morning there was fish for Jimmy. As Mother cooked the fish in their barrack, Taro's belly rumbled. He realized how much he too had missed the fresh food of home.

"Are these Pacific fish?" Jimmy asked. "Did they come from far away like us?"

Mother laughed as Jimmy ate at last. Taro had forgotten the sound of his mother's laugh, and it was beautiful.

332

With bellies full, Taro and Jimmy went outside to draw pictures in the dusty earth. And when other children came by, Jimmy went off to play with them.

Many months later Father was released from prison and was permitted to join the rest of the family at the camp. Taro showed Father how, each week, he would creep beyond the fence to the free air of the mountains to find fish for Jimmy.

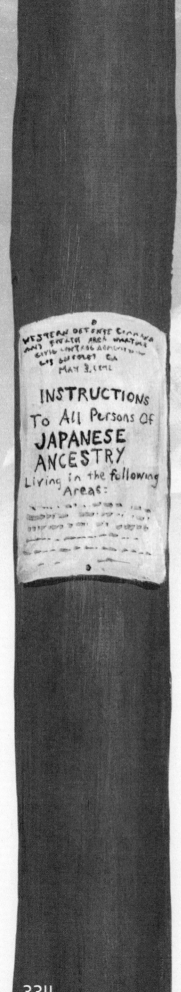

Dear Reader,

This story is based on a true story from my own family's history in the Japanese internment camps. In the real story, my grandfather's cousin snuck out of the camp to find fish for his very young son. In the book, what happened to Taro and Jimmy's father is based on what happened to my great-grandfather Anko Hirashiki.

On December 7, 1941, the Japanese bombed Pearl Harbor, in Hawaii. Many American soldiers were killed, and the next day the United States declared war on Japan. The years that followed were extremely hard times for people of Japanese descent. More than 110,000 American citizens of Japanese descent and Japanese resident aliens, including my great-grandparents, aunts, and uncles, lost their homes and were sent to live in internment camps in desolate parts of the country. They were sent there because the government feared people of Japanese descent couldn't be trusted. Many innocent Japanese men, such as my great-grandfather, were also arrested and sent to prison the night of Pearl Harbor for fear they were spies for Japan.

The camps were closed in 1945, and in 1988 the United States government admitted it had made a mistake and offered a formal apology to the victims of the internment.

Katie Yamasaki

KATIE YAMASAKI's great-grandmother Toshi Hirashiki, great-aunt Akiko Hirashiki, and great-grandfather Anko Hirashiki interned at the Granada Relocation Center in Amache, Colorado

Granada Relocation Center, Amache, Colorado

335

Shaped by Words

by Margarita Engle
illustrated by Ashley Mims

My ancestors were born
in Asia, Africa, and Europe,
but sometimes I feel like a bird
that has migrated across the vast ocean
to this one
small island,
as if I am
shrinking.

I don't know my *africana* mother's language.
I hardly even know her enslaved relatives.
I only know the *chino* half of my family.

Teachers call me a child of three worlds,
but I feel like a creature of three words:
Freedom.
Liberty.
Hope.

Write the answers to the questions on these pages in your notebook. Use evidence and details from the text to support your answers.

Text Connections

1. Describe why Taro risks leaving the camp.
2. With what similes does the speaker in "Shaped by Words" describe himself?
3. Compare and contrast the effects that going to the internment camp and eating fresh fish have on Jimmy and his family.
4. In what ways is familiar food important in both "Hope and Tears" and "Fish for Jimmy"?
5. How are the "The Unbreakable Code" and "Fish for Jimmy" similar to each other? How are they different?
6. Using knowledge you have gained from "Fish for Jimmy" and the other selections in this unit, describe the relationship between the concept of freedom and the United States.

Did You Know?

In spite of discrimination, Japanese Americans fought for their country during World War II. Of the 33,000 who volunteered to serve, 2,100 came from internment camps. In 2010, the U.S. government honored the service of Japanese Americans in World War II with the Congressional Gold Medal.

Look Closer

Keys to Comprehension

1. Why does Jimmy stop eating after arriving at the camp? What clues does the author give?

2. What themes does the author explore in "Fish for Jimmy"? Cite examples from the text.

3. Describe the area surrounding the internment camp using details from the text.

Writer's Craft

4. How does the text layout of stanzas in "Shaped by Words" visually communicate some of the poem's ideas?

5. From what point of view is "Fish for Jimmy" told, and how does it compare to "Fiona's Lace"?

Concept Development

6. Compare and contrast the role of older children toward younger children during times of trouble as portrayed in "Fiona's Lace" and "Fish for Jimmy."

Write

How does Taro define freedom? How do you define freedom? Choose between poetry and prose, and write what freedom means to you.

Connect | Science

Read this Science Connection. You will answer the questions as a class.

Text Feature

Figures are illustrations, photographs, or other visuals that provide additional information.

One Novel Navigator

"Swimming upstream" is a common expression. It describes a difficult situation in which one has to work very hard for a long period of time. This expression is based on how salmon swim. Wild salmon around the world all share something interesting in common. They navigate thousands of miles of waterways each year. From the Pacific and Atlantic oceans, salmon swim inland to spawn, or reproduce.

As if fighting against the flow of rivers and streams was not interesting enough, salmon do something even more intriguing. They return to the exact stream in which they were first born. How do they know which stream to return to?

Scientists in the early 2010s proved that sockeye salmon follow Earth's magnetic field. Earth's core is surrounded by molten, or liquid hot, iron. Earth's solid inner core spins faster than the liquid outer core. This produces streams of flowing, molten iron in the outer core. Earth's magnetic field is a region of magnetism produced in part by the flow of molten materials in the outer core (see figure 1). Certain rocks, the atmosphere, plants, and animals are all affected by this magnetism (see figure 2).

When young sockeye salmon make their first journey to the ocean, they imprint, or automatically remember for life, the magnetic forces they experience. When they are ready to spawn, this memorized magnetized map permits them to find their way home. They swim back up the stream where they were born (see figure 3).

Birds, turtles, and other fish also have a magnetic sense. Researchers do not know for sure what structures these animals use to sense Earth's magnetic field. Future research might reveal these structures and how they function.

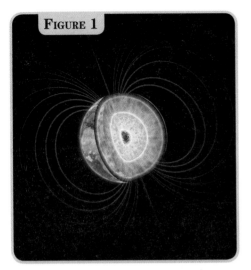

Earth's magnetic field, illustrated as red and blue lines, helps salmon find their way home.

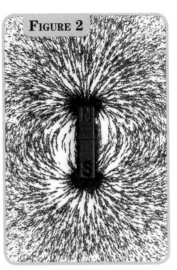

Iron shavings show the field of a common magnet.

Sockeye salmon spawn in a shallow pool.

1. Based on the text, what do salmon do? What makes the sockeye salmon unique?

2. Will scientists discover how sockeye salmon sense Earth's magnetic field? Construct an argument for why or why not.

3. Using Figures 1 and 2, describe the pattern formed by Earth's magnetic field.

 Go Digital

Many animals instinctively imprint some experience from their early lives. Humans experience imprinting too! Choose an animal to research. Find information about its imprinting instinct and how this behavior helps the species survive.

Adaptations in Action

BIG Idea

How do adaptations help plants and animals?

Theme Connections

How do adaptations help these plants and animals survive?

 Background Builder Video

connected.mcgraw-hill.com

Genre Folktales

Essential Question
How have people used stories to explain nature?

How & Why STORIES

by Martha Hamilton and Mitch Weiss
illustrated by John Joven

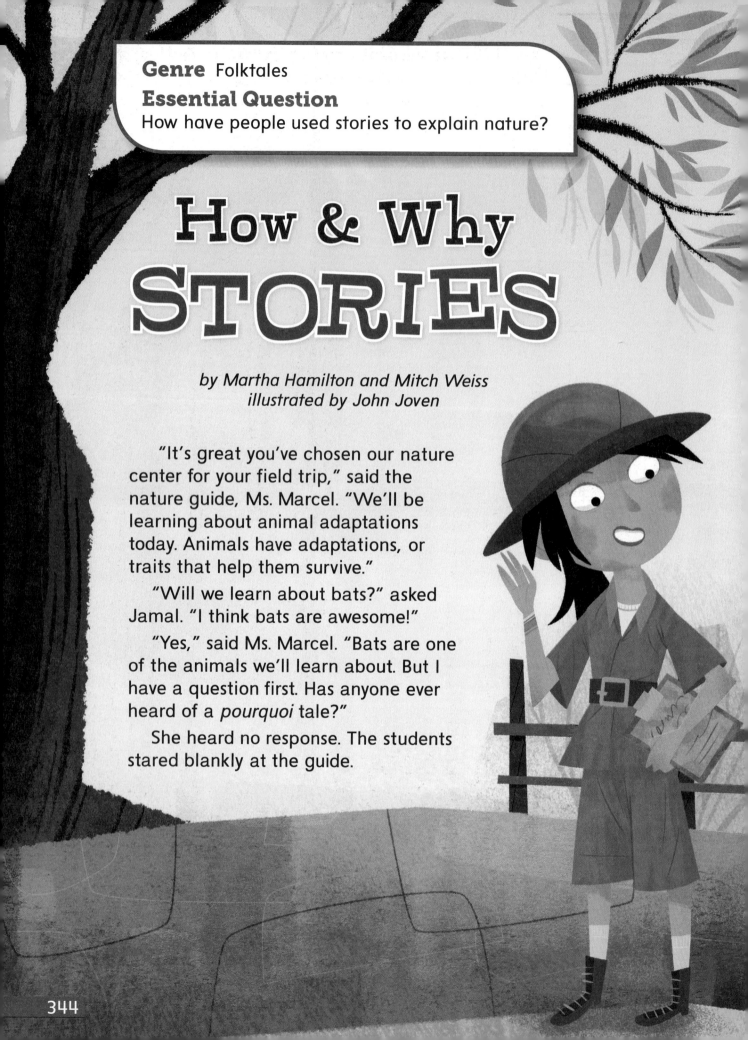

"It's great you've chosen our nature center for your field trip," said the nature guide, Ms. Marcel. "We'll be learning about animal adaptations today. Animals have adaptations, or traits that help them survive."

"Will we learn about bats?" asked Jamal. "I think bats are awesome!"

"Yes," said Ms. Marcel. "Bats are one of the animals we'll learn about. But I have a question first. Has anyone ever heard of a *pourquoi* tale?"

She heard no response. The students stared blankly at the guide.

"Well, then," said Ms. Marcel, "A *pourquoi* tale is a how-and-why story. The word *pourquoi* is French for 'why.' When ancient cultures couldn't explain how or why something was the way it was, they'd invent a story in an attempt to explain it. I like to use these stories when I explain certain traits our animals have. I think you'll understand what I mean when I tell you some of these stories."

The guide showed the students a picture of a bat, wings outstretched, and a picture of an owl sitting on a branch. "What do these two animals have in common?"

Several hands shot up.

"They come out at night!" Grace said.

"That's right," said Ms. Marcel. "Anyone want to tell me why that is?"

"That's when they hunt and eat," Jamal said.

"Right," Ms. Marcel said. "Both bats and owls are nocturnal animals. That means they sleep during the day and are active at night. Do you ever wonder why that might be? Well, the two *pourquoi* tales I'm going to tell you explain why these animals are nocturnal."

WHY BAT FLIES ALONE AT NIGHT
A Story of the Modoc Indians

Long ago, the birds and the animals were at war. They fought many battles. During one battle, Bat fought on the birds' side. But things didn't go well for the birds that day. When Bat realized the birds might lose, he flew up into a tree and hung upside down.

When the fighting was over and the animals had won, Bat decided to go home with them. Lion noticed this and said, "Bat, why are you coming with us? You were fighting against us!"

"Oh, no," said Bat. "I wouldn't do that. I'm one of you. I'm an animal. Look at my teeth. None of the birds have teeth."

The animals agreed that this was true, so they let Bat go with them. Not long after that, there was another battle.

When the birds started to win, Bat hid under a log and waited till the fighting was over. As the birds flew home, Bat went right along with them.

"Wait a second," said Eagle. "You're one of our enemies! I saw you fighting on the animals' side."

"Oh, no," said Bat. "You're wrong. I'm not an animal. Just look at my wings. Have you ever seen an animal with wings?"

The birds had to admit that this was true, so they let Bat go home with them.

As long as the war lasted, Bat went home with the winning side each day. By the end of the war, the animals and birds were furious with Bat. They got together and held a big council to decide what to do. At last they said, "Bat, you lied to us. We don't want to see you again. From now on, you will fly only at night."

To this day, the birds and animals have not forgiven Bat. He still flies alone at night.

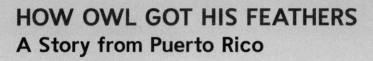

HOW OWL GOT HIS FEATHERS
A Story from Puerto Rico

Long ago, the animals gave large parties and balls. Everyone was invited. They wore their finest outfits and had a great time dancing and feasting.

One day, the birds decided to have a grand ball. They wanted every bird to be there. They sent Hawk to knock on all the birds' doors to invite them.

When Hawk got to Owl's house and gave him the invitation, Owl was worried. You see, back then Owl did not have feathers. Owl said, "All the other birds will be there in their fine feather suits. They'll make fun of me. I can't possibly go."

Hawk told the other birds what Owl had said. They decided each one of them would lend Owl a feather so that he could have a fine suit of feathers and come to the ball. Hawk collected the feathers of different colors and gave them to Owl. He warned Owl that each feather had to be returned to its owner after the party.

Owl arranged the feathers very carefully. Everyone at the ball agreed that Owl looked quite handsome in his new suit. He was so pleased. But during the ball he kept thinking about how he would look when it was over. He hated the thought of having to return the feathers. So when no one was looking, he stole away from the ball and hid in the forest.

When the party was over, the other birds looked for Owl so they could get their feathers back. But he was nowhere to be seen.

To this day, Owl still wears that same fine suit, and the other birds are still looking for him. That is why Owl is never seen by day. He comes out only at night when the other birds are sleeping.

"Some animals fly like our bat and owl, and some animals crawl," Ms. Marcel said. "Here's our ant farm and our collection of beetles, two creatures that crawl."

"We had ants in our kitchen," said Lucia. "We got rid of them, but it was hard. They were everywhere!"

"The beetles look kind of cool," said Sergio. "Their shells are very colorful."

"Yes, we can find ants everywhere, and beetles have colorful shells," said Ms. Marcel. "And I have two more *pourquoi* tales that explain why these adaptations came about. Who wants to hear the tales?"

"We do!" the students cheered.

WHY ANTS ARE FOUND EVERYWHERE
A Story from Burma

One day, Lion, the king of the beasts, ordered all the other animals to honor him. One by one, Tiger, Elephant, Snake, Lizard, and many other animals came to bow before Lion.

Even Ant set out on the long journey. It was not an easy trip for him. Whenever he came to a rock or vine, he had to crawl up one side and down the other. As a result, Ant was the last to arrive. When the animals saw Ant coming, they made fun of him. Lion roared with laughter and said, "It's about time you got here!"

350

Ant crawled away in shame. He told the Queen of the Ants how badly Lion had treated him. The Ant Queen was furious. She asked her friend Worm to crawl in Lion's ear and torture him.

Worm crept into Lion's ear. He twisted and turned. He wiggled and jiggled. Lion roared. He shook his head back and forth trying to get Worm out. The other animals offered to help, but none was small enough. Lion knew he would go crazy if he didn't find a way to get rid of Worm.

At last he realized there was only one animal that could help him. Lion sent a messenger to the Ant Queen. He asked her to send someone to crawl in his ear and get Worm out. The Ant Queen decided Lion had been punished enough, so she sent Ant to help.

When Ant finally arrived, Lion was rolling on the ground in pain. Ant crawled into his ear and called out, "Thank you, Worm. You can come out now."

Lion was so relieved that he rewarded Ant. He said, "Well done, Ant. I have decided that from now on you and your people may live anywhere you'd like."

And that is why, to this day, even though some animals can live only in the jungle, some only in the desert, and others only in the rain forest, ants live everywhere.

HOW BRAZILIAN BEETLES GOT THEIR GORGEOUS COATS
A Story from Brazil

Long ago in Brazil, beetles had plain brown coats. But today their hard-shelled coats are gorgeous. They are so colorful that people often set them in pins and necklaces like precious stones. This is how it happened that Brazilian beetles got their new coats.

One day a little brown beetle was crawling along a wall. Suddenly a big gray rat darted out of a hole in the wall. When he saw the beetle, he began to make fun of her.

"Is that as fast as you can go? What a poke you are! You'll never get anywhere! Just watch how fast I can run!"

The rat dashed to the end of the wall, turned around, and ran back to the beetle. The beetle was still slowly crawling along. She had barely crawled past the spot where the rat left her.

"I'll bet you wish you could run like that!" bragged the gray rat.

"You certainly are a fast runner," replied the beetle. Even though the rat went on and on about himself, the beetle never said a word about the things she could do. She just kept slowly crawling along the wall, wishing the rat would go away.

A green and gold parrot in the mango tree above had overheard their conversation. She said to the rat, "How would you like to race with the beetle? Just to make the race exciting, I'll offer a bright colored coat as a reward. The winner may choose any color coat and I'll have it made to order."

The parrot told them the finish line would be the palm tree at the top of the hill. She gave the signal to start, and they were off.

The rat ran as fast as he could. When he reached the palm tree, he could hardly believe his eyes: there was the beetle sitting beside the parrot. The rat asked with a suspicious tone, "How did you ever manage to run fast enough to get here so soon?"

"Nobody ever said anything about having to run to win the race," replied the beetle as she drew out her tiny wings from her sides. "So I flew instead."

"I didn't know you could fly," said the rat with a grumpy look on his face.

The parrot said to the rat, "You have lost the contest. From now on you must never judge anyone by looks alone. You never can tell when or where you may find hidden wings."

Then the parrot turned to the brown beetle and asked, "What color would you like your new coat to be?"

"I'd like it to be green and gold, just like yours," replied the beetle. And since that day, Brazilian beetles have had gorgeous coats of green and gold. But the rat still wears a plain, dull, gray one.

The students moved on to some exhibits showing rabbits and foxes.

"Isn't that fox's tail beautiful?!" Grace exclaimed.

"I'm sure the rabbit wishes it had a tail like that," added Rosa.

"Yes," said Ms. Marcel, "some animals need long tails to help them survive. For example, a monkey has a long tail so it can swing from tree to tree in a hurry. Some animals started out with long tails, but over time, their tails adapted to become shorter. Their long tails weren't necessary for the animals to survive. I happen to know two more *pourquoi* tales—about tails!"

RABBIT COUNTS THE CROCODILES
A Story from Japan

Long ago, Rabbit had a fine, long, bushy tail like a raccoon's. Back then, just as now, he was always up to one kind of trick or another. It was one of his tricks that caused him to lose his long tail. Let me tell you how it happened.

Rabbit lived on the island of Oki, just off the coast of Japan. Although he had a good life, Rabbit longed to see what it was like on the mainland. He would spend hours staring across the sea, wishing he knew how to swim.

One day when Crocodile swam near the shore, an idea came to Rabbit. He called out, "Crocodile, do you realize I have hundreds of rabbits in my family? It's a shame you have so few crocodiles in yours."

"Who told you that?" snapped Crocodile. "Why, there are hundreds, maybe even thousands, of crocodiles in my family!"

This reaction was just what Rabbit had hoped for. "So far, so good," Rabbit thought to himself. "My plan just might work." Then he said to Crocodile, "Well, if there are so many in your family, how come I only see one of you now and then?"

"That's easy," replied Crocodile. "Because we're usually hidden below the water."

"Well, I won't believe it until I see it. Why don't you call all your crocodile family here so I can count them?"

Crocodile was furious. She shouted, "Fine, you little ball of fur, you stay right here. I'll show you just how many crocodiles are in my family." Crocodile then dove under the water and disappeared.

Soon many crocodiles began to appear. Before long, there were hundreds and hundreds of crocodiles swimming toward the island.

Rabbit then said to Crocodile, "I must admit that you have a lot of crocodiles in your family. But I can't count them when they're in a big clump like this. Tell them to get in a long line."

The crocodiles made one long, straight line that stretched all the way to the mainland. Rabbit began to hop across the backs of the crocodiles. As he did, he counted, "One, two, three, four, five . . ." and on and on until he was almost to the mainland.

When he was just about to step on the last crocodile, he couldn't keep from laughing and shouting, "Oh foolish crocodiles, thanks so much for making a bridge for me!"

When the last crocodile heard this, she opened her jaws wide to eat Rabbit. But all she managed to bite off was Rabbit's tail. That's why, to this day, all rabbits have short tails.

WHY BEAR HAS A STUMPY TAIL
A Story from Norway

One cold winter morning, Fox stole a long string of fish from a fisherman's cart. As she was on her way back to her den, she met Bear. Bear's eyes grew big when he saw the fish. His tail began to swing back and forth in excitement. You see, this was a long time ago when bears had long, bushy tails instead of the short, stumpy ones they have today.

Bear said to Fox, "Goodness! What a tasty-looking catch you have there! Would you share it with me?"

"No!" Fox snapped. "These are my fish. It took a long time to catch them. If you want some, you'll have to catch them yourself."

Bear asked with a suspicious tone, "How did you catch them? The water's frozen solid."

With a sly gleam in her eye, Fox replied, "Why, just come with me, Bear. I'll be glad to show you."

Fox led Bear down to the lake and said, "It's easy, Bear. First, you must cut a hole in the ice. Then stick your tail in. Hold it there as long as you can. It will hurt when the fish grab on, but the longer you hold it there, the more fish you'll catch. When you think you've caught enough, just give a strong, hard pull."

Bear did just what Fox had told him. Soon he felt what he thought was a bite. "You're right, Fox!" he cried excitedly. "I'm already catching fish."

Fox ran off laughing to herself. She knew what Bear was feeling was the water beginning to freeze around his tail.

356

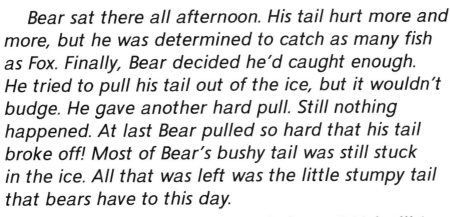

Bear sat there all afternoon. His tail hurt more and more, but he was determined to catch as many fish as Fox. Finally, Bear decided he'd caught enough. He tried to pull his tail out of the ice, but it wouldn't budge. He gave another hard pull. Still nothing happened. At last Bear pulled so hard that his tail broke off! Most of Bear's bushy tail was still stuck in the ice. All that was left was the little stumpy tail that bears have to this day.

Bear roared with pain. He cried out, "Wait till I get my hands on that no-good, lying Fox!" He dashed off to find her. What happened when Bear finally caught up to Fox? . . . That's another story!

"You can search 'pourquoi tales' online and learn more about them," said Ms. Marcel. "And as you think about them—including the ones I told you today—you'll be able to see the lesson, or moral, in them. Thanks, and au revoir! That means 'good-bye' in French!"

Write the answers to the questions on these pages in your notebook. Use evidence and details from the text to support your answers.

Text Connections

1. Why does Ms. Marcel use *pourquoi* tales during the nature center tour?

2. The folktale "How Owl Got His Feathers" actually tries to explain two things about owls. What are they?

3. Which of Ant's traits made him the only one who could help Lion?

4. Contrast the explanations about rabbit tails in the Read Aloud "Peter and Jumper Go to School" and "Rabbit Counts the Crocodiles."

5. With which folktale character do you feel the most connection, and why?

6. Why do you think modern people, like the children in "How & Why Stories," still enjoy *pourquoi* tales, even if they know they are not scientifically factual?

Did You Know?

Books of folktales and fairy tales, along with plays and poetry, are actually usually shelved with nonfiction in the library.

Look Closer

Keys to Comprehension

1. Based on the folktales in "How & Why Stories," make an inference about the types of things *pourquoi* tales usually explain.

2. Summarize "How Brazilian Beetles Got Their Gorgeous Coats," and identify one theme of this story.

3. Using details from the text, compare and contrast the character traits of Rabbit and Fox in "Rabbit Counts the Crocodiles" and "Why Bear Has a Stumpy Tail."

Writer's Craft

4. Explain what *pourquoi* means, and use it to define *pourquoi* tale.

5. How do you know "How & Why Stories" is prose and not a poem?

Concept Development

6. Compare and contrast how two of the folktales cover the topic of nocturnal animals.

Write

Write a short *pourquoi* tale involving a tricky animal, like the rabbit in "Rabbit Counts the Crocodiles." Make sure it explains something in nature.

Science

Why Do Animals Have Tails?

Read this Science Connection. You will answer the questions as a class.

Text Feature

A **bulleted list** organizes related items that do not belong in a particular order.

You've certainly noticed that many kinds of animals have tails. Many scientists believe the first tails helped early animals move through the water. But why do land animals have them today?

There isn't just one answer to this question. It depends on the animal. For example:

- A primate is a monkey, and not an ape, if it has a tail. Some monkeys have prehensile tails, used for grabbing and holding. Interestingly, the only monkeys that have tails that can do this are the ones found in Central and South America.
- Birds have many different shapes and lengths of tails, many of which play an important part in flying. Like the tails on airplanes, bird tails help create stability. Bird tails balance movements left and right. Bird tails help with lift and turning. Bird tails also help slow birds for landing.
- Many four-legged grazing animals like horses and zebras have tails with hair they can use for swatting insects.
- Kangaroos actually use their tails like a fifth "leg." Their tails help propel them forward when they walk slowly and graze.
- Some ground squirrels wave their tails from side to side when they see a snake. Scientists think this signal may be an attempt to either tell the snake that its hiding place is not a secret or that the squirrel is really good at watching for snakes.

Not all animals have tails, of course—and some types of animals had tails long ago but lost them over time. For many animals, however, their tails have important jobs.

Kangaroos graze while using their tails as a fifth "leg."

1. Why did early animals first have tails?

2. Why do scientists call a kangaroo's tail a fifth "leg"?

3. Using the information from the connection, construct an argument supporting the claim that tails are important to many animals' survival and behavior.

 Go Digital

Research ways cats and dogs use their tails. Why is this behavior important?

Genre Informational Text
Essential Questions
What types of animals must defend themselves?
What kinds of adaptations serve as defenses?

ANIMAL
Defense Academy

by Nicole Gill
illustrated by Scott Brooks

So, you don't want something to eat you, right?
Totally understandable. Here at Animal Defense
Academy, we can teach you plenty of ways to
avoid becoming someone else's lunch.

1. RUN!
2. ARMOR
3. POISON
4. STINK
5. HIDE!
6. LIE

RUN AWAY!

The first line of defense is pretty simple—run away! Of course, it helps to have strong legs, a speedy body, or wings.

Thomson's gazelles are fast. They can run 40 miles (64 km) an hour. Cheetahs like to eat gazelles and are just a bit faster. But cheetahs do not have the stamina to keep running for as long as gazelles can, so the gazelles often get away.

It also helps to have plenty of friends around to keep an eye out for prowling carnivores. Gazelles and ostriches are two such friends on the African grasslands. Taller and with much better eyesight than gazelles, ostriches keep a lookout for predators. Gazelles, on the other hand, have better senses of smell and hearing than ostriches. Both animals warn each other when they sense danger.

Most birds fly away from danger. But ostriches can't fly. Instead they run away on long, powerful legs. And they're quick! An ostrich in a hurry can run as fast as a gazelle.

Other animals use different forms of escape. To get a head start, why not leave behind a decoy, like, say, a tail? Some lizards can detach their tails and keep on running. The tail tidbit distracts a predator long enough for the lizard main course to escape. Later, the lizard simply grows a new tail.

Rabbits run in zigzags which make them difficult to catch. Flying fish have a great escape trick. They leap right out of the water and glide through the air on oversized fins that act like wings. The big fish chasing them in the water must wonder where they've disappeared.

SPINES, QUILLS, AND HORNS

If you cannot run away, a nice suit of spines or quills can make you look like an unappealing meal.

When a porcupine senses danger, it curls itself up into a prickly ball. Its sharp quills will poke the tender nose of anything that tries to eat it. A baby porcupine is born with soft quills, but these harden within a short time, making the porcupine unappetizing almost immediately. A predator who tried to bite one would drop it like a hot potato.

Puffer fish stick out their spines and gulp in water until they look like large spiky balls that would be impossible to swallow.

Sea urchins also have sharp spines. Some sea urchins have venom or poison in their spines. The attacker gets not only pierced, but also poisoned!

Many plants protect themselves with thorns and spines. A cactus may look soft and juicy, but things are not always what they seem. Their sharp spines are modified leaves that feel like needles in your skin if you touch one. Imagine what it would feel like in your mouth if you were an animal that tried to eat a cactus!

Some animals have horns they can use for protection. A bighorn sheep has a large heavy curved horn on each side of its head. A black rhino has two sharp horns on the front of its head. Both of these animals will ram anything that threatens them.

The male rhinoceros beetle has a set of sharp horns too. It can use its horns to protect itself but also to dig itself a quick hole to hide from an attacker.

You might think you would have to be awfully hungry to eat a tarantula, but some animals do. Some tarantulas respond by rubbing stinging hairs on their predators. These hairs have barbs that are like fishhooks and are difficult to remove.

ARMOR OR SLIME?

Many soft-bodied animals, such as this garden snail, grow hard shells to protect themselves from becoming an easy dinner. Other soft-bodied animals with shells include turtles, oysters, crabs, and scorpions.

The decorator crab actually decorates its shell to disguise itself. First it cuts pieces of seaweed with its claws. Next it chews an end of the seaweed to make it sticky. Then it sticks the seaweed to its shell. If it moves to an area with another kind of seaweed, it can give itself a makeover with the camouflage.

Hard, scaly plates cover the body of the pangolin, or scaly anteater, like a suit of armor. Like the pangolin, the armadillo is covered in hard, leathery plates. *Armadillo* is a Spanish word that means "little armored one." In the heat of the moment, both pangolins and armadillos roll themselves up into bite-proof balls when they feel threatened.

The Indian rhino has thick, bumpy, tough skin that hangs like a suit of armor and provides protection from predators.

In contrast, the chuckwalla lizard does not have a shell or armor, but it knows how to create some armor. When frightened, the chuckwalla runs to a rock crevice and crawls in. Then it puffs itself with air. It packs itself so tightly into the crevice that it acts as armor until the predator gives up and goes away.

The hagfish uses slime as its armor. If a shark strikes, it immediately lets go because the hagfish releases a thick, suffocating slime into the shark's mouth and gills. As the shark thrashes around in the water, clouds of slime come out of its mouth. Meanwhile, the hagfish swims safely away with strings of slime trailing behind it.

POISON

Poisonous animals often sport bright colors to warn predators to STAY AWAY! Tiny poison arrow frogs look adorable, but just one has enough poison to kill 10 adult humans. The saying "curiosity killed the cat" comes true if a feline predator is curious enough to eat one of these frogs.

If something bothers the bombardier beetle, it sprays out a boiling hot, stinging jet of acid. The attacker will think twice before biting another one.

Monarch caterpillars do put all their eggs in one basket by eating only the milkweed plant. Milkweed contains a poison that does not hurt the caterpillars, but it does hurt many other animals. As the caterpillars eat more and more milkweed, enough of this poison is stored in their bodies to make a bird that eats one of these caterpillars quite sick.

Many plants protect themselves with poison, and you do not always have to eat one to suffer. Just touch poison ivy or poison oak, and your skin may break into itchy blisters. If you realize you have touched one of these plants, wash immediately!

A poison doesn't always kill or make an animal sick; sometimes it tastes absolutely awful. Most birds and spiders avoid ladybugs. They know the leg joints of a ladybug give off a terrible-tasting liquid.

STINK

Another great defense is to make yourself smell really, really bad. Skunks are champion stinkers, and their stripes let you know who they are. When threatened, they raise their tails, hiss, and stamp their feet as a warning. If the predator does not back off, the skunk shows no mercy. Other animals quickly learn not to bother the black-and-white stripes, or risk being squirted with the smelly liquid from a gland near the skunk's tail.

Fulmar birds leave their chicks alone in the nest while the parents hunt for fish. But appearances often are deceiving. These are no helpless babies. They can protect themselves by vomiting a sticky, stinky goo on any would-be attackers.

Hoopoe chicks can also defend themselves if the parent birds are not around. However, the chicks' stinky stuff comes out the other end. They squirt foul-smelling feces out of their tiny rumps.

Birds such as turkey vultures eat dead animals. Animals that have been dead for a while smell horrible. A predator that eats dead smelly animals tends to smell horrible as well. To make itself even more stinky, a turkey vulture in danger will vomit the rotting meat. Phew!

Some plants also use odor as protection. Deer and rabbits often avoid marigolds because of the smell of the flowers. However, this does not protect the flowers from animals with little sense of smell, such as most birds.

HIDE!

Predators cannot eat what they cannot find. Hiding is an excellent defense—and many animals excel at it. Leaf insects are hide-and-seek champions.

An underground burrow offers a great place to hide. When prairie dogs look for food, one always keeps watch for predators. If the lookout barks, all the prairie dogs scurry for the tunnels.

Many other animals hide in burrows or holes, including chipmunks, badgers, foxes, and ferrets. But have you ever heard of the burrowing owl? One burrowing animal even has a special day dedicated to it—February 2, Groundhog Day!

Can you spot this cleverly disguised octopus? Octopuses, squids, and cuttlefish can change the color and texture of their skin to match different backgrounds.

Animals living in a snowy climate have little to hide behind. The bushes and trees have lost their leaves, and the snow covers rocks and holes. But some animals that live in snowy areas can hide out in the open. Both the snowshoe hare and willow ptarmigan turn white in winter and are almost impossible to see in snow.

Potoo birds burn the midnight oil; that is, they are nocturnal birds of Central and South America. Their wailing cry, "potoo," sounds just like their name. During the day they sleep upright on dead branches or stumps. Their gray, black, and brown feathers look just like the branches or stumps where they roost. No potoo bird here—just an old tree stump.

LIE

In the animal kingdom, honesty is not always the best policy. Sometimes the best defense is a clever deception.

Like this twin-spot goby, many fish have big spots on their fins that look like eyes. This confuses larger, predatory fish who cannot tell if the goby is coming or going.

The opossum play acts extremely well. When threatened, the opossum keels over and pretends to be dead. Its body goes stiff and it lies perfectly still. Sometimes the opossum will even ooze out a bit of stinky green mucus, so it smells like it has been dead for a while.

Killdeer birds will pretend to have a broken wing to lead predators away from their nests. Then—ha, ha, fooled you! The not-really-hurt bird flies away, safe.

Some animals protect themselves by copying the colors of more dangerous relatives. Still others protect themselves by pretending to be something completely unappetizing. The harmless Pueblan milk snake looks enough like a deadly coral snake that snake-eating animals leave it alone. Lithops, also called "living stones" or "pebble plants," keep plant-eating animals away by looking like rocks. Instead of being colored green like most plants, lithops come in a range of colors such as white, gray, pink, purple, and beige. The cunning swallowtail caterpillar has coloring exactly like a pile of bird feces. Would YOU eat it?

We hope this class at the Animal Defense Academy has taught you plenty of ways to protect yourself. We can use this chart to review:

Run	gazelle, ostrich, lizard, flying fish
Spines	porcupine, puffer fish, sea urchin, cactus
Armor	armadillo, snail, Indian rhino, decorator crab
Poison	poison arrow frog, bombardier beetle, monarch caterpillar, poison ivy
Stink	skunk, fulmar chick, hoopoe chick, turkey vulture
Hide	prairie dog, octopus, snowshoe hare, potoo bird
Lie	twin-spot goby, opossum, killdeer bird, lithops

Now hopefully you can avoid becoming someone else's breakfast, lunch, or dinner. Be careful out there!

Write the answers to the questions on these pages in your notebook. Use evidence and details from the text to support your answers.

Text Connections

1. Explain why a certain defense only works for social animals that live in groups.

2. Why do you think baby fulmar birds and hoopoe chicks use bad-smelling goo and feces as a defense, rather than running?

3. Describe the defense ladybugs and monarch caterpillars have, and explain the downside of this defense if one of them meets a predator that's never seen its kind before.

4. Think about "Animal Defense Academy" and "How & Why Stories." What is the difference between how these texts explain different animals' behaviors?

5. Describe a defensive behavior you read about. What about it will make you think twice about getting near a particular animal? Explain why.

6. Why do you think so many of the defenses the text describes are ways of avoiding conflict, rather than fighting back against predators?

Did You Know?

Opossums aren't the only animals that can play dead; some predators do the same thing. The Central American cichlid fish not only lies on the lake bottom, pretending to be dead, but also its colors mimic a rotting animal. When a small fish comes to eat it, the cichlid attacks and finds its own meal.

Look Closer

Keys to Comprehension

1. Why do animals use the defense they do in a snowy climate, according to the text?

2. Describe the details that support the concept that an animal's first line of defense is running away.

Writer's Craft

3. What is the fictional setting for "Animal Defense Academy"? Connect it to the way the text is structured.

Concept Development

4. What text information from "Animal Defense Academy" does the chart on page 373 help you better understand?

5. How does the author use reasons to support the idea that "honesty is not always the best policy" in the animal kingdom?

6. Integrate information from the Read Aloud "Peter and Jumper Go to School" and "Animal Defense Academy" to describe ways a rabbit can escape predators.

Write

Write an opinion paragraph about the animal defense adaptation you think is the most effective. Be sure to include reasons from "Animal Defense Academy" to support your opinion.

Read this Science Connection. You will answer the questions as a class.

Text Feature

A **caption** is a sentence or phrase that tells more about a photograph.

A Shark Repellent?

Researchers have been trying to develop a shark repellent for over sixty years. Fishers have long said sharks avoided shark necromones, found in the rotting remains of other sharks. Using this information, the Navy in the 1940s created survival vests with a stinky mixture. Unfortunately, it did not work. Then, in the 1970s, a biologist named Eugenie Clark discovered that the Moses sole secretes a powerful shark repellent from glands along its fins. The toxin can cause a shark to back away just as its open mouth is about to close over the Moses sole. People were not able to use this toxin in commercial repellents, however.

In 2004, a chemist named Eric Stroud accidentally made a discovery. While working near a pool with small sharks, he dropped a large magnet into the water. It bothered the sharks. Further experimentation proved a strong, moving magnet is a great shark deterrent. The reason for this has to do with sharks' adaptation of electrical sensors. These sensors help sharks find swimming prey. They also allow sharks to use Earth's electromagnetic field like a map. A magnet's field disrupts a shark's sensors, annoying the shark.

Companies are developing a range of shark repellents. Containers of liquid necromones are exploded underwater to send sharks scurrying away. People hope magnetized fishhooks can keep sharks from getting caught by accident. Not all related products work well. Some are expensive. Still, inspired by repellents found in nature, people continue to try and figure out ways to protect people and sharks from each other.

Sharks' heads have electrical sensors known as ampullae of Lorenzini.

1. Why do magnets bother sharks?

2. Create a model to see the power of magnetic fields.

   a. You need two small strong magnets, tape, a plastic or wooden toy train car, and straight train track.

   b. Tape one magnet on the train's front with the magnet's north pole facing out. Tape the other magnet to the bottom of a wall with its north pole facing out.

   c. Line up the track so it ends at the wall magnet.

   d. Push the train on the track until it touches the wall magnet. Let go. What happens?

3. In this model, the train has energy of motion (kinetic energy) when you push the train car forward. The kinetic energy briefly converts into magnetic potential energy when the two magnetic fields collide. Based on your observation, did the magnetic potential energy then convert back into kinetic energy? Explain how you know.

 Go Digital

Research some of the natural solutions people use to keep pests out of their gardens. Which methods mimic predators?

Genre Informational Text
Essential Question
How is camouflage an adaptation?

MASTERS OF ILLUSION

by Jean Enicks
illustrated by Peter Bull

Not all masters of illusion are magicians. Many animals outdo
humans in their ability to create illusions and disappear.

LIVING LONG

Animals that live long enough to reproduce pass their genes to their young. Ever wonder why albino animals are so rare? Their lack of color makes them stand out and an easy target for predators. Few albino animals live long enough to reproduce.

How do animals increase their odds of surviving? One way is through camouflage. Camouflage is when an animal uses coloring or covering to blend in with the world around it. Predators have a hard time finding an animal they cannot see.

Camouflage is an animal adaptation that is developed over many generations. There are hundreds of kinds of katydids throughout the world. They are often called leaf insects because their wings look like leaves. Some look like healthy green leaves. Others look like brown dead leaves. Each kind of katydid that survived did so by adapting to its surroundings.

Suppose at one time most katydids were green, but then some brown ones came along. The brown ones that stayed on the green leaves most likely were eaten, but the brown ones that moved to the dead leaves most likely survived. They had young that developed to look even more like dead leaves.

Generation after generation the ones that stood out in the crowd were eaten, but the ones that blended in survived and reproduced. They adapted to their surroundings by changing what they ate, how they moved, and how they acted. Each kind of katydid that survived did so by adapting to its surroundings.

MATCHING COLORS

Many animals, such as katydids, adapt over time to match the color of their surroundings. Most animals that live in the desert are sandy shades of brown. They look like the sand and rocks they live on or under. The horned lizard is not only the color of the desert rocks, but also it has spines on its back that make it look rough like the rocks.

Camouflage helps animals from being eaten, and it also helps the animals who want to eat. Predators can be as well camouflaged as the prey. Scorpions, rattlesnakes, desert mice, and roadrunners are all the same colors as the sand and rocks.

Few plants live in the desert, so most desert animals eat other animals. The horned lizard eats ants, spiders, and grasshoppers. Scorpions eat ants, spiders, and grasshoppers too, but they also eat lizards.

The southern grasshopper mouse does not look ferocious, but it eats scorpions. This mouse is immune to the poison of the scorpion's sting. Rattlesnakes eat mice and lizards. Roadrunners eat mice, lizards, scorpions, and rattlesnakes. All use camouflage to catch their prey.

DESERT FOOD WEB

A food web is two or more food chains that are connected.

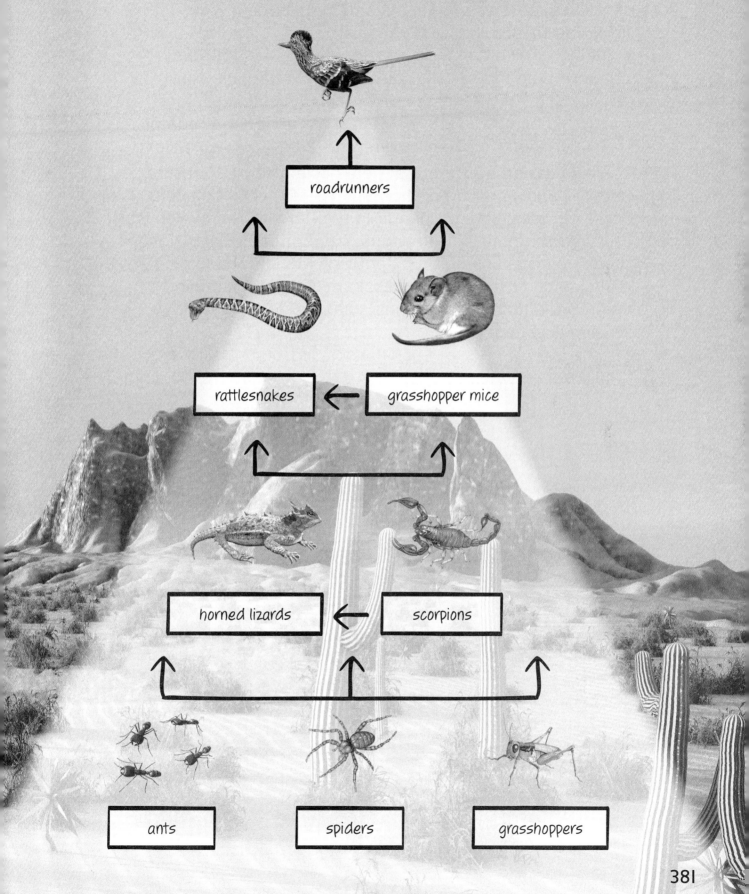

roadrunners

rattlesnakes ← grasshopper mice

horned lizards ← scorpions

ants

spiders

grasshoppers

CHANGING COLORS

Some animals can change colors to match their surroundings. Not only can an octopus change its skin color, but it can also change its skin texture. Sharks, dolphins, and eels like to eat octopuses. An octopus may not have time to hide, so it disappears! Patterns of color appear on its skin in less than a second. Its skin becomes rough and bumpy like the sand or rocks near it. A predator no longer sees it and moves on.

How does an octopus disappear? Scientists are not sure, but they know an octopus has millions of special skin cells. Each of these cells can change to a different color, which is great because most environments are not one color. At one time scientists thought an octopus saw its surroundings and changed its color to match. Later they studied blind octopuses and found they could change to match their surroundings too.

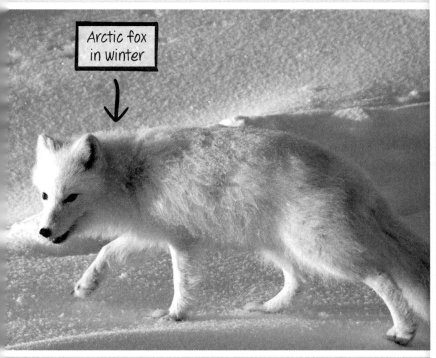

Arctic fox in winter

Arctic fox in summer

Some animals change colors to match the seasons. They are brown in the summer and white in the winter. Summer is short in the Arctic, but it does come. Arctic animals would be easy targets if they stayed snow white through the summer.

In the summer the collared lemming is grayish brown. It blends in with the ground and rocks. In the winter, it grows white fur and blends in with the snow. How does it change like this? Scientists think the shorter, colder days of fall trigger chemicals in the lemming's brain. These chemicals cause white fur to grow under the gray-brown fur. The collared lemming sheds its gray-brown fur, and by the time winter arrives, the animal is snow white.

Other Arctic animals change in a similar way. The Arctic fox is one of these animals. Arctic foxes eat lemmings. They also follow polar bears and eat their leftovers. They do not follow too closely, though, because polar bears eat Arctic foxes.

SEEING RIGHT THROUGH

There are some animals with very little color at all. They do not match their background. They do not change colors. Instead, they are see-through, or transparent.

Most butterflies are colorful, but not clearwing butterflies. Clearwing butterflies have clear wings. Some are completely clear, and some have black or colored edges. When a clearwing butterfly is sipping nectar from a flower, predators see the flower showing through its wings. They do not see the butterfly.

Glass catfish have see-through bodies. If they are near rocks, predators see rocks. If the catfish are swimming through the water, they look like reflected light or a ripple in the water. Having a see-through body is great camouflage!

Some shrimp are colorful, but others are almost as transparent as the water. They may have a few brightly colored markings, but these often look like sparkles in the water. Fish, turtles, and water birds like to eat shrimp, but these predators have a hard time catching what they cannot see. If you visit a rock pool and see nothing, look closer. It may contain ghost shrimp that seem invisible at first.

glass catfish

ghost shrimp

USING PATTERNS

Stripes and spots are bold in a photograph, but they can actually make animals harder to see. A zebra's stripes stand out in a photo or when you see a zebra at the zoo. But in the tall grass of a savanna, the stripes help zebras blend in. Zebras also stand in groups. Their stripes make it hard to see a single animal. Predators become confused and do not know where to strike.

Many fish have stripes. The stripes of butterfly fish, clownfish, and lionfish make them stand out in a fish tank, but their stripes help them blend in with the colorful coral reefs they live in naturally.

Snow leopards live high in the mountains and mainly eat mountain sheep. Snow covers the mountains, but it does not hide all the rocks. The leopards' spots help them blend in with the rocks. The sheep do not see them until it is too late.

You might think a fawn would be easy prey for a predator. A mother deer often leaves it, but she stays within hearing distance. The fawn stays very still. Its spots help it blend in with the forest floor and the spots of sunlight coming through the trees. A fawn also has another trick to protect itself. It has very little scent. A predator has a difficult time finding something it cannot see or smell!

snow leopard

ANIMALS WITH STRIPES AND SPOTS*

	STRIPES	SPOTS
PREDATORS	tiger striped hyena coral snake	leopard cheetah moray eel
PREY	zebra tapir caterpillar	giraffe fawn ladybug

*These are only some of the animals with stripes and spots.
 There are many more.

ACTING IT OUT

Walking sticks are extremely well camouflaged. They look like the twigs they rest on. Walking sticks are nocturnal. That means they sleep during the day and are active at night. They are very still when they sleep. They do not move and give themselves away, so predators pass them by.

Thorn bugs look like the thorns on a plant. They stay very still and suck juices from the plant. Most predators do not notice them.

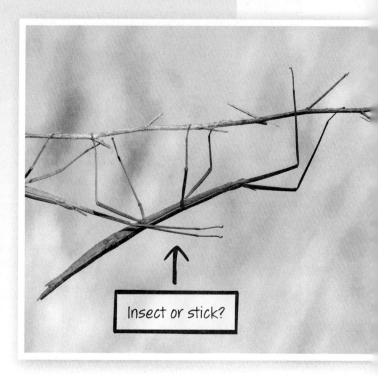

Insect or stick?

Many animals stay still, but some put on an act. Several caterpillars have markings that make them look like a snake, but some caterpillars go one step further. A giant swallowtail caterpillar moves red parts on its body to look like a snake's forked tongue. When a predator approaches a hawk moth caterpillar, it rears up and makes movements like a striking snake.

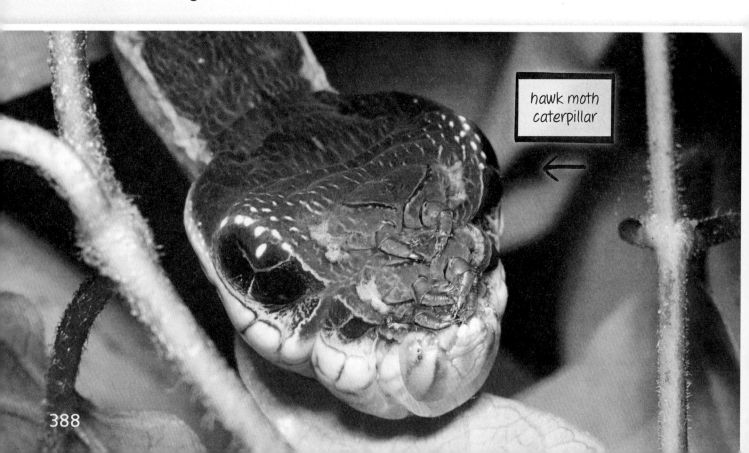

hawk moth caterpillar

The bittern is a wading bird with a striped neck. The stripes look like the reeds it stands in. The bittern lifts its head and stands still, unless the wind blows. Then the bird sways back and forth with the reeds. Because its back is not as well camouflaged as its neck and chest, the bittern keeps its chest toward enemies. The bittern knows how to act the part.

The alligator snapping turtle has a dark shell that blends in with the mud at the bottom of a lake. It can stay underwater for up to fifty minutes. It opens its mouth and wiggles its tongue. Its tongue looks like a worm. The turtle plays the part well. When a curious fish swims near the turtle's tongue, the turtle snaps its mouth shut and swallows the fish.

People can learn much from animals. To get close enough to study these animals, some scientists and wildlife photographers wear camouflage. They sit very still. Some wildlife photographers will wait days for a great shot!

alligator snapping turtle

Ghost Crab

by David L. Harrison
illustrated by Giles Laroche

List of words
ghost crabs know:
danger, freeze,
blend, slow,
look, run,
stop, go.

Sea, food,
wave, tide,
eat, fast,
scurry, hide,
dig, hole,
dive, inside.

Gull, danger,
sand, white,
disappear,
plain, sight,
sun, burn,
safe, night.

Write the answers to the questions on these pages in your notebook. Use evidence and details from the text to support your answers.

Did You Know?

The field of biomimicry involves creating human-made materials and systems that imitate things in nature. For example, scientists recently created a flexible material that can automatically change color to match patterns of light. The technology is inspired by the way cephalopods, such as the octopus, do the same thing.

Text Connections

1. Explain why you are unlikely to find a bright pink prey animal in the desert.

2. Explain how the words in "Ghost Crab" could also be seen as descriptions of a series of events and actions.

3. Why do some animals have patterned camouflage instead of solid-colored camouflage? Give an example.

4. Based on the information from "Masters of Illusion" and "Animal Defense Academy," why do you think monarch caterpillars have coloring that makes them stand out?

5. What do you think people can learn from studying animal camouflage, aside from making better camouflage clothing?

6. Which adaptation in "Masters of Illusion" do you think is the most impressive, and why?

Look Closer

Keys to Comprehension

1. Using the information about the giant swallowtail caterpillar and the alligator snapping turtle, explain why the caterpillar imitates a predator's tongue, while the turtle makes its tongue appear to be a kind of prey.

2. Relate the main idea of "Masters of Illusion" to the selection's title, and summarize how the text supports this main idea.

Writer's Craft

3. Define *camouflage,* and use details from the text to explain how animals develop it.

4. Compare and contrast the way authors use lists of words in "Ghost Crab" and the poem "Shaped by Words" from the previous unit.

Concept Development

5. How does the food web diagram on page 381 help you better understand interconnections of camouflaged desert animals?

6. Using information from both "Masters of Illusion" and "Animal Defense Academy," compare and contrast the ways an octopus, collared lemming, and snowshoe hare use color to hide from predators.

Write

Make up a story about an animal that finds itself in a situation where its usual kind of camouflage doesn't work. For example, what if the walking stick from "Masters of Illusion" could not find a stick or a tree branch? How does the animal solve its problem?

Read this Science Connection. You will answer the questions as a class.

Text Feature

Informational text often includes **pronunciations** for difficult words.

Hiding from an Extinct Predator

Sometimes an adaptation can be a window into the past, showing how an organism avoided ancient predators. This appears to be true for the New Zealand Araliaceae (ə rālē′ āsē ē) tree. This tree once used color to hide—a type of camouflage most often used by animals.

For a long time, scientists found the Araliaceae tree puzzling. The plant's leaves change dramatically as it grows. As a seedling, its leaves are mottled brown. At about 6 inches (about 15 centimeters) tall, it starts growing leaves that look completely different. These juvenile leaves are thin and stiff. Their edges have sharp indentations with bright green marks. Then, when the tree is about 3 yards (about 3 meters) tall, ordinary green leaves suddenly appear.

To understand why these changes developed, you have to look back generations. For millions of years, giant moa birds roamed New Zealand. These birds ate only plants. Over time, the Araliaceae tree developed adaptations to fend off hungry moa birds. For example, the seedling leaves match dead leaves and would have been overlooked. Once the tree was taller, though, this strategy wouldn't have worked. So instead, the juvenile leaves are spiky and difficult to swallow— the bright green marks serve as a warning. Once over 3 yards (about 3 meters) tall, the tree would have been too tall for a moa to reach. The tree no longer needed special coloring to survive.

Of course, times have changed. People hunted the moa birds into extinction nearly 600 years ago. But the Araliaceae tree has not gotten the message yet. It is still hiding from a predator that is not coming back.

A juvenile New Zealand Araliaceae tree

1. What is unusual about the New Zealand Araliaceae tree's leaves?

2. Why are the New Zealand Araliaceae tree's leaf changes no longer useful as a defense?

3. If the moa bird suddenly came back to New Zealand, would the New Zealand Araliaceae tree have adaptations that would allow it to survive? Give facts to support your argument.

 **Go Digital**

Conduct research about Australian mistletoe plants. How do they use mimicry to hide?

Genre Narrative Nonfiction

Essential Questions
What kinds of adaptations might help plants?
Where can you see plant adaptations?

Plants Found a Way

by Lynn Williams

illustrated by James Haskins and David Hovey

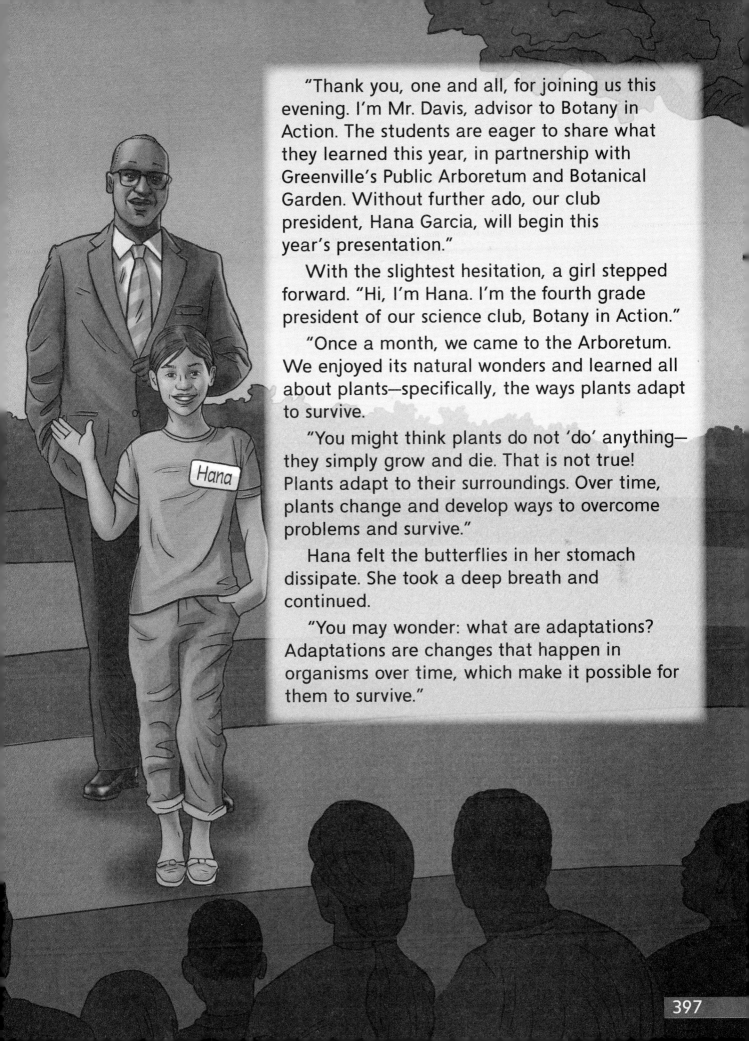

"Thank you, one and all, for joining us this evening. I'm Mr. Davis, advisor to Botany in Action. The students are eager to share what they learned this year, in partnership with Greenville's Public Arboretum and Botanical Garden. Without further ado, our club president, Hana Garcia, will begin this year's presentation."

With the slightest hesitation, a girl stepped forward. "Hi, I'm Hana. I'm the fourth grade president of our science club, Botany in Action."

"Once a month, we came to the Arboretum. We enjoyed its natural wonders and learned all about plants—specifically, the ways plants adapt to survive.

"You might think plants do not 'do' anything— they simply grow and die. That is not true! Plants adapt to their surroundings. Over time, plants change and develop ways to overcome problems and survive."

Hana felt the butterflies in her stomach dissipate. She took a deep breath and continued.

"You may wonder: what are adaptations? Adaptations are changes that happen in organisms over time, which make it possible for them to survive."

At that, Lucia, Arturo, Dana, and Tariq stepped forward holding posters. Hana continued, "Adaptations can

- protect plants from being eaten.
- aid plants with reproduction.
- help plants remain safely in the same place.
- help plants receive more Sunlight, Water, Air, or Nutrients (SWAN)."

For each word in SWAN, a fellow member of the club lifted their poster board to reveal a cleverly illustrated letter sign. The students held their signs high over their heads, spelling out the acronym.

"There are two basic kinds of plant adaptations. Structural adaptations involve the plant's physical features, such as its color, shape, or size. For example, flowers have developed bright colors to attract bees or butterflies that help with reproduction.

"The second type of adaptation is behavioral. It is hard to imagine that plants 'behave,' but they do! Plants respond to changes in their environments. One example of this is the sunflower. Young sunflower stems grow rapidly in response to sunlight, causing the head of the flower to turn and appear as if it is following the sun across the sky. Sunflowers that do this grow larger and outcompete sunflowers that do not.

"Tariq Bari will now tell you more about flowers."

Hana and Tariq bumped fists as they traded places onstage. Tariq had practiced his part of the presentation over and over in front of his bathroom mirror every night for a week. He felt extra confident, and his voice boomed out to the crowd.

"Have you ever thought about why flowers bloom in the spring? Blooming is a behavioral adaptation. Flowering plants compete with other plants for resources, such as rain and pollinating insects. Over time, flowering plants have adapted to bloom when conditions over eons have proven best for them to produce seeds.

"Flowering plants need to be pollinated to produce seeds," Tariq continued. "That happens when a flower's pollen is transferred to the flower's reproductive parts, such as the stigma. However, a flower cannot move the pollen on its own. It needs help!"

"Flowers," Tariq explained, "have developed structural adaptations to attract the help they need.

- **Color.** Bright colors often act as a signal that nectar can be found within a flower. Red flowers, such as the cardinal flower, invite hummingbirds. Yellow or orange daisies invite butterflies. Violet or blue flowers, such as lavender, draw bees to the plant.

- **Shape.** Flowers such as buttercups are shaped like open bowls. Insects rest on the flower petals as they gather nectar. Pollen in the bowl sticks to the insect and moves with it from flower to flower.

- **Size.** Pollinators can see and are attracted to the large flowers on hibiscus, banana trees, and cacti.

- **Odor.** Some flowers release strong scents to appeal to pollinators. This is especially true of many night-blooming flowers such as the chocolate-scented daisy. Insects may not see the plants well in the dark, so the odor helps guide them to the flowers' nectar.

- **Nectar.** Flowers produce nectar, a sweet substance consumed by pollinators. When pollinators access the flower's nectar, they also pick up pollen on their legs, beak, or other body parts. They transfer that pollen to the next flower they touch. Hummingbirds favor honeysuckle; zinnias draw butterflies near; and bees swarm to black-eyed Susans."

Color — Cardinal flowers

Shape — Buttercups

Size — Flowering cactus

Odor — Chocolate daisy

Nectar — Zinnia

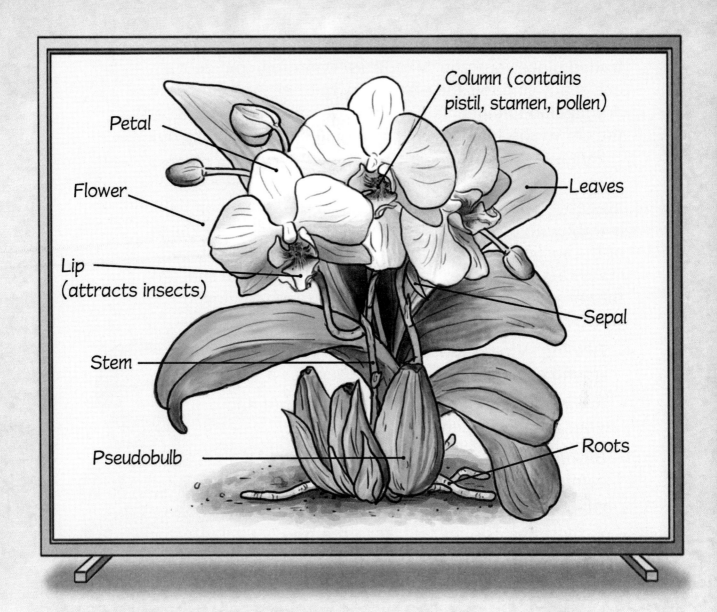

Petal

Flower

Lip
(attracts insects)

Stem

Pseudobulb

Column (contains
pistil, stamen, pollen)

Leaves

Sepal

Roots

Tariq then focused on one particular flower. "One flower with an incredible track record is the orchid. Orchids are some of the most abundant and adaptable species on the planet, and they have been around for millions of years. Plus, more than twenty thousand varieties of the plant exist.

"Adaptability is the key to the orchid's success! Some orchids can grow in soil, some on trees, and some on rocks. One variety has even adapted to live underground. Some orchids have flowers that resemble bees, flies, or spiders to attract pollinating insects. Other orchids have thick, bulb-like stems that retain water to keep the plant alive during dry spells.

"That is all for flowers! Dana Meyer is up next to explain all about vines."

Dana and Tariq gave each other a high-five as they traded places onstage. Like Tariq, Dana felt confident and ready. She felt the jitters, too, but her experiences in drama club told her they would fade away. As Dana faced the crowd she took a deep breath, smiled, and spoke out.

"Vines are also incredible plants. They grow in places other plants cannot, making the best of whatever space is available. This is especially evident in the rain forest, which is thick with competing vegetation. Tall trees block much of the sunlight from reaching the forest floor. As a result, many rain-forest vines can climb trees to get the sunlight they need. These vines climb trees to reach the forest canopy in several different ways.

- *Twining.* Vines grow around and up, winding around a support of some kind, such as a tree.

- *Tendrils.* Small parts of the vine grow out and wrap around and up the support.

- *Thorns, hooks, and rootlets.* These grow from a vine and into the tree.

- *Sticky tips.* These vine growths secrete resin on their tips. The resin sticks to the tree."

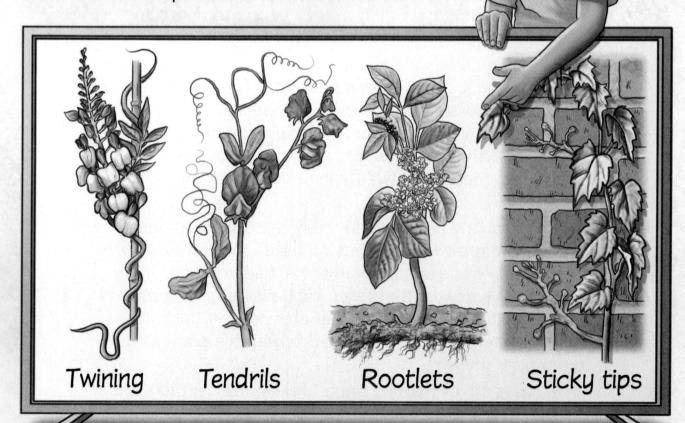

Twining   Tendrils   Rootlets   Sticky tips

Shallow roots

Buttress roots

Prop and stilt roots

"Many plants in and around the world use these adaptations. Wisteria and honeysuckle plants have the twining adaptation. Sweet peas and grapes have tendrils. Poison ivy has rootlets, and Boston ivy has sticky tips.

"Plant roots are another important rain-forest adaptation. Rain-forest topsoil is thin. Most of the nutrients are close to the surface. Rain-forest trees get more nutrients if their roots spread out horizontally instead of growing downward. Even trees that are more than a hundred feet tall may stand on shallow roots that are only a few feet deep.

"Tall rain-forest trees may develop buttress roots. These large, woody ridges provide support and stability. They grow at the base of the tree and spread across the ground. Buttresses can grow as tall as fifteen feet or more before they merge back into the main trunk of the tree.

"Other trees, such as mangroves, develop prop and stilt roots. These above-ground roots grow downward into wet soil and along the edges of waterways. Such roots anchor plants in areas that flood frequently or have regular tides that flood the shore."

"I hope I've *anchored* your understanding of vines and roots. Arturo Diaz will share his knowledge of seeds." The audience clapped as Dana waved to the crowd and skipped offstage, winking at Arturo as he stiffly stepped forward.

Arturo smiled, nodded, and relaxed as he took his place. Arturo felt gratified by Dana's support. He wanted to do well for his new classmates.

"Many plants grow from seeds, so it is no surprise that seeds have adapted too. For plants to thrive, they must spread to new areas where the seeds can grow. Plants have adapted to use wind, water, and animals to carry them to new places.

- *Wind.* Some seeds are lightweight and have special shapes that 'catch' the wind and help them 'fly.' Dandelion seeds are like tiny, fluffy parachutes; they float far away on the wind to grow elsewhere.

- *Water.* Plants that live in or near water often have seeds with structural adaptations that help them float. Coconuts, for example, are large seeds that have a lot of air inside. Because they are less dense than water, they can easily float away to a new destination. Plus, the coconut water and "meat" inside keep the seed alive during its journey.

- *Animals.* Animals carry many seeds to far-off locations. Burrs with seeds inside catch onto the fur of passing animals. Rodents gather nuts and seeds and bury them in new places. Birds and other animals eat berries and other fruits with seeds. The seeds that pass through their bodies undigested land somewhere else when the animals defecate."

Wind

"Many seeds have adapted over time to become very durable. They can last for years until conditions are right and then germinate to grow into a new plant. Desert plants, for example, have seeds that resist heat and drought. They lie dormant for months or even years until rains return. Even seeds discovered buried for thirty thousand years in the icy tundra have grown to produce plants!

"Other seeds are protected by tough outer coverings. The hard shells of acorns protect oak seeds. Pods, from plants such as honey locust and acacia trees, keep seeds safe inside until the growing season. Spruce, fir, and other conifer trees produce bushels of pine cones that serve the same purpose. Each woody scale of a pine cone harbors two seeds. That adds up to dozens of seeds per cone!"

Water

Animals

405

The sun dipped below the horizon, and the amphitheater dimmed in the twilight. While Arturo spoke to the audience, the other members of the botany club sprang into action. Tariq and Dana switched on two spotlights. Hana looked around to make sure the safety and walkway lights glowed.

Mr. Davis and Lucia worked behind Arturo to set up the next visual aid. Arturo gave her a cue, and Lucia pressed a "play" button. The screen, which Mr. Davis had set up next to Arturo, flickered to life. At that moment, now flanked by a video of a burning and smoldering forest floor, Arturo exclaimed, "Behold, the renewing power of fire!"

The audience oohed and awed. As he continued, the video showed a superheated pinecone opening in a blaze.

"Some pine cones," continued Arturo, "such as those from lodgepole pines and redwoods, are so tough that only fire can release the seeds inside. When forest fires sweep through boreal forests, the heat melts the resin holding the pine cone scales closed. The scales pop open, releasing their seeds. Such fires also wipe out old or diseased plants. This opens the land for new, healthy trees to grow. Lucia Rodríguez will now nurture your knowledge of spines, other plant defenses, and one surprising and rare adaptation."

Lucia rushed to the stage, eager for her turn to share. "Deserts are some of the most extreme climates in the world," she began. "Plants have adapted to survive the high temperatures and lack of rain. As a result, many desert plants flourish! One of those is the cactus. It has a very important structural adaptation: spines! Cacti spines serve many purposes.

- **Protection.** Spines protect the cactus from hungry or thirsty animals that would damage the plant.

- **Regulation of temperature.** Spines help cool the plant by shading its surface. White or light-colored spines also reflect heat away from the plant. This helps keep the plant cool too.

- **Conservation.** Because spines are small, they use little water.

"Like the cactus, plants in other biomes also rely on adaptations that are sharp. These include thorns, needles, and hooks. Roses, blackberries, and other plants have thorns for protection. Conifers, such as fir trees, have tough, pointy needles that deter animals and people. Burdock burrs are covered with tiny hooks. These prickly balls protect the seeds inside and help the seeds spread to other places by clinging to the fur, feather, and clothing of unsuspecting travelers."

Spines

Needles

Thorns

Hooks

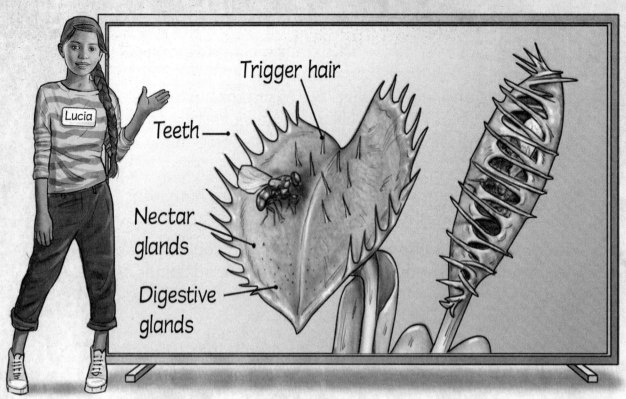

Trigger hair

Teeth—

Nectar glands

Digestive glands

Lucia

"Finally, I will end this evening's presentation by describing one curious adaptation. We all think of plants as food some creatures eat. Botany in Action learned that some plants eat too!

"These plants have adapted to their environments by becoming carnivorous. The famous Venus flytrap is one of these. Its habitat is mainly along the coast and in the wetlands of North and South Carolina. The soil there has few nutrients that can support growing plants. The Venus flytrap has adapted to obtain those nutrients elsewhere. It has developed a structural and behavioral adaptation: special leaves that catch and digest insects and even small animals.

"The insides of the leaves are brightly colored to attract prey. In addition, glands along the outer edge make nectar to lure prey. These leaves have microscopic 'trigger hairs' that sense motion. When prey touches these hairs, the plant snaps shut in less than one second, which is not enough time for the prey to escape. The edges of the leaves also have 'teeth' that lock together, trapping the prey inside. After the trap closes, other glands release juices that break down and dissolve the prey so the plant can absorb it. A Venus flytrap digests an insect in five to twelve days."

Tariq, Dana, Arturo, and Hana joined Lucia onstage as she continued, "The next time you step outside, look at the plants around you."

"Get curious! Investigate!" cheered Tariq.

"Ask questions to find out what you might already know about a familiar plant," said Dana. "For example . . ."

"How has the plant adapted to its environment?" interjected Arturo. "How has it adapted to weather such as droughts or extreme cold?"

"How does the plant take in food, water, and light? How does it protect itself? And does it have special adaptations that help it reproduce?" asked Hana.

"In nearly every environment, plants have found a way!" finished the group together. As they bowed, the audience, filled with friends, family, and teachers, gave a standing ovation.

The Trees Speak

by Maggie Smith-Beehler
illustrated by Ka Botzis

In the rain forest, I am tall and broad, umbrella-like,
my leaves large, some large as elephants' ears,
to soak up sunlight. They're thick and waxy,
pointed, with "drip tips" to let the warm
rain drain off. I arrange my leaves
at different angles to keep them
out of the shade, to keep them
glowing, lapping up the light.
Some of my roots — called
prop roots or stilt roots —
grow above the ground.
They help me stand
in the rich wet soil
of the rain
forest.

In the taiga,
my wide, shallow
roots are poor anchors,
so I grow near the others,
clustered together, keeping
protected from wind and cold.
In winter, my roots can't drink
from the frozen ground. My thin
leaves are needle-shaped, compact,
coated in wax. They keep water inside
them like a secret. They are dark green
to sip more sunlight here. Evergreen, I am
tall and cone-shaped to bask in every golden ray,
to keep my branches from breaking under the wet
weight of snow. It slides down my sides in the taiga.

Write the answers to the questions on these pages in your notebook. Use evidence and details from the text to support your answers.

Text Connections

1. Explain why occasional controlled forest fires are necessary in redwood forests.

2. Do you think hummingbirds and insects can see at least some colors? Explain how you know, using information from "Plants Found a Way."

3. Explain the differences between the roots of the rain forest and taiga trees in "The Trees Speak."

4. Describe the main defense cacti use. Based on "Plants Found a Way" and "Masters of Illusion," why do you think desert plants need strong defenses against animal predators?

5. What life lesson do you think a person could learn from the orchid?

6. Explain some ways that plants move.

Did You Know?

Venus flytraps aren't the only carnivorous plants—there are over 600 such species! For example, pitcher plants have deep pools into which insects slip. Sundew plants catch insects with drops of sticky goo on their leaves—tentacles then wrap and smother the insects. Carnivorous adaptations let these plants survive in low-nutrient areas.

Color

Shape

Size

Cardinal flowers

Buttercups

Flowering cactus

Look Closer

Keys to Comprehension

1. Infer whether burrs with seeds inside are typically light or heavy. Support your inference using details from the text.

2. Explain why and how a rain-forest vine climbs trees.

Writer's Craft

3. Define *adaptation* and explain the two basic kinds of plant adaptations.

4. Explain how one of the visual aids helped you better understand the science club's presentation in the text.

Concept Development

5. How does the visual organization of "The Trees Speak" reflect its subject matter?

6. Using information from both "Plants Found a Way" and "Animal Defense Academy," explain how flowers can use odor to both entice and ward off certain animals.

Write

A shape poem, like "The Trees Speak," both describes an object and is sometimes shaped like the object. Choose a plant and write your own shape poem about it.

Read this Science Connection. You will answer the questions as a class.

Text Feature

A **caption** is a word or sentence that tells more about illustrations and photographs.

An Unusual Heritage

What do a quillwort plant and a lump of coal have in common? More than you might think. These two things share history with plants that lived long ago.

Modern-day quillwort plants are related to a family of plants that once filled Earth's swamps. At that time, most of Earth was warm and humid. Shallow water covered much of the land.

Tree-like plants called lycopsids flourished in these conditions. These ancient organisms were an early type of vascular plant. Vascular plants have roots that absorb water from the soil, as well as stiff stems with leaves to collect sunlight. Lycopsids had a huge advantage over plants that lacked vascular systems. Their stems grew tall, raising their narrow, spiny leaves above the other plants, capturing more sunlight. At the same time, their roots anchored them so they resisted falling over. Tree-like lycopsids didn't reproduce using seeds. Instead, they reproduced using spores, similar to the way modern ferns reproduce.

When lycopsids died in the swamps, the decaying plants became peat. Peat is similar to soil, but among other characteristics, it contains plant and animal materials that are only partially broken down. Over long periods of time, sediment buried the peat, pressing out the water. As more sediment piled on top over a long period of time, pressure and heat changed the peat into coal. Some coal still bears traces of fossilized leaves—reminders of its origins.

Over time, the lycopsids became extinct. Their smaller relatives survived and changed over many generations to become modern quillwort plants. We use coal, which the long-dead lycopsids have become, as a source of fuel.

Tree-like lycopsids grew and decayed in swampland during the Carboniferous period. The land depicted in this illustration is now beneath the surface of the Eastern United States.

1. Explain how coal and quillwort plants are related.

2. Why is the supply of coal on Earth limited? Make an inference based on the connection.

3. Complete the Go Digital section below. Create a three-column chart comparing and contrasting the natural resources from which coal, crude oil, and natural gas came. Include the processes that formed these substances.

 Go Digital

Research how living things formed crude oil and natural gas. What similarities do they share with the plants that formed coal?

Genre Informational Text
Essential Questions
What animals can be found in cold habitats?
What adaptations are necessary to survive there?

Survival at 40 Below

by Debbie S. Miller
illustrated by Jon Van Zyle

Along the Koyukuk River, towering mountains guard the magnificent valley. Their sheer faces watch the seasons change.

Click . . . click . . . click. Snapping hooves and grumbling voices fill the autumn air. With heads held high, a herd of caribou follows the river through Gates of the Arctic National Park.

These regal deer wear new coats of dense fur, with velvet antlers curving toward the sky. Ready for winter, the caribou have gained a thick layer of fat from summer grazing on the tundra.

GATES OF THE ARCTIC
NATIONAL PARK AND PRESERVE

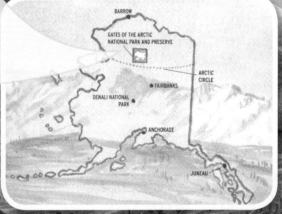

BARROW

GATES OF THE ARCTIC
NATIONAL PARK AND PRESERVE

ARCTIC
CIRCLE

FAIRBANKS

DENALI NATIONAL
PARK

ANCHORAGE

JUNEAU

Other arctic animals scurry and prepare for the coming eight months of snow. Chickadees and gray jays cache seeds and morsels of carrion, hiding the food in cracks beneath tree bark. Red squirrels pluck spruce cones and hurl them to the ground. They will tear open the cones and eat the spruce seeds through the winter. A weasel snatches a brown lemming and carries it to an underground food cache.

Nights grow colder. A thin layer of ice creeps across a pond near the river. Snug in their lodge, beavers rest after cutting many saplings for their underwater cache. Near their food pile, an Alaska blackfish paddles slowly through pond vegetation, searching for insect larvae. This bottom dweller can survive the winter in shallow frozen ponds with little oxygen. Along with gills, the blackfish has an unusual esophagus that can work like a lung, absorbing oxygen from the air. During the winter, this fish will find holes in the ice and breathe through its mouth.

Leaves rustle softly as a wood frog burrows into the duff of the forest floor. Suddenly, the frog feels its skin freezing. Its heart begins to beat rapidly. The frog's liver quickly produces lots of glucose. This sugary fluid, which the frog pumps through its body for several hours, will protect the insides of the cells from ice crystals. When more than three-quarters of its body freezes, the frog stops breathing and its heart stops beating.

But, like magic, the frog is still alive. Beneath the insulating layers of duff and snow, this frozen amphibian will hibernate until spring. It's a live frogsicle!

Farther up the valley, a small golden mammal is plump after a summer diet of tundra plants and seeds. As days grow shorter, the male arctic ground squirrel tunnels into the earth to prepare its burrow. He digs an underground chamber, about the size of a basketball, and stuffs it with grasses and tufts of caribou fur. Then he collects and stores seeds and berries.

Sik . . . sik . . . sik. The squirrel chatters a warning signal. Across the river, a grizzly bear browses on berries and digs up thick potato-like roots with her sharp claws. Alarmed by this huge predator, the squirrel dashes beneath the tundra. Like the squirrel, this grizzly will soon dig her winter den on a mountain slope.

As snowflakes swirl, the squirrel is ready to hibernate. He curls into a ball in his burrow, then slowly supercools his body, lowering his temperature to just below the freezing point of water. His heart rate gradually drops to three beats per minute, and his brain activity ceases. This ice-cold furry squirrel looks dead, but, amazingly, he is only in the inactive state of torpor.

After three weeks, something triggers the squirrel to wake up. His heart rate increases. He warms his body by burning brown fat. This insulating fat protects his vital organs and acts like a heating pad. Within several hours, his heartbeat and temperature are normal.

After rearranging his nest, the squirrel curls back into a ball and falls asleep. He dreams and sleeps soundly for about twelve hours. Then his body supercools again. Like a yo-yo, the squirrel warms himself, sleeps, and supercools about a dozen times during the winter to conserve enough energy to survive.

Above the squirrel's burrow, an arctic fox searches for prey. The fox picks up the scent of voles beneath the snow. These mouselike animals are huddling in their nest to keep warm. Like an acrobat, the fox springs high into the air and pounces on the voles. Breaking through the snow, he traps one by surprise.

The arctic fox keeps warm in frigid temperatures because he wears two winter coats. His dense underfur insulates him like the down in a fluffy sleeping bag. His thick outer coat has tiny air pockets inside the hair shafts, instead of color pigment. The snow-white coat perfectly camouflages the fox for hunting prey and escaping predators. Fur also covers the soles of his paws, and his big, bushy tail provides extra warmth.

Inch by inch, the layer of snow deepens with each winter storm. On a frigid January day, the temperature plummets to 40 below zero. Thick pond ice cracks and makes eerie sounds. The fluffy quilt of snow insulates and protects the many animals, plants, and insects beneath it. It is much warmer under the snow layer than in the open air.

Other animals are well adapted to survive the colder air temperatures above the ice and snow. Snowshoe hares and ptarmigan zigzag between the willow bushes. Both animals can travel lightly across the snow with insulated feet that help spread out their weight. But the ptarmigan can't survive the lethal night temperatures and fly off at dusk to seek shelter.

Puff! They dive into a drift of powdery snow. Invisible to the world, the ptarmigan roost inside their snow burrows, protected from predators and the extreme cold.

Another bird combats the deep freeze. A black-capped chickadee flits from tree to tree, eating his cached food. He must gain enough fat each day to survive the night.

But this small bird needs more than food to survive. He fluffs up his dense feathers for better insulation. Tiny muscles control the angle of each feather, while other muscles shiver to produce heat. The chickadee can also lower his temperature and metabolism to save energy. He roosts in a thick forest or in tree cavities that give him the best shelter.

423

While birds roost beneath a full moon, all is not quiet. A wolf howls on a distant ridge as caribou crunch through the snow with their broad hooves. These deer are well insulated for the Arctic by dense fur and hollow guard hairs. They sniff the snow and detect the smell of ashes from an old forest fire. Turning away, the caribou avoid this burned area.

Muzzles to the ground, the caribou later detect the mushroomlike scent of lichens. They dig craters and forage on clumps of these rootless plants. Their hooves and thin legs are well adapted for digging. A special liquid fat protects their joints. Blood traveling directly to the hooves helps warm the returning blood to the heart. This circular flow protects the legs and reduces heat loss.

While caribou wander, the grizzly bear is snug in her den with two newborn cubs. The drowsy bear nurses them and rests to save energy. The three survive off her large storehouse of fat. As she sleepily feeds her fast-growing cubs, she doesn't notice the faint sound of steps across the snow.

Sure-footed and agile, Dall sheep pick their way across the mountain slope. Fierce winds have blown snow off the alpine tundra, exposing frozen grasses and sedges. The sheep graze on these withered plants, then seek shelter from the wind by bedding down in the lee of some rocky crags.

425

Month by month, winter passes slowly. Backs to the wind, a group of musk oxen stands on the snow-covered tundra, conserving energy. Short legs, small ears, and fluffy underwool, known as *qiviut*, insulate musk oxen from even the deepest cold. As a newborn calf suckles milk from its mother, one musk ox sees wolves approaching and senses danger. Immediately, the musk oxen gather together. Shoulder to shoulder they form a circular wall of thick fur and horns. As one wolf draws near, a large bull lowers his deadly sharp horns. With a sudden burst, he charges the wolf.

Wheeling away, the wolf quickly retreats. The musk oxen continue to work as a team, charging and driving off the hungry wolves.

Trickle . . . tinkle . . . drip. The snow and ice begin to melt. As temperatures rise, bumblebees, butterflies, and other dormant insects begin to stir. A woolly bear caterpillar basks in the sun after being snow-covered for eight months. His dark, furry body traps the sun's heat. Inching his way to a budding willow, he chews on a tiny leaf.

These fuzzy creatures, and other northern insects, have antifreeze substances that prevent ice crystals from forming in their bodies. The woolly bear will spend up to fourteen winters in the Arctic as a caterpillar. Then this amazing survivor will transform into a moth, but for only one short summer!

427

One by one, moist leaves rustle near the pond. The wood frog slowly thaws out, and its heart beats once again. *rrrrRuk . . . rrrrRuk*. The frog begins calling for a mate, making a ducklike sound near the pond's edge. Slapping their tails in the open water, the beavers dive while the blackfish dart after prey on the pond's bottom. Farther up the valley, the male ground squirrel eats his stored cache of food, then leaves his burrow in search of a mate.

Hour by hour, day by day, the pulse of life increases with warmer June days and greening plants. Caribou feast upon a summer buffet, while playful grizzly bear cubs tussle and explore the tundra as their mother searches for prey. Birds that migrated south for the winter return to their birthplace, building nests on the tundra and filling the air with music. For more than two months the days will be endless, as the top of the world tilts toward the sun and the magical Land of the Midnight Sun explodes with life.

Write the answers to the questions on these pages in your notebook. Use evidence and details from the text to support your answers.

Did You Know?

Gates of the Arctic National Park and Preserve protects plants and animals living on over 8 million acres of land. This designated wilderness is in the Brooks mountain range. It is the second-largest national park in the United States.

Text Connections

1. How do musk oxen survive the Arctic winter without needing to hibernate?

2. Give an example of an adaptation that provides insulation, and explain why insulation is so important in the Arctic.

3. Why doesn't the mother grizzly bear need to eat food during the winter?

4. Using information in "Masters of Illusion," what color change occurs for many Arctic animals in the summer that is not mentioned in "Survival at 40 Below"? Explain why it is necessary.

5. Name a way people could imitate an animal adaptation when doing things outside during the Arctic winter.

6. Why is it important for so many Arctic animals to limit movement during the winter?

Look Closer

Keys to Comprehension

1. Infer why a cold Arctic winter with little snow would cause problems for many animals, based on details in the text.

2. Compare and contrast the processes by which the wood frog and male arctic ground squirrel hibernate.

Writer's Craft

3. Explain what *antifreeze substances* are, based on examples from the text.

4. How does the author organize animal adaptation facts in "Survival at 40 Below"?

Concept Development

5. With what evidence does the author support the point that during summer the Arctic "explodes with life"?

6. Describe adaptations the snowshoe hare and ptarmigan have to help them survive the Arctic. Combine information from both "Survival at 40 Below" and "Animal Defense Academy" in your answer.

Write

Imagine you are visiting Gates of the Arctic National Park during the late autumn described in "Survival at 40 Below." Write a short letter to a friend describing your experience.

Text Feature

Informational text often includes **maps** that relate to content.

The Creation of Nunavut Territory

The United States and Canada both have lands in the Arctic. The Arctic has long been home to polar bears, snowshoe hares, and ptarmigan. The Inuit people of the Arctic have also lived there for thousands of years. Their way of life has long been tied to the geography and climate of the land.

For many years the Canadian government left the Inuit mostly to themselves. However, increasing contact with fur traders, whalers, and other nonnative people affected the Inuit. By the 1950s, the Canadian government was encouraging the Inuit to cease their nomadic lifestyle. The government thought it would be better if the Inuit adapted to a Western lifestyle. The government built housing projects intended for Inuit families. Some Canadian leaders thought native peoples should no longer be left to themselves.

In response to all of this, the Inuit formed a national group. Among other things, the group asked the Canadian government to recognize a land claim. The claim covered parts of two Canadian provinces—the Northwest Territories and northern Quebec. It took many years, but in 1999, Canada divided the Northwest Territories. The eastern part of it, along with many nearby islands, became Nunavut. *Nunavut* means "our land" in Inuktitut, the Inuit language. Although still a part of Canada, Nunavut has its own territorial government. The people there continue to face many challenges. Still, Nunavut's creation honors the Inuit people's claim to Arctic lands.

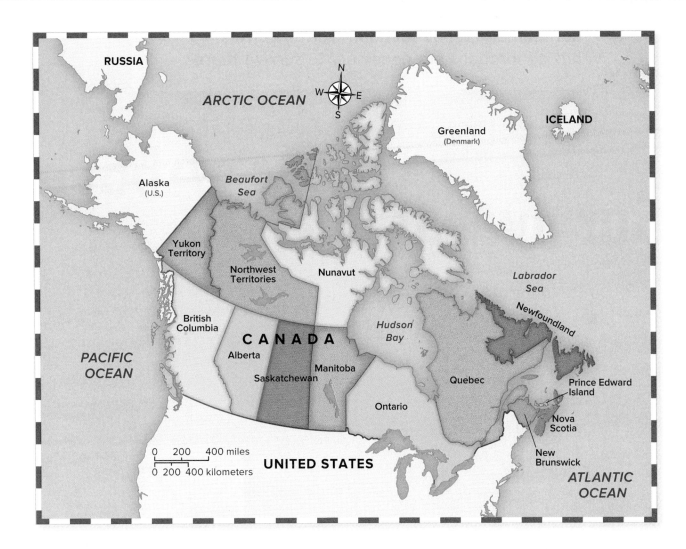

1. About how long have the Inuit lived in the Arctic regions?

2. How is the creation of Nunavut an example of a government responding to the needs of individuals and groups?

3. How does the creation of Nunavut allow the Inuit to govern themselves?

 Go Digital

Research the history of the Athabaskan people, another native people of the Arctic. In which parts of the Arctic do they live? How did they come to live there?

Survival at 120 Above

by Debbie S. Miller
illustrated by Jon Van Zyle

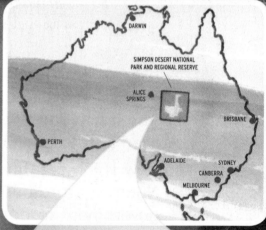

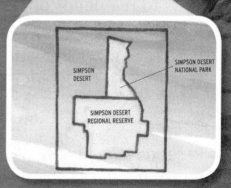

As the night sky melts away, the Simpson Desert horizon glows like a campfire. Creaking voices of crickets grow faint. The dawn air is dry and warm when the chiming wedgebill sings its five-note song, "Time to get up now . . . time to get up now."

A brilliant sun peeks above the longest parallel sand dunes in the world. As soft as powder, the stunning sand is the color of a red brick. In early days, people called this arid land the "Great Ribbed Desert" because of the long, wind-shaped dunes that finger across Australia for hundreds of miles (hundreds of kilometers). This vast, rippled desert bakes beneath a dome of a forever-blue sky.

Reptiles stir. A sand goanna (go-AN-a) swaggers into the bright sunshine from an underground burrow. His 2-foot (61 centimeter)-long tail cuts S-turns into the velvety sand of the dune. A maze of black patterns decorates the tan skin of this large lizard. His camouflaged body blends in with the dry grasses of the spinifex. Many round humps of this needle-sharp grass cover the dunes.

The goanna's forked tongue explores the ground. Acting like a nose, the tongue discovers the scent and location of food or predators. A shiny emerald beetle scurries across the sand. Flicking his tongue, the goanna laps up a good meal of protein. Above him, a huge wedge-tailed eagle circles. The goanna detects the shadow of this predator with the tiny sensor eye on top of his head and immediately bolts into a clump of spinifex.

By noon the sand is blistering hot
beneath a cloudless sky. The temperature
rises to more than 120 degrees Fahrenheit
(50 degrees Celsius). For seven years the
desert has faced a great drought, with only
an occasional sprinkling of rain. Seeds lie
dormant, lacking enough moisture to sprout.
During this scorching time, the goanna
moves to a grove of gidgee trees. With
barbed claws, he climbs a tree seeking
shade and a breeze. Other reptiles tunnel
beneath the sand to find cooler ground.

Near the goanna, a mob of red
kangaroos rests in the shade of the trees.
Some of the kangaroos lick their arms and
paws to cool themselves. When a breeze
drifts through the open woodland, moisture
evaporates from their fur, which lowers
their body temperature. The world's largest
marsupial also has special hair that helps
reflect sun rays. Each shiny strand acts like
a tiny mirror.

In the afternoon, a blustery wind signals a change in weather. Puffy clouds run across the sky with veils of rain streaming beneath them. These misty curtains of rain, known as virga, evaporate before reaching the ground due to rising heat. The scattered clouds bring cooler temperatures and a patchwork of shade to the red sand.

At last, a few drops reach the ground, then some sprinkles. Suddenly, as though someone turned on a faucet, the light drizzle changes to pouring rain. Each drop finds a home on a grain of sand, a leathery leaf, or the fur of a kangaroo. Withered roots welcome the rain like a dry kitchen sponge. Now the desert is really wet!

Parched creek beds turn into bubbling streams, fingering across the desert. Dry claypans, wrinkled with cracks, turn into swamps. Patient fairy-shrimp eggs hatch after baking in the dry clay for seven long years. Triops erupt from this new source of life. These minnow-like crustaceans grow domed shells that look like tiny horseshoe crabs. Rainbowfish squiggle up the meandering creeks, migrating to new ponds.

Bonk . . . bonk . . . bonk. It sounds like someone is playing a distant bongo. Filling her throat pouch with air, a female emu makes a drumming sound as she strides across the open woodland. She smells water.

This huge, flightless bird looks like a grass hut walking on scaly stilts. Like an ostrich, her round body is stacked with feathers. Well adapted to the heat, her loose, open feathers allow air to pass through them. They shade and cool her body. As she moves toward the distant water, her giant three-toed feet support her in the soft sand.

While emus saunter across the dunes, herons, pelicans, and other waterbirds fly overhead. Sensing the distant rain, these birds fly hundreds of miles from the coast to feast on the explosion of life in the desert swamps. It is a mystery how these birds sense the rain, sometimes from 1,000 miles (1,610 km) away.

Wearing a spiny coat of armor, a thorny devil crawls slowly from his burrow. Only 8 inches (20 cm) long, this unique lizard looks like a miniature ankylosaurus dinosaur. The top of his body is completely covered with thorny spikes, protecting him from predators. Soon he discovers a highway of tiny black ants, his only food source. Thrusting out his sticky tongue, he devours the ants one by one. The thorny devil can eat as many as three thousand ants in one day.

Standing in a patch of wet sand, the thorny devil reveals his drinking secret. Through capillary action, this lizard can drink this water from his feet. The water moves upward along narrow grooves on the skin's surface from his toes, up his legs, to the corners of his mouth, similar to the way a plant drinks water from its roots.

A blue-tailed skink searches for a bright patch of sunshine. Darting across the sand, this striped lizard discovers a basking spot that offers a good lookout for possible predators. As the skink warms himself, a venomous western brown snake is slithering toward him.

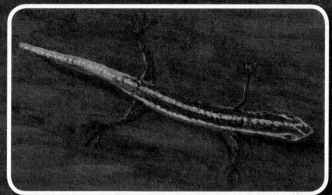

The well-camouflaged snake draws closer, curving through the grasses. Suddenly, the skink hears a rustling sound. Immediately he begins waving his blue tail. It looks like the lizard is performing a hula dance. Attracted by the movement, the snake's head races forward. Her gaping mouth tries to bite the dancing tail. Instantly, the end of the lizard's tail breaks off, and the skink dashes away into the safety of the spinifex. The skink will grow a new tail, a special adaptation for survival. Some lizards lose and regrow their tails several times during their lives.

As the sun slips below the horizon, a peach sky deepens to the shade of strawberries. The dunes begin to cool. An Australian raven closes the day with his moaning call: *Ah . . . Ah . . . Ahhhhhhhhhhh*. On cue, the voices of crickets loudly fill the air like thousands of castanets.

Nocturnal animals grow restless in their burrows. A brush-tailed mulgara (mul-GAR-uh) cautiously peeks out of an exit hole, sniffing the air. She smells the faint scent of a dingo, but no worries—the wild dog's tracks are several days old.

The mulgara has sensitive black eyes designed for night vision. In the soft moonlight this predator detects a sandy inland mouse. The quick mulgara scampers along the trail of tiny round footprints. *Pounce!* She snatches the mouse as he feeds on some dried seeds. No longer hungry, the mulgara returns to her burrow. This hamster-size marsupial plays an important role in controlling rodents and keeping the diversity of desert life in balance.

Pockets of sand begin to move. Brown heads speckled with orange spots brush through the surface of the sand. After many dormant months of rest, known as estivation, desert spadefoot frogs explode from the ground. Near midnight, hundreds of these amphibians begin cooing for their mates near the edge of a pond.

The chorus of frogs attracts other animals. White wings suddenly flash through the darkness. A spotted nightjar cuts swiftly through the air. He dives at a frog, attempting to snatch her from the ground. The warty frog quickly protects herself by secreting a milky liquid from her poison glands through the skin of her neck. When the nightjar bites the frog, this sticky white goo acts like glue. The goo cements the mouth of the nightjar so he can't eat the frog. She's a superglue frog!

The moon casts soft light on new seedlings that will turn dust bowls into lush carpets of plants.

A mouse-size dunnart (DUN-art) senses the new moisture. He scurries beyond the spinifex that shields him. Dashing quickly, he is watchful for mulgaras and other lurking predators. His ink-black, beady eyes allow him to see clearly in the darkness. This nocturnal marsupial also has a keen sense of smell. The dunnart knows the scent of rain-soaked ground means there will be more plants and many invertebrates to feed on.

Tracing the scent, the dunnart zigzags through the maze of spinifex, scurrying mile after mile to reach the swamp area. Along the way he spots the sparkling eyes of a hefty spider. He races past an emu bush and catches this midnight snack. The dunnart absorbs enough water from spiders and other prey so that he can survive without drinking water.

Through the night he journeys. His tiny feet become swollen and blistered. By the time the dunnart reaches the swamp, he will have traveled nearly 2 miles (3.2 km) during one night. Given the dunnart's short 1-inch (2.5 cm) stride, this distance would be the equivalent of a human walking 20 miles (32.2 km) in one night!

A ningaui (nin-GOW-ee) stirs. She feels the cool night air and leaves her underground home. This thumb-size creature, one of the smallest marsupials, weighs as little as six paper clips. Dashing between the spinifex, her tiny cone-shaped head and flattened ears allow her to squeeze through thick clumps of grasses. As she hunts for beetles and spiders, the sound of a running animal startles her. She spots the fleeting shadow of a doglike creature.

The panting dingo is chasing a large feral house cat. Sand flying, the sleek cat races through the obstacle course of spinifex. While the dingo is a larger animal, the wild cat is quick and nimble. He slips away, springing over bushes, escaping over the crest of the dune. The ningaui is lucky. Feral cats are fierce predators, feeding on many small marsupials and reptiles. The dingo helps control cats and other feral animals so that native species, such as ningaui and mulgara, can survive.

444

While the thorny devil and sand goanna rest in their burrows, a spinifex hopping-mouse scurries through a network of underground tunnels. The mouse cautiously peeks outside, then dashes toward a clump of dead grasses that camouflage him.

This nocturnal mouse hops across moon shadows, his long feathery tail arching behind him. Sniffing the cool red sand, he finds spinifex seeds. Like many other desert animals, this well-adapted mouse can take enough liquid from his food to survive without drinking water.

As night fades away, a boobook owl suddenly dives from her perch toward the mouse. The cautious mouse reacts immediately to the faint shadow of this predator. Springing off his strong hind legs, he leaps to the shelter of the spinifex.

445

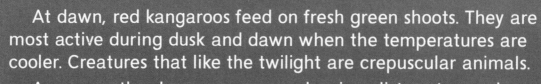

At dawn, red kangaroos feed on fresh green shoots. They are most active during dusk and dawn when the temperatures are cooler. Creatures that like the twilight are crepuscular animals.

As one mother kangaroo grazes, her joey listens to a pair of Australian magpies singing their beautiful duet. Joining the magpies is a loud chorus of cooing frogs and creaking crickets.

Beyond the kangaroos a lone camel plods over the dune, leaving plate-size tracks in the sand. This one-humped dromedary camel can live for months without water, yet he smells the rain-fed swamp and marches toward it. Like other desert animals and plants, the camel will thrive on the gift of rain.

The desert is a sea of green and red in the early morning light. Like cresting waves, the dunes rise and fall above green swales and newly formed swamps. The endless ridges of red sand create a land similar to the wavy texture of corduroy.

The emus discover a swamp after traveling many miles. They kneel in the shallow water, splashing themselves with their stubby wings. Surrounding them are white-necked herons, avocets, and pink-eared ducks. These birds are feasting on the fairy shrimp, triops, and other aquatic invertebrates. The long seven-year drought is over. For a short time life will flourish in this vast and beautiful land of red.

Write the answers to the questions on these pages in your notebook. Use evidence and details from the text to support your answers.

Did You Know?

The continent of Australia, with 70 percent of it desert or nearly desert, is the second driest continent on Earth. So what is the driest continent? Antarctica—because not all deserts are hot!

Text Connections

1. What strategies do Simpson Desert animals use to find shade, and why is shade important? Give examples to support your answer.

2. Why do many birds travel hundreds of miles to a newly formed desert swamp?

3. Based on information in the text, what would happen if the mulgara suddenly became extinct?

4. Explain one way an animal can take in water without actually drinking it.

5. What do "Survival at 120 Above" and "Plants Found a Way" both say about dormant seeds?

6. What are the main challenges faced by animals that live in places like the Simpson Desert?

Look Closer

Keys to Comprehension

1. Using text details, describe the actions of the red kangaroos over the course of one day in the Simpson Desert. How do they relate to the kangaroos' desert adaptations?

2. What is a main idea of "Survival at 120 Above"? Summarize how the text's details support this idea.

Writer's Craft

3. What does the word *dormant* mean?

4. How do both the illustration on page 439 and the simile "this unique lizard looks like a miniature ankylosaurus dinosaur" work together?

Concept Development

5. How does the text support the idea that rain causes a desert to spring to life?

6. Compare and contrast the ways frogs deal with extreme temperatures, based on information from "Survival at 120 Above" and "Survival at 40 Below."

Write

Describe the nimble actions of a particular animal from "Survival at 120 Above," but do not name the animal. Do you think other people would be able to identify it based on your description?

Read this Science Connection. You will answer the questions as a class.

Text Feature

A **numbered list** organizes related items that belong in a particular order.

The Sand Dunes of the Simpson Desert

Dune fields characterize most of Australia's Simpson Desert. The colors of the dunes' sand range from white to dark red. Where did all this sand come from? Why is it so many different colors?

The sand in the Simpson Desert is made of tiny pieces of white quartz rock mixed with varying amounts of clay. In general, the color of the sand changes as it ages through this process:

1. The sand nearest to the usually dry Lake Eyre is nearly white. Over time, iron in the clay begins to rust, turning to iron oxide. This sand might look orange.

2. Once sand is very old, the iron oxide covers the sand grains, turning them dark red.

Although it might be hard to imagine, these dunes are relatively young by geological standards. Long ago, this area was very wet and covered by large rivers. Over time the climate dried out. During glacial periods, wind eroded the now dry ground. Some of that erosion formed sand.

Prevailing winds, or winds that typically blow from one direction, moved the sand south-to-north across Earth's surface. Over time, the interactions of winds formed linear dunes, which are dunes that look like straight or nearly straight meandering lines. The ancient river system is still there, but today it is buried deep below the colorful sands of the Simpson Desert.

This NASA photo was taken from 35,000 miles above Earth. It shows a nearly dry Lake Eyre, its white sand, and the older sand that has turned orange and red over time.

1. How has the area where the Simpson Desert is now changed over time?

2. Explain how wind erosion forms dunes.

3. Do an experiment to model wind erosion. Put a cup of sand on a paper plate, and use your hands to form a dune shape. Measure and record your dune's height. Blow gently on the dune for 10 seconds, and measure it again. Reform the dune to its original height, and repeat the experiment, but this time blow for 20 seconds. Repeat, blowing for 30 seconds. Organize all your information into a chart to show the effects of wind erosion.

 Go Digital

Research the dune fields of Death Valley National Park. How do these dunes compare to the ones in the Simpson Desert?

BIG Idea

What makes a national treasure?

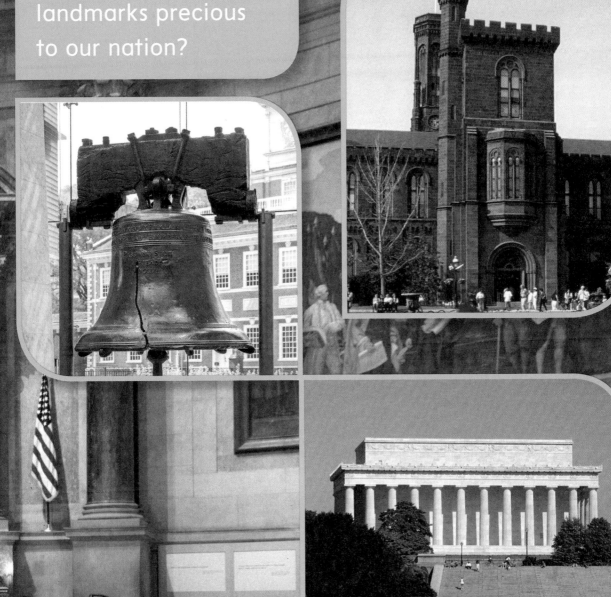

Theme Connections

What makes these landmarks precious to our nation?

 Background Builder Video
connected.mcgraw-hill.com

Genre Narrative Poem

Essential Questions

How did patriots contribute to our country's founding?

How can a story become a national treasure?

Paul Revere's RIDE

by Henry Wadsworth Longfellow
illustrated by Jose Flores

Listen, my children, and you shall hear
Of the midnight ride of Paul Revere,
On the eighteenth of April, in Seventy-five;
Hardly a man is now alive
Who remembers that famous day and year.

He said to his friend, "If the British march
By land or sea from the town to-night,
Hang a lantern aloft in the belfry arch
Of the North Church tower as a signal light,—
One, if by land, and two, if by sea;
And I on the opposite shore will be,
Ready to ride and spread the alarm
Through every Middlesex village and farm,
For the country folk to be up and to arm."

Then he said, "Good night!" and with muffled oar
Silently rowed to the Charlestown shore,
Just as the moon rose over the bay,
Where swinging wide at her moorings lay
The Somerset, British man-of-war;
A phantom ship, with each mast and spar
Across the moon like a prison bar,
And a huge black hulk, that was magnified
By its own reflection in the tide.

Meanwhile, his friend, through alley and street,
Wanders and watches with eager ears,
Till in the silence around him he hears
The muster of men at the barrack door,
The sound of arms, and the tramp of feet,
And the measured tread of the grenadiers,
Marching down to their boats on the shore.

Then he climbed the tower of the Old North Church,
By the wooden stairs, with stealthy tread,
To the belfry-chamber overhead,
And startled the pigeons from their perch
On the sombre rafters, that round him made
Masses and moving shapes of shade, —
By the trembling ladder, steep and tall,
To the highest window in the wall,
Where he paused to listen and look down
A moment on the roofs of the town,
And the moonlight flowing over all.

Beneath, in the churchyard, lay the dead,
In their night-encampment on the hill,
Wrapped in silence so deep and still
That he could hear, like a sentinel's tread,
The watchful night-wind, as it went
Creeping along from tent to tent,
And seeming to whisper, "All is well!"
A moment only he feels the spell
Of the place and the hour, and the secret dread
Of the lonely belfry and the dead;
For suddenly all his thoughts are bent
On a shadowy something far away,
Where the river widens to meet the bay, —
A line of black that bends and floats
On the rising tide, like a bridge of boats.

Meanwhile, impatient to mount and ride,
Booted and spurred, with a heavy stride
On the opposite shore walked Paul Revere.
Now he patted his horse's side,
Now gazed at the landscape far and near,
Then, impetuous, stamped the earth,
And turned and tightened his saddle girth;
But mostly he watched with eager search
The belfry-tower of the Old North Church,
As it rose above the graves on the hill,
Lonely and spectral and sombre and still.

And lo! as he looks, on the belfry's height
A glimmer, and then a gleam of light!
He springs to the saddle, the bridle he turns,
But lingers and gazes, till full on his sight
A second lamp in the belfry burns!
A hurry of hoofs in a village street,
A shape in the moonlight, a bulk in the dark,
And beneath, from the pebbles, in passing, a spark
Struck out by a steed flying fearless and fleet:
That was all! And yet, through the gloom and the light,
The fate of a nation was riding that night;
And the spark struck out by that steed, in his flight,
Kindled the land into flame with its heat.
He has left the village and mounted the steep,
And beneath him, tranquil and broad and deep,
Is the Mystic, meeting the ocean tides;
And under the alders, that skirt its edge,
Now soft on the sand, now loud on the ledge,
Is heard the tramp of his steed as he rides.

It was twelve by the village clock,
When he crossed the bridge into Medford town.
He heard the crowing of the cock,
And the barking of the farmer's dog,
And felt the damp of the river fog,
That rises after the sun goes down.

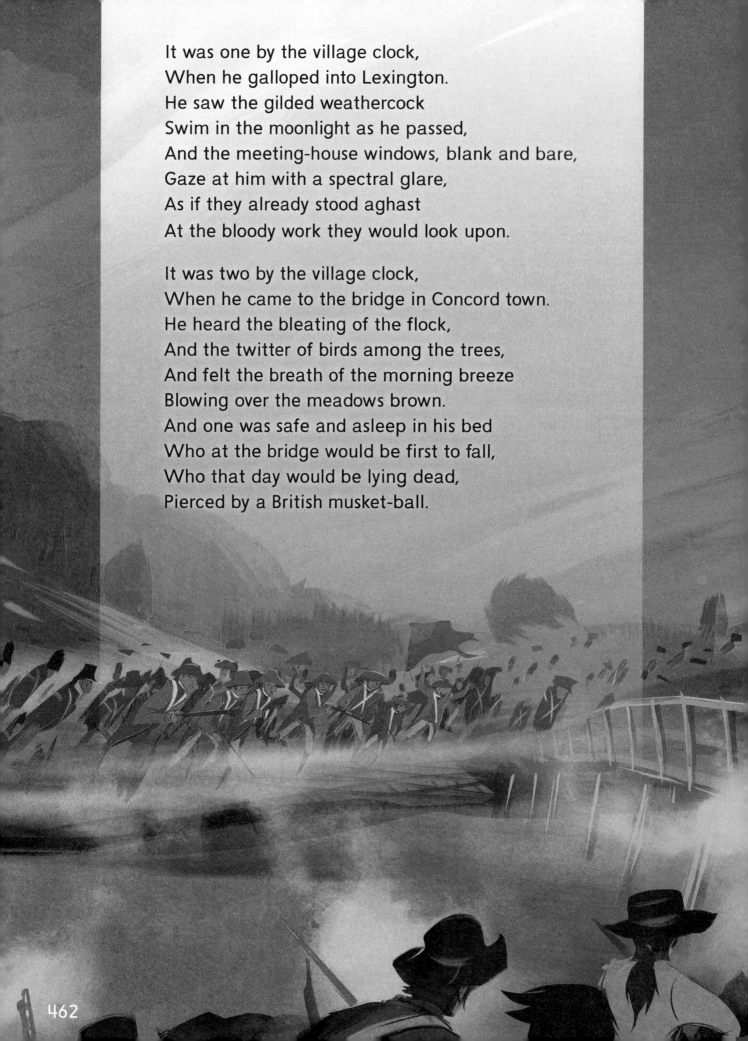

It was one by the village clock,
When he galloped into Lexington.
He saw the gilded weathercock
Swim in the moonlight as he passed,
And the meeting-house windows, blank and bare,
Gaze at him with a spectral glare,
As if they already stood aghast
At the bloody work they would look upon.

It was two by the village clock,
When he came to the bridge in Concord town.
He heard the bleating of the flock,
And the twitter of birds among the trees,
And felt the breath of the morning breeze
Blowing over the meadows brown.
And one was safe and asleep in his bed
Who at the bridge would be first to fall,
Who that day would be lying dead,
Pierced by a British musket-ball.

You know the rest. In the books you have read,
How the British Regulars fired and fled, —
How the farmers gave them ball for ball,
From behind each fence and farm-yard wall,
Chasing the red-coats down the lane,
Then crossing the fields to emerge again
Under the trees at the turn of the road,
And only pausing to fire and load.

So through the night rode Paul Revere;
And so through the night went his cry of alarm
To every Middlesex village and farm, —
A cry of defiance and not of fear,
A voice in the darkness, a knock at the door,
And a word that shall echo forevermore!
For, borne on the night-wind of the Past,
Through all our history, to the last,
In the hour of darkness and peril and need,
The people will waken and listen to hear
The hurrying hoof-beats of that steed,
And the midnight message of Paul Revere.

Text Connections

1. What is Paul Revere's plan?

2. Why is the night wind's whispered message "All is well" not truthful?

3. Describe what Paul Revere does as he waits for the signal. Why does he act this way?

4. How did both Paul Revere in "Paul Revere's Ride" and the grandfather in Unit 3's "The Unbreakable Code" act as patriotic messengers?

5. Describe a time you had an important job to do and how it made you feel.

6. What word or message do you think "shall echo forevermore" in the minds of people who remember Paul Revere's ride? Explain.

Did You Know?

Popular legend says Paul Revere shouted, "The British are coming!" as he rode. However, it is likely he would have ridden quietly so as not to alert the British troops nearby. Also, that phrase would have confused the colonists, who still considered themselves British at that time.

Look Closer

Keys to Comprehension

1. Who do you think the narrator of "Paul Revere's Ride" is, and to whom is he or she speaking? Make an inference, using details from the text.

2. What is a theme of "Paul Revere's Ride"? Explain how it relates to events in the text.

3. Describe in depth the setting Revere's friend views from the "tower of the Old North Church" as he waits to give the signal.

Writer's Craft

4. What is the meaning of the phrase "the fate of a nation was riding that night"?

5. Explain how you know "Paul Revere's Ride" is both a poem and historical fiction.

Concept Development

6. How does the illustration on pages 456 and 457 help you better understand what the Somerset is?

Write

Reread page 448. Write a description of a dark place that fills a character with dread, like the belfry in the poem was filled with dread. Be sure to include descriptive adjectives and adverbs.

Read this Social Studies Connection. You will answer the questions as a class.

Text Feature

Informational texts often include **maps** that relate to their content.

The Real Midnight Ride

Henry Wadsworth Longfellow's poem "Paul Revere's Ride" made this event famous. However, his version of events is not entirely accurate.

In the years leading up to Revere's ride, the British government had angered many colonists. The Stamp Act of 1765, a tax on printed material, seemed unfair. Some colonists formed stealthy "Sons of Liberty" resistance groups across the colonies, and their defiance pressured the British government. Parliament took away the Stamp Act but made it clear that it could create any laws it liked. Colonial anger grew.

Samuel Adams, a legislator in Boston, came up with Committees of Correspondence. They were to organize resistance against Great Britain. Committee riders would take messages between the colonies. Paul Revere was one such messenger.

In 1775, tensions were building. On the night of April 18, Joseph Warren told Paul Revere to warn Samuel Adams and John Hancock that British troops planned to arrest them. Revere had a friend hang two lanterns in a church. This was a message to other Sons of Liberty warning of the troops' approach "by sea." Revere and two other men rode out. Revere managed to warn Adams and Hancock. Although one rider, Dr. Samuel Prescott, did make it to Concord, Revere was briefly arrested before arriving there, and the other, William Dawes, turned around to avoid arrest. The troops took Revere's horse. As he walked back to Lexington, the Battles of Lexington and Concord were under way.

Longfellow's poem changed some of these facts, and it is likely Longfellow knew it. However, Longfellow told the story in a way that, to him, was more exciting and satisfying.

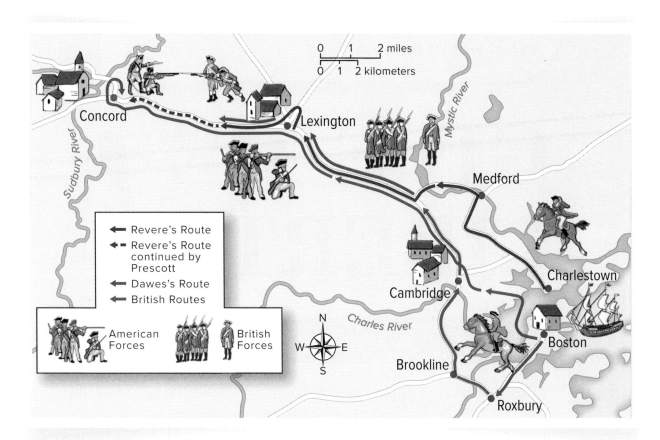

This map shows the routes of Paul Revere and the two other riders who joined him on April 18, 1775.

1. Why did Longfellow likely choose to change the facts of Paul Revere's ride?

2. What are the pros and cons of learning about the past from historical fiction?

3. How can we evaluate the usefulness and reliability of various pieces of historical fiction?

 Go Digital

Research the Battles of Lexington and Concord. How did they relate to the Revolutionary War?

Genre Informational Text

Essential Questions
Who wrote the Declaration of Independence?
What was its purpose?

GIVE ME LIBERTY!

The Story of the Declaration of Independence

by Russell Freedman

By June 1776, the thirteen American colonies had been at war with Great Britain for more than a year. Representing each colony, members of the Continental Congress met in Philadelphia. They debated General Washington's needs for the war effort as well as what to do about the colonies' relationship with Britain.

In January of that year, a writer named Thomas Paine had published a pamphlet, Common Sense. Many colonists read it and agreed with its message: the time had come for independence. So it was that in June 1776, the Continental Congress agreed to draft what would become a historic statement.

At age thirty-three, Thomas Jefferson was one of the youngest delegates to the Continental Congress. A tall, slim, quiet man with gray eyes and reddish hair, he could be lively and even vivacious among his friends. But in public he was so reserved, so soft-spoken and shy, he often seemed stiff or aloof. "During the whole time I sat with him in the Congress," said John Adams, "I never heard him utter three sentences together."

Though Jefferson did not say much, he was an avid scholar and an accomplished writer. Ever since his student days, he had practiced writing by condensing everything he read, striving to develop what he considered "the most valuable of all the talents, that of never using two words when one will do."

Thomas Jefferson

COMMON SENSE;

ADDRESSED TO THE

INHABITANTS

OF

AMERICA,

On the following interesting
SUBJECTS.

I. Of the Origin and Design of Government in general,
with concise Remarks on the English Constitution.

II. Of Monarchy and Hereditary Succession.

III. Thoughts on the present State of American Affairs.

IV. Of the present Ability of America, with some miscellaneous Reflections.

Man knows no Master save creating HEAVEN,
Or those whom choice and common good ordain.
THOMSON.

PHILADELPHIA;
Printed, and Sold, by R. BELL, in Third-Street.
MDCCLXXVI.

▲ Thomas Paine's pamphlet,
Common Sense

Adams wanted Jefferson to write the first draft of the statement we know today as the Declaration of Independence—a tough job, since the writer would have to come up with a document that all thirteen colonies could accept.

It seems that Jefferson tried to get out of the assignment. He wanted Adams to write the first draft. But Adams refused. Years later Adams recalled the following conversation:

"You should do it," said Jefferson.

"Oh, no!"

"Why will you not?"

"I will not."

"Why?" pressed Jefferson.

"Reasons enough," said Adams.

"What can be your reasons?"

"Reason, first, you are a Virginian and a Virginian ought to appear at the head of this business. Reason second, I am obnoxious, suspected and unpopular. You are very much otherwise. Reason third, you can write ten times better than I can."

A draft of the Declaration of Independence with edits

The earliest U.S. national flag

So it was settled. Jefferson went to work in his rented rooms on the second floor of a brick house at the corner of Market and Seventh Streets in downtown Philadelphia. Every morning he would rise before dawn, soak his feet in a basin of cold water, have tea and biscuits, then sit down at a small portable desk he had designed himself and start writing.

"I did not consider it part of my charge to invent new ideas," he said later, "but to place before mankind the common sense of the subject."

There were plenty of ideas in the air for Jefferson to draw on. He was familiar with the writings of John Locke, an influential English philosopher who argued that people are born with certain natural rights and that governments should be run for the benefit of everyone, not just for their rulers. Like most Americans, Jefferson had read Thomas Paine's *Common Sense* and other revolutionary pamphlets. A number of state and local governments, including Virginia's, had already issued declarations of rights and resolutions on independence that could serve as his models.

Scratching away with his quill pen, he worked on the Declaration for about two weeks while attending daily meetings of the Congress—constantly writing and rewriting, ripping up his earlier drafts as he made changes. On one draft that still exists, he changed nearly one third of the words. Finally he showed his work to John Adams and Ben Franklin, who suggested additional changes before the draft was submitted to Congress on June 28.

While Jefferson worked on his many drafts, news reached Philadelphia that British warships had bombarded Charleston, South Carolina, the South's most important seaport. A large British fleet had also been sighted off New York. And there was terrible news from Canada, where the invading Americans had been forced to retreat in total disorder, suffering from smallpox, malaria, and dysentery. Some five thousand American troops had been killed or wounded during the disastrous ten-month Canadian campaign.

With these alarming reports as a background, Congress began its final debate on independence. Before the delegates could consider Jefferson's declaration, they had to vote on Richard Henry Lee's resolution stating "That these United Colonies are, and of right ought to be, free and independent States."

On the steamy afternoon of July 1, John Dickinson of Pennsylvania rose to speak for the moderates. His voice trembled with emotion as he warned the delegates that independence was risky and premature. To abandon the protection of Great Britain would be "like destroying our house in winter and exposing a growing family before we have got another shelter." He argued that a way must be found to get along with England.

THE DECLARATION COMMITTEE.

THOMAS JEFFERSON of Virginia, JOHN ADAMS of Massachusetts, BENJAMIN FRANKLIN of Pennsylvania, ROGER SHERMAN of Connecticut, ROBERT R. LIVINGSTON of New York, were appointed June 11th 1776 a Committee to draw up a Declaration in accordance with the resolution offered in Congress, June 7th 1776, by Richard Henry Lee, of Virginia, (who being suddenly called to the bedside of his sick wife, was unable to serve personally upon the Committee,) the Declaration was prepared by the Chairman, Thomas Jefferson, and with few alterations reported by the Committee to the Congress July 1st, and at mid-day July 4th 1776, the Thirteen Colonies were declared, Free and Independent States, under the name of the United States of America.

The Declaration Committee, from left to right: Thomas Jefferson, Roger Sherman, Benjamin Franklin, Robert R. Livingston, and John Adams

As John Adams began his reply, a summer storm crackled and exploded in the heavens above Philadelphia. Thunder shook the statehouse windows and lightning flashed against the darkening sky while Adams pleaded the cause of independence. No record of his words exists, but Jefferson remembered that Adams spoke "with a power of thought and expression that moved us from our seats."

When the vote was taken, only nine colonies voted for independence. Pennsylvania and South Carolina were opposed. Delaware's two delegates were divided. And New York's delegates abstained, saying they had no instructions from home.

The delegates who favored independence got busy behind the scenes. After a night of intense negotiations, Pennsylvania and South Carolina agreed to change their votes and go along with the other colonies. An absent Delaware delegate, Caesar Rodney, who also favored independence, rode eighty miles through heavy rain to reach Philadelphia and break the tie in his delegation's vote. New York, still lacking instructions, abstained again.

The final vote on July 2 was twelve colonies in favor of independence, none opposed. Two weeks later, New York's delegates were able to add their colony's approval, making the vote for independence unanimous.

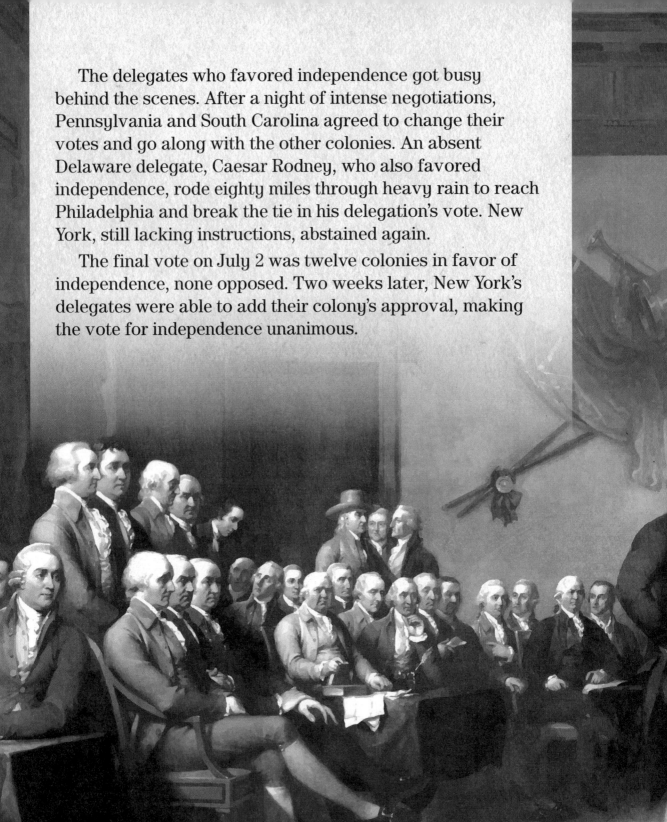

Congress then turned to the wording of Jefferson's draft. During a three-day period, from late Tuesday, July 2, through Thursday, July 4, the delegates went over the document word by word. Jefferson, justly proud of his composition, squirmed in his seat, listening in unhappy silence as whole paragraphs were taken out, as new words and phrases were added. In all, nearly one hundred changes were made. Jefferson's text was cut by about a fourth. John Adams believed that Congress worked some real improvements into the text, but also "obliterated some of the best of it."

The Declaration Committee presents the first draft to the Continental Congress.

The most hotly contested change concerned a long passage Jefferson had written attacking the slave trade and blaming King George III for imposing slavery on America. Jefferson himself lived in a slave society. He owned more than two hundred slaves. His plantations and way of life depended on the labors of the human property he had inherited. Yet he considered slavery an evil that should gradually be abolished. More than once, he had proposed plans to end the slave trade in Virginia. In his draft of the Declaration, he denounced slavery as "a cruel war against human nature itself, violating its most sacred rights of life and liberty."

At that time in America, it was easier to denounce slavery than to put an end to it. Southern slave owners in the Continental Congress, particularly those from Georgia and South Carolina, refused to sign a document that included Jefferson's tough anti-slavery passage. They "had never attempted to restrain the importation of slaves," Jefferson wrote later, but "still wished to continue it." The Southerners were backed by some of the delegates from New England, whose merchants had grown rich shipping slaves from Africa to the colonies. "For though their people had very few slaves themselves," said Jefferson, "yet they had been pretty considerable carriers of them to others."

John Adams, Ben Franklin, and other revolutionary leaders had spoken out strongly against slavery, but for the sake of unity, they agreed to compromise. The anti-slavery passage was eliminated. The explosive question of slavery was put aside and would not be resolved until America's Civil War nearly a century later.

Monticello, Thomas Jefferson's estate

MONTICELLO, THE EAST PORTICO.

On July 4, 1776, swarms of horseflies from a nearby stable invaded the assembly room, encouraging the delegates to bring their deliberations to a close. The final version of the Declaration of Independence was voted on and approved unanimously. As soon as the vote was taken, a boy stationed at the statehouse door began to clap his hands and shout, "Ring! Ring!" At nearby Christ's Church, the old bellman was waiting for that signal.

That afternoon, the Declaration of Independence was signed by John Hancock, president of the Continental Congress. He said he would make his signature large enough so that King George would be able to read it without his glasses. Most historians believe that no other signatures were added until August 2, after the document had been copied onto a sheet of durable parchment, when every member present signed it. The remaining members added their signatures at later times.

One signer, Stephen Hopkins of Rhode Island, had a condition called palsy that caused his hands to shake. As he took up his pen to add his name to the Declaration, he said, "My hand trembles, but my heart does not."

Each man among them knew that by signing the Declaration of Independence, he had become a traitor to England. If captured by the British, he could pay with his life. The outcome of the Revolutionary War would decide whether the signers would be remembered as the founders of a nation or be hanged by the British for treason.

John Hancock signs the Declaration of Independence.

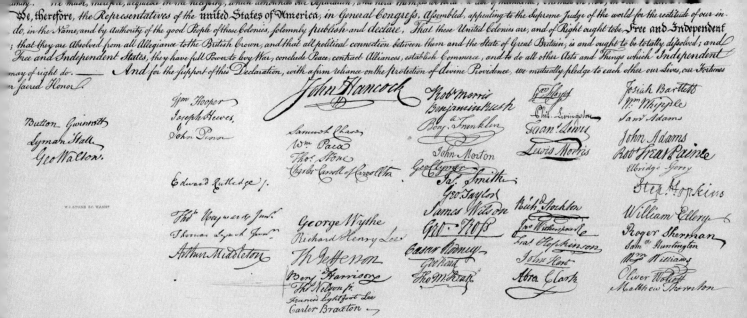

DECLARATION OF INDEPENDENCE SIGNATURE KEY

GEORGIA
Button Gwinnett
Lyman Hall
George Walton

NORTH CAROLINA
William Hooper
Joseph Hewes
John Penn

SOUTH CAROLINA
Edward Rutledge
Thomas Heyward, Jr.
Thomas Lynch, Jr.
Arthur Middleton

MASSACHUSETTS
John Hancock

MARYLAND
Samuel Chase
William Paca
Thomas Stone
Charles Carroll of Carrollton

VIRGINIA
George Wythe
Richard Henry Lee
Thomas Jefferson
Benjamin Harrison
Thomas Nelson, Jr.
Francis Lightfoot Lee
Carter Braxton

PENNSYLVANIA
Robert Morris
Benjamin Rush
Benjamin Franklin
John Morton
George Clymer
James Smith
George Taylor
James Wilson
George Ross

DELAWARE
Caesar Rodney
George Read
Thomas McKean

NEW YORK
William Floyd
Philip Livingston
Francis Lewis
Lewis Morris

NEW JERSEY
Richard Stockton
John Witherspoon
Francis Hopkinson
John Hart
Abraham Clark

NEW HAMPSHIRE
Josiah Bartlett
William Whipple

MASSACHUSETTS
Samuel Adams
John Adams
Robert Treat Paine
Elbridge Gerry

RHODE ISLAND
Stephen Hopkins
William Ellery

CONNECTICUT
Roger Sherman
Samuel Huntington
William Williams
Oliver Wolcott

NEW HAMPSHIRE
Matthew Thornton

479

▲ Colonists pull down a statue of George III.

▼ Richard Henry Lee reads the Declaration of Independence in Philadelphia.

Meanwhile, copies of the Declaration were printed and carried by express riders and coastal schooners to towns and villages in each of the thirteen states, where the text was read aloud amid "great demonstrations of joy." General George Washington and his troops heard it read in New York City on July 9. That evening a jubilant crowd pulled down a fifteen-foot-high gilded statue of George III on horseback. Later, the statue was melted down and the metal molded into 42,000 bullets for Patriot guns.

We hold these truths to be self-evident,

that all men are created equal, that they are endowed by their Creator with certain unalienable Rights, that among these are Life, Liberty and the pursuit of Happiness. — That to secure these rights, Governments are instituted among Men, deriving their just powers from the consent of the governed, — That whenever any Form of Government becomes destructive of these ends, it is the Right of the People to alter or to abolish it, and to institute new Government, laying its foundation on such principles and organizing its powers in such form, as to them shall seem most likely to effect their Safety and Happiness. . . .

Essential Questions
How did people react to the Declaration of Independence?
Why is it important for so many people?

LET *Independence* RING

by Tanya Anderson
illustrated by Nancy Lane

For days and days, we watched them gather,
Men from places near and far,
Discussing war and independence.
I listened through the door ajar.

The heat of summer filled the statehouse,
Open windows helped a bit.
I heard them shout, heard them argue,
Convincing holdouts to commit.

Throughout the city, tension mounted,
As people waited for the news.
Blood's been shed, war's been started,
Now all that's left is which to choose:

A future under British power,
Forced to bow down to their king?
Or something new, something greater,
Freedom to forever ring?

July the Fourth, a vote was taken,
"Approved!" I heard John Hancock say.
I ran to tell all who'd listen—
Our independence starts today!

News spread fast among the folks
As they took their evening stroll.
Four days passed by and then we heard
The bells throughout the city toll!

We all gathered at the statehouse,
Its grand bell chimed loud and true,
Then stopped before a man began
To read what hearts already knew.

"We hold these truths," he started out,
And we stood silent through the rest,
The weight of words, their impact clear,
At last, our liberty professed.

Whenever now I hear those bells,
It's this day that I recall,
Birthing freedom, a brand-new nation,
Life and liberty for all.

Write the answers to the questions on these pages in your notebook. Use evidence and details from the text to support your answers.

Text Connections

1. In June 1776, what was not yet clear to the Continental Congress?

2. How can reading poetry, such as "Let Independence Ring," help you better understand historic events?

3. Describe Thomas Jefferson in the summer of 1776, based on the text.

4. Based on the information in "Give Me Liberty!" and the Read Aloud "Sleepover at the National Archives," why is preserving the original Declaration of Independence so important?

5. Explain reasons why working with a large group like the Continental Congress can be difficult, based on your experience.

6. Why did signing the Declaration of Independence require a certain amount of courage?

Did You Know?

The night of July 4, 1776, a man named John Dunlap printed copies of the Declaration of Independence to distribute to leaders and troop commanders. Today, these copies, called broadsides, are rare and very valuable. Fewer than 30 are known to still exist. Historical artifacts, thought lost, sometimes surface in unexpected places. For example, in 1989, a man bought an old framed painting at a flea market. When he later took it apart, he found one of the Dunlap copies hidden inside!

Look Closer

Keys to Comprehension

1. Based on details about John Adams, make an inference about his importance to the Declaration of Independence.

2. What is a main idea of "Give Me Liberty!" and how do details support it?

3. Describe and explain the procedure by which the delegates of the Continental Congress adopted the Declaration of Independence.

Writer's Craft

4. Describe the structure and rhyme scheme of "Let Independence Ring."

Concept Development

5. How does the image of the signatures on the Declaration of Independence on page 479 help you better understand the related text?

6. How does the author support the idea that the delegates were divided over the question of slavery during the revision of the Declaration of Independence?

Write

Reread page 473. Then, write a paragraph in which you imagine some of what John Adams might have said when he "pleaded the cause of independence" the afternoon of July 1, 1776.

Read this Social Studies Connection. You will answer the questions as a class.

Text Feature

A **bulleted list** groups items that belong together but do not need to be in a particular order.

The Thinkers behind the Declaration

Thomas Jefferson wrote the first draft of the Declaration of Independence. When asked about the Declaration's origins, Jefferson said the authority of its ideas rests "on the harmonizing sentiments of the day." In other words, his work was based on popular ideas of the time. He then gave examples of places to find those ideas: "in conversation, in letters, printed essays, or in the elementary books of public right, as Aristotle, Cicero, Locke . . ."

Who were these men? Which of their ideas made it into the Declaration of Independence?

- **Aristotle** was an ancient Greek philosopher. Philosophers deliberate about the meaning behind things. One of his ideas involved countries being governed by the rule of law. The law, for him, was based only on good thinking, not on strong emotions. He wrote about what makes laws fair, or just.
- **Cicero** was an ancient Roman philosopher who studied Aristotle. One of his ideas was a sense of right that all people have inside them. This sense can lead people to follow a law that is "according to nature."
- **John Locke** was a British philosopher in the 1600s. He helped create the ideas of individual rights and limited government. In his view, people had rights, but must also respect others' rights. Governments owe their citizens certain things.

In the first version of the Declaration of Independence, Jefferson took and combined ideas from great thinkers of the past. As we now know, the result of this work had powerful consequences.

ARISTOTLE

LOCKE

CICERO

Aristotle, Cicero, and Locke were all sources of inspiration for Thomas Jefferson as he wrote the Declaration of Independence.

1. How did ideas spread between societies in Thomas Jefferson's time, and how do they spread today?

2. How did the spread of ideas affect the delegates of the Continental Congress?

3. Compare and contrast Jefferson's firsthand account quoted in the Social Studies Connection with information about sources of Jefferson's ideas in "Give Me Liberty!"

 Go Digital

Research to find images of Independence Hall in Philadelphia, where the delegates signed the Declaration of Independence. If possible, take a virtual tour of this important building.

Genre Informational Text

Essential Questions
What was the purpose of the Constitution? What does the Bill of Rights protect?

OUR CONSTITUTION
A BLUEPRINT FOR GOVERNMENT

by William Bale
illustrated by Josh Brunet and R. Schuster

In the spring of 1787, the United States of America was still a brand-new country. Not long before, it had been a group of colonies ruled by Great Britain and its king. The colonists had strongly disliked being ruled by an all-powerful king. They thought the king's rules were unjust and unfair. They believed the people, and not the king or queen, knew best the kinds of laws that would lead to a good life. They also objected when the British parliament, where they were not represented, placed taxes on them. Therefore, they went to war to break free of Great Britain. After they won the war, the Americans now had the freedom to make their own laws. They no longer had to live under the rules and orders imposed by the king of England.

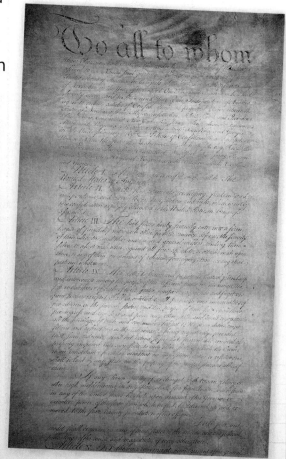

The Articles of Confederation

A FLAWED SYSTEM

The new nation's leaders called their first system of government the Articles of Confederation. Articles are explanations of rules. *Confederation* means a group of separate states that work together. The articles guided the separate states that composed the new country.

In some ways, the Articles of Confederation worked well. Under the Articles of Confederation, the United States agreed to a peace treaty with Great Britain. The US government also passed two important laws that set the rules for creating new states in lands to the west. In many other ways, the Articles worked poorly. The states were only loosely connected. No strong national government existed to assume important tasks to help the states run smoothly. For example, the national government could not raise money by taxing the people. It did not have the power to set up rules to ensure trade between the states operated fairly. It also lacked enforcement power to make sure the people obeyed the law. The national government could not support its paper money, making the money worthless. The state governments all printed their own money, causing confusion in the money system.

All these weaknesses at the national level and differences at the state level began to lead to chaos. The new country, its leaders believed, was in danger of falling apart. It soon became clear that the Articles of Confederation needed to be revised, and soon.

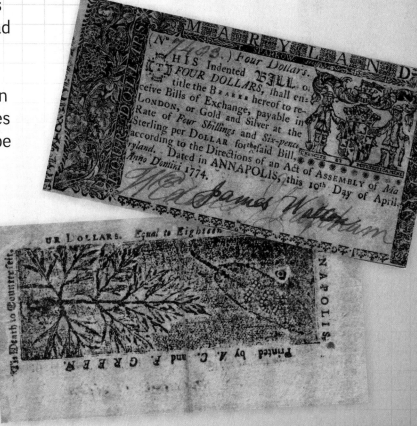

Each state had its own money under the Articles of Confederation.

CALLING FOR A CONVENTION

Chief among those concerned leaders were George Washington, Alexander Hamilton, and James Madison. In February 1787, Congress—the government body that made the laws—agreed that changes needed to be made to fix the government. They decided to hold a convention, or special meeting, to do the job. Congress invited each of the thirteen states to send delegates—representatives who had the experience and knowledge—to the convention.

In the spring, delegates departed from their home states to meet in Philadelphia. All the states except Rhode Island sent delegates. They were wealthy, well-educated businessmen, lawyers, bankers, and landowners. The first delegate to arrive in Philadelphia was James Madison, of Virginia. On May 25, he began to outline a new government. He called it the Virginia Plan. It called for a government that separated power into three branches. The legislative branch would make the laws. The executive branch would enforce the laws. The judicial branch would decide whether the laws were just and fair.

George Washington

Alexander Hamilton

Believing they needed privacy to speak freely, the delegates agreed to keep their work secret. They allowed no reporters or interested citizens inside the convention. After a few weeks, the delegates realized their original plan, to revise the Articles of Confederation, would not do enough to solve all the government's problems. The delegates decided they needed a constitution, or written plan for government. The new constitution would detail how the government would be structured and how it would operate. Their meeting came to be known as the Constitutional Convention. Today we call the men who wrote it the Framers of the Constitution, also knows as the Founders. James Madison, for his leadership and heroic effort in crafting the document, became known as the Father of the Constitution.

James Madison

The Virginia Plan

DISAGREEMENT AND COMPROMISE

The Framers' job was not easy. The summer heat was intense and the building stuffy. Tempers often ran hot, too, as the Framers disagreed on important points. At times, they were tempted to give up. But the future of their new nation was at stake, and they kept working.

The Great Compromise

One of the most serious disagreements was about Congress. Congress had representatives from all the states. But what would determine how many representatives each state would send? The large states believed that the bigger the population of a state, the more representatives it should have. The small states realized this plan gave them little chance of having an equal say in lawmaking. They wanted each state to send the same number of representatives, regardless of the size of their populations.

The Framers found a compromise. A compromise is an agreement in which each side gives up a little of what it wants. The Framers decided Congress would be bicameral, or made of two groups, called houses. In the lower house, called the House of Representatives, representation would be based on population. In the upper house, called the Senate, each state would be equally represented. This agreement was called the Great Compromise, because without it, the states would not have agreed to a union.

House of Representatives
- Number of members based on state population
- 435 voting members today

Both Houses
- Write laws
- Vote on laws written by the other house

Senate
- Each state has two senators
- 100 senators today

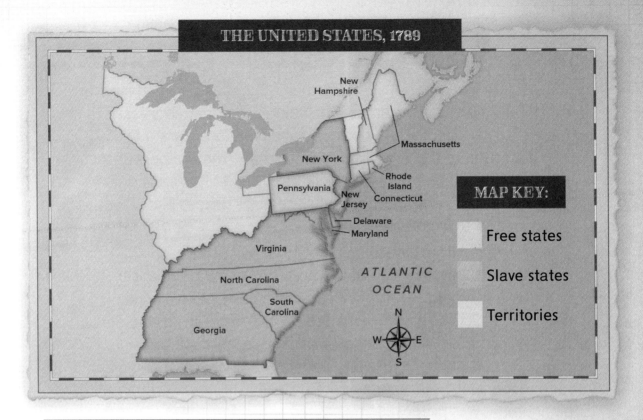

THE UNITED STATES, 1789

New Hampshire

Massachusetts

New York

Rhode Island

Pennsylvania

New Jersey

Connecticut

Delaware

Maryland

Virginia

North Carolina

ATLANTIC OCEAN

South Carolina

Georgia

N
W E
S

MAP KEY:

Free states

Slave states

Territories

The abolition of slavery was gradual in the free states.

The Three-Fifths Compromise

The Framers also disagreed about the matter of human slavery. At that time, enslaving people from Africa was legal. Some Northern states had already made slavery illegal, but because the Southern states depended on this unpaid labor, they would not yield on the question of outlawing slavery. Southern delegates also wanted to count enslaved people toward their populations in determining representation. Yet they did not want enslaved people to count in determining taxes owed to the national government. What they wanted would give Southern states more power in the House of Representatives and a smaller tax burden.

Delegates from the Northern states wanted the exact opposite, knowing that outlawing slavery was not an option. In the end, the delegates agreed to count three of every five enslaved persons when determining state representation and taxes. This agreement, called the Three-Fifths Compromise, still resulted in more power for the Southern states in the House of Representatives. The Three-Fifths Compromise would stay in place until after the Civil War, in 1865, when slavery was abolished in all states, and formerly enslaved people were made citizens.

WRITING THE CONSTITUTION

Through the long, hot summer, the Framers established several other rules for the government, including some that addressed the issue of trade. Making sure goods flowed easily from state to state was important to the new country's economy. The Framers agreed the states had to respect the laws of the other states and could not charge each other tariffs. Tariffs are taxes or fees placed on goods imported from other places.

The Framers also determined how the constitution could be amended, or changed, in the future. They wanted the ability to make important changes while also discouraging trivial, or unimportant, changes. They allowed for two ways an amendment could be proposed. It could be passed by two-thirds of the members of both the House and Senate. Alternatively, it could be recommended by two-thirds of the state legislatures. After an amendment was proposed and passed, three-fourths of the states would have to ratify, or approve, it.

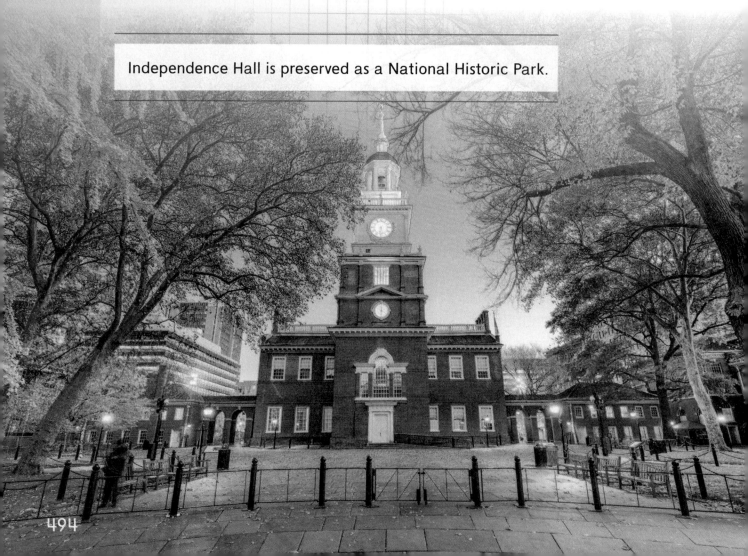

Independence Hall is preserved as a National Historic Park.

At the beginning of September 1787, the draft of the Constitution included twenty-three articles, or sections. The Framers sensed it was too long, so they appointed a committee to make sure the document was clear, concise, and well written. The committee edited and shortened the document from twenty-three articles to seven. The committee wrote a preamble, or introduction:

We the People of the United States, in Order to form a more perfect Union, establish Justice, insure domestic Tranquility, provide for the common defense, promote the general Welfare, and secure the Blessings of Liberty to ourselves and our Posterity, do ordain and establish this Constitution for the United States of America.

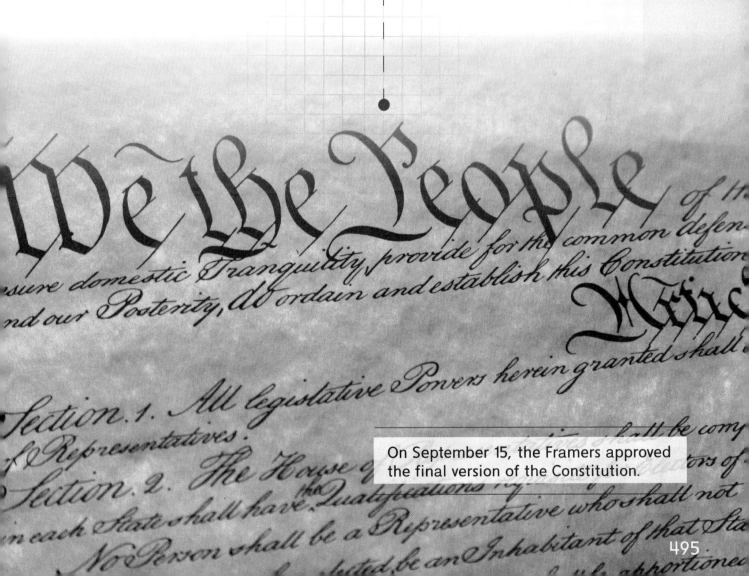

On September 15, the Framers approved the final version of the Constitution.

SIGNING THE CONSTITUTION

No computers or even typewriters existed in the 1700s. People wrote official documents on parchment. A skilled clerk named Jacob Shallus copied the final version of the Constitution in elegant handwriting on parchment. For his pen, he used a sharpened quill, or bird's feather. His ink was made from various plant materials. When he made a mistake, he scraped the ink off the parchment using a small knife. This painstaking work took Shallus an entire weekend.

By the third week of September, Shallus completed the final parchment document. One by one, thirty-nine Framers lined up to sign at the bottom of the last page. George Washington was the first to sign. Then each state delegation added their signatures in order of their state's location from north to south. Alexander Hamilton stood by and labeled each group of delegates with the name of their state.

At the same time, the Framers hired a printer to make hundreds of copies of the Constitution. Delegates would take some of the copies home with them to their legislatures. Other copies were bound for the Continental Congress.

Of the forty-two delegates present, only three refused to sign the document. George Mason, Elbridge Gerry, and Edmund Randolph believed the document did not include enough to protect the rights of individual citizens. After the Constitution became the law of the land, the First Congress would grant Mason, Gerry, and Randolph's wish for a bill of rights. But first, the Framers had to convince the American citizens the new Constitution would be good for the country.

DEBATING THE CONSTITUTION

The Framers included instructions for ratification, or approval, of the Constitution in the Constitution itself. They agreed that nine of the thirteen states would need to ratify the Constitution for it to be adopted. The Framers returned to their home states to lead the effort. Most wanted to convince Americans the new government would be good for the people. However, a few delegates believed the Constitution should not be ratified. On September 28, Congress told each state to hold conventions to decide whether to ratify the Constitution.

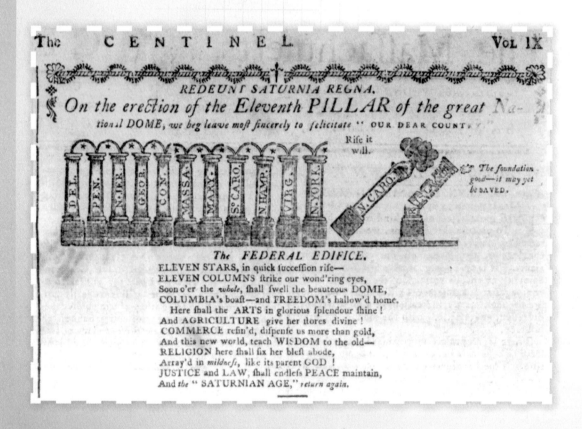

This illustration shows the order in which the states ratified the Constitution.

At the start of the Revolution, Patrick Henry gave a famous speech. He proclaimed, "Give me liberty, or give me death!"

The Anti-Federalists

Throughout the thirteen states, Americans held spirited debates over the Constitution. Those against it were called Anti-Federalists. Anti-Federalists opposed the formation of the federal government described in the Constitution. The most famous of the Anti-Federalists were Patrick Henry and James Monroe. Henry had been a hero of the Revolution, and Monroe later became president. Another active Anti-Federalist was the governor of New York, George Clinton. He wrote letters against the Constitution to newspapers under the pen name Cato.

Anti-Federalists mistrusted the idea of a strong, national government. Many Anti-Federalists argued that breaking free from a powerful government was exactly why they had fought the war against Britain. They feared a strong government would trample people's rights. They also believed the Constitution favored the wealthy instead of ordinary people. They thought the states and individuals should be given more power.

The Federalists

Those supporting the Constitution were writing letters too. These people were called Federalists. Thoughtful, detailed letters supporting the Federalist cause began to appear in newspapers. They were signed *Publius*. The letter writers chose this name carefully. Publius was a leader in ancient Rome. He helped change Rome from a monarchy, a land ruled by an all-powerful king, to a republic. In the republic of Rome, the people's rights were protected. The citizens of Rome also elected their leaders.

Few people knew it at the time, but the authors writing under the name Publius were three of the Framers. Between fall 1787 and summer 1788, James Madison, John Jay, and Alexander Hamilton wrote eighty-five letters to explain and support the Constitution. They wanted to send a message that the new Constitution was creating a republic, not a monarchy. Their aim was to convince Americans the new government was by the people and for the people.

The letters answered the Anti-Federalists' objections to the Constitution. The Federalists argued the states had more common interests than differences. A strong national government was the best way to protect and further those interests. Publius pointed out the three branches of government offered a system of checks and balances. Each branch could limit the other two branches in certain ways. This three-branch system would ensure no branch became too powerful. This system remains the cornerstone of government in the United States today.

Collectively, the Publius letters are known as the Federalist Papers. Judges and scholars still use the Federalist Papers to understand what the Framers planned for the government.

The Federalist Papers

THE FEDERALIST. 217

Nothing remains but the landed interest; and this in a political view, and particularly in relation to taxes I take to be perfectly united from the wealthiest landlord to the poorest tenant. No tax can be laid on land which will not affect the propietor of millions of acres as well as the proprietor of a single acre. Every land-holder will therefore have a common interest to keep the taxes on land as low as possible; and common interest may always be reckoned upon as the surest bond of sympathy. But if we even could suppose a distinction of interest between the opulent land-holder and the middling farmer, what reason is there to conclude that the first would stand a better chance of being deputed to the national legislature than the last? If we take fact as our guide, and look into our own senate and assembly we shall find that moderate proprietors of land prevail in both; nor is this less the case in the senate, which consists of a smaller number than in the assembly, which is composed of a greater number. Where the qualifications of the electors are the same, whether they have to choose a small or a large number their votes will fall upon those in whom they have most confidence; whether these happen to be men of large fortunes or of moderate property or of no property at all.

It is said to be necessary that all classes of citizens should have some of their own number in the representative body, in order that their feelings and interests may be the better understood and attended to. But we have seen that this will never happen under any arrangement that leaves the votes of the people free. Where this is the case, the representative body, with too few exceptions to have any influence on the spirit of the government will be composed of land-holders, merchants, and men of the learned professions. But where is the danger that the interests and feelings of the different classes of citizens will not be understood or attended to by these three descriptions of men? Will not the land-holder know and feel whatever will promote

T.9.

Alexander Hamilton, James Madison, and John Jay wrote The Federalist Papers.

RATIFICATION

After a period of debate, delegates at state conventions were ready to vote on ratification. In each state, voters elected delegates to their state conventions to decide whether to ratify the Constitution. In some states, the voters elected more Anti-Federalist than Federalist delegates. In others, they elected more Federalists. This imbalance put ratification in doubt. Some state conventions ratified the Constitution fairly quickly. On December 7, 1787, Delaware became the first to do so. Pennsylvania, New Jersey, Georgia, and Connecticut soon followed.

Other state conventions argued over ratification of the Constitution for many weeks. Anti-Federalist delegates held fast to their demand for a guarantee of rights for the people. In Massachusetts, the delegates reached a compromise with the Anti-Federalists. They agreed to ratify if Congress promised it would add amendments to the Constitution protecting people's rights. Because this compromise applied to all states, Massachusetts, Maryland, and South Carolina then voted to ratify. Now only one more state was needed for the Constitution to become law. New Hampshire became the ninth and deciding state on June 21, 1788. By July, Virginia and New York had ratified as well.

The new Constitution took effect on March 4, 1789. The United States government as we know it today began. However, two states, North Carolina and Rhode Island, still had not ratified. North Carolina wanted rights, amendments, and more to preserve slavery. But North Carolina put aside its demands and ratified in November 1789. Rhode Island did not want the federal government to control the money supply. It also was deeply against slavery and opposed the Three-Fifths Compromise. In the end, the US government told Rhode Island it would not trade with the state if it did not ratify. With no other choice, on May 29, 1790, the tiny state became the thirteenth, and last, state to ratify the Constitution.

NORTH CAROLINA

• Wanted protections for slavery

RHODE ISLAND

• Opposed slavery and Three-Fifths Compromise
• Opposed federal control of money supply

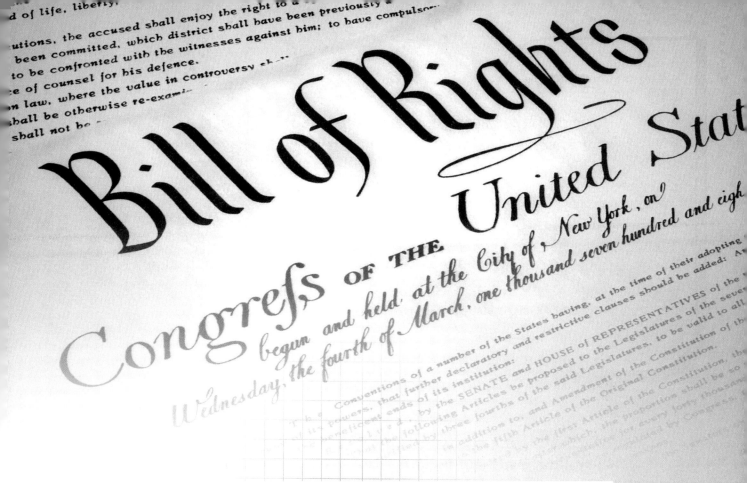

THE BILL OF RIGHTS

The Bill of Rights is the name for the first ten amendments to the US Constitution. These amendments name the basic rights of the people. The Founders had discussed the idea of a bill of rights for many years. George Mason, a delegate from Virginia, had written the Virginia Declaration of Rights in 1776. This declaration was a list of rights the government could not take away from the people. At the Constitutional Convention, the Framers had considered adding a list of rights to the Constitution. But the idea was voted down. In the end, Mason refused to sign the Constitution because it lacked a bill of rights.

Mason continued his push for a bill of rights after returning to his home state of Virginia. Many people supported having a bill of rights, and the idea played a large role in the debates in the ratifying conventions. Some states agreed to ratify only on the promise of a bill of rights. On September 25, 1789, the newly formed Congress approved twelve amendments. Congress sent these amendments to the states for ratification. The states ratified ten of the twelve amendments, and on December 15, 1791, the Bill of Rights became part of the Constitution.

In general, the Bill of Rights guarantees the people will be safe from harm or mistreatment by the government. Each amendment guarantees a different freedom.

- **AMENDMENT I.** The First Amendment protects the people's freedoms of religion, speech, and the press. It also promises to the people the right to peacefully assemble and to petition the government.

- **AMENDMENT II.** The Second Amendment protects the right of the people "to keep and bear Arms."

- **AMENDMENT III.** The Third Amendment guarantees the military will not illegally force private citizens to house soldiers. This had been a major grievance in the years leading to the Revolution.

- **AMENDMENTS IV–VIII.** The Fourth through Eighth Amendments protect the people from unfairness in the way the government enforces the law, called due process. The Sixth Amendment protects the right to have a fair trial.

- **AMENDMENTS IX AND X.** The Ninth and Tenth amendments limit the power of the federal government by protecting unnamed rights and giving unstated powers to the states and the people.

George Mason's strong, steady support for the rights of Americans earned him the title of Father of the Bill of Rights.

THE CONSTITUTION TODAY

The Constitution of the United States forms the basis for all the laws that govern our nation. Every law, written by Congress and signed by the president, must follow the Constitution. It is the job of the Supreme Court to decide whether laws are constitutional. The Supreme Court is the country's highest court, so it has the last word.

In the Constitution, the Framers created a strong but flexible document. With the amendments process, the Framers ensured the Constitution would be able to change with the times. For this reason, the Constitution has stood the test of time. Today, it is the world's oldest written plan of government.

The Supreme Court hears arguments in this building.

The president lives and works at the White House.

Congress meets at the United States Capitol.

Write the answers to the questions on these pages in your notebook. Use evidence and details from the text to support your answers.

Text Connections

1. Who were the delegates at the Constitutional Convention, and what was their job?

2. What physical circumstances made the Framers' job even harder?

3. Why does the author describe Jacob Shallus's work as "painstaking"?

4. Consider both "Our Constitution" and "Give Me Liberty!" How did the need for unity and disagreements about slavery affect both the Declaration of Independence and the Constitution?

5. How would your life be different if you couldn't easily buy things from other states?

6. Why is it important for constitutional amendments to be possible but not easy?

Did You Know?

The Constitution's Preamble originally began, "We the People of the States of New-Hampshire, Massachusetts," and so on, listing all 13 original states. Framer Gouverneur Morris was given the task of editing the Preamble. It was Morris who came up with the much shorter and now famous beginning: "We the People of the United States."

Look Closer

Keys to Comprehension

1. In what way was the Bill of Rights the key to state ratification of the Constitution?

2. Summarize the information under the heading "A Flawed System," and explain its main idea.

3. Explain what the Great Compromise was and why it was needed.

Writer's Craft

4. Explain what the term *Framers* means.

5. How did the author of "Our Constitution" structure the information in this selection?

Concept Development

6. Using information from "Our Constitution" and "Give Me Liberty!," summarize the process by which the colonies officially formed a country with a constitution.

Write

Write a petition asking for a change in a state or federal law. Explain your reasons thoroughly. Cite evidence from "Our Constitution" to show that your proposed law would not go against the Constitution.

Read this Social Studies Connection. You will answer the questions as a class.

Text Feature

Numbered titles and **sections** help to organize complicated text.

Article 5

When the Framers created the U.S. Constitution, they included seven articles, or sections. Article 5 tells how to change the Constitution. The Framers knew changes, or amendments, would be needed. They would preserve the future usefulness of the Constitution. Some very important changes have followed over the years. Two examples are:

Amendment XIII
Section 1. Neither slavery nor involuntary servitude, except as a punishment for crime whereof the party shall have been duly convicted, shall exist within the United States, or any place subject to their jurisdiction.
Section 2. Congress shall have power to enforce this article by appropriate legislation.

Amendment XV
Section 1. The right of citizens of the United States to vote shall not be denied or abridged by the United States or by any state on account of race, color, or previous condition of servitude.
Section 2. The Congress shall have power to enforce this article by appropriate legislation.

When writing a proposed amendment, language is important. Proposers of amendments choose individual words with care.

XIII and XV are Roman numerals for 13 and 15. Like many others, amendments 13 and 15 are divided into sections. The 13th Amendment says slavery and forced labor are not allowed. The 15th Amendment says no one can keep a man who is a citizen from voting. Section 2 of both amendments ensures Congress can make related laws.

Thirty-Eighth **Congress of the United States of America;**

At the _second_ Session,

Begun and held at the City of Washington, on Monday, the _fifth_ day of December, one thousand eight hundred and sixty-_four._

A RESOLUTION

Submitting to the legislatures of the several States a proposition to amend the Constitution of the United States.

Resolved _by the Senate and House of Representatives of the United States of America in Congress assembled,_ (two-thirds of both houses concurring), that the following article be proposed to the legislatures of the several States as an amendment to the Constitution of the United States, which, when ratified by three-fourths of said legislatures shall be valid, to all intents and purposes, as a part of the said Constitution, namely: Article XIII. Section 1. Neither slavery nor involuntary servitude, except as a punishment for crime whereof the party shall have been duly convicted, shall exist within the United States, or any place subject to their jurisdiction. Section 2. Congress shall have power to enforce this article by appropriate legislation.

Speaker of the House of Representatives.

H. Hamlin
Vice President of the United States.

When Congress suggested the 13th Amendment, it created a proposal in the form of this joint resolution.

1. Why did the Framers of the U.S. Constitution include Article 5?

2. Using an example amendment, explain how one change affected ordinary people.

3. What role do you think ordinary citizens have in this process?

 Go Digital

Research other important Constitutional Amendments. How did each change life in the United States?

Genre Fantasy

Essential Questions
What is a treasury? Why did the United States need a mint?

Mice in the Mint

by Karen Martin • illustrated by Gerald Kelley

"Welcome to the Mint!" Penny Mouse cried as she hugged her grandson Bill and ushered him into the three-story brick building. "I can't wait to give you a tour of the place . . . right after you settle in and we have a nice cup of tea."

510

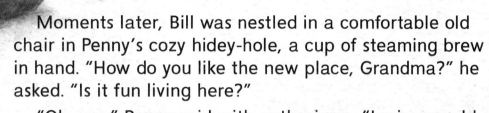

Moments later, Bill was nestled in a comfortable old chair in Penny's cozy hidey-hole, a cup of steaming brew in hand. "How do you like the new place, Grandma?" he asked. "Is it fun living here?"

"Oh, yes," Penny said with enthusiasm. "I miss my old place sometimes, but life is interesting here at the Mint."

As Bill took a long sip of tea, his eyes scanned the room, pausing at a portrait of a man hanging on the wall.

"Who is the man in the painting?" Bill asked.

"That's my good friend, Alexander Hamilton," she answered, rocking contentedly in her chair. "Hamilton and I go way back—all the way back to the Revolutionary War."

"You have known him since the Revolutionary War? Now I *am* curious. Will you tell me more?" Bill asked. He loved hearing stories about the remarkable people his grandma had known and the exciting places she had been in her life.

"Alexander Hamilton was a Revolutionary War hero, and now he has a very important job! He is the Secretary of the Treasury."

"The Treasury? You mean his job is to make treasure?" Bill looked excited, and Penny chuckled.

"Yes, in a way. The Treasury makes the money people use to buy things, and it also collects taxes and manages government debts. Alexander Hamilton is in charge of all of that for the entire nation."

Bill's eyes widened with interest. "That sounds important. Will you tell me how you met him, Grandma?" asked Bill.

She smiled fondly and replied, "Let me dig out some old mementoes, and I will tell you the story."

Penny began to speak as she crossed the room to retrieve a small trunk packed with souvenirs from a lifetime of adventures. "I was a young field mouse when I first encountered Hamilton. It was during the early days of the Revolutionary War, in 1775. He was only eighteen years old."

She said, "I would watch Hamilton and his friends as they performed drills and prepared to fight the British." Penny pulled a green jacket out of the trunk. "Here is the jacket I made to blend in, so I could move among the soldiers.

"I decided to leave the field and travel with Hamilton," she said. "By the time he was nineteen years old, he was captain of an artillery company defending New York City against the British.

"He was a brilliant commander," Penny continued, "and it wasn't long before people took notice. One of those people was General Washington."

"Do you mean George Washington, the president?" asked Bill.

"That's right, the very man who was sworn in for his second term last week. But he wasn't president then," Penny said. "He was the commander in chief of the Continental army. Washington singled out Hamilton for his intelligence, his clever ideas, and his many skills. Washington made Hamilton his personal aide-de-camp. That's a soldier who works as an assistant to a high-ranking military officer. This picture shows the two of them in the field," she said, taking a paper out of the worn trunk and pointing to a sketch of two figures in uniform.

"Hamilton spent the next four years of the war by Washington's side. He advised the general on battle tactics and military strategy, wrote letters for him, and delivered important messages. Sometimes even I would help deliver messages! These two great men developed a deep loyalty that continues to this day.

"After four years, though, Hamilton was not happy working behind the scenes anymore. He was aching to go back into battle, but Washington did not want to let him go—he was too valuable as his aide-de-camp. After many requests, Washington finally relented, and Hamilton took command of his own battalion.

"When we arrived in Yorktown, Virginia, it was the eve of what was called the Battle of Yorktown. The entire army was tense with nervous energy, but Hamilton was focused and ready for the battle. He once wrote, 'There is a certain enthusiasm in liberty, that makes human nature rise above itself in acts of bravery and heroism.' We won that battle at Yorktown, and it was the last one of the war. The British General Cornwallis surrendered, and our country was truly independent at last. What an exciting time!"

"Wow, Grandma! What happened after the war?" asked Bill.

"After the war, Hamilton decided to return to New York to practice law, and of course I went with him. I did not want to miss any of the action! And I was not disappointed. Hamilton jumped into politics with both feet after we arrived in New York. In fact, in 1787 he became a New York delegate to the Constitutional Convention. Hamilton thought it was important to address the problems the government faced under the Articles of Confederation and to help write a new guiding document. For that, we traveled to Philadelphia.

"During the Constitutional Convention," Penny continued, "delegates argued about who should hold the power in this new country: the individual states or a central government. Some people wanted the states to have the power to govern themselves. Other people wanted the federal government to hold the power. Hamilton was one of those—a Federalist."

"Why did he want the government to hold the power?" asked Bill.

"Well, above all, Hamilton didn't want the country to fail. If the country failed, we could lose the liberty we had fought to win. Hamilton worried the United States would fall apart if it didn't have a strong central government. For him, maintaining the Union was more important than providing for individual states' rights, and he believed the Constitution would help uphold the Union."

"That makes sense, I guess, but I can see how the states would be nervous about it. They had won their independence from the British, so giving lots of power and control to the federal government might be scary."

"Right," said Penny. "That was Thomas Jefferson's stance, along with many others. Jefferson did not take part in the Constitutional Convention at all. Neither did several of the men who were deeply involved in the Revolution, such as John Adams, Samuel Adams, Patrick Henry, and John Hancock. They were all absent from the convention. Even Hamilton's fellow delegates from New York left the convention early, because they did not agree with what was being written."

"You mean the states didn't want the rules to change?" asked Bill.

"Some did, but not all of them," answered Penny. "Remember, the United States was founded by thirteen individual states, each with its own ideas about how the country should be run. Convincing them to all work together has sometimes been like trying to herd thirteen cats!"

Bill giggled, and his grandmother grinned.

"The delegates at the convention were determined to produce a constitution that would unite the thirteen colonies, so they kept working on the document. Almost everyone agreed on one point: the country needed one national currency."

Bill interrupted and said, "The country had different kinds of money? That had to be confusing."

"Very confusing," said Penny. "Before the war, each state had its own money, and afterward, under the Articles of Confederation, the country had federal notes too. The entire financial system was a mess. The humans were all very frustrated by it."

"What did they do?" asked Bill. Mice do not have much use for human money. However, Bill was always curious about everything. He enjoyed learning, simply for the sake of knowing something new.

"Hamilton," continued Penny, "and the other delegates took the first steps toward fixing this problem as they drafted the United States Constitution. They included a clause that called for one national currency, and they also gave only Congress, not the states, the right to produce money."

Bill nodded and said, "That sounds like a smart idea. Then what happened?"

"After a lot of debate from both sides, the United States Constitution was ratified in 1788. Much more needed to be done, though, before the United States would be on stable footing."

"What does that mean?" asked Bill.

"Stable footing? A footing is a foundation, the stone a building sits on. It's a metaphor," responded Penny. She continued. "The following year, the First Federal Congress met in New York City."

"But isn't the capital in Washington, D.C.?" asked Bill.

"It is now," responded Penny. "The nation had several capitals before the humans built the District of Columbia. One of the most important things the Framers did was to create the Department of the Treasury. President Washington appointed Hamilton as the leader of the department. Hamilton started immediately on a plan to clean the financial mess—especially the debt from the Revolutionary War, which totaled millions of dollars."

Bill frowned. "Why was the debt such a big problem?"

"That's a good question, Bill," responded Penny. "It's complicated, but the short answer is credit. Credit is someone's financial reputation."

"I know what a reputation is!" exclaimed Bill. "It's what others think about someone, based on their past behavior."

"That's right," agreed Penny. "A financial reputation, or credit, is whether you're known for paying your debts. No one will lend you more money if you don't pay back the original loan.

"Governments need a lot of money to function, and they usually borrow it. That's how the states and the central government assumed so much debt during the war. This is what Hamilton was worried about—America's credit."

REPORT
OF THE
SECRETARY OF THE TREASURY
READ TO THE
HOUSE OF REPRESENTATIVES
OF THE
UNITED STATES
JANUARY 19th 1795

PUBLIC CREDIT

Penny rummaged through the papers in the trunk and retrieved another document to show Bill. "Hamilton wrote a report on the subject for the new Congress in 1790. Hamilton knew if the United States didn't pay back our loans from the war, we would have poor credit. No one would respect or trust us if that happened, and they probably wouldn't loan our government more money."

"Did Hamilton have a plan for solving the debt problem?"

"He did, but it was controversial. He suggested the federal government should not only pay off its own debt from the war, but also that it should assume the states' debts."

Bill looked confused. "Why not let the states pay off their debts themselves?"

"For Hamilton, consolidating the debt was a way to gather power for the federal government," Penny said. "Hamilton wrote, 'A national debt, if it is not excessive, will be to us a national blessing. It will be a powerful cement of our Union.'"

"That sounds like another metaphor," said Bill. "Did he mean that the national debt would bind the nation like glue?"

"Yes!" responded Penny. "You see, the states mostly owed money to rich, powerful men, and Hamilton wanted those men to conduct business with the federal government instead of the states. If the federal government owed these men money, they would have a personal stake in its success or failure."

"Because . . ." Bill thought a moment. "If the government failed, they wouldn't get their money back?" asked Bill.

"Exactly," Penny confirmed.

"It still sounds like a good arrangement for the states," Bill mused. "Their debt is paid, and the nation grows stronger too."

"Not everybody looked at it that way," Penny said. "Many people thought the Federal government was interfering in state matters, that it was trying to grab too much power. Thomas Jefferson especially opposed Hamilton's plan to take over the states' debts. Actually, the idea made Hamilton unpopular with many members of Congress, but he finally managed to persuade Jefferson and others to support it. Hamilton had more work to do, though, to fix the financial crisis."

"Really? What more could he do?" asked Bill, amazed.

"Hamilton proposed a national bank that could conduct business on behalf of the federal government. Many people supported the idea, many were against it too."

"But if it were good for the nation, why would anyone be against it?" asked Bill.

"They cared about the people's freedoms and worried about the power of a national bank. Opponents such as Jefferson and James Madison argued Congress did not have the power to create a bank," explained Penny.

"Why would they think that?" asked Bill.

"That claim was based on the 10th Amendment to the Constitution, which is in the Bill of Rights." Penny showed Bill a page tacked to the wall and read aloud, "'The powers not delegated to the United States by the Constitution, nor prohibited by it to the states, are reserved to the states respectively or to the people.'"

"Oh!" mused Bill. "The Framers really thought of everything, didn't they!"

"Almost," mused Penny.

Bill thought for a moment and said, "Then according to the Constitution, the states hold all powers except for those specifically named as federal powers."

"Yes, that's how Jefferson saw it," said Penny. "But the Constitution is quite complex, and people often interpret it differently."

"Let me guess," said Bill. "Hamilton interpreted it differently. Do those two agree on anything?"

Penny laughed. "Not much. Hamilton cited Article One of the Constitution to support his position," she said, reading aloud from yet another sheet of paper. "'The Congress shall have Power . . . To make all Laws which shall be necessary and proper.' Hamilton believed a national bank was absolutely necessary, and therefore, proper."

"Who won the argument this time, Jefferson or Hamilton?" asked Bill.

"Hamilton did, and Congress approved the plan for a national bank in 1791. Now the government had both the exclusive right to make money and a national bank. They needed one more item to establish the country's financial system. Can you guess what it was?" Penny spread her arms out and gestured at the building around them.

"The Mint!" Bill replied quickly. "Everything was already in place except for the actual money—they had to make the money!"

"That's right!" exclaimed Penny. "In 1792, Congress passed the Mint Act to do just that. The Mint Act set the dollar as the nation's currency and designated the first coins that should be produced, from gold eagle coins worth ten dollars down to copper half-cent coins. The act also authorized the building of the Mint itself—and here we stand today. The Mint was the first federal building constructed under the United States Constitution, which speaks highly about how important this place is. I feel very lucky to live here."

"Amazing," Bill said. "It's a lot of work starting a new country. Thank goodness I'm a mouse and not a human!"

Penny laughed and put her arm around her grandson's shoulders. "Me too, Bill, me too. Now let's go take that tour . . . I have a good friend I would like you to meet."

Text Connections

1. What do the United States Treasury and the Mint each do?

2. Infer how George Washington seemed to view Alexander Hamilton, and explain how you know.

3. Why did Hamilton and Jefferson disagree about the formation of a national bank? Explain each side's argument.

4. Based on information from "Mice in the Mint," what was Alexander Hamilton likely doing during the Continental Congress of the summer of 1776 described in "Give Me Liberty!"?

5. Which of Penny's experiences sounds the most exciting to you and why?

6. What traits did Hamilton and Jefferson share, even as they disagreed about details of the Constitution and what it means?

Did You Know?

Since the 1860s, Alexander Hamilton's face has appeared on various bills. In 2015, the Treasury Department considered removing him from the ten-dollar bill, but public outcry kept Hamilton on it.

Look Closer

Keys to Comprehension

1. Summarize Alexander Hamilton's journey from soldier to Secretary of the U.S. Treasury, using details from the text.

2. Describe in depth the character of Penny in "Mice in the Mint." Use details to support your description.

Write

Do you agree with Hamilton or Jefferson when it comes to the idea of a strong central government? Using the facts in "Mice in the Mint," explain your opinion.

Writer's Craft

3. Explain the type of figurative language Penny uses when she says, "much more needed to be done, though, before the United States would be on stable footing." What does this phrase mean?

4. Contrast the genres of "Mice in the Mint" and "Paul Revere's Ride," using details from each text.

5. Compare the points of view from which "Paul Revere's Ride" and "Mice in the Mint"are told.

Concept Development

6. Compare and contrast how "Mice in the Mint" and "Our Constitution" cover the topic of Hamilton's work at the Constitutional Convention.

Read this Social Studies Connection. You will answer the questions as a class.

Text Feature

A **caption** is a phrase or sentence that gives more information about a photograph.

The Story of "Greenbacks"

When you think of United States money, you probably picture both coins and paper bills. However, did you know that until the 1860s, the green paper bills we use today did not exist?

The Bank of the United States received its charter in 1791, and the U.S. Mint began coining money in 1792. For the most part, however, the federal government did not print paper money. Instead, state banks did. The Bank of the United States did control the money supply. It regulated how many notes state banks could print. However, in 1811 the federal bank was not renewed, and disappeared for several years.

From 1837 to 1861, only state-chartered banks issued paper bills. These paper bills were like bills of credit. The idea was that you could trade them in for gold or silver. However, some state banks printed many more paper bills than they could back up. Because of this, the bills were worth less and less. Storekeepers had to track the values of all these different bills. At the same time, many people created counterfeit, or fake, bills. It was a complex mess.

In the 1860s, the Civil War forced a change. The federal government needed money to finance the war. It began creating federal banks, though they did not take modern form until many years later. The federal government also started printing a uniform national paper currency. People called these bills "greenbacks." It put taxes on state bank notes, and this tactic got people to stop using them. It also created a special division to fight counterfeit money. Today, the Bureau of Engraving and Printing produces and develops the only paper money used in the United States.

This 1839 example of a state bank bill was issued by Texas.

1. How was money different in the United States before the 1860s?

2. How did the function of the U.S. government gradually change after the 1860s, in regard to money and banking?

3. Do you think federal governments should have the authority to control a country's money? Why or why not?

 Go Digital

Research techniques the Bureau of Engraving and Printing uses to protect paper money from being counterfeited. How and why have their techniques changed over time?

Genre Narrative Nonfiction

Essential Questions
Who contributed to the Statue of Liberty? Why
are they an important part of the American story?

LADY LIBERTY
A BIOGRAPHY

by Doreen Rappaport
illustrated by Matt Tavares

DOREEN RAPPAPORT
New York City, Today

One hundred twenty years ago,
my grandfather fled his home in Latvia,
thousands of miles away.
He left his mother and father and
brothers and sisters and
aunts and uncles and cousins
to come to a country where he knew no one.
He came to build a better life.

As the ferry nears the Statue of Liberty,
I try to imagine his ocean journey and
how he felt when he saw her for the first time.

He was on a ship packed with people
from many different countries,
speaking languages he did not understand.
For days the ocean bucked and roared.
He slept in steerage with others who had no money,
longing for fresh air.
Most days his stomach hurt too much to eat.

Then early one morning, shouts of
"The Lady! The Lady!" awakened him.
He raced up to the deck.
The ship was pulling into New York,
and there was Lady Liberty greeting them all.

Arms reached out as if to caress her.
People lifted babies so they could see her.
Tears ran down my grandfather's face.
People around him were crying, too.
And then a wave of cheering and hugging
swept over the ship.

I wonder if my grandfather ever thought
about how she came to be.

ÉDOUARD DE LABOULAYE

Professor of Law
Glatigny, France, 1865

It is a warm summer night.
After dinner, we move into the parlor.
The talk turns to our dear friend, America.

We speak of how the Marquis de Lafayette
fought side by side with George Washington.
Ever the historian, Henri Martin reminds us
that the Americans would not have won
the final battle at Yorktown
without Count de Grasse's navy
and Rochambeau's soldiers.
Our countrymen died for America's freedom.

The American Revolution fired our revolution.
Their Declaration of Independence inspired our
Declaration of the Rights of Man and of the Citizen.
I often tell my own students that the
American Constitution is a model for the world.

Soon America will be one hundred years old.
I share my dream of a birthday gift.
Auguste Bartholdi listens intently when
I suggest a monument from our people to theirs
to celebrate their one hundred years of independence
and to honor one hundred years of friendship
between our countries.

Henri says such a gift is not possible now.
Emperor Napoleon III rules France.
This dictator would not allow such a gift.
I will wait for things to change, I say.
I will not give up my dream.

534

AUGUSTE BARTHOLDI
Sculptor
40 rue Vavin, Paris, France, 1875

Laboulaye's dream has become my dream, too.
Now after ten years of dreaming,
we can make it come true—
Napoleon III rules France no more.

I went across the sea to America to share the dream.
Laboulaye gave me letters of introduction.
I met many famous people,
including President Ulysses S. Grant.
Everyone was polite and seemed interested.
But no one offered to raise money to build her.
I am not worried.
We will raise the money in France.

Everything in America is so big.
The mighty Niagara Falls pounds liquid thunder.
Tall grasses stretch across a never-ending prairie.
Jagged peaks soar in the Rocky Mountains.
California's giant redwoods cover the sky.
In this New World of colossal natural wonders,
I found the perfect place for her.
She will rise on an island in New York's harbor,
welcoming everyone to America.

I have sketched Liberty many times
and made clay models.
Laboulaye helped me at every stage.
She will be massive but elegant,
as grand as any one of the
Seven Wonders of the Ancient World.
Liberty will rival the Great Pyramid of Egypt,
and the gold and ivory statue of Zeus at Olympia,
and the colossus of Helios in Rhodes.

MARIE SIMON

Bartholdi's Assistant
25 rue de Chazelles, Paris, France, 1876

After months of work,
we have finished the right arm and torch.
Now we start on the left hand.
We go back to Bartholdi's four-foot clay model.

The pointers measure her forearm, wrist,
fingers, nails, and tablet.
They multiply each part by two
to build a model twice as big.

Again, they measure and multiply,
this time by four.
Slowly. Carefully. Section by section,
the workers build a bigger model.
Bartholdi moves about like a prowling tiger,
reminding everyone to be precise.

Again, measure and multiply by four.
This third model pleases Bartholdi.
The workers divide it into twenty-one parts.
Each part will be enlarged another four times.

Now the carpenters begin.
Day in, day out, buzzing and sawing.
Wood chips and sawdust litter the floor.
Narrow wooden strips are bent and
nailed together to form the giant molds.
Some wood is carved to make softer lines.

White dust clings to the workers
as they pour plaster over the wood
until the shapes are just right.
Bartholdi waits impatiently
for the plaster to harden.

536

New wooden molds have been set on the plaster.
Now the coppersmiths begin their work.

"I will not cast her like ancient statues
from bronze cannons taken from enemies,"
Bartholdi says.
"She will be of pure copper,
made by workers in an era of peace."

Liberty's copper skin will not rust
in the salt air of the New York harbor.
Copper is light and easy to work.
It bends without cracking.

Day in, day out, rapping and banging,
as the copper is pounded on the molds
until the shapes are perfect.
Bartholdi stalks about the studio
from station to station,
hurrying the workers along,
oblivious to the noise.

Finally the hollow copper shells
are lifted off the wooden molds.
Now it is Eiffel's turn.
He must make sure Liberty stands tall.

GUSTAVE EIFFEL
Structural Engineer
25 rue de Chazelles, Paris, France, 1883

Lady Liberty is the talk of Paris.
Every day hundreds of people come
to watch her grow.

To keep Liberty upright is a challenge
as great as any I have faced in building bridges.
Her copper shell weighs more than 179,000 pounds.
So I made her a skeleton—
a ninety-six-foot-high iron tower
of beams and ribs
upon which to bolt her copper skin.

Iron rusts when it touches copper.
Some say my brilliance is having
the beams pass through fittings
so the iron does not fasten directly to the copper.
The fittings also let her copper skin move,
to expand and contract with the weather.

I listen to the people talk as they watch
her skin being riveted onto her skeleton.
She inspires them. She inspires me.
Liberté, *égalité*, and *fraternité* are in the air.

EMMA LAZARUS

Poet
New York City, November 1883

A gala auction is being held
to raise money for Liberty's pedestal.
Famous artists are donating paintings.
I was asked to write a poem
to be sold along with poems
by Longfellow and Whitman.
It is a great honor to be asked.
I can write about anything I want.
But I have had trouble writing lately
because I feel too sad.

In the past few years in Russia,
hundreds of Jews have been killed.
Thousands have been persecuted,
their homes burned, their shops destroyed.
They trek hundreds of miles across Europe
with only the clothes on their backs,
hoping to find ships to take them to America.

We Jews are not new to hatred.
Almost two hundred years ago
my ancestors fled Europe, too.
America was a land of hope for them.
It is still a land of hope.

Soon when people arrive in the New World,
they will be welcomed
by a caring, powerful woman.

Give me your tired, your poor,
Your huddled masses yearning to breathe free,
The wretched refuse of your teeming shore.
Send these, the homeless, tempest-tost to me:
I lift my lamp beside the golden door!

CHARLES P. STONE

Construction Supervisor
Bedloe's Island, March 1884

Sweat and grime cover the workers' bodies.
Their muscles bulge from months of digging.
They grunt and call out to one another
in words foreign to my ears
as they hack away with pickaxes
at old cisterns and stone walls,
until the hole is thirteen feet deep
and ninety-one feet square.

They mix and pour cement and sand
and large and small stones
to fill the huge hole.
They pour more concrete on top,
27,000 tons in all, until the foundation
rises sixty-five feet from the ground.
They test each layer to be sure
it is hard before they pour again.

Over and over, sixteen hours a day,
their rhythms never change,
only the weather.
Every part of their bodies aches,
but no one complains.
There were no jobs in their villages
in Italy.

When the sun goes down, they eat,
then stumble off to sleep
in makeshift tents on the island.
But I believe they are content, for
they are building new lives in this country.

543

JOSEPH PULITZER
Publisher, New York World
New York City, March 1885

More than one hundred thousand French people—
shopkeepers, artisans, farmers, and children—
gave their hard-earned money to build Liberty.
Americans have been giving money, too.
One hundred thousand dollars is still needed
to build her pedestal.
Some Americans criticize the French
for not giving *all* the money, since it is a gift.
I read with disgust newspaper editorials
mocking their generosity.

Some people call Liberty a "national disgrace."
Others call her "New York's lighthouse."
The mayor of New York City does not want her.
Congress has refused to give money for her pedestal.
I cannot understand why politicians do not understand
her power as a symbol of freedom.

I say she belongs in New York City.
New York is the gateway to the New World,
the door of hope for immigrants.
I know.
I landed here penniless twenty-one years ago.

We have more than a hundred millionaires in this city
who could write a check for the full amount.
But no one has.
I shall ask my readers to help.
They are not millionaires,
but I know *they* will care,
for they will understand her importance.

FLORENCE DE FOREEST
Metuchen, New Jersey, June 1885

Mr. Pulitzer's campaign is working.
More than one hundred thousand
Americans have given
pennies, nickels, dimes, and dollars.
When you send money,
Mr. Pulitzer prints your name
and how much you gave in his paper.

I am sending my two pet roosters.
Mr. Pulitzer can sell them and
use the money for the pedestal.
I can't wait to see my name in print.

People as far away as Texas have sent money—
soldiers, factory workers, miners, bank tellers,
actors, doctors, farmers, shopkeepers.
Even gamblers have given money.
The most money has come from
veterans of the Civil War.
They gave fifteen hundred dollars.

Two boys sent a dollar that
they had saved for circus tickets.
Another boy sent twenty-five pennies.

Mr. Pulitzer pokes fun
at the rich people who don't give.
He calls them "croakers" and "laggards"
and prints their names in his paper, too!

JOSEPH PULITZER
Publisher, New York World
New York City, August 1886

Liberty's skeleton is now anchored
to the pedestal,
bolted to huge girders
that protrude from the concrete.
Eighty-nine feet tall, twenty feet thick,
and faced with granite,
the pedestal is more majestic than I had hoped.
I am humbled by my readers' generosity.
Many who have so little gave so much
to build this noble structure.

Liberty arrived in 214 crates.
On her trip across the ocean,
vicious storms buffeted the ship.
Labels fell off crates.
Pieces of her copper skin were shaken.
Many need to be reshaped.

Slowly each copper sheet
is hoisted up with heavy ropes.
The workers sit on the crossbars,
fitting her copper skin to the skeleton.
When one piece doesn't fit,
they haul up another and try it,
then another,
until they find the right one.
The first piece of copper skin attached
to the skeleton is named "Bartholdi."
The second piece is christened "Pulitzer."

Each day she grows more beautiful.
I predict that those who once mocked her
will soon love her and understand
her power and significance.

549

JOSÉ MARTÍ

Journalist, Poet
New York City, October 28, 1886

Today is Liberty's day.
Up and down the Hudson River,
French and American flags stretch
from mast to mast, from bow to stern,
on hundreds of tugboats and yachts and
scows and steamers and ships-of-war.

Rain is falling, but no one cares.
The red, white, and blue of the Stars and Stripes
and the French tricolors fly
from buildings and stores and arches.
Sidewalks, doorways, windowsills, and roofs
bulge with people.
Adults stand on wooden boxes and scaffolding.
A million Americans have come to welcome her.

Grand Marshal Charles Stone,
astride a black horse, leads
five miles of red, gray, blue, and green.
Regiment after regiment.
Soldiers and sailors, young and old,
march in lockstep.
Eyes front, chests out, arms swinging.
Left, right, left, right.
Legs strut and splash themselves.

The militias dip their colors in tribute
at Pulitzer's building and the viewing stand.
The Rochambeau grenadiers raise
their glistening swords to their lips.
President Grover Cleveland salutes
the bullet-torn flags of past wars.
"Bartholdi! Bartholdi!" people cry
as they see him on the viewing stand.
Three girls race up to give him flowers.

550

Children in school uniforms,
heavy-footed policemen with shiny brass buttons,
firemen decked out in red shirts
alongside their horse-drawn steam engines,
cheering, "Hi-yi-yi-hi."
Navy men with big white hats.
Zouaves with fire-red pants.
Soldiers wounded in past wars ride
in carriages with judges and governors.

And the marching bands,
so many, all playing at once.
O say can you see . . .
Arise, ye sons of France, to glory . . .
I wish I was in the land of cotton . . .
I'm a Yankee Doodle Dandy . . .
A din of drums and horns and tubas.

Finally, General Washington's carriage,
drawn by eight dappled gray horses.
Yays and hoorays for the Continental Guards.
The city is one vast cheer.

Liberty! The most important word in the world.
I know that all too well.
I was deported from my country, Cuba,
for fighting to free my people from Spanish rule.

AUGUSTE BARTHOLDI
Sculptor
Bedloe's Island, October 28, 1886

Liberty's face is hidden beneath our tricolors.
I see easily through to her magnificence.

I wend my way through the crowd
to climb up to Liberty's crown.
Surrounded by her beams and ribs,
I mount the 354 steps, remembering
the hundreds of thousands of people—
French and American—
who helped realize my dream.
If only Laboulaye were alive to see her.

I crouch to look through her windows.
I wave to the boy below who will signal me
at just the right moment.
Tugboat whistles and trumpet fanfares
clash in the damp air.
Cannons fire deafening salutes.

Finally quiet. A blessing.
One speech. A second speech.
I cannot hear anything over
the shrieking tugboats.

The boy waves his hand.
At last, it is time.
I loosen the cord holding the tricolors
over Liberty's face.

The flag falls.
Lady Liberty is visible in all her glory.
Cheering and shouting rip the air.
Roaring cannons, belching foghorns,
drumrolls, trumpet flourishes.
Arise, ye sons of France, to glory . . .
O say can you see . . .

Every part of her shouts freedom.
In one hand she holds a tablet,
engraved with July 4, 1776.
In her other hand she holds a torch.
These flames do not destroy.
Mon Américaine does not conquer with weapons.
True liberty triumphs through Truth and Justice and Law.

She wears a flowing robe
like the ancient goddess *Libertas*.
Her right foot is raised.
Liberty walks.
Freedom never stands still.
A broken shackle and chain lie near her feet.
America broke the links of slavery
to fulfill its promise of equality for all.

President Cleveland steps forward.
The crowd quiets.
"We will not forget that Liberty
has made her home here," he says.

More cheering and shouting.
On and on, a glorious explosion of noise.
Like a hundred Bastille Day celebrations.

I feel perfect happiness.
This symbol of unity and friendship
between two great republics will last forever.
It has taken more than twenty years, but
the dream of my life is accomplished.

553

The New Colossus

by Emma Lazarus

Not like the brazen giant of Greek fame,
With conquering limbs astride from land to land;
Here at our sea-washed, sunset gates shall stand
A mighty woman with a torch, whose flame
Is the imprisoned lightning, and her name
Mother of Exiles. From her beacon-hand
Glows world-wide welcome; her mild eyes command
The air-bridged harbor that twin cities frame.
"Keep, ancient lands, your storied pomp!" cries she
With silent lips. "Give me your tired, your poor,
Your huddled masses yearning to breathe free,
The wretched refuse of your teeming shore.
Send these, the homeless, tempest-tost to me,
I lift my lamp beside the golden door!"

Write the answers to the questions on these pages in your notebook. Use evidence and details from the text to support your answers.

Text Connections

1. How did connections between the United States and France lead to the idea for the Statue of Liberty?

2. Why do you think immigrants and regular people, rather than very wealthy people, were the ones who gave money to create the Statue of Liberty's pedestal?

3. On the day the statue is unveiled, why do you think marching soldiers honor Joseph Pulitzer by dipping "their colors in tribute at Pulitzer's building"?

4. How does the section about Emma Lazarus in "Lady Liberty: A Biography" connect with the poem "The New Colossus"?

5. Describe a time you worked on a long-term project, and connect your experience to that of the design and building of the Statue of Liberty.

6. Why does the Statue of Liberty still inspire people today?

Did You Know?

Gustave Eiffel, who created the frame for the Statue of Liberty, next helped create the Eiffel Tower in Paris. As workers began the tower in 1887, many protested, saying it would be ugly. However, as with the Statue of Liberty in the United States, the Eiffel Tower is now an important symbol of France.

Look Closer

Keys to Comprehension

1. Why didn't workers digging the foundation on Bedloe's Island complain about the rough work? Use details from the text to support your inference.

2. What is a theme of "The New Colossus"? Explain how details support it.

3. Explain the procedure workers used to create the full-sized statue, using Bartholdi's four-foot clay model.

Writer's Craft

4. Describe the structure the author uses to tell Lady Liberty's biography.

Concept Development

5. How do the illustrations on pages 548 and 549 help you better understand the process workers used to fit copper sheets on the skeleton?

6. Using information from Doreen Rappaport's account in "Lady Liberty: A Biography" and Pearl Libow's account in Unit 3's "Hope and Tears," describe what the Statue of Liberty meant to immigrants who came through Ellis Island.

Write

In one kind of acrostic poem, the first letter of each line spells out a word. Create an acrostic poem about the theme of freedom, with lines that spell out the word *liberty*. Use at least two words from "The New Colossus," like "welcome" and "free," in your poem.

Read this Science Connection. You will answer the questions as a class.

Text Feature

A **figure** in informational text is a visual that helps you understand the content.

Fighting Corrosion

When Frederic Auguste Bartholdi designed the colossal Statue of Liberty, he knew it would need to be able to withstand rain and salt spray. Much of the statue weathered well. However, Lady Liberty's torch was another story. For the monument's first hundred years, the torch was a source of trouble. The reason for the problems relates to the science of corrosion.

Bartholdi wisely chose copper for the statue's outer layer. This metal develops a patina, or film, that protects it. Originally, the torch was also to be protected with a solid "skin" of copper. However, at the last minute, people cut holes in the torch. They put lights inside it so the torch would actually shine. It didn't work. One newspaper at the time said it was "more like a glow worm than a beacon." In 1916, artist Gutzon Borglum redesigned the torch. He cut apart the copper and installed colored glass windows, with electric lights shining out (see figure 1).

A glowing torch might have seemed like a good idea, but the changes caused a big problem—leakage. Over time, water seeped in through cracks around the windows. Under the copper layer, the statue is made of iron. When water, oxygen, and iron come into contact, an oxidation reaction happens, forming rust. Rust causes corrosion, making the metal come apart. Rust ate away at the insides of the torch.

In the 1980s, the National Park Service renovated Lady Liberty. Workers removed the corroded torch and replaced it with one based on Bartholdi's original plan. Today, the torch is completely covered with copper, and the flame's copper layer has a layer of gold, which never corrodes (see figure 2). It is protected from the corrosive power of rust.

1. How did installing windows in the Statue of Liberty's torch cause problems?

2. What affects the rate of erosion caused by rust? Test this using the following experiment:

   a. Gather 3 pieces of steel wool, 3 paper cups, and a small amount of cooking oil. Fill Cups 1 and 2 halfway with water. Leave Cup 3 dry.

   b. Place 1 piece of steel wool in each cup. Push it under the water in Cups 1 and 2. Pour a layer of oil on top of the water in Cup 2.

   c. Observe the cups over several days. Which metal rusts the fastest? Why do you think that is, based on the Connection information?

Figure 1: The torch, with Gutzon Borglum's windows, removed during the restoration

Figure 2: The torch after its replacement in 1985

 Go Digital

The copper on the outside of the Statue of Liberty was originally a reddish brown, but over the years a chemical reaction resulted in its green patina. Research why this happens to copper.

The Smithsonian Institution

by Elliot Young
illustrated by Peter Bull

Who wouldn't like to climb inside a spacecraft that flew to the moon and back? Many people might like to see dinosaurs fight one another! Film buffs worldwide might be interested in gazing at a pair of glittery ruby slippers worn long ago. Visitors to the Smithsonian Institution can have these experiences and many more!

The Smithsonian is a series of museums and research centers based in Washington, D.C. Its purpose is to preserve United States history and heritage. Smithsonian historians and curators constantly collect new information. In addition, they share their knowledge with everyone in the United States and people around the world.

The Smithsonian Institution is the largest museum in the world. The Institution includes nineteen separate museums, in addition to galleries, gardens, and a zoo. It also supports facilities in other places—from bustling New York City to the small village of Bar Harbor, Maine.

The first Smithsonian building was designed to house artwork and laboratories for study. It also included a library and a lecture hall. The building was large and inspiring, and it opened to the public in 1855.

The Smithsonian Institution Building, also known as The Castle, was its first building. It houses the visitor center and is located close to the White House and the Capitol.

ESTABLISHING THE SMITHSONIAN

The Smithsonian would not exist without an Englishman named James Smithson. Smithson studied science, especially chemistry and minerals.

Smithson believed that science could improve the way people lived, especially for individuals at a disadvantage in society. When he died in 1829, he left the United States all his money and belongings. His only requirement was that the country had to create "an establishment for the increase and diffusion of knowledge" named the Smithsonian Institution.

It was a curious act, for Smithson had never even visited the United States! No one knows why he would leave such an enormous sum to a foreign country. He left no clues, and he confided to no one. He merely asked that in addition to housing world treasures, the Smithsonian should discover new knowledge and share it with the world.

Smithson did not clarify what the Smithsonian should be. Should it be a university? Should it be a library or research center? Should it be a publishing house? Should it be an observatory? It took ten years of debate to decide. In the end, it has become all these things, except one. The Smithsonian is not a university.

1829 James Smithson names the United States government in his will.

1890 The Smithsonian founds the Astrophysical Observatory.

1891 The National Zoological Park opens.

1850

1900

1846 Congress passes Smithsonian Act of Organization.

1910 The National Museum of Natural History opens.

1855 The Smithsonian Institution Building opens.

562

Early in its history, the Smithsonian made a big impression. In 1848, the Smithsonian began a project that would become the National Weather Service. Scientists began tracking storms and studying weather patterns. This service still exists today. By 1878, people regarded it as the leader in scientific research. More important, the institution fulfilled its purpose of sharing its knowledge with people all over the world.

Leaders realized if the public were to benefit from the Institution, its rooms would have to be filled with exhibits. Scientists began collecting and preserving wild animals. Teams gathered samples of rocks. Citizens donated documents, books, scientific tools, and works of art.

Curators designed exhibits of the collected artifacts and specimens. Finally, in 1881, the United States National Museum opened, and people could view the collections. This museum is now known as the Arts and Industries Building of the Smithsonian. Over the next ten years the Secretary and Board of Regents authorized the building of an observatory and a national zoo. After that, the Smithsonian grew with the addition of more and more facilities and museums.

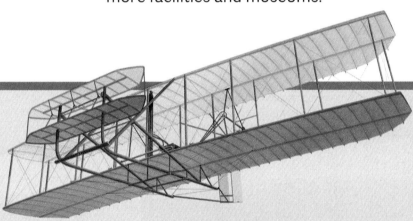

2004 The National Museum of the American Indian opens.

1976 The National Air and Space Museum opens.

2016 The National Museum of African American History and Culture opens.

1950   2000

1993 The National Postal Museum opens.

1964 The National Museum of American History opens.

1967 The Anacostia Community Museum opens.

BRINGING A NEW MUSEUM TO LIFE

The National Museum of African American History and Culture is the most recent Smithsonian museum to open. On September 24, 2016, it became the nineteenth museum, but it took more than a hundred years to establish! How did this museum come to be?

To create a new museum, Congress must approve a proposal and agree to the funding. In 1915, African Americans who had fought in the Civil War asked for a memorial and museum in Washington, D.C. Congress was open to the idea, and fourteen years later, the president signed a bill that would create a memorial. However, that was 1929, the same year that the country fell into the Great Depression. Banks failed, people lost their jobs, few people could pay taxes, and the federal government had little money. The idea was shelved, and later, forgotten—at least for a while.

In the 1960s, 1970s, and 1980s the idea arose again and again. In 1988, Congress concluded that honoring African American history in a museum was a worthy idea, but again, they had no money to fund it. The idea for funding the museum was reintroduced in each Congress for the next thirteen years.

Then, in 2001, Congress passed and the president signed a new law. It finally gave the Smithsonian permission to plan a new museum. This new museum would honor the contributions made by African Americans to the history and culture of the United States.

The next tasks were not simple. A director had to be named. A location had to be identified. Funding had to be secured. The building had to be designed. The museum's founding director became responsible for guiding all of these tasks. Over more than a decade, with enormous diligence, effort, and teamwork, the museum took shape.

At the same time, a team of curators sought items for the collection that would highlight the history and contributions of African Americans. People across the nation donated items from their own lives or ones handed down to them by their ancestors. The curators carefully considered each artifact and its story.

In 2016, a dream came true when the National Museum of African American History and Culture opened to the public. People have flocked to the museum—so many that visitors must reserve passes far in advance.

CURATING THE COLLECTIONS

Where have the artifacts on display come from? Scientists and historians contributed many items in the Smithsonian's collections. Some artifacts in the museum have been on expeditions to the depths of the oceans and outer space. Still more artifacts have come from the general public. Anyone with a rare artifact can contact the Smithsonian to donate it. However, the Smithsonian museums do not accept everything. Museum curators only save artifacts they do not already have or are especially unique.

Innovating the Preservation Process

Inside a museum's doors, one may find a dinosaur skeleton looming down from the ceiling. The dodo, a flightless bird now extinct, might be on display. Or a Stone Age axe used more than two million years ago might be available for study. These are real-life artifacts.

Not all artifacts can, or should, be brought to a museum for display, however. Some must be left where they are found. Technology makes it possible for the Smithsonian to preserve and display such artifacts. As a result, the Smithsonian also has a virtual collection.

For example, the Smithsonian is working to preserve stone monuments in Mongolia. These monuments, called Deer Stones, show pictures of deer flying, which are important to the cultural heritage of the Tsaatan people who live nearby. In Mongolia, these monuments are outside and unprotected. Instead of removing them from Mongolia and displaying them in a museum, scientists are protecting them in another way.

Scientists take laser scans of these monuments. The scans can capture images of bird droppings and small growths of plants. At the museum, scientists can watch the scans for changes. For example, lichen eats away at stone when it secretes an acid as it grows. By virtually simulating this growth, scientists can decide how much of a threat these plants are. If the shape of the virtual stones begins to change, the lichen can be removed.

Scientists at the Smithsonian save the scans. They are a record of the cultural heritage of the Tsaatan people. These scans preserve the artifacts as a digital copy, in case something later happens to the actual stones.

EXPLORING THE MANY MUSEUMS

The Smithsonian museums are vast, and it would take months to explore them all. The following is a small taste of what some of the museums have to offer.

National Air and Space Museum

The National Air and Space Museum is dedicated to the study of flight. It holds the most important flight machines and artifacts since humankind first entered the air above Earth.

Wright Flyer. Orville and Wilbur Wright had a dream: They wanted to fly the first machine-powered airplane. In 1899, they wrote to the Smithsonian asking for information about aeronautics, the science of flying. The brothers used this information to design their first glider, a machine that flies without engines. Later, they used wind data from the U.S. Weather Bureau. They decided that Kitty Hawk, North Carolina, was the best place to test their invention. Finally, in 1903, they made the first mechanical flights—the last one flying eight hundred fifty-two feet in fifty-nine seconds. They had indeed flown!

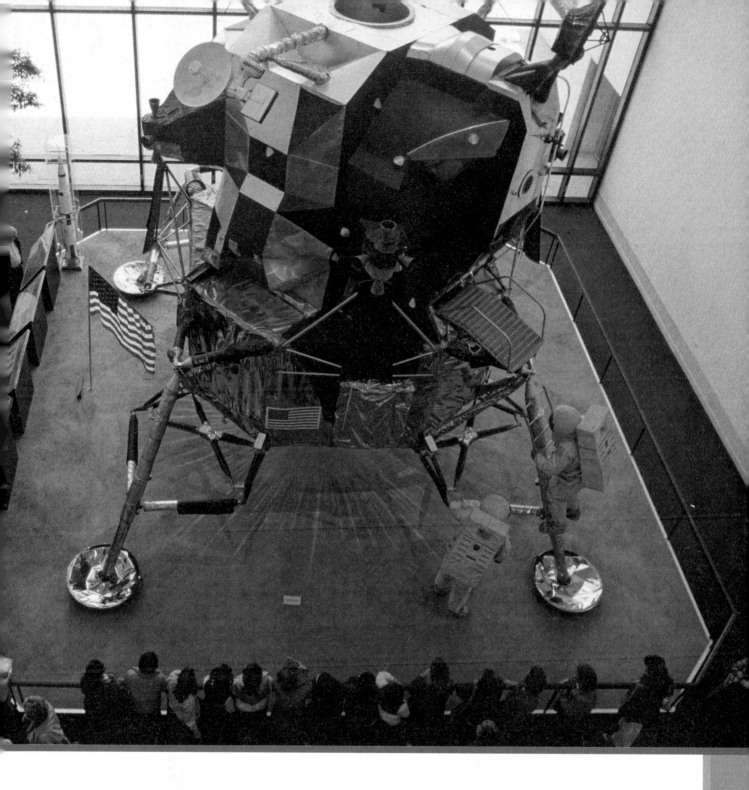

The Apollo Lunar Module. The Apollo Lunar Module 2 is on display at the National Air and Space Museum. Although it was never launched, the module was used for ground testing. Then it was modified to resemble the Apollo 11 Lunar Module and put on display at the museum. The Apollo 11 Lunar Module carried the first astronauts to the moon. The landing portion of that spacecraft cannot be displayed on Earth because it is still on the moon!

Steven F. Udvar-Hazy Center

Some aircraft are too large to display at the Smithsonian's National Air and Space Museum, so the Steven F. Udvar-Hazy Center was built in Virginia to show off these huge artifacts.

Lockheed SR-71. Called the Blackbird, this huge aircraft was a spy plane for twenty-four years. On its last flight, it broke a speed record. It averaged 2,134 miles an hour (3,434 kilometers an hour) flying from Los Angeles to Washington, D.C.! The aircraft landed in Washington on March 6, 1990. Then the United States Air Force turned the Blackbird over to the Smithsonian.

Space Shuttle *Discovery*. This spacecraft flew more miles than any other space shuttle—more than 136,000,000 miles! *Discovery* began flying in 2005 and flew for six years. It carried 145 astronauts in its thirty-eight flights. It hauled parts for the *International Space Station (ISS)*. It also transported food, supplies, satellites, and astronauts to the *ISS. Discovery* found its final stop at the Smithsonian after its last flight in 2011.

National Museum of Natural History

Inside the National Museum of Natural History, an African bush elephant stands in a large circular room. It even frightens some, because it looks like it might charge at any moment. Visitors encounter sea creatures as well, such as the blue whale. Dinosaurs don't roam the earth anymore, but exhibits of them exist at this museum. The museum's many displays feature creatures still alive today and those that are extinct.

Some objects are truly out-of-this-world. Visitors gaze at moon rocks or meteorites that have fallen to Earth. If it is a living thing or object found in nature, this museum will house it.

National Museum of American History

The National Museum of American History focuses on the history of the United States. This museum displays artifacts of war, the first American cars, ball gowns worn by the First Ladies at the White House, and so much more.

The Civil War. Artifacts from the Civil War, 1861-1865, include muskets used in the war. You can see the blue uniforms worn by the Union soldiers and the gray uniforms worn by the Confederates. Exhibits explain how the war started, how it was fought, and how it was won.

America Moves. Americans have traveled in so many ways. They've used bicycles, airplanes, trains, subway cars, boats, and automobiles. Americans are known worldwide for their love of cars, and many are on exhibit at the National Museum of American History. The museum features one of the first cars, the 1894 Balzar. The museum shows how automakers have kept improving automobiles, from the 1903 Cadillac and the 1913 Model T to the first electric car in the 1990s, called the EV1.

Anacostia Community Museum

The focus of the Anacostia Community Museum is on urban communities. The exhibits explore what has happened to shape the ways in which people in cities live. Researchers also observe and record trends today.

Photographs, artwork, and maps help tell the stories of past urban events. Past exhibits have shown how immigrants came to cities. Other exhibits have featured the folk-art forms practiced by people in cities. Still another has explained how waterways serve cities in the United States.

National Postal Museum

The US Postal Service is known for quick and efficient mail delivery. Packages sent from hundreds of miles away usually arrive within a few days' time. However, mail delivery has not always been so timely. The National Postal Museum shows how the US mail system has improved since the early days of the Pony Express.

The National Postal Museum houses the largest stamp gallery in the world. The museum also features vehicles used to carry the mail, such as three early mail airplanes. A railway car used to carry the mail is on display, as is a 1931 Ford Model A postal truck.

The National Zoo

Smithsonian's zoo is world renowned. It features about two thousand animals. For example, the zoo is home to giant pandas, Asian elephants, tigers, gorillas, and cheetahs.

One of the zoo's missions is to protect animals all over the world. Scientists and researchers educate and train people to save animals from extinction. During the spring, winter, and summer, students can attend camps at the zoo. There they learn how scientists work to save wild animals.

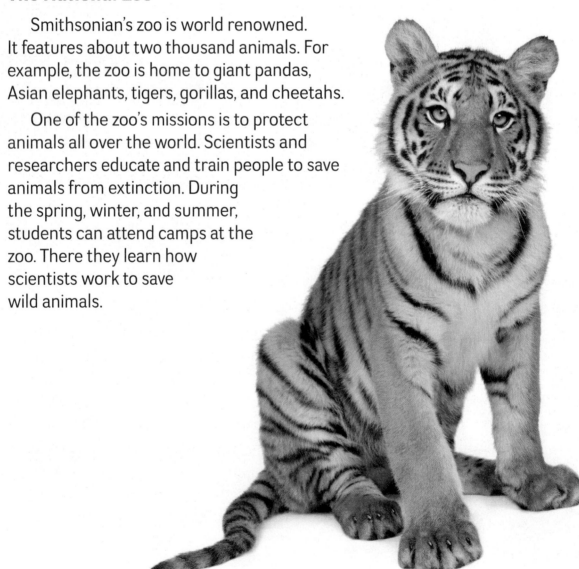

National Museum of the American Indian

Before Europeans arrived in what are now the Americas, Native Americans lived on the land. The National Museum of the American Indian has two museums—one in Washington, D.C., and one in New York City. The exhibits in these museums educate visitors about native peoples from Hawaii to Alaska to Florida. Visitors can see artifacts of clothing, jewelry, weapons, and artwork from Native American tribes.

However, the museum isn't a place only to honor past cultures and heritage. It is also where visitors can learn about the modern traditions and experiences of Native American nations.

THINKING INTO THE FUTURE

Part of the funding for each of the museums and the zoo is for a research department. Researchers in these departments discover new information or seek answers to lingering questions. They research the past, record the present, and look forward, thinking about the future.

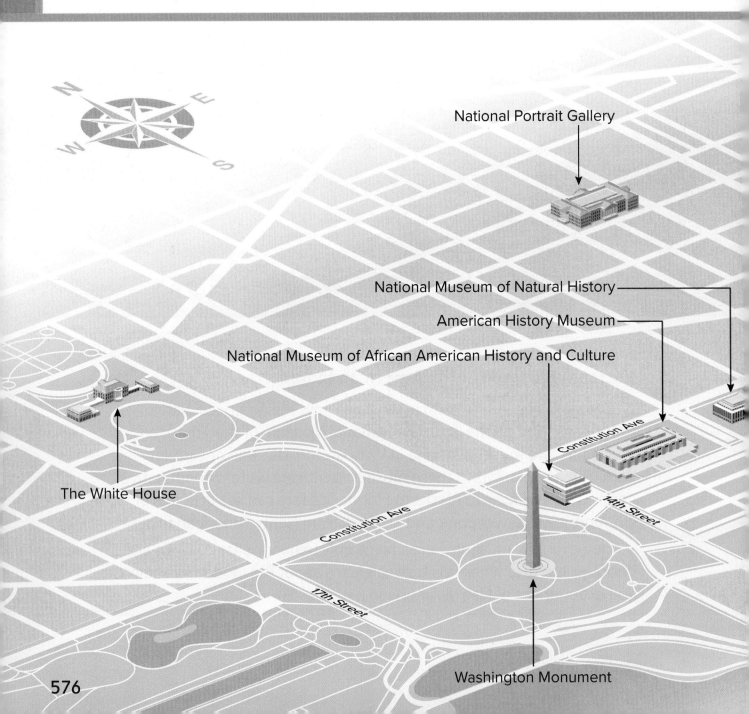

National Portrait Gallery

National Museum of Natural History

American History Museum

National Museum of African American History and Culture

The White House

Constitution Ave

14th Street

Constitution Ave

17th Street

Washington Monument

For example, scientists at the National Air and Space Museum are studying Mars. They are mapping the planet's surface, studying how water once flowed on it, and studying the impact of craters on its surface. At the National Museum of American History, researchers and curators are examining new trends in American culture.

The Smithsonian Institution continues to grow and expand. Following the intent of its benefactor, the Smithsonian Institution fosters curiosity and exploration for all!

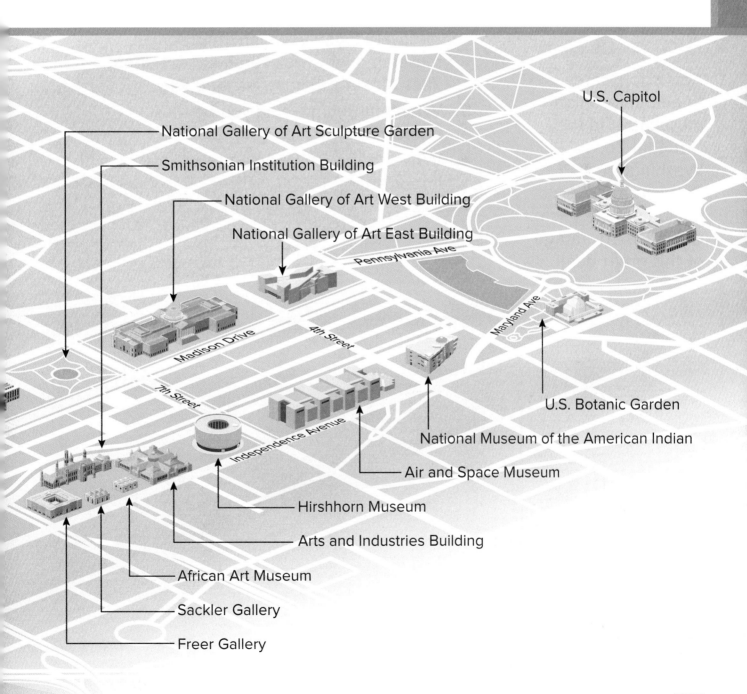

National Gallery of Art Sculpture Garden

Smithsonian Institution Building

National Gallery of Art West Building

National Gallery of Art East Building

Pennsylvania Ave

Madison Drive

4th Street

7th Street

Maryland Ave

U.S. Capitol

U.S. Botanic Garden

National Museum of the American Indian

Independence Avenue

Air and Space Museum

Hirshhorn Museum

Arts and Industries Building

African Art Museum

Sackler Gallery

Freer Gallery

Write the answers to the questions on these pages in your notebook. Use evidence and details from the text to support your answers.

Did You Know?

Admission is free to all Smithsonian museums and the National Zoo in Washington, D.C. On average, 30 million people each year take advantage of this great deal!

Text Connections

1. How do virtual collections help historians protect certain kinds of artifacts?
2. In which two museums could a special book owned by Dr. Martin Luther King, Jr., be housed, and why?
3. If you thought you had a rare item for the Smithsonian, how could you donate it?
4. Based on information in Unit 2's "The Discovery Fair," in which Smithsonian museum might you see an exhibit about Ynés Mexía's discoveries, and why?
5. Which museum would you be most interested in visiting? Explain.
6. Why are the Smithsonian museums important?

Look Closer

Keys to Comprehension

1. What is the story behind the creation of the Museum of African American History and Culture?

2. Explain the procedure by which people create a new Smithsonian museum.

Writer's Craft

3. Based on context in "The Smithsonian Institution," what is a curator's job?

4. Using information from "The Smithsonian Institution" and "The Diary of Orville Wright, 1903," compare and contrast the secondhand and firsthand accounts of the story of the Wright Flyer.

Concept Development

5. How does the map on pages 576 and 577 help you better understand all the types of museums the Smithsonian has to offer?

6. In what ways was James Smithson's gift a puzzle? Give evidence from the text to support your answer.

Write

Write a paragraph explaining which Smithsonian museum you would like to help curate and why. Use examples from "The Smithsonian Institute" to explain why you chose that museum.

Read this Social Studies Connection. You will answer the questions as a class.

Text Feature

A **block quotation** is a longer quotation that is set off from the main text. It does not include quotation marks.

The First National Weather Service

Can one man's passion for science change daily life for people across a country? In the case of Joseph Henry, first secretary of the Smithsonian, the answer is yes.

Henry was keenly interested in the beginnings of meteorology, or weather science. As soon as he began leading the Smithsonian, he called for "a system of meteorological observations for solving the problem of American storms." He recruited volunteers to make observations.

The great game changer of that time was the recent invention of the telegraph system. Henry realized that people could now send weather observations over the telegraph. This might make it possible to predict weather patterns across the country. The Civil War, however, caused problems for Henry's weather report network. Once the war ended, Henry decided to hand over his project to the federal government.

In 1870, a law was passed to create a national weather service. For the first twenty years, the U.S. Army Signal Service ran it. They sent weather forecasts on a regular basis.

In 1890, Congress gave the weather service to the Department of Agriculture. It became the U.S. Weather Bureau. Joseph Henry's dream had grown into a successful reality. As author and judge Charles P. Daly said,

> Nothing in the nature of scientific investigation by the national government has proved so acceptable to the people, or has been productive in so short a time of such important results, as the establishment of the Signal Service Bureau.

Washington, D.C., was the location of the U.S. Weather Bureau Signal Service's headquarters.

FIG. 143.—The U. S. Weather Bureau Station at Washington, D.C.

1. In what way did Joseph Henry and the Smithsonian change everyday life for U.S. citizens from the 1860s on?

2. How did the telegraph change the science of meteorology?

3. How are changes in communication technology affecting the way people learn about the weather today?

 Go Digital

Research other museums that are part of the Smithsonian Institution but are not mentioned in the selection "The Smithsonian Institution." How do they also fulfill James Smithson's mandate to increase and diffuse knowledge?

BIG Idea

Where do you see literature and art together?

Theme Connections

What themes of art and literature do you see here?

 Background Builder Video
connected.mcgraw-hill.com

Genre Tall Tale

Essential Questions
How do tall tales come to be?
How can tall tales influence art?

PAUL BUNYAN

by Dennis Fertig • illustrated by Olga and Aleksey Ivanov

A BIG, BIG BABY

For folks living on the coast of Maine, seeing heavy-looking clouds drift in from the sea isn't unusual. So on a day long ago, Papa Bunyan didn't think twice about the big cloud floating in the sky. He didn't even think twice about the group of birds flying around it. Of course, Ma Bunyan did.

Suddenly, Papa yelled, "Wait, that's not a cloud. It's a giant blanket!"

Ma smiled. "Yes, and those birds are storks."

"You mean our baby's coming?" yelled Papa, as he counted the storks. "It's a five-stork baby!"

Ma grinned. It WAS a five-stork baby.

Now it may not have happened just this way, but that's how most folks think Paul Bunyan came into this world.

Like any baby, Paul needed a cradle to sleep in. Papa made one, but Paul grew too fast and shattered it.

Papa cut down some tall trees, and the sound of Paul's howls knocked down a few more. Papa and Ma used that wood to make the largest cradle the world will ever see!

The Bunyans set the cradle in the water a little off shore. The gentle waves rocked the baby to sleep, but Paul's size made the cradle rock faster and faster. Soon the rocking caused great waves to crash into the coast! The colossal waves carved out big chunks of Canada just north of Maine. The gap formed a new body of water called the Bay of Fundy. Folks who don't believe it should look at a map!

PAUL ROAMS

As Paul grew, Papa taught him how to be a lumberjack. Soon Paul was toppling more trees than a spinning tornado.

Like most youngsters, Paul had dreams. One summer morning, teenaged Paul packed some tools and bade Papa and Ma good-bye. Paul traveled west to find tall trees and good lumberjack work.

Paul walked with long strides through Maine. After he crossed into New Hampshire, he hiked up and down the rugged White Mountains. He even jumped over a towering peak or two! Then Paul walked through the Green Mountain Forest on the border between Vermont and New York. In New York, Paul reached a forest clearing and went to sleep. After all, he had walked nearly three hundred fifty miles since leaving home that morning.

The next day, Paul woke up as thirsty as a mule, so he drank all the water in a nearby pond. It was a small pond, though, that covered only three acres.

Paul walked with huge steps across the state of New York. Some folks claimed they felt earthquakes as he walked. Then when Paul slipped and fell, he actually did cause an earthquake! His hands hit the ground so hard that they left long, deep ditches in the dirt. After rain filled those ditches, they became known as the Finger Lakes.

Paul walked quickly and covered another three hundred fifty miles by late afternoon. When he reached the Niagara River, he was very hot, so he made a cannonball jump into the water. His splash was so large that it took five days for the water to fall back to Earth. When the water fell, it created Niagara Falls!

Paul loved the falls and spent time digging out a large pit for the water from the falls to flow into. The pit is called Lake Ontario.

BIGGER AND STRONGER

Paul Bunyan was a strong, tall teen when he left Maine. Over the next few years, he grew into a stronger, taller man. Some folks say he was bigger than two tall men—maybe three men, maybe more—stacked on top of each other.

Paul had herculean strength, too, and used it. When he was in Pennsylvania, for example, he decided he liked digging new lakes, so he dug another one, which became Lake Erie. Paul dug fast, tossing huge shovelfuls of dirt up into the high west winds.

When Paul stopped digging, he looked up and discovered he was now in the state of Ohio.

Paul also dug the other three Great Lakes. When he was digging Lake Huron next to the state of Michigan, he noticed a huge forest of tall trees. Paul dug around the forest. That piece of land sticks out into Lake Huron. It forms the thumb in the mitten-shape of Michigan.

Curiosity and lake digging took Paul into Wisconsin. He spent some time working in Wisconsin logging camps. With his own crews, he cut down huge trees and floated them on wide rivers to sawmills. He logged so many trees that even today, almost every wooden building, bench, table, wagon, and doghouse contains drops of Paul Bunyan's sweat.

Paul worked with dozens of different lumberjacks. The lumberjacks made Paul into a legend of sorts. They swapped stories with each other about all the remarkable things Paul did. Some folks say those stories were exaggerations. Some tales might have been exaggerated, but not many.

A BLUE OX NAMED BABE

When Paul was lumberjacking with his crew in Minnesota, he made a special discovery. It was in the Winter of Blue Snow. The deep, drifting snow that year was actually blue! Look it up!

The snow was so deep that only a giant like Paul could trek through it. The good news was that lumberjacks didn't need to cut down trees. Heavy snows made them topple over.

One day, Paul spotted a patch of shivering blue snow. *Wow! It's really cold when the snow shivers,* he thought.

Paul brushed away the snow and discovered a half-frozen, teeth-chattering baby ox.

Paul noticed two strange things about this ox. First, it was as blue as the sky, maybe from the cold or maybe from the snow. Second, it was the biggest baby ox Paul had ever seen. It might even have been a five- or six-stork baby ox! Paul named the ox "Babe."

Babe grew quickly and soon was as long as Paul was tall. Babe was happy to work with Paul and his crew. Babe would pull heavy logs or wagons filled with tons of water and grub. Folks had always said Paul was as strong as an ox. Now they talked about an ox that was as strong as Paul!

Paul and Babe had some fine adventures. The best one was when they chased each other all over Minnesota. Their running, stomping game of tag created footprints that formed the ten thousand lakes of Minnesota!

After some years in Minnesota, Paul felt the urge to travel again. He loaded tools, food, cooking equipment, and large vats of water on a big sled that Babe pulled. As they crossed into Iowa, the big sled cleared acres of land for farmers to use.

GOOD DEEDS

For some time, Paul and his crew worked in the Missouri forests, near the Mississippi River. Paul did more than cut trees. When the river flooded, he had Babe drink river water while Paul built a huge dam. But Babe gulped so much water that the dam wasn't needed!

Folks in Kansas heard how Paul and Babe cleared farmland in Iowa, so they sent one hundred twenty-eight officials to Missouri to ask Paul to do the same in Kansas. Paul agreed, and Babe gave all one hundred twenty-eight officials a free ride back to Kansas on his big sled. The sled cut a deep, wide path in Missouri. Folks say the Lake of the Ozarks now fills part of that path.

From Kansas, Paul and Babe and their crew traveled west. Paul still could walk as fast as a pronghorn antelope could run. Babe was a bit slower, so Paul let the ox rest in the middle of Nebraska. Paul wanted to see what was ahead, so he built a three-hundred-foot tall tower to stand on. Today, folks call it Chimney Rock.

The friends traveled through South and North Dakota, and had a few small adventures along the way. One time big, big Paul helped a family find a lost child. Paul found the boy on top of Black Elk Peak, the highest mountain east of the Rockies, and jumped to the top of the mountain to rescue him. That boy grew up to be the governor of South Dakota.

Paul also stopped a charging herd of buffalo from destroying a small town in North Dakota. He lassoed all one hundred of the beasts with one giant rope!

A SAD TIME

Paul and his lumberjack crew worked all over the West. It was hard, but it was work Paul loved. Babe loved it, too, but Paul knew work was getting harder for his old friend. One summer evening in Montana, Paul could tell Babe was feeling under the weather. That night, Babe died in Paul's big arms.

Paul thought back to the day he found Babe shivering in the snow. The discovery was a blessing. Babe had become his best friend.

Paul started to weep big, big tears and did not stop for days. His tears pooled up and flowed south. Folks say Paul's tears were the beginning of the Missouri River. The incredible thing is that the new river flowed past or through many of the places Paul and Babe had logged.

Paul and his crew moved on to Wyoming. It was hot and dry. The crew needed water. Paul looked for an underwater spring. With mighty swings of his ax, he dug holes in the ground. On the third swing, he hit a gusher, but it was not cool drinking water that burst out. It was a geyser of hot water and steam. Paul had just opened Old Faithful! He used the hot water to make tea for the crew.

While traveling in Colorado, Paul visited the Rocky Mountains. He was shocked when he read a wooden sign at the top of the highest peak. It said:

These Rocky Mountains were formed by dirt
Paul Bunyan flung miles into the air when
he dug the Great Lakes.

PAUL STILL FEELS YOUNG

The Rocky Mountains also reach into New Mexico. Paul planned to log the forests there. In Colorado, Paul told his crew to meet him in a New Mexico forest near Wheeler Peak. Paul planned to jump from one Rocky Mountain peak to the next until he reached Wheeler Peak.

Paul and his crew left on the same day. The crew worried Paul was too old to leap from mountain to mountain. Paul was a bit worried too.

As the crew took wagons full of supplies along snow-packed roads, Paul jumped from one mountain peak to another. At first, he was careful. Soon, though, he was jumping from peak to peak as fast as possible. He was as strong as in the old days!

The peaks were snow-covered and slippery, and Paul slid down a mountainside feet first! His huge body knocked down trees and made a wide, smooth path into a valley. Today, that route is called the Taos Ski Valley. That's on a map too. People today probably never think about Paul Bunyan as they ski down the mountain.

The most important thing for Paul was arriving in the forest before his crew. In fact, Paul had logged half the trees by the time they arrived.

Paul did feel a tad tired for a time after his race to Wheeler Peak. This may be why he dragged his big ax behind him as he visited Arizona, Utah, and Nevada. By the way, that's how Paul and his heavy ax carved out the Grand Canyon.

A NEW FRIEND

As Paul grew older, life became more difficult. In California, he fell out of a gigantic redwood tree. He wasn't hurt much, but trees crashed all around him. Folks say his fall created a long, deep crack along the West Coast. It's called the San Andreas Fault.

Over the years, Paul heard about a big, strong lumberjack in Canada named Big Joe Mufferaw. Folks told almost as many stories about Big Joe as they told about Paul. By chance, Paul met Big Joe in the Cascade Mountains, which stretch from California to Canada.

Like Paul, Big Joe enjoyed jumping from mountaintop to mountaintop. They met because both Paul and Joe jumped onto the same mountain at the same time. That mountain shrunk about twenty feet! The two men stared at each other. They weren't sure they liked each other. It was good they both knew not to judge a book by its cover.

After Paul and Big Joe had a brief mountain-jumping contest, they talked. They swapped stories as they walked through Oregon and Washington. They cooked suppers over mountaintop campfires and put the flames out with huge rocks. Folks say they created two big volcanoes that way— Mount Hood and Mount Rainier.

They talked so much that they walked right into Canada and didn't know it!

The two became good friends. Folks say they continue to swap stories even to this day as they hike together through the Cascade Mountains.

Write the answers to the questions on these pages in your notebook. Use evidence and details from the text to support your answers.

Did You Know?

Many places across the United States have enormous statues of Paul Bunyan, as well as Babe the Blue Ox. Two towns—Bemidji, Minnesota, and Bangor, Maine—not only have huge statues of Paul Bunyan, but also claim to be the place he was born. Some Paul Bunyan statues, such as the one in Bemidji and another in Portland, Oregon, are on the National Register of Historic Places.

Text Connections

1. How does Babe get its name?
2. What are the main landforms Paul Bunyan creates?
3. According to the author of "Paul Bunyan," how does Paul Bunyan's work in Wisconsin lead to the first stories about him?
4. Why do you think Paul Bunyan and Big Joe become such good friends?
5. How are Paul Bunyan stories similar to the *pourquoi* stories in Unit 4's "How & Why Stories"?
6. What kind of people do you think might especially love Paul Bunyan stories?

Look Closer

Keys to Comprehension

1. How does digging Lake Ontario lead to a new hobby for Paul Bunyan? Give details from the text to support your answer.

2. Why do you think Babe the Blue Ox is the only pet Paul Bunyan ever has? Use text examples to support your inference.

3. Based on details from the text, describe the character of Paul Bunyan in depth.

Writer's Craft

4. Look up "Hercules" in an encyclopedia. What does the text mean when it says Paul Bunyan has "herculean strength"?

5. What genre is "Paul Bunyan" and how do you know? How might it have been different if it had been written as a poem?

Concept Development

6. How does the illustration on page 588 help you better understand Paul Bunyan's physical qualities? Connect it to the description in the text on that page.

Write

Choose another United States landform and write a short Paul Bunyan tall tale to explain how it was formed. How does your story compare to one found in "Paul Bunyan"?

Read this Social Studies Connection. You will answer the questions as a class.

Text Feature

A **caption** gives more information about a photograph.

Advertising a Folk Hero

As an American folk hero, Paul Bunyan had an unusual journey to fame. Although he began as the subject of stories told by lumberjacks in the 1800s, he actually became popular because of an advertising campaign.

In 1913, a logging company was expanding. They began in Minnesota but had started running a sawmill in Westwood, California. They wanted to get out the word that they could handle really big orders.

Into this situation walked a man named William B. Laughead. Laughead had worked in the logging business. However, Laughead was interested in advertising and loved drawing cartoons. By chance, he came up with the idea of putting the logging stories about Paul Bunyan into a little booklet advertising the lumber company. At first, no one liked it. Laughead realized the problem was that, outside lumber camps, no one had heard of Paul Bunyan.

As a result, Laughead and the logging company created ads to educate people about Paul Bunyan. The company taught their salespeople how to spread the stories. Quite suddenly, Laughead's pamphlet, "The Marvelous Exploits of Paul Bunyan," took off in a big way. People all over the country began reading Laughead's stories and cartoons.

Before Laughead's advertising campaign, a story and poem had already been published about Paul Bunyan. However, it was Laughead that made him famous. Laughead also created Babe the Blue Ox as well as many other characters. It was a lumber company's ad campaign that made Paul Bunyan a well-known character across the United States.

1. What people first told stories about Paul Bunyan?

2. How do advertising designs and storytelling influence American popular culture?

3. How do media like television and the Internet spread cultural ideas today?

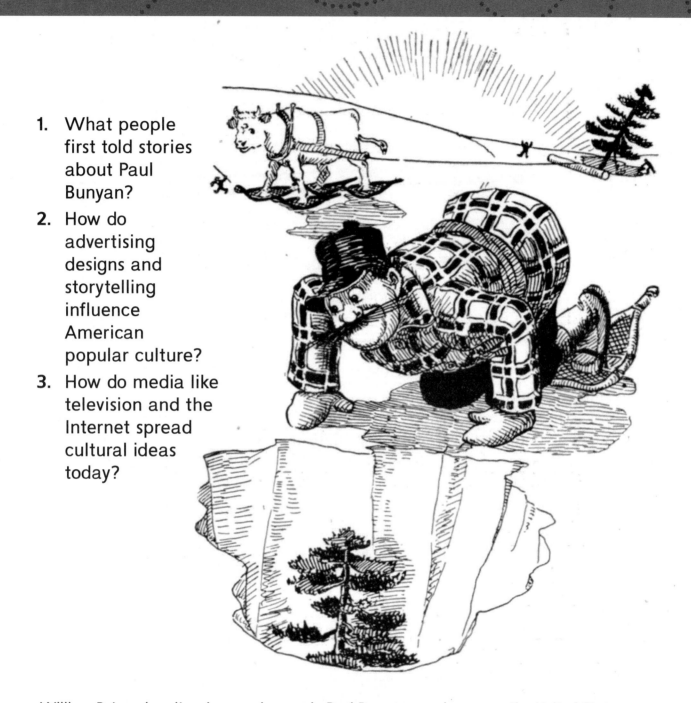

William B. Laughead's ad campaign made Paul Bunyan popular across the United States. The story that goes with this illustration begins, "The Winter of the Deep Snow everything was buried. Paul had to dig down to find the tops of the tallest White Pines."

 Go Digital

Research places across the United States that feature statues of Paul Bunyan and Babe the Blue Ox. Why might a community build such a statue?

Genre Myth
Essential Questions
What kinds of stories are told in mythology?
How can mythology influence art?

The Labors of HERCULES

by Vidas Barzdukas
illustrated by Olga and Aleksey Ivanov

Hercules was the greatest hero in all of Greece. Although his mother was mortal, his father was the almighty Zeus, the king of the gods. When Hercules was a baby, the goddess Hera sent two snakes into Hercules's crib. Despite his being an infant, Hercules was already as strong as an ox, so he seized both snakes before they could harm him. When his mother heard the commotion and rushed into the nursery, she found a giggling Hercules clutching a wriggling snake in each hand.

As Hercules grew, so did his courage and prowess with the bow and sword. He became the greatest wrestler in Greece, defeating any opponents who dared challenge him. By the time he was a young man, Hercules was the strongest man on Earth.

Hercules married Megara, and they had three sons.
Although his marriage to Megara brought him great
happiness, it also brought him unbearable sorrow. The
goddess Hera, still jealous of Hercules, knew she could not
defeat the mighty hero in battle. Instead, Hera caused a
horrible accident that killed Megara and her sons.

When Hercules discovered what had happened, he was
overcome with grief. In his distress, he prayed to the god
Apollo, who told him that for his penance he must visit his
cousin, Eurystheus, the King of Mycenae.

"A horrible tragedy has been brought down upon my
family because of me," Hercules told King Eurystheus, who
looked upon Hercules with pity. "I must cleanse myself of the
guilt I feel in my heart."

King Eurystheus thought for a moment. "To relieve
yourself of the guilt you feel, you will perform labors that
help others," he said. "But I won't lie to you, Hercules. These
labors are nearly impossible to complete and involve great
risk. However, if you complete these labors and help others,
you will become Greece's greatest hero."

Hercules picked up his bow and sword. "I'll do them."

The Lernaean Hydra

One of the first labors Hercules had to complete was to defeat the dreaded hydra, a nine-headed dragon that lived in a swamp and terrorized the countryside. Hercules traveled to the swamp with his nephew, Iolaus. The swamp was a furnace with leafy green flora that covered the soggy ground like a blanket. Poisonous fumes rose from the brackish water, making Hercules gag. Covering their mouths and noses with pieces of cloth, Hercules and Iolaus tried to protect themselves from the toxic fumes. Iolaus waved his torch about, searching for any fauna that might be dangerous.

Finally, the two men came to the hydra's lair, a dark cave located in a large hill. Using Iolaus's torch, Hercules lit an arrow and fired the flaming arrow into the cave.

Suddenly, the hydra shot out of the cave and rushed toward Hercules. For a moment, panic gripped his heart as the charging monster neared. Then Hercules remembered that fortune favors the brave and pulled out his sword. With a mighty swing, the sword cut through the air and chopped off one of the hydra's heads. Whatever satisfaction Hercules and Iolaus felt quickly evaporated as two heads suddenly sprang up from the severed stump!

"I have an idea!" Iolaus yelled. As Hercules cut off another head, Iolaus sprang forward and used his torch to burn the spot where the head once grew. Now additional heads could not sprout. Using this method, Hercules and Iolaus were able to defeat the hydra.

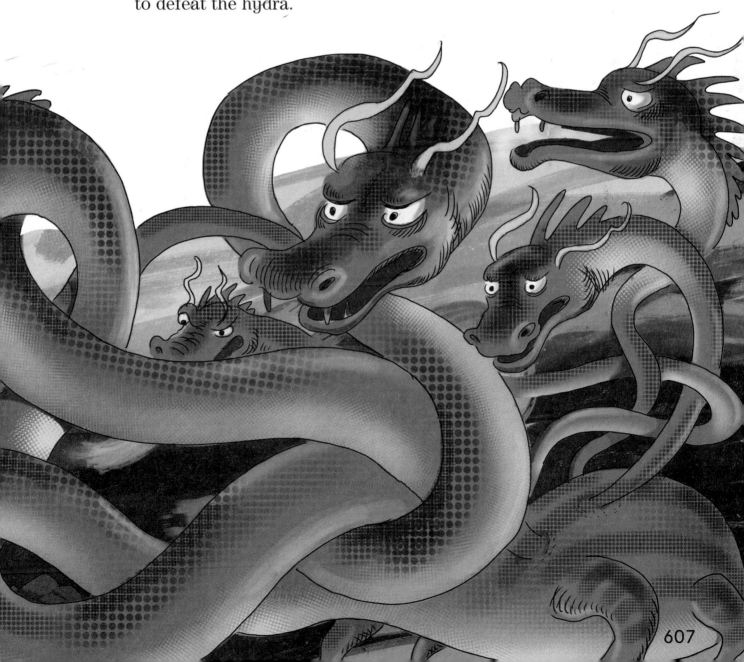

The Hind of Ceryneia

The next labor took Hercules an entire year to complete. King Eurystheus tasked Hercules with capturing the hind of Ceryneia, or a female red deer living north of Eurystheus's palace. Normally capturing a deer was an easy task for Hercules, who was a master hunter. However, the hind of Ceryneia had golden horns and bronze hoofs, which made it so fast it could outrun an arrow. In addition, the hind was sacred to Artemis, the goddess of hunting. Hercules knew that hurting the hind would bring Artemis's wrath down upon him. What was he to do?

Hercules chased the hind for an entire year, stalking it across Greece and not giving it a chance to rest. Finally, the hind became too exhausted to run away and lay down near a stream, where Hercules captured it easily with a net. On the way back to King Eurystheus's palace, however, Hercules saw Artemis approaching.

"What are you doing with my hind?" Artemis asked angrily. Her brow darkened as she prepared to unleash her wrath and punish Hercules. However, Hercules quickly explained the tragedy that befell his family and the labors he had to complete for King Eurystheus. Artemis felt sorry for Hercules and let him go.

The Erymanthian Boar

For Hercules's next labor, King Eurystheus commanded him to capture the Erymanthian boar, a vicious, titanic pig with a nasty temper and tusks as sharp as daggers. Every morning, the boar charged out of its cave high atop a mountain and gored people and animals living in the countryside, ripping up crops and gouging holes in people's homes on its rampage.

Hercules tracked the boar through the snow to its lair inside the cave. At first he considered charging into the cave with his spear. Then he remembered that discretion is the greater part of valor. Instead, Hercules screamed as loud as he could into the cave, causing the boar to rush out in terror. Hercules chased the boar, whooping and hollering, and waved his spear over his head. Finally, he drove the boar into a snowbank and trapped it with a net.

When Hercules returned to the palace with the wriggling boar slung over his wide shoulders, King Eurystheus shrieked and ran out of the room.

609

The Augean Stables

The next labor on the odyssey took place at the Augean Stables. Hercules smelled the stables before he came within ten miles of them. That is because the owner, King Augean, had more than a thousand bulls, sheep, cows, and horses that he kept in the stables. To make matters worse, the filthy stables had not been cleaned in many years. And to make matters even worse than that, King Eurystheus gave Hercules only a single day to clean them!

Hercules pinched his nose and sat on a tree stump. He was deep in thought as flies buzzed around his head. Hercules was gazing at the animals drinking from two nearby rivers when the solution finally hit him like a ton of bricks. His idea would require a lot of work. But he remembered that a journey of a thousand miles begins with a single step, so he sprang to his feet and went to work.

First, Hercules grabbed a large axe sitting nearby and chopped a giant hole into one wall of the stable. Then he ran to the opposite wall of the stable and chopped a hole directly across from the first opening. Next, Hercules picked up a shovel and ambled over to the rivers, the sheep and cows scattering as he drew near. Finally, he dug a deep trench from the rivers to one of the openings he'd cut in the stable wall. The sun was a golden ball that rolled from one end of the sky to the other as Hercules worked.

When all was ready, Hercules dug out the last bit of dirt from the trench. With a mighty roar, the rivers gushed through the trench and flowed through the stables in a great flood. Hercules had diverted the rivers so they flowed through the stables instead. In a matter of minutes, all the filth left from thousands of animals washed away. After the stables were clean, Hercules put the rivers back as he had found them.

The Cretan Bull

Hercules did not have much time to rest, however. His next labor took him to the island of Crete off the coast of Greece. It was there that Minos, the king of Crete, had promised to sacrifice a bull to Poseidon, the god of the sea. However, King Minos thought the bull was too beautiful to give to the god, so he kept the bull for himself and sacrificed another bull instead. When Poseidon found out about this deception, his anger exploded like a volcano. The god cursed the bull with madness so it would run wild and terrorize people living in Crete.

When Hercules arrived to capture the bull, he tracked it to its hiding place. The bull spotted Hercules and put down its head, showing its curved horns, and pawed at the ground in anger. Then it charged.

Hercules stood as still as a statue and held his ground as
the bull rushed at him. Seconds before the horns could impale
him, the hero grabbed the bull's horns and twisted his wrists,
wrestling the bull to the ground. The bull was stunned. Before
it could react, Hercules quickly tied its hooves together with a
piece of rope and brought it back to King Eurystheus.

"Well done," King Eurystheus said, eying the bull warily.
"But your labors are not yet complete. Your next task may be
the most dangerous one yet. You must visit King Diomedes of
Thrace and capture his horses."

"What's so dangerous about a few horses?" Hercules asked.

"These horses eat people," King Eurystheus answered.

Hercules thought for a moment. "Maybe I'll take some
warriors with me."

The Horses of Diomedes

The next day Hercules sailed to Thrace with a group of warriors. As they neared the stables, Hercules and his band of warriors heard music coming from within. Hercules peeked inside and discovered several grooms tending the horses. One of the grooms was playing a flute. When Hercules gave the signal, the warriors rushed inside and overpowered the grooms.

"Tie the mares' mouths shut," Hercules commanded. "It's better to be safe than sorry. And then take the horses to our boats on the beach."

Hercules and the warriors quickly led the horses out of the stable and toward the beach where their boats sat in the sand. However, before Hercules could load the horses onto the boats, they heard a shout. It was King Diomedes. Behind him was an entire army of his finest soldiers!

"What are you doing with my mares?" King Diomedes yelled. "Release them at once!"

Hercules laughed and pulled out his sword. Behind King Diomedes, his army of soldiers pulled out their swords too. Even an entire army of armored soldiers was no match for Hercules and his band of warriors. The battle was over quickly, and the defeated King Diomedes and his army retreated to the safety of their homes. When the last soldier was over the hill, Hercules led the mares onto his boats and sailed back to King Eurystheus.

"Excellent job," King Eurystheus said, eying the man-eating mares warily as they ran around the stable and gnashed their teeth at the stable hands. "Your next labor will take you to the far-off island of Erytheia. Your task is to bring back the cattle of Geryon."

"What's so bad about Geryon?" Hercules asked.

"You'll find out when you get there," King Eurystheus said, and quickly hurried back to the palace.

Geryon's Cattle

The next morning, Hercules boarded his ship and set sail across the shining sea. After several days, he came across a large mountain jutting into the water. Hercules decided to commemorate his journey by splitting the mountain in two. These mountains became known as the Pillars of Hercules.

When Hercules arrived on the island of Erytheia, he heard a loud bark that rumbled across the sky like thunder. It came from a gigantic two-headed dog that bounded toward him. Hercules defeated the dog easily and then heard a commotion behind him. When Hercules finally spotted Geryon coming toward him over a hill, his noble heart fell.

Geryon was part man and part monster, with three heads, six arms, and six legs. The monster was armed with three shields and three spears that flashed in the morning sun as it charged Hercules. Even worse was the monster's bad breath. Hercules raced to a river to escape the monster, but then realized his way was blocked. Hercules turned and pulled an arrow from his quiver, aiming it at the monster. He let loose the arrow and thus defeated Geryon. With the monster and his watchdog defeated, Hercules loaded the cattle onto his ship and returned to King Eurystheus.

When King Eurystheus spotted Hercules entering the palace, he was jubilant.

"Congratulations, Hercules! You have completed the labors!" the king said. "Your penance for the deaths of your family is over. Because you completed the labors, the gods have given you the gift of immortality!"

Hercules would go on to have many great adventures and perform more amazing deeds. However, none were as great as the labors he completed for King Eurystheus. After he performed his last glorious feat, the gods took Hercules to Mt. Olympus. There he lives today beside his father, Zeus, entertaining the gods with stories of his adventures.

ODE ON A HERCULEAN VASE

by Andreas Chryssos

Though hearts adorn this terracotta jar,
No love from Hera flowed to Hercules.
Instead, her hatred marked him like a scar
To live his days without one thought of ease.
Consigned to serve a king who forged a plan
Impossible—for any other man.

So, on the hardened surface painted here
A scene plays out (though none upon it move),
Nine-headed Hydra, monster most severe,
Brave Hercules, with knife in hand, must prove
The stronger one, despite its poison bite,
And sever all its heads by firelight.

The helper for this task, his brother's son,
Who grasps the serpent's head within his fist,
While Hercules, whose work has just begun,
Is taunted by a crab, but must persist.
A wingéd sphinx observes behind a bloom,
Waiting for the epic battle to resume.

For centuries this story will be told
By poets and in choruses sublime.
A hero rendered here in black and gold,
His chore a mythic message for all time.
One labor out of twelve, forever still,
To honor both his wisdom and his skill.

Write the answers to the questions on these pages in your notebook. Use evidence and details from the text to support your answers.

Did You Know?

Greek myths helped create many English words. For example, the word *herculean,* meaning "of great size" or "very difficult," comes from *Hercules.* Because of a character named *Echo* whose longing turned her into nothing but a voice, we have the English word *echo.* Other English words from mythology include *atlas, east, west, helium, museum,* and *night.*

Text Connections

1. King Eurystheus tells Hercules that if he completes the labors and helps others, he will become "Greece's greatest hero." Was the king right? Explain.

2. Look up and define the words *discretion* and *valor.* How did Hercules's method of catching the Erymanthian boar prove the meaning of the saying "discretion is the better part of valor"?

3. Which labor do you think was the most difficult, and why?

4. In both "The Labors of Hercules" and "Paul Bunyan," each hero is said to be "strong as an ox." Name one way each proves this claim as a baby.

5. Based on the Read Aloud "Inspiring Connections: Art and Literature," why do you think artists so often portray Greek myths like "The Labors of Hercules"?

6. What character qualities make Hercules a hero?

Look Closer

Keys to Comprehension

1. How does the meaning of the proverb "a journey of a thousand miles begins with a single step" help Hercules as he cleans the Augean stables?

2. Describe in depth the character of Artemis, based on her actions.

Writer's Craft

3. Explain the double meaning of the title of the poem "Ode on a Herculean Vase."

4. Describe how "The Labors of Hercules" would have been different if Iolaus had told the story in the point of view of Unit 2's "My Brothers' Flying Machine."

Concept Development

5. How are both "The Labors of Hercules" and "Paul Bunyan" examples of quest stories? How are their quests different?

6. Compare and contrast how "The Labors of Hercules" and "Ode on a Herculean Vase" tell about Hercules and Iolaus fighting the hydra.

Write

Write your own description of one of the monsters Hercules faced. Be sure to use plenty of descriptive adjectives and adverbs, including at least two adjectives or adverbs from the selection.

Connect | Social Studies

Read this Social Studies Connection. You will answer the questions as a class.

Text Feature

A **numbered list** organizes information that belongs in a particular order.

Ancient Pottery Tells a Tale

Sometimes, the materials from which art is created can be as important as its subject matter. This is certainly true for ancient Greek pottery. Although ancient artisans also created wooden carvings and painted murals, few have survived. Pottery, however, was sturdy enough to last. By studying it, modern historians can see how Western art developed.

In the city of Athens during 600–500 B.C., two important changes came to pottery:

1. **Eastern cultures changed Greek art.** Up until that time, artists decorated vases with geometric designs. However, when Greece began trading with Asian cultures, they saw new kinds of pottery. Many Greek artists began imitating it. They painted pottery with animals and monsters, as well as myths.

2. **Athenian artists invented new techniques.** Around the same time, artists in Athens started making black-figure pottery. Potters formed red-clay vases using a wheel. They created a special slip, or liquid clay, and painted and decorated the vases. They then used a three-step firing process. It made the special slip turn black.

The new techniques led Athenian artists to create complex, detailed scenes few others could match. Many showed stories of the titanic hero Herakles, later called Hercules by the Romans. Historians today can see how Athenian artists became better and better at showing realistic human forms. By studying this artwork, we can learn both about ancient Greek values and the growth of their artistic techniques.

This cup is an example of black-figure pottery. It shows Herakles and his patroness, Athena.

1. Why did Athenian vases survive when wooden carvings did not?

2. How and why did Asian artistic forms spread to ancient Greece?

3. What is a benefit of contemporary artists being able to easily share their art with a worldwide audience?

 Go Digital

Research to find a map of Greece and its surroundings, and locate the real-life places related to the labors of Hercules, including the villages of Erymanthia, Keryneia (Ceryneia), the Lerna region of springs, the island of Crete, and the area of Thrace.

Genre Folktale

Essential Questions
What themes are found in literature around the world? Why do different cultures have literature with similar themes?

Little Red RIDING HOOD

by Brothers Grimm retold by Karen Martin
illustrated by Christine Kornacki

Once upon a time a young, carefree girl whom everyone loved lived in a small village in the country. One year, the girl received a gift from her beloved grandmother. It was a red velvet riding cloak with a sweet, little hood. Everywhere she went, the girl put on the cloak to protect herself from the sun, the wind, the rain, and the snow. Soon, the villagers called her Little Red Riding Hood.

The girl lived with her mother in a tidy little cottage. Her mother worked hard to support them. Little Red Riding Hood did everything she could to help. She baked bread and swept the floor. She did the laundry too.

Everyone in the village helped take care of each other. Almost every day, neighbors stopped by to help the girl and her mother with difficult tasks. Mr. Goodly helped them fix their fence. Farmer Able helped them plow their field. The girl and her mother repaid their neighbors as best they could. They gave Mr. Goodly, who had no cow, several quarts of fresh milk for his children. Farmer Able, a widower who didn't like to cook, took home a basket full of fresh-baked tarts and bread.

One blustery spring day, Little Red Riding Hood was hanging shirts to dry in the morning sun. A woman hailed her from the road that passed by the cottage. It was Mrs. Barley, a friendly woman who lived in the village.

"Little Red Riding Hood," Mrs. Barley called out loudly, "where is your mother? I have important news!"

Right away, the girl became concerned. After all, it wasn't every day that someone had "important news" in their village. "What's the matter, Mrs. Barley?" she asked, hurrying over to the garden gate to speak with the woman. "Mother has gone to the market, and she won't return for another hour."

"I've been to visit your grandmother, my child, and she is quite ill, I'm afraid. She has a terrible cold and is at home in bed, coughing and sneezing. I thought your mother would want to know."

"Oh, that *is* important news," Little Red Riding Hood exclaimed. "Thank you, ma'am. I'll be sure to let my mother know as soon as she comes home."

Soon after her mother returned, the girl left the cottage with a large basket in hand. Her mother had packed it full of her grandmother's favorite things: a crock of chicken soup, a loaf of crusty bread, and a little pot of butter too. Her grandmother lived in the next village, on the other side of the dark forest. Little Red Riding Hood knew the way, but she had never walked there by herself.

"Stay on the path," her mother advised in a serious tone, "and come straight home after you've delivered the basket. Don't dawdle, and don't talk to any strangers on the way."

"I won't, Mother," the girl agreed as she pulled up the hood of her cloak and stepped outside.

Little Red Riding Hood had not traveled far on the path into the forest when she encountered a wolf.

"Greetings, young lady!" the wolf addressed her in a pleasant voice. Having never met a wolf, the girl did not know he was a dangerous, untrustworthy creature. She remembered her mother's warning about talking to strangers. *But he seems perfectly nice*, she rationalized to herself. *Surely it would be rude to ignore him.*

"Where are you going in such a hurry?" he asked slyly, sizing up the girl. *How delicious she looks!* thought the wolf. *What a fine, plump meal she would make!*

"I'm taking a basket of food to my sick grandmother in the next village," the girl replied. "She lives in the stone cottage with the three large oak trees in front."

"The poor woman!" the wolf exclaimed. "How terrible it is to be sick. But look here, many beautiful flowers grow in the woods. Why don't you pick some and take them to her with the food? Flowers will surely cheer her, and it won't take long to gather some."

"I really shouldn't . . ." Little Red Riding Hood said reluctantly, looking around at the lovely blossoms not far off the path. "But Grandmother *would* like them, so I suppose a few minutes wouldn't hurt." She stepped off the path into the thick forest and began gathering flowers one by one. Each flower she gathered took her farther into the woods, farther away from the path.

Meanwhile, the devious wolf slipped away to find the grandmother's house. *Foolish girl!* he thought. *Now I will eat them both!* He hustled down the path toward the village and the stone cottage with the three oak trees in front.

Soon the wolf stood before the cottage, where he lifted a hairy paw to knock on the wooden door. He heard a cough and a sneeze from inside the house.

"Who is it?" a soft voice called out.

The wolf pitched his voice high and answered, "Grandmother, it is your granddaughter, here with food for you. Open the door, and let me in."

"I am too sick to get out of bed," the unwell woman answered feebly. "Lift the latch, and the door will open."

The wolf lifted the latch, and immediately the door swung open. There lay the girl's grandmother, looking sickly and miserable. Without a word, the wolf sprang toward the bed and swallowed her whole! Then he slunk to the nearby chest of drawers and selected a nightgown and cap to help hide his coarse hair and big ears. The crafty wolf crawled under the covers to await the arrival of the little girl.

Back in the forest, Little Red Riding Hood soon realized how much time she had spent picking flowers.

"I am dawdling, just as Mother told me not to do. I must go to Grandmother's!" she exclaimed anxiously, as she pushed through the snarled brush to find her way back to the path. Suddenly, a large figure loomed in front of her, and she screamed in fright.

"Don't be alarmed, Red Riding Hood. It's only I, out snaring rabbits for my family's table."

"Huntsman Grady!" the girl breathed a sigh of relief, recognizing the kindhearted man who lived in her village. "You startled me."

"My apologies, miss. Tell me," he said, sounding concerned, "where are you going all by yourself through these woods?"

"Mother has sent me to the next village with a basket of food for my grandmother, who is ill."

"I see," he nodded, and then inquired, "Did I see you speaking with some creature on the path not long ago?"

"It was a wolf," she answered, as she put the flowers she had gathered into her basket.

"I thought so," he said gravely. "Red Riding Hood, did you tell the wolf where you were going?"

"Yes . . ." the bewildered girl hesitated, "I didn't think . . ."

The huntsman offered her a hand and quickly assisted her back to the path. "We don't have a moment to lose, then, because that wolf is not to be trusted. Your grandmother is in danger—he may already be at her house!"

They hurried down the path as quickly as the girl's legs would allow. As they proceeded, Little Red Riding Hood and Huntsman Grady devised a plan to capture the wily wolf.

When they arrived at her grandmother's cottage a few minutes later, the door was open.

"It is just as I feared," the huntsman grimaced. "The wolf has beaten us here. You know the plan, Red Riding Hood. Entice the wolf to come outside, but don't go near him! I will lay the trap and be ready for him when he comes out."

"I will!" she cried resolutely. She set the basket of provisions beneath one of the giant oak trees in front of the house. Then Little Red Riding Hood drew in a breath and stepped bravely across the door's threshold.

The room was dim, for the windows were all closed, but Little Red Riding Hood could make out a figure lying in her grandmother's bed. "Grandmother!" she called. "Are you well, Grandmother? Come out into the light where I can see you."

"Come closer, child," croaked the wolf from under the bedcovers. "I am too ill to get out of bed."

Little Red Riding Hood took two steps toward the bed but stayed well out of reach of the wolf. "Grandmother, your voice sounds so strange!"

"It's only because I have this terrible cold, my dear," the wolf said, coughing loudly and dramatically.

"Why then, you should come outside, for the fresh air and sunshine will do you good!" the girl tried to persuade the wolf.

"Oh, no," the wolf resisted, "I need to stay here in this warm, cozy bed. Come closer, child, and speak into my ear, for I can hardly hear you."

Red Riding Hood took one step closer to the wolf, still out of reach, and then cupped her hands and shouted, "But Grandmother, what big ears you have! You should be able to hear me from the next village!"

The wolf was growing impatient now. "Did you bring me anything tasty to eat? Bring it to me here in bed; I am famished, and I could use a good meal!" he lied, his belly stretched to fullness by the woman he had just swallowed whole. Even now, she was wiggling around in his stomach, punching and poking him from the inside.

Little Red Riding Hood took one more step toward the wolf, yet still out of reach of his hairy paws. "Yes, Grandmother, I have a wonderful picnic waiting for us outside. There's a crock of chicken soup, a loaf of crusty bread, and a little pot of butter I churned myself yesterday. Come outside, and let us enjoy it together," she cajoled the beast, not fooled by his act for one minute.

The wolf grinned broadly, showing his sharp, pointed teeth. *Now she is within my grasp,* he thought. *And I shall eat her in one bite!*

"Grandmother, what terrible, pointy teeth you have!" the girl said loudly, pretending to be afraid.

But the wolf was through pretending. "All the better to eat you with!" he snarled, flinging off the covers and jumping out of bed toward his prey.

The girl was ready, though, and quickly jumped away, making her escape through the front door and into the yard, where the huntsman was hiding. The wolf raced out after her, unaware of the trap waiting for him on the other side of the door.

Red Riding Hood sped across the yard toward the three big oak trees. A loop of rope, which she carefully avoided as she raced by, lay hidden amid the tall grass. The huntsman peered out from behind one of the trees, holding the other end of the rope.

Now the wolf came barreling after Little Red Riding Hood at full speed. *I will not let this tasty little morsel get away!* he vowed to himself, completely focused on the girl. He did not see the huntsman hiding behind the tree. Nor did he see the coiled rope hidden in the swaying grass. He stepped directly into the concealed loop as he chased after the girl.

At that moment, Huntsman Grady pulled with all his might. The loop closed around the wolf's ankle, stopping him in his tracks. He fell to the ground with a hard thud. Seconds later, the creature found himself hanging upside down as the huntsman pulled on the rope and dragged him upward into the air.

So swift and sudden was the yank of the rope that out fell the grandmother from inside the wolf's stomach! She landed in the patch of grass, looking dazed and rather frightened. Little Red Riding Hood rushed over and embraced her.

"Grandmother, Grandmother!" she cried. "Thank goodness you're safe! And as for you," she stood up and addressed the wolf, who was now dangling pathetically from the tree by one foot. "Shame on you for trying to trick me like that! And shame on you for eating my grandmother!"

The wolf answered her with a proud look, not sorry at all. "I am a wolf," said he. "That is what I do; it is my nature."

"Well, you won't be doing it here anymore," the huntsman growled at him. He threw a sack over the wolf and tied it shut firmly with the rope. "I'm taking you somewhere you can't hurt the good people of this land ever again!" He slung the sack over his shoulder and strode away, leaving Red Riding Hood to tend to her ill grandmother.

"My goodness, that was unpleasant!" the woman sputtered, coughing roughly and shaking her head.

The girl removed her cloak and spread it carefully across a patch of soft grass. "Come, Grandmother, sit down," she coaxed. "I've brought you a picnic from Mother—all your favorite foods."

Opening the basket, she neatly laid out the soup, bread, and butter on the cloak. She surrounded the meal with the pretty flowers she had gathered in the woods.

"How wonderful! I *am* rather hungry after all the excitement." Red Riding Hood's grandmother settled onto the cloak. She broke off a hunk of bread and slathered it with creamy butter from the little pot, and then took a bite.

"Have some soup, too, Grandmother," Little Red Riding Hood urged as she handed her a bowlful. "It will make your throat feel better." As her grandmother ate, the girl related the entire adventure to her, from first meeting the wolf in the woods to how Huntsman Grady captured him in the snare.

Grandmother harrumphed, and said, "Well, I hope you learned a lesson today, my girl. Not everyone can be trusted!"

Sweet words may be easy on the ear
But think carefully on what you hear.
Do you know the person speaking?
Do you know just what they're seeking?
Do they want your harm or good,
Or are they telling a falsehood?
'Tis better by far to cautious be
Than become the dinner of one like he!

Write the answers to the questions on these pages in your notebook. Use evidence and details from the text to support your answers.

Did You Know?

By studying the many versions of "Little Red Riding Hood," some scholars now suspect that the oldest forms of this story may have been told about 2,000 years ago. The story changed as it spread throughout Europe and into Asia.

Text Connections

1. Describe the kind of people that mostly surround Little Red Riding Hood. How do her actions imply this?

2. Why does the wolf want Little Red Riding Hood to pick wildflowers?

3. Describe the plan Little Red Riding Hood and the huntsman use to catch the wolf. Do you think they expected to save her grandmother as well? Why or why not?

4. How are Fox in Unit 4's "How & Why Stories" and the wolf in "Little Red Riding Hood" alike?

5. If you were in Little Red Riding Hood's place, what would you do the next time you met a wolf in the woods?

6. How is the huntsman an example of a hero?

Look Closer

Keys to Comprehension

1. How does Little Red Riding Hood learn of her grandmother's illness? Give details from the text to support your answer.

2. Summarize "Little Red Riding Hood," and explain a theme of the story.

Writer's Craft

3. Explain the meaning of the Grandmother's advice, "Not everyone can be trusted," based on the story's context.

4. What section of "Little Red Riding Hood" is structured as a poem, and how do you know?

Concept Development

5. How do the text and the illustration on page 624 work together to help you better understand what a "riding cloak" and "hood" are?

6. How do Hercules in The Cretan Bull story of "The Labors of Hercules" and the huntsman in "Little Red Riding Hood" demonstrate the power of good over evil? Compare and contrast their actions.

Write

Write an explanation telling how "Little Red Riding Hood" is a useful story for teaching children to be *cautious.* Use evidence from the text.

Read this Science Connection. You will answer the questions as a class.

Text Feature

A **caption** is a phrase or sentence that gives more information about a photograph.

Wolves: Myth and Reality

Wolves are understood as villains in popular culture. Stories like "Little Red Riding Hood" show a lone wolf as a devious trickster. We use expressions like a "wolf in sheep's clothing" to describe a fraud.

Prejudice against wolves has had a real impact on ecosystems. In 1872, Yellowstone National Park became a protected wildlife area. Grey wolves were an important part of its ecosystem. Grey wolves usually live in packs. They communicate with one another through special sounds and care for their young. They hunt elk, deer, and small mammals, keeping their populations under control. Leftovers from wolf kills feed other animals.

However, people did not like wolves. They thought wolves should not prey on other park animals. Nearby farmers feared wolves would kill livestock. As a result, early park managers in Yellowstone helped kill off the park's wolves.

By the 1980s, similar policies across the country placed the wolves in danger of extinction. Scientists noticed ecosystem problems due to the missing wolves. In 1994, the U.S. Fish and Wildlife Service began reintroducing wolves to Yellowstone National Park. By 2016, hundreds again lived in the park and surrounding areas.

Park employees now work to educate the public. They produce informational literature with technical art—visual aids such as maps, charts, and graphs. Yellowstone also has a website with multimedia. Yellowstone workers persuade people that wolves are neither good nor bad. They are simply animals that function as part of an ecosystem.

A wolf in Yellowstone National Park

1. Explain some of the reasons people in the United States have traditionally disliked wolves.

2. Suppose someone told you that wolves in Yellowstone live alone and do not help the ecosystem. Construct an argument explaining in what ways that person's information is inaccurate.

 Go Digital

Research to find the fable connected to the expression "a wolf in sheep's clothing." How long have people been telling this story?

Genre Folktale

Essential Questions
How can themes be the same in literature from different cultures? How can they be different?

The Sun and the Moon

by David Park
illustrated by Jennifer Kindert

A very long time ago when the world was still covered in darkness, a mother and her two children, a boy and a girl, lived in a faraway valley. They were very poor, and the mother worked hard to take care of her little family. She made the most delicious rice cakes in all the land. Every day she carried fresh rice cakes to the closest village many miles away. She sold her cakes in the market, but she always held back a few for her children to eat when she returned home.

The son and daughter loved their mother and listened to her wise words. She warned them of the dangerous tigers in their region. "Never, ever open the door for anyone while I'm away," she told them. She knew how clever the tigers could be. Because her children were so good and obedient, the mother knew they would be safe while she was gone.

While their mother sold her rice cakes, the children did their daily chores. Big brother and his little sister were hungry by the end of the day. The rice cakes their mother brought home filled their stomachs and made them happy indeed.

One cold day, the mother left with her cakes as usual. She wrapped her head in a scarf and pulled on a coat for the long walk to the village. She went to the market and greeted everyone with a smile, selling her delicious rice cakes. Soon the market emptied, and the mother gathered her things to return to her home in the valley. She counted the remaining cakes—one, two, three, four—and put them in her basket. One rice cake for each of them and another to share as a special treat!

The mother walked the path she had traveled so many times before. She thought about the work she had to do after the children went to bed. It would be a long night of making more rice cakes. She grew tired just thinking about it but then thought of her son and daughter. They were the joy of her life. She picked up her feet and walked faster, eager to get home.

As she walked over the first of many hills on the way to her house, the mother saw a tiger walking toward her. She gathered her coat tightly around her, walked faster, and hoped he would not see her. But he did. The tiger let out a soft growl—or was that his stomach? He was hungry. He stopped in the path in front of the woman.

"What do you have in that basket?" he asked her.

"I am taking rice cakes home to my children," she answered, hoping he would let her pass without harm.

"I am very hungry, and I could eat you," he said. "But I will let you go in exchange for one of your rice cakes."

The mother remembered she had four, so she could give up the extra one without a second thought. She handed the tiger a cake, and he thanked her and let her go on her way.

Step by step, the woman hurried toward home, continuing on the path that was well-worn from all her days of making the same journey.

She was halfway home when the same tiger pounced onto the path again.

"I could eat you," he repeated, "but if you give me another rice cake, I will let you go."

"I will give you one more," the woman answered, "for I can sacrifice my meal. But I must keep the last two cakes for my children."

Two children, the tiger thought to himself. *Rice cakes are good, but children are extra delicious!* "I give you my word," said the tiger, who was not an honorable creature at all.

The woman took one cake from her basket and threw it toward the tiger. He swallowed it in one gulp and ran off.

When the mother was within view of her safe home where her dear children were waiting, she was frightened when she saw the tiger pacing the path between her and the house. She thought of the two remaining rice cakes in her basket. Would the tiger be so cruel as to take her children's food?

"Ah, we meet again," said the tiger, who had only grown hungrier after eating the small cakes.

"I will give you my last cakes if you will leave me alone," the woman cried.

"Yes, hand me those cakes," the tiger told her. She took them from her basket and held them toward the tiger. He took them and added, "Now give me your coat and scarf, for I am very cold."

The woman wondered how a tiger with such thick orange-and-black fur could be cold, but she knew better than to argue with him. She shivered as she handed the tiger her clothing.

647

Then the great creature pounced on her and carried her to a place where vines covered the trees. There he tied her up, tangling her in the vines so she could not escape. She would make a fine meal for another day. This day, however, the tiger was hoping to feast on children.

He put on the woman's scarf and coat, placing the two rice cakes in a pocket. He arrived at the door to her house and called out, "Children, your mother is home. Please, let me in!"

The brother and sister listened carefully to the voice at the door, but they did not open it.

"You do not sound like our mother," said the boy through the door. "We cannot let you in."

"I have caught a cold on my way home," the tiger answered, "and that is why my voice sounds so low. Please, let me in."

"You must prove you are our mother," the boy replied. "Our mother has warned us about tricksters who mean to do us harm."

"I have proof," said the tiger, and he slipped the two rice cakes under the door. "Here are the rice cakes I always bring home for dinner."

The boy and girl picked up the cakes and tasted them. Yes, indeed, they were their mother's delicious cakes! They unlatched the door.

As the tiger walked in standing upright, he held his head low so the children could not see his face. When the boy walked behind the tiger to close the door, he noticed a long, striped tail sticking out from his mother's coat.

"Sister! It's a tiger! Run, run, run!" he cried.

The girl was quick and dashed past the tiger before he could grab her. Her brother took her hand, and together they ran toward a grove of tall trees. They found a tree with many branches and climbed as fast as they could. Below, they could see the tiger charging toward them over the ground below. Up, up, up they climbed until they were at the very top of the tree.

When the tiger reached the trunk of the tree, he looked up through the branches.

"Come down, little ones!" he called. "I mean you no harm!"

But the children knew tigers could not be trusted. They also knew tigers were not the best tree climbers. They watched as the animal used his mighty claws to scramble up the trunk, only to slide back down because of his great weight.

"How did you climb so high?" he asked the children, hoping to learn their tree-climbing secret.

The boy was just as clever as the tiger, and he winked at his sister as he answered, "We used a special tar that is in that barrel beside our house. We covered the bark with it, and it helped us climb the highest tree!"

The tiger raced to the barrel and rolled it to the tree. He opened the lid and reached in, filling his paws with the substance inside.

He covered the tree trunk with tar and tried to climb. But it was not tar at all. It was thick, slippery oil! The tiger was enraged as he slid off the tree, unable to get any grip on the bark. He roared until the trees shook with the sound.

"I will not climb up to you," growled the tiger. "Instead, I will bring you down to me!" Then he went back to the house where he had seen an axe propped beside some firewood. The children watched as the tiger carried the axe toward the tree.

"What will we do?" cried the sister as she clung to the tree.

"Help! Help!" screamed the brother, hoping someone would hear and come rescue them from certain death.

Chop! Chop! Chop! The tiger kept hacking at the tree, making huge gashes in the trunk and shaking the tree with every strike.

"Help us! Oh, help us, please!" cried both children, who by now were terrified and wept at the thought of never seeing their mother again. Not far away, their mother heard their pleas and struggled to free herself. She became even more entangled and feared no one could save her son and daughter.

Even in the darkness, the children could tell the tiger had very nearly finished cutting the tree. They wailed louder and louder, knowing that within minutes, time would run out, and they could not be saved.

As they embraced each other, tears falling, they suddenly felt a thick rope beside them. It had appeared from the sky just in time! They grasped the rope and held on as it lifted them from the tree, from the earth, and beyond the clouds.

The tiger wondered why he no longer heard the children's cries. He looked up and saw a last glimpse of the children in the treetop. He saw the rope and realized his prey had escaped him again. Being a clever tiger, he thought perhaps if he sounded desperate, the giant rope would lift him, too, and take him to the children.

He wept, and he cried, and he howled. Just as he hoped, a thick rope dropped from above and landed at his feet. *Aha!* he thought. *You cannot get away from me!*

The tiger grabbed the rope, and it lifted him higher than he had ever been. Far above the treetops he climbed, hanging on with his sharp claws. As he climbed, the rope grew thinner and thinner, until it was just a few threads wound together. He was too heavy for the rope to hold him, and it snapped with a great POP! He fell like a rock into a field of millet. Exhausted and injured, the tiger returned to his lair to lick his wounds, determined never to bother with humans again.

The mother grieved, thinking her children had become victims of the tiger's hunger. Imagine her surprise when a bright circle in the sky appeared. She shaded her eyes with her hand and looked up. There she saw her daughter's face shining down upon her. She had become the sun, bringing light to the earth. In the light, the mother could see the vines that held her. She spent a full day unraveling them until she was free.

As the sun moved across the sky, the earth darkened again. Then another circle appeared above the clouds. The mother cried in joy when she recognized her son's face. He had become the moon, shining a soft light throughout the night. Now, in day and in night, the mother would forever see her children smiling down at her.

Write the answers to the questions on these pages in your notebook. Use evidence and details from the text to support your answers.

Did You Know?

Tigers are an important part of Korean culture and stories. Unfortunately, however, the Amur tiger of the Korean peninsula is endangered. It is likely only a few live in wild areas of North Korea, and today the greatest wild population is in Russia.

Text Connections

1. The children in "The Sun and the Moon" promise to never open the door to anyone but their mother. Do you think they broke their promise? Why or why not?

2. How do you know the tiger is a liar?

3. How does this mother's relationship with her children change because of this story's adventure?

4. Based on the explanation of *pourquoi* tales in Unit 4's "How & Why Stories," do you think "The Sun and the Moon" is a *pourquoi* tale? Explain.

5. Do you think there is anything the children or mother could have done differently in order to avoid the situation with the tiger? Explain.

6. Why do you think people all over the world tell stories like "The Sun and the Moon" and "Little Red Riding Hood" to their children?

Look Closer

Keys to Comprehension

1. Explain why rice cakes were important to the family in "The Sun and the Moon." Give text details to support your answer.

2. Describe in depth the setting of the confrontation between the tiger and the children at the end of "The Sun and the Moon."

3. How did the character of the tiger change at the end of "The Sun and the Moon"? Explain, using details from the text.

Writer's Craft

4. Explain what the mother meant when she thought about her children being "the joy of her life."

5. Describe changes you could make to turn "The Sun and the Moon" into a play.

Concept Development

6. Compare and contrast the patterns of events in "The Sun and the Moon" and "Little Red Riding Hood."

Write

Write a poem describing the son's or daughter's experience of coming to live in the sky. Use details from pages 652 and 653 when describing their journey.

657

Read this Social Studies Connection. You will answer the questions as a class.

Text Feature

A **table** organizes information related to informational text.

Have You Eaten Rice?

Rice has long been a central part of Korean culinary arts, or the art of making delicious food. One of the most common ways to greet someone in South Korea is to use a phrase that means, "Have you eaten rice?" In Korean, different words describe rice in various stages. Once cooked, rice is called *bap,* which can also mean "meal" or "main food."

Long ago, people in Korea began the art of making sweet rice cakes called *tteok*. These were a special treat. As rice became more available, Korean cooks invented many types of *tteok*. Some are stuffed with honey, bean paste, or other fillings. Some are coated with bean powders. Many became foods eaten at times of celebration like the New Year's festival or weddings.

Over the last sixty years, South Korean eating patterns have shifted. Rice consumption has gone down. (See Table 1.) A complicated set of reasons lie behind this change. In the 1970s, the South Korean government wanted to stop depending on rice from other countries. For a time, it required Koreans to mix other grains with rice. When these rules were lifted, rice consumption did not rise. By then, many people lived in cities. Many ate convenience foods made with wheat. Rice was sometimes more expensive than other food options.

Despite these changes, South Koreans still embrace rice and related foods like *tteok*. They are part of traditional celebrations, cultural meals, and memories. For many people there, the answer to "Have you eaten rice?" will continue to be "yes."

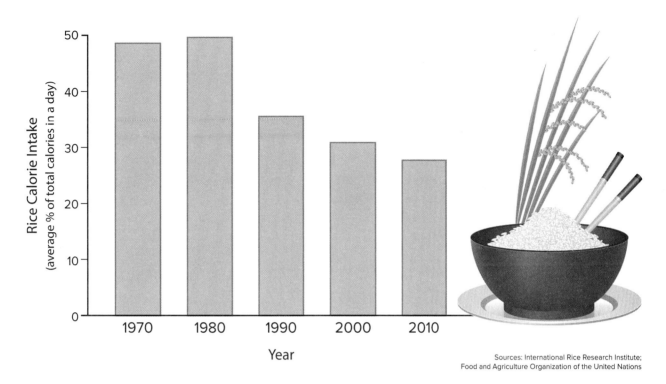

Table 1: South Korean Yearly Average Consumption of Rice

Sources: International Rice Research Institute;
Food and Agriculture Organization of the United Nations

1. How does rice relate to people's basic needs?
2. What influences have changed South Korean consumption of rice?
3. Based on the information in the connection and the table above, make a prediction about South Korean rice consumption in the next few years. Explain.

 **Go Digital**

Research to find images of *tteok,* or Korean sweet rice cakes. Compare these cakes with other kinds of celebration foods from various cultures.

Genre Fairy Tale

Essential Questions
What kinds of stories are told in fairy tales? How can fairy tales influence art?

Sleeping Beauty

*As retold in The Fairy-Tale Princess:
Seven Classic Stories from
the Enchanted Forest*

*sculptures by Su Blackwell
retelling by Wendy Jones
photographs by Tim Clinch*

Long, long ago, and far, far away, there was a king and a queen who lived in a splendid castle. Every day the queen said, "All I want is a child," but a child didn't come.

One day the queen was lying in a deep, warm bath when a great fat frog leaped out of the water.

"Your Majesty," it croaked. "Soon you will have a daughter."

"A daughter!" exclaimed the queen and smiled.

And so it came to pass. Within a year, the queen had a baby girl. The king was so delighted that he ordered a feast to celebrate.

"Invite all the lords and ladies, dames and knights," commanded the king. "And the wise women of my kingdom shall be the princess's fairy godmothers."

But there were thirteen wise women and only twelve silver plates so the thirteenth wise woman was not invited.

The feast was splendid, the hall magnificent and the food delicious. At the end of the feast, each wise woman gave the baby princess a magical gift. The first gave the gift of goodness, the second the gift of beauty, the third gave wealth, and the fourth gave kindness. When the last was about to give her gift, the thirteenth wise woman – the one who had not been invited – burst into the hall.

In a terrible, terrifying voice, she said, "In her fifteenth year, this princess will prick her finger on the needle of a spinning-wheel and she will die!" Then she turned and left.

The hall fell silent.

Fortunately, the twelfth wise woman had yet to give her gift. Although she could not undo the wicked curse, she could soften it.

"The princess won't die," she promised, "but she will fall asleep for a hundred years."

The king cried, "Burn all the spinning-wheels in my kingdom. At once!"

The princess grew up and was blessed with all the magical gifts the eleven wise women had bestowed upon her. She was beautiful, kind and full of grace. The wicked wish was forgotten.

And so it happened that on the princess's fifteenth birthday, the king and queen went out hunting and the princess was left alone. She wandered through the castle until she came to a tall tower. She climbed its narrow winding staircase and at the top found a small door. In the door was a rusty key. She turned the key, and inside the dark room, there was an old woman.

"Good day to you, old woman. What do you have there?" the princess asked, for she had never seen a spinning-wheel before.

"It's a spinning wheel for spinning wool," the old woman replied.

"And what is that?" asked the princess as she reached out to touch the spindle. But no sooner had she touched the wheel than she pricked her finger on the needle. The princess fell on the bed and into the deepest sleep.

The wicked wish had come true.

665

As the princess slept, so did the entire castle. The king and queen, returning home, fell asleep on their golden thrones. The horses fell asleep in the stable. The cook, who at that moment was reaching out to punish the kitchen boy, fell asleep, and so did the kitchen boy. The dog slept on the floor, and the cat too. The flies slept on the wall. All the servants, wherever they were, fell asleep. And the roast stopped sizzling when the fire stopped flickering.

Around the castle grew the thickest thorn trees, which reached higher and higher with every passing year, until only the tops of the tall towers could be seen.

Throughout the land people spoke of the sleeping beauty. Many princes tried to enter the castle, but they got caught in the thick thorns and could never free themselves and died.

Almost one hundred years later, a handsome prince was riding through the land when he met an old man, who told him about the castle behind the wall of thorns, and the sleeping princess within.

"Her name is Briar Rose," said the old man. "She is said to be as beautiful as she is graceful." And then he told the prince what had happened to the other princes before him.

"I am not afraid," the prince said. "I will see this princess."

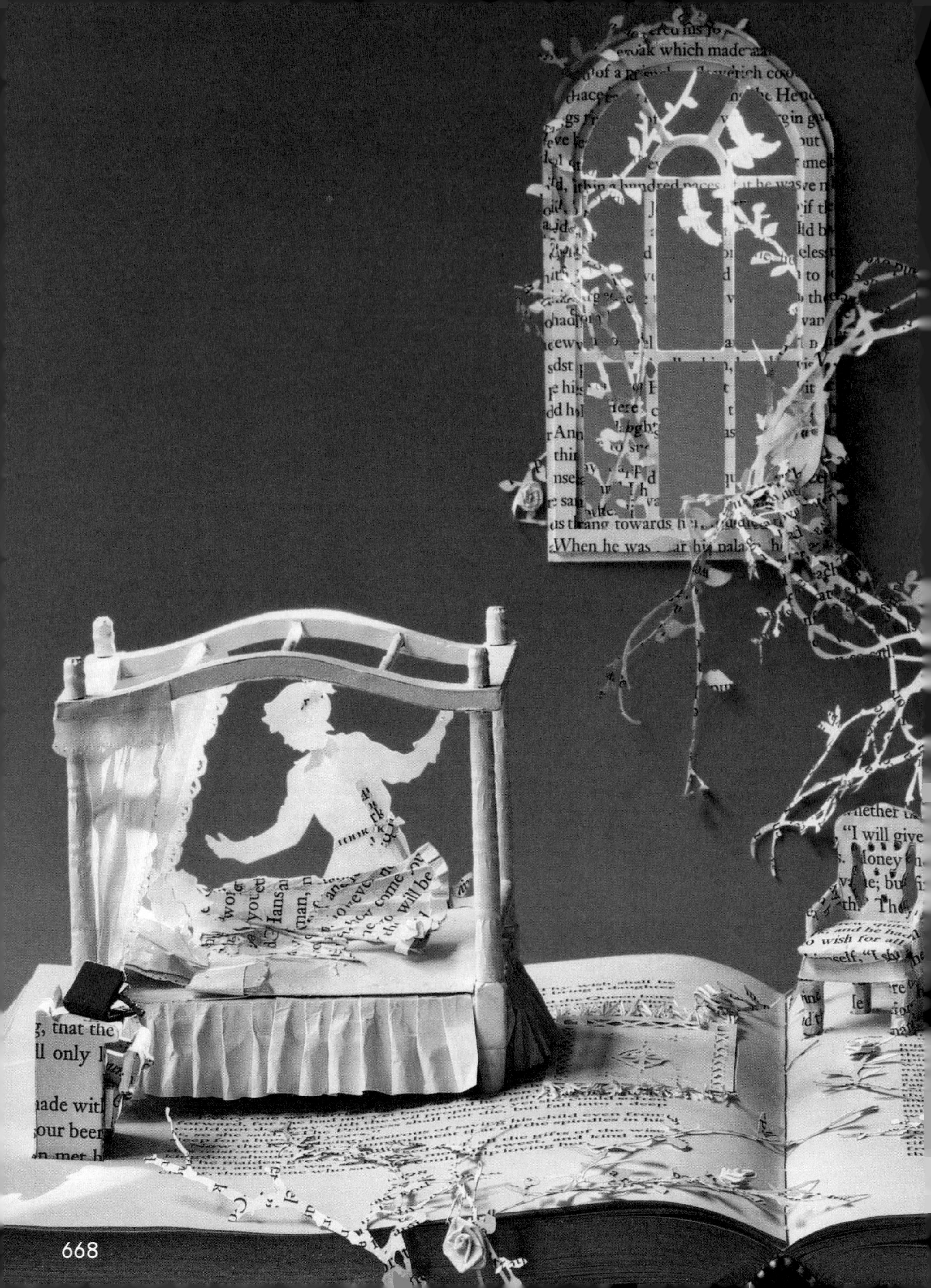

It so happened that on the day the prince reached the castle, exactly one hundred years had passed. As the prince cut at the forest of thorns with his axe, the thorns magically turned into beautiful flowers that swayed aside to make a path for him to enter.

Once inside the castle, the prince saw the king and queen asleep on their golden thrones, the horses asleep in the stable and the pigeons on the roof with their heads under their wings. The flies slept on the wall. The dog slept on the floor, and the cat too.

Everyone was sleeping; everywhere was silence. As the prince walked further and further into the castle, all he could hear was the sound of his own breath.

At last the prince came to the tallest tower. He climbed the narrow winding stairs until he reached the small door with the rusty key. He turned the key and opened the door. And there lay Briar Rose asleep on the bed. He was overcome with her beauty.

The prince kissed Briar Rose. She awoke and looked at him kindly.

Together the prince and princess left the small room in the tall tower and walked through the castle.

The king and queen awoke and were astonished. The horses in the stable shook themselves and the dog jumped up and chased the cat. The pigeons took their heads from under their wings and flew to the fields. The flies buzzed around. The kitchen boy dodged the cook. The fire in the hearth broke into flames and the roast sizzled again.

And so the prince married the princess. The wedding was splendid and the feast was delicious. And they lived happily ever after.

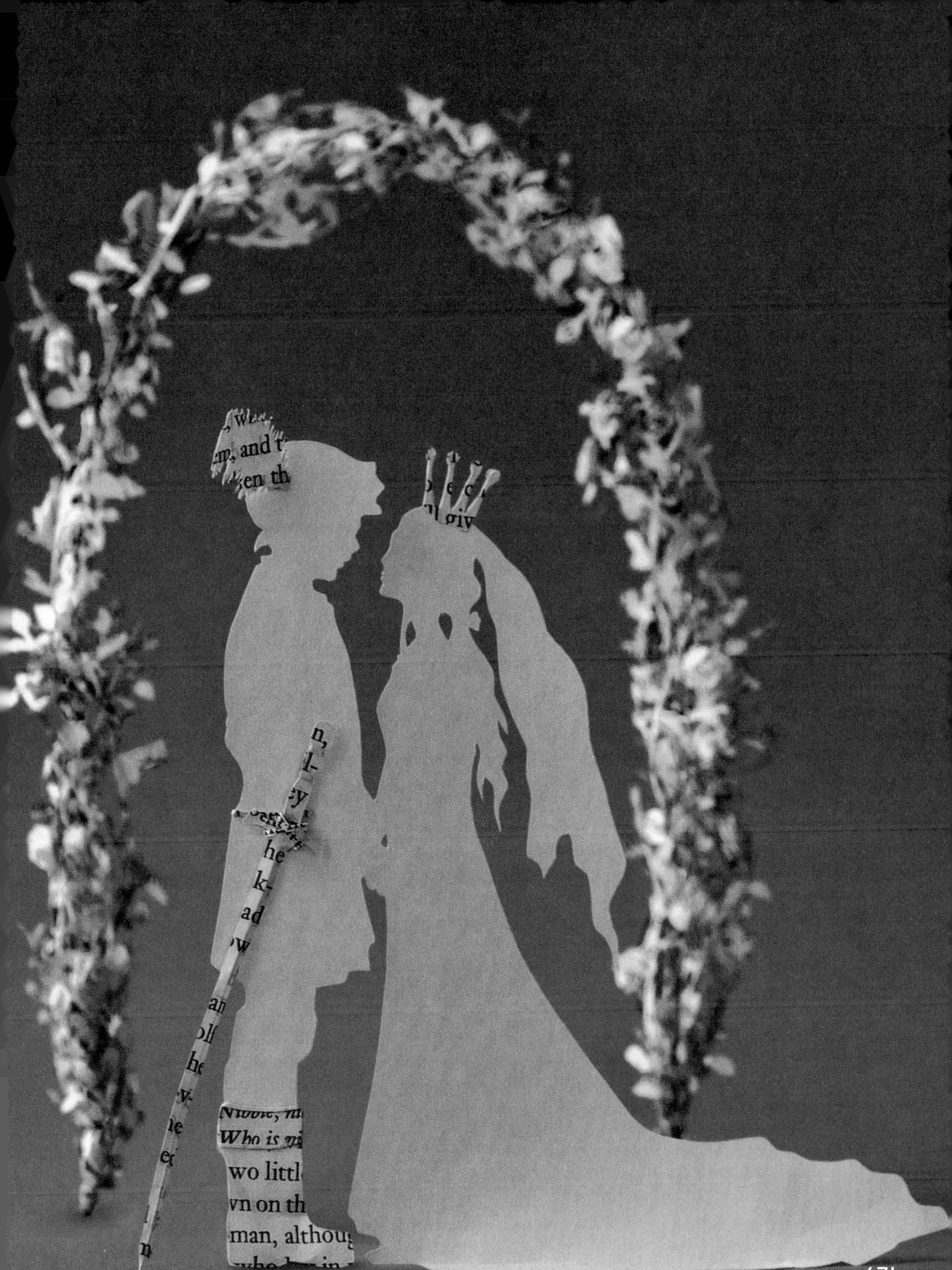

Old Books,
New Ideas

by Jack Oliver

What happens to old books? That depends. Many people save them to read again or to share with friends and family. Many more old books fill libraries so that communities can use and reuse them. Charities sometimes receive donations of old books; in other cases, people sell their old books to used-book stores. Almost every garage sale or yard sale has books to sell. Also, environmentally conscious people also choose to recycle old books to make new products—even new books.

Over the last few decades, some artists have given old books a second life in exciting, surprising ways. They have folded, shaped, glued, painted, or cut countless pages to change the books into something different, something new. These artists have recycled their books into fresh works of art.

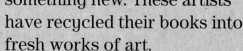

The kind of art created using old books goes by many names: bookwork, sculpted books, carved books, transformed books, and altered books. Altered books may be the most inclusive name for this new art form. It says that a book has been changed from one kind of art into another.

The art of altering books is relatively new. A few artists began reshaping books in the 1960s and 1970s. They were at the forefront of this new discipline. It took decades for other artists to follow their example.

Interest Grows with the Internet

The digitization of books began in the earliest days of the Internet—in the 1970s. Talk of electronic media replacing traditional print media began to increase in the 1990s and 2000s, when more books became available through computerized devices. Once more and more readers could easily access their books on a computer, printed books acquired a new kind of value for many people. They liked that a real book could be held. They liked that its pages could be touched and turned. The printed book became more than printed words on a page to them. It began to symbolize something.

As digital books increased in use, some artists began altering paper books to convey their feelings about the special nature of printed books and writing in general. Altered books helped people celebrate the importance of books and stories. They still do.

Artists also altered books to recycle them and keep them from being discarded in landfills. As a result, some altered book art is made from old phone books, catalogs, and reference books.

The highly publicized work of some artists has inspired many other people to alter old books and create something new. Today, more and more young artists around the world do exactly that. Often their works are full of incredible detail. The artwork may reflect a book's original story. The characters of the book may seem to spring from its pages!

Other artists alter books to create something completely different from the original story. Such artists reshape the pages from these books to convey their own messages or tell unique stories. They use the old books only as media to make new art. The old books are truly altered, sometimes beyond recognition.

Some artists use many pages from many books to construct one piece of art. Or artists may alter books by using them as building blocks in large statues or sculptures. The artist might glue, wire, or bolt together many books to form the artwork.

Interest in altered books continues to grow. Museums, libraries, and colleges have held special altered-book exhibits. Also, many adults and children create altered books of their own.

Making Altered Book Art

Artists use many methods to alter old books into something new. For them, the easy part is getting old books. The hard part is creating something fresh.

For even a book-art novice, the hardest part might simply be finding discarded or inexpensive old books available for purchase to alter. Changing the old book into new art can be simple and fun.

Once one finds the right old book, the simplest way to make it into something new is to fold the book's pages. Fold each corner of a page to its center to form a triangle. After doing that to many pages, close the book and press firmly to fix the shapes in place. The book is now thicker. The cover of the book rises at an angle. Viewing the book from the side reveals the shape formed by the folded pages. One might alter the book further by painting the triangles in a colored motif or scheme.

Novice artists can try additional techniques. With practice, one may learn to fold pages to make words or simple shapes. Blogs and Internet videos show how to do this. How-to books are also available at the library.

As more young artists investigate and experiment with altered-book art, some may find they have a latent talent for it. An exceptional few may go on to nurture this new tradition of giving old books new life!

Inspiration

by Maggie Smith-Beehler
illustrated by Yevgenia Nayberg

I was lost inside a fairy tale,
book in my lap, when inspiration
struck me like a spell—
the kind of spell you find
in fairy tales: I could make art
from the story itself.
I could open a book—
any book from my shelf—

and scissor the setting
to life. I could cut the teeth
of mountains, those serrated
peaks, or the pine forest's
tall triangles—the trees
where creatures dwell,
or I could cut the palace,
or an enchanted well.

I could sharpen my blades
and fill the landscape
one by one with flitting fairies.
I could people the kingdom,
carve characters out of the pages
and into each scene—
the silhouette of a princess,
perhaps, or an evil queen.

Once I was lost inside a fairy tale
when inspiration struck me,
dazzled me, like a spell.
My art is a kind of magic too—
transforming something old
into something new.

Write the answers to the questions on these pages in your notebook. Use evidence and details from the text to support your answers.

Text Connections

1. Describe the cause-and-effect chain that leads to Briar Rose's hundred-year sleep.

2. How does the twelfth wise woman protect Briar Rose's family when Briar Rose falls asleep?

3. How do the illustrations in "Sleeping Beauty" and the topic of "Old Books, New Ideas" connect to the theme of "Literature Meets Art"?

4. How do colorful verbs in "Inspiration" help you better imagine its subject matter?

5. How does "Inspiration" connect to the illustrations in "Sleeping Beauty"?

6. In literature, can happy endings come about partly by chance? Use an example from "Sleeping Beauty" to explain your answer.

Did You Know?

In the illustrations of most versions of "Sleeping Beauty," the spinning wheel is a Saxony wheel invented in the 1500s. However, though an older type of spinning wheel has a sharp spindle, Saxony wheel spindles do not actually have sharp ends.

Look Closer

Keys to Comprehension

1. Why is the castle preparing for a feast the day Briar Rose pricks her finger? What kind of feast does it eventually become? Give details to support your inference.

2. What is a theme of "Sleeping Beauty"? Summarize details to support your answer.

Write

Find where the word "splendid" is used on pages 660 and 663. Then, describe a *splendid* meal you once had. In what way was it an example of a feast?

Writer's Craft

3. Explain the meaning of the phrase "inspiration struck me" from the poem "Inspiration."

4. Explain the structural differences of the poem "Inspiration" and the fairy tale "Sleeping Beauty."

Concept Development

5. Describe how one illustration in "Sleeping Beauty" shows a setting described in the text.

6. Compare and contrast how "Sleeping Beauty" and "The Sun and the Moon" demonstrate the opposition of good and evil.

Read this Social Studies Connection. You will answer the questions as a class.

Text Feature

Book titles are **italicized** in informational text, while story titles have **quotation marks** around them.

Folklore and the Brothers Grimm

Many of the most famous European folktales come to us today because of the work and ideas of two brothers: Jacob and Wilhelm Grimm. Although you have probably heard of the Brothers Grimm, you may not realize that their influence goes beyond the stories they published.

Jacob and Wilhelm lived in Germany in the late 1700s and early 1800s. The brothers planned originally to become lawyers like their father. However, while at the University of Marburg from 1802 to 1806, they came upon some new ideas. The brothers were overcome by an interest in folk poetry and studies of the past. At that time, many people were talking about the ideas of Johann Gottfried von Herder. Herder was a philosopher who argued that language and cultural traditions form the way people think. A culture's traditional poetry, to him, was a key to understanding its people.

The brothers set aside their pursuit of law. Instead, they started doing something few people had done before: collecting songs, poetry, and folktales. They met with people who knew many traditional stories and wrote them down. In their first book, *Children's and Household Tales,* were the original versions of many stories we still tell today, including "Sleeping Beauty," "Rapunzel," and "Snow White."

What was important about the *Tales'* first volumes was that the stories were unchanged. Rather than adapt each story to teach a particular lesson, the brothers simply recorded how people had told each story for hundreds of years. Because of this, people call them pioneers in the science of folklore studies.

Children's and Household Tales by the Brothers Grimm inspired countless additional artistic interpretations and retellings. The illustration and text shown is from "Rapunzel" by Otto von Spekter, published in 1898.

1. How did Jacob and Wilhelm Grimm express their interest in folklore?

2. In what way can *Children's and Household Tales* help people learn about the past?

3. How did the Brothers Grimm influence folklore collectors? Why is the past still important to such collectors today?

 Go Digital

Research Charles Perrault, an author who also wrote a version of "Sleeping Beauty." How was his writing method different from the Grimm Brothers' method?

Genre Play

Essential Questions
Where do stories come from?
Why might a story be unfinished?

The Doomed Prince

An Egyptian Tale Retold in Two Acts

by Paul Thompson
illustrated by Diana Magnuson

Characters

NARRATOR	YOUNG MAN
KING	PRINCESS
QUEEN	MAID
PEOPLE	KING II
MESSENGER	GUARD
SEVEN HATHORS	GREYHOUND
NASSIR	CROCODILE
PRINCE	GIANT

Setting: *Egypt*

ACT 1

SCENE 1

SETTING: *The Great Hall of the Palace*

(KING and QUEEN sit on their thrones. QUEEN coos over her newly born child who lies in her arms.)

NARRATOR. A celebration honoring the infant prince is about to begin.

KING. What a joyous day this is!

QUEEN. Our prince is such a lovely child, so happy and content. See how he smiles at me?

PEOPLE *(outside).* Long live the prince! Long live the prince!

(A MESSENGER enters and bows before KING.)

MESSENGER. The Seven Hathors insist on seeing you, Your Majesty.

QUEEN *(upset)*. No, turn them away. They arrive only when they have bad omens, and I just won't hear them. My son, our son, will not be harmed by these Hathors!

KING. We must allow them to tell us whatever news they have.

QUEEN. I fear bad news, so we must turn them away. What you don't know can't hurt you!

KING. Hathors can also bring good tidings and give us sage advice, my queen. Besides, whether we meet with them or not, whatever they say will happen anyway. Shouldn't we know our fate? Living in a bubble of ignorance is never a good idea.

KING *(to MESSENGER)*. Introduce the seven goddesses!

(SEVEN HATHORS enter and bow to KING. They peer into QUEEN's bundle and smile.)

KING. Goddesses, you honor us with your presence! Now speak!

SEVEN HATHORS *(chanting)*.

The winds blew hard, the seas have churned,
Bringing a message that we have learned.
They tell of a son, so newly born,
But alas, his fate you will mourn.

The snapping jaws of a crocodile,
The fatal bite of a poisonous snake,
The treachery of a loyal dog,
One of these, your son's life will take.

(SEVEN HATHORS back away from KING.)

KING. Wait, Hathors! Tell us more!

(SEVEN HATHORS disappear in a cloud of smoke. QUEEN hugs the baby tightly and cries.)

KING. Worry not, my queen. We must fear three things only: a crocodile, a snake, or a dog. Surely we can protect the prince from these things.

QUEEN *(hopefully)*. Yes! We can build a castle in the mountains where no wild dog or crocodile or snake could ever reach.

KING. Yes, it will be done. But for now, let us celebrate with our people!

(KING stands and beckons QUEEN.)

SCENE 2

SETTING: *A castle hidden in the mountains*

NARRATOR. Years pass, and the prince becomes a strong and clever young boy of twelve. This scene begins on the roof of the castle, where the prince is sewing a piece of canvas.

NASSIR. Your father will not be happy to hear of your invention.

PRINCE. Nonsense! He will praise me for my cleverness.

NASSIR. If only you had not been caught scaling these castle walls.

PRINCE. I am forbidden to climb them—it is no matter. Climbing castle walls is child's play. Now I'm going to fly!

NASSIR. Only birds fly, my lord. You dream too much, I'm afraid.

PRINCE *(throws canvas on the ground).* What am I to do? Sit around all day and read books about a life I'm not even allowed to lead? This castle is a prison. I might as well be chained inside a dungeon or locked in a tower.

NASSIR. Your father has given you everything you need.

PRINCE *(picks up canvas again).* Except freedom, and that is all I have ever wanted. *(He points down to a boy and his dog below.)* See that peasant boy with his stick? What is that animal with him?

NASSIR. It is a greyhound, my lord. They are playing fetch.

PRINCE. That boy has more joy in this moment than I have had in my entire life.

(PRINCE holds up his canvas glider.)

PRINCE. With this, I can soar in the wind. Warm drafts of air will carry me, and I will escape this prison.

(Royal bugles announce KING.)

NASSIR. Your father is here!

PRINCE. Welcome, father! You are here to see my latest feat.

KING. What are you doing? What is that thing?

PRINCE *(holding up the canvas).* Behold, my wings of flight!

KING. What do you mean? Those will help you fly?

PRINCE. Yes, oh, yes. I've already tried it. The canvas catches the wind currents, and I fly safely to the ground. One time, a warm current caught me, and I floated upwards!

KING. But you do not leave the castle grounds, do you?

PRINCE. Not yet, but that is my goal. Practice makes perfect, you know.

KING. I have kept you here for your own protection. If you leave the castle walls, you will perish.

PRINCE. You want me to live in the shadow of your fears?

PRINCE *(points to dog and boy below).* Look there, father! That boy with his greyhound has more joy in his little finger than I have in my entire life.

KING. Is that what you want, son? A dog? Because that is not wise.

PRINCE. Father, fear is like a disease. It rots from within, eating away all happiness in the soul.

(PRINCE flies down and then soars upward and lands in the courtyard.)

KING *(yelling to his son below).* This is madness! Fine! I'll find you a small puppy, one that you can train to love and protect you. Please, no more flying!

Act 2

SCENE 1

SETTING: *A stone plaza outside a castle tower*

NARRATOR. And so the prince grew and grew. When he came of age, his father granted him his freedom. The prince and Nassir traveled to Nahrin, a city in another kingdom, to find his fortune and a new life, where he resigned to face his fate. He joins a mob of young men who are looking up at a tower window and talking amongst themselves.

PRINCE. Look, Nassir, at all the people gathered around this tower. I wonder what is going on?

(PRINCE approaches a YOUNG MAN.)

PRINCE. What is the commotion about?

YOUNG MAN. We are all here to court the princess. The king says whoever can fly to her can have her hand in marriage. Of course, many have tried, but flying is impossible. Look, there, that man has put feathers on his arms.

(The man flaps his arms, jumps, and then falls. The crowd roars in laughter.)

YOUNG MAN. We all believe the king wants his daughter to wither away and never marry.

PRINCE. We mustn't let that happen, must we?
(to NASSIR) We must go and prepare!

691

SCENE 2

SETTING: *Inside the castle tower*

NARRATOR. Meanwhile, the princess does needlework with her maid.

PRINCESS. What is all the commotion outside?

MAID. Every single man in the kingdom is below. One of them is hoping to find a way to fly to your window, so he may marry you.

PRINCESS. My father is such a silly man to make such a requirement.

MAID. I believe he does not want you married, my lady.

PRINCESS. And that is very selfish indeed. *(She stands and looks at a tower across the castle.)* Come, quickly! That man has a huge canvas cloak! Now he's on the edge of the tower, and oh my! *(She backs away from her window. PRINCE lands on her windowsill.)*

PRINCE. Good day, my beautiful princess! I have come to rescue you from a life of imprisonment!

PRINCESS. What would you know about a prison?

PRINCE. I have just been released from one. My father protected me from the outside world, just as you have been.

PRINCESS. I see that we are kindred spirits, and I pledge my allegiance to you.

702

(*KING II enters with GUARD, and PRINCE bows.*)

KING II. Who is this man? Guard, seize this man!

PRINCE. I am the son of a chariot fighter from a distant kingdom. I left home because my father remarried, and my stepmother hates me. I am here to make a new life.

KING II. You flew here? What trickery is this?

PRINCE. I learned to fly when I was a young boy.

PRINCESS. He did fly here, father. I watched him soar from yonder tower.

KING II (*turns to his daughter*). And do you wish to marry this man?

PRINCESS. Most certainly. He has won your frivolous contest and has also won my heart.

KING II. Very well, I will keep my word. So it shall be.

693

SCENE 3

SETTING: *A living area of the castle*

(The PRINCE sits on the sofa with the PRINCESS. The GREYHOUND fetches a small ball as the PRINCESS tosses it.)

NARRATOR. And so the next week, the king held a great celebration in honor of the princess and the prince. The prince still did not reveal his true identity to the king, but the prince's conscience did weigh heavily upon him.

PRINCE. My darling wife, I am so happy, and you are so beautiful.

PRINCESS. Beauty fades, my husband.

PRINCE. Perhaps, but you also have a heart of gold. That will never fade. *(He sighs.)* To think that my life could change into something so wonderful and so quickly.

PRINCESS. And mine also!

PRINCE. There is something I have not told you, my princess. *(pause)* I must explain why my father put me in a castle away from everyone. First, I am not the son of a chariot fighter. I am the Prince of Egypt. I wanted you to love me as a man, not as a prince.

PRINCESS. You are a silly man, my husband. Love does not seek rank or privilege.

PRINCE. There's more. When I was born, the Seven Hathors predicted a snake, a crocodile, or a dog would kill me. I call them the three dooms.

PRINCESS *(shrinking from the GREYHOUND).* Then we must banish your pet, my dear! A dog is a threat to you!

PRINCE. No, I have had him since he was a puppy. He will never hurt me, and I will not harm a hair on his head.

PRINCESS. Very well, but we must keep you safe from other harms. We have a crocodile in the river nearby, but you are not to worry about that. My father ordered a giant to guard the beast so that it will not harm any human.

PRINCE. My wife, if I have learned one thing in my short life, it is not to live in fear. You and I, we deserve better.

PRINCESS. You are very wise, but you should rest now, my dear. The hour is late, and you are very tired.

(PRINCE rests, and PRINCESS warms herself beside the fire.)

NARRATOR. As they rest, a poisonous snake slithers into the room, as silent as the night air. The prince is in a heavy slumber, but the princess senses danger and searches the room until she spies the deadly serpent. As the snake approaches the bed, the princess strikes the snake with the poker from the fireplace. The snake dies.

PRINCESS. Husband, awake!

PRINCE. What has happened?

PRINCESS. All is well, and I have happy news! I have killed one of your dooms, the snake. For now, you are safe.

PRINCE. What a courageous and loyal wife! I shall treasure you forever.

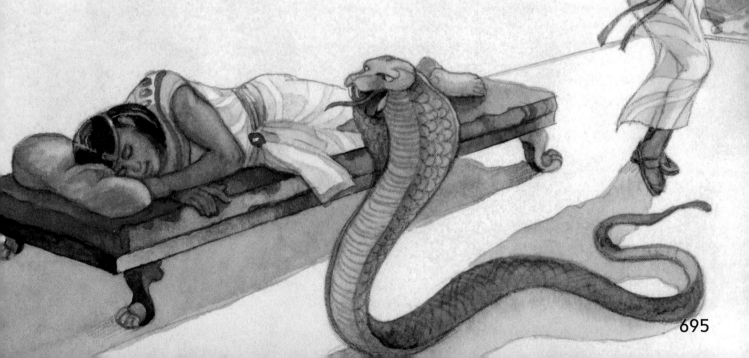

SCENE 4

SETTING: *Outside the castle walls*

NARRATOR. Buoyed by the destruction of one of his dooms, the prince leaves the castle to play with his dog. The prince tosses a ball to the greyhound. He fetches it several times, but on the last toss, the greyhound chases a rabbit. The prince follows the dog until he jumps into the Nile. The dog struggles in the water.

GREYHOUND. Help, Master, I did not know that I could not swim!

PRINCE *(jumping into the river).* Your paws are not meant for swimming, my dear pet. *(PRINCE grabs his pet. As they reach the shore, a CROCODILE emerges from the water and snags PRINCE's shirt.)* Stop, Crocodile! Where is your master, the giant?

CROCODILE. Ah, he sleeps during the day. Did not anyone advise you?

PRINCE. Let me go!

CROCODILE. Give me your dog, and I will leave you alone. I am hungry for dog meat.

PRINCE. Never! I will fight you to the death!

CROCODILE. Not only will I kill and eat you and the dog, I will do it in front of my jailor's very home!

(CROCODILE drags PRINCE to GIANT's hut. CROCODILE and PRINCE fight fiercely. GIANT awakens from his sleep and emerges from his hut.)

GIANT *(bellowing)*. Stop this foolishness, Crocodile! Must I watch you both day and night? Release the dog and the prince, or I will destroy you!

(CROCODILE releases PRINCE and GREYHOUND. PRINCE holds GREYHOUND to his chest, who shivers in fear.)

CROCODILE *(backing away)*. You have escaped me today, Prince, but I am still your doom. One day I will kill this giant who guards me and pursue you to the ends of the earth. Mark my words, you, the Doomed Prince. I will destroy you and that wretched dog.

NARRATOR. This Egyptian tale has no end. Does the crocodile prevail and kill the prince? Does the Princess again save the prince from the crocodile or the dog? Perhaps the dog sacrifices his life for that of his master. Or maybe the dog accidentally bites the prince and an infection causes his death. It is up to you to determine the fate of the Doomed Prince.

THE END

Did You Know?

The papyrus that contains the beginning and middle of "The Doomed Prince" is housed today in the British Museum. The document is over 3,000 years old.

Text Connections

1. Why does the prince choose to go out in the world, rather than stay safe in the castle?

2. In "The Doomed Prince," how are the prince's and princess's fathers alike?

3. Which danger do you think is the greatest threat to the prince at the end of the story, and why?

4. Describe the connection a main character has with an animal in "The Doomed Prince" and "Paul Bunyan."

5. Would you have left the castle if you were the prince? Why or why not?

6. In "The Doomed Prince," how does love lead to fear for the king and queen? Do you think this can happen in real life? Explain.

Look Closer

Keys to Comprehension

1. How does the prince's wife save him from one of his dooms? Give details from the text to support your answer.

2. Describe in depth the setting of "The Doomed Prince."

Write

Reread the last page of "The Doomed Prince." Then, write your own ending to the story.

Writer's Craft

3. Near the beginning of "The Doomed Prince," the queen says, "What you don't know can't hurt you!" What does this idiom mean, and do you think it was true in her case?

4. Contrast the different structural elements of the drama "The Doomed Prince" and the poem "Ode on a Herculean Vase."

5. How would "The Doomed Prince" have been different if the prince were the narrator in the play?

Concept Development

6. Compare and contrast how parents try to protect a child from fate in "The Doomed Prince" and "Sleeping Beauty."

Read this Science Connection. You will answer the questions as a class.

Text Feature

A **figure** is a visual that gives more information about an informational text.

Science and Art: Making Papyrus

Modern knowledge of ancient Egypt is tied to the history of a grass-like plant. Thousands of years ago, this plant grew wild in quiet waters of the Nile River Valley. At some point, ancient Egyptians made a discovery. They found that, by using a special method, they could make a material for storing writing.

Tall papyrus stalks carry water up from the plant's roots (see figure 1). Inside the stalks is something called the pith. The pith layers together two kinds of cells: tough cell bundles that pull up water and air-filled cells that let the stalk bend in the wind.

Ancient Egyptians would carefully take the pith out of a section of stalk. By either peeling or slicing the pith, they created long, thin strips. They would make a bottom layer of a row of vertical strips. Then they would make a second layer on top of this by putting strips across it horizontally. At some point in the process they wetted the pith. Then they would press these layers together, before hammering and drying them (see figure 2).

Modern paper made from wood pulp contains a kind of glue that holds it together. However, papyrus fibers, when treated in this way, did not need glue. Their cells and sap cemented the layers into a strong, white writing surface.

Because of Egypt's dry climate, old pieces of this substance have survived. The oldest have lasted over 4,000 years. As scholars study these written fragments, the stories and information they contain give us a window into the identity of an ancient people.

Figure 1. Ancient Egyptians used the papyrus plant to make a writing surface.

Figure 2. This image of handmade papyrus shows the strands of pith laid across each other.

1. Explain how ancient Egyptians made a writing surface out of papyrus.

2. Plan a test to see what layering patterns make the strongest writing substance.

   a. Gather paper, scissors, glue, water, a plastic cup, a paintbrush, three plastic sandwich bags, duct tape, and dry beans.

   b. Cut the paper into narrow strips of the same length and width. In the cup, mix the glue and water. Apply the glue solution to one side of the strips using the paintbrush.

   c. Using three different layering patterns, create three "papyrus" sheets. Keep the number of strips used and layers the same in each test. Let dry.

   d. Tape a plastic bag to the bottom edge of each sheet. Test the strength of Sheet 1 by putting beans into the bag ten at a time. Lift Sheet 1 by its top two corners after each set of ten. Record how many beans it takes to break the sheet. Repeat with the other two sheets. Which pattern created the strongest sheet?

 Go Digital

Research the Rosetta stone. How did it help unlock the meaning of writing used on ancient Egyptian papyrus like the one containing the story of "The Doomed Prince"?

Glossary

Pronunciation Key

a	as in **a**t	**ô**	as in br**ou**ght and r**a**w	**ə**	as in **a**bout, chick**e**n, pen**ci**l, cann**o**n, circ**u**s
ā	as in l**a**te	**oi**	as in c**oi**n		
â	as in c**a**re	**o͝o**	as in b**oo**k	**ch**	as in **ch**air
ä	as in f**a**ther	**o͞o**	as in t**oo**	**ng**	as in ri**ng**
e	as in s**e**t	**or**	as in f**or**m	**sh**	as in **sh**op
ē	as in m**e**	**ou**	as in **ou**t	**th**	as in **th**in
i	as in **i**t	**u**	as in **u**p	**t͟h**	as in **th**ere
ī	as in k**i**te	**ū**	as in **u**se	**zh**	as in trea**s**ure
o	as in **o**x	**ûr**	as in t**ur**n, **g**erm, l**ear**n, f**ir**m, w**or**k		
ō	as in r**o**se				

The mark (´) is placed after a syllable with a heavy accent, as in **chicken** (chik´ ən).

The mark (´) after a syllable shows a lighter accent, as in **disappear** (dis´ ə pēr´).

abolition (ab´ ə lish´ ən) *n.* the act of ending or stopping

absorbed (əb sorbd´) *adj.* very interested in; focused on

abstained (ab stānd´) *v.* past tense of **abstain:** to keep oneself from doing something

abundant (ə bun´ dənt) *adj.* more than enough; plentiful

access (ak´ ses) *n.* providing a way to get to something

accomplished (ə kom´ plisht) *v.* past tense of **accomplish:** to do something successfully; to complete

adapt (ə dapt´) *v.* to change in order to make suitable

addressed (ə dresd´) *v.* past tense of **address:** to speak or give a formal speech to

agency (ā´ jən sē) *n.* a company or person that does business for other companies or people

aghast (ə gast´) *adj.* feeling shocked or horrified

702

ahead (ə hed´) *adv.* in front

aim (ām) *n.* goal

aloof (ə lōōf´) *adj.* having or showing little or no concern or friendliness

already (ôl red´ ē) *adv.* by a certain time

alter (ôl´ tûr) *v.* to make or become different; change

amid (ə mid´) *prep.* in the middle of

angle (an´ gəl) *n.* the figure formed by two lines or flat surfaces that extend from one point

apartheid (ə pärt´ tīd) *n.* the government policy of racial segregation that used to be followed in South Africa

appear (ə pîr´) *v.* to come into sight; be seen

application (ap´ li kā´ shən) *n.* a formal written request to attain something, such as a job

apprenticed (ə pren´ tist) *v.* past tense of **apprentice:** to take on, or place as an assistant, a person who is hoping to learn a skill or art

aquatic (ə kwä´ tik) *adj.* growing or living in water

arranged (ə rānjd´) *v.* past tense of **arrange:** to put in order or position

arthritis (är thrī´ tis) *n.* a painful inflammation of a joint or joints of the body

articles (är´ ti kəlz) *n.* plural form of **article:** a separate section of a formal document

artifacts (är´ ti fakts) *n.* plural form of **artifact:** an old tool, weapon, or other thing made by people in the past

aside (ə sīd´) *adv.* on or to one side

astride (ə strīd´) *adv.* with one leg on each side

at stake (at stāk) *prep. phrase* in a position to be lost if something goes wrong

atmosphere (at´ məs fîr) *n.* the layer of gases that surrounds Earth

attempt (ə tempt´) *n.* a try; effort

attend (ə tend´) *v.* to be present at

auction (ôk´ shən) *n.* a public sale at which things are sold to the person who offers the most money

awkwardness (ô´ kwûrd´ nəs) *n.* a difficult or embarrassing moment; clumsiness

bade (bād) *v.* past tense of **bid:** to say, such as when meeting or leaving someone

badges (baj´ əz) *n.* plural form of **badge:** something worn to show that a person belongs to a certain group or has received an honor

barracks (ber´ əks) *n.* plain, usually temporary, buildings in which people live in large groups

703

based on (bāst on) *v. phrase* past tense of **base on:** to use something as a base or foundation for something else

battered (bat´ ûrd) *adj.* worn and weathered

beloved (bi luvd´) *adj.* loved very much

bewilderment (bi wil´ dûr´ mənt) *n.* the state of being confused

bind (bīnd) *v.* to tie together; fasten

blistering (blis´ tûr ing) *adj.* very intense or severe

blundered (blun´ dûrd) *v.* past tense of **blunder:** to move in a clumsy way

blustery (blus´ tûr ē) *adj.* violently windy

border (bôr´ dûr) *n.* a line where one country or other area ends and another begins; boundary

bore (bôr) *n.* a person or thing that is dull

botany (bot´ ə nē) *n.* the study of plants

bountiful (boun´ tə fəl) *adj.* more than enough; abundant

boycotts (boi´ kots) *n.* plural form of **boycott:** a planned joining with others in refusing to buy from or deal with a person, nation, or business

brace (brās) *v.* to prepare for a shock

breathless (breth´ lis) *adj.* out of breath

brief (brēf) *adj.* short in time

broadcasting (brôd´ kast ing) *v.* form of **broadcast:** to send out music, news, or other kinds of programs by radio or television

bronze (bronz) *n.* a reddish-brown alloy made by melting together copper and tin

browses (brouz´ əz) *v.* form of **browse:** to feed or nibble on

bundle (bun´ dəl) *n.* a number of things tied or wrapped together

by chance (bī chans) *adv. phrase* accidentally

C

cache (kash) *v.* to place or store something in a hidden or secret place

cakes (kāks) *n.* plural form of **cake:** a flattened or shaped mass

carnivores (kär´ nə vôrz´) *n.* plural form of **carnivore:** an animal that eats the flesh of other animals

catalyst (ka´ tə ləst) *n.* a condition or event that causes or speeds another condition or event

caution (kô´shən) *n.* close care; watchfulness

cautious (kô´shəs) *adj.* careful or watchful

ceases (sēs´əz) *v.* form of **cease:** to come or bring to an end; stop

cell (sel) *n.* a small enclosed part or space

cement (sə ment´) *n.* something serving to unite firmly

centers (sen´tûrz) *n.* plural form of **center:** a facility providing a place for a particular activity or service

century (sen´chə rē) *n.* a period of one hundred years

certain (sûr´tən) *adj.* sure; positive

charities (châr´ə tēz) *n.* plural form of **charity:** a fund or organization for giving help to those who need it

citation (sī´tā shən) *n.* a formal public statement that praises a person for doing something good or brave

citizen (sit´ə zən) *n.* a person who was born in a country or chooses to live in and become a member of a country

civil (siv´əl) *adj.* polite but not friendly; courteous

cleanse (klenz) *v.* to make clean

clerk (klûrk) *n.* a person who sells goods to customers in a store

code (kōd) *n.* any set of signals, words, or symbols used to send messages

coiled (koild) *adj.* curled or wound into rings or spirals

colossal (kə lä´səl) *adj.* of great size

command (kə mand´) *n.* the ability to use or control

complex (kəm pleks´) *adj.* hard to understand or do

comrades (kom´radz) *n.* plural form of **comrade:** a friend who shares the same work or interests with another

conditions (kən dish´ənz) *n.* plural form of **condition:** the state something is in

conducted (kən dukt´id) *v.* past tense of **conduct:** to control; manage

confidence (kon´fi dəns) *n.* trust that a person will not tell a secret

conquer (kon´kûr) *v.* to overcome; to defeat

conserve (kən sûrv´) *v.* to keep and protect from harm, loss, or change

contact (kon´takt) *v.* to get in touch with; to communicate with

contagious (kən tā´jəs) *adj.* able to spread from person to person

contract (kon´trakt) *n.* an agreement

controversial (kän trə vər´shəl) *adj.* of or relating to a topic that causes the exchange of opposing ideas, often with strong feelings

converse (kən vûrs´) *v.* to talk together

coordinated (kō ôr´də nāt´id) *adj.* able to do well with physical work or sport

coral (kôr′ əl) *n.* a hard substance like stone, found in the tropical seas

corrupt (kə rupt′) *adj.* able to be bribed; crooked; dishonest

council (koun′ səl) *n.* a group of people called together to discuss a problem or other matter

court (kôrt) *v.* to try to win the favor or love of a person

crack (krak) *n.* a break or narrow opening between the parts of something

cradle (krā′ dəl) *n.* a small bed for a baby, often on rockers

creased (krēst) *adj.* marked by folds or wrinkles

crock (krok) *n.* a thick clay pot or jar

cue (kū) *n.* a signal that tells someone when to do something

culture (kul′ chûr) *n.* way of life for a group of people at a certain time

cunning (kun′ ing) *adj.* good at fooling or deceiving others

customs (kus′ təmz) *n.* plural form of **custom:** a way of acting that has become accepted by many people

decades (dek′ ādz) *n.* plural form of **decade:** a period of ten years

decoy (dē′ koi) *n.* something or someone used to draw attention away from another

defeating (di fēt′ ing) *v.* form of **defeat:** to win a victory over

defiance (di fī′ əns) *n.* bold refusal to obey or respect authority

degree (di grē′) *n.* a title given by a school or college to a student who has finished a course of study

delegates (del′ i gits) *n.* plural form of **delegate:** a person who is chosen to act for others; representative

deliberations (di lib′ ə rā′ shənz) *n.* plural form of **deliberation:** careful discussion before a decision

delivered (di liv′ ûrd) *v.* past tense of **deliver:** to take to the proper place or person

demand (di mand′) *n.* something that is asked for forcefully

demonstrate (dem′ ən strāt′) *v.* to explain, prove, or show clearly

denounced (di nounst′) *v.* past tense of **denounce:** to speak out against; object to

dense (dens) *adj.* packed closely together; thick

depths (depths) *n.* plural form of **depth:** a place far below a surface or inside something

descent (di sent´) *n.* the origin or background of a person in terms of family or nationality

deserve (di zûrv´) *v.* to have a right to; be worthy of

designated (dez´ ig nāt´ id) *adj.* marked, separated, or called by a particular name or title

desolate (des´ ə lit) *adj.* without people; deserted

desperately (des´ prət´ lē) *adv.* with great urgency

despite (di spīt´) *prep.* in spite of; regardless of

determined (di tûr´ mind) *adj.* firm in sticking to a purpose

developed (di vel´ əpt) *v.* past tense of **develop:** to bring or come gradually into being

devious (dē´ vē əs) *adj.* sneaky or untrustworthy

dictator (dik´ tā tûr) *n.* a person who rules a country without sharing power or consulting anyone else

discipline (di´ sə plin) *n.* a field of study

disguises (dis gīz´ əz) *n.* plural form of **disguise:** something that changes or hides the way one looks

disrupting (dis rupt´ ing) *v.* form of **disrupt:** to break up or apart

distinctly (di stingkt´ lē) *adv.* in a clear manner

distress (di stres´) *n.* great pain, sorrow, or misery

dormitory (dôr´mi tôr´ ē) *n.* to a building in which there are many bedrooms

draft (draft) *v.* to make a sketch, plan, or rough copy of something

dread (dred) *n.* a feeling of great fear

dream (drēm) *n.* a hope or ambition to do or succeed at something

drift (drift) *v.* to move because of a current of air or water

drowsed (drouzd) *v.* past tense of **drowse:** to almost be asleep or lightly asleep

due to (doo too) *adj. phrase* because of

durable (dûr´ ə bəl) *adj.* able to last a long time in spite of much use or wear

earnestly (ûr´ nis lē) *adv.* done in a serious and sincere manner

efficient (i fi´ shənt) *adj.* able to get the results wanted within a minimum of time or effort

emancipation (i man´ sə pā´ shən) *n.* freedom from slavery or control

embraced (em brāsd´) *v.* past tense of **embrace:** to take or hold in the arms as a sign of love or friendship; hug

enraged (en rājd´) *v.* past tense of **enrage:** to make very angry; put into a rage

ensure (en shûr´) *v.* to make sure or certain; guarantee

equivalent (i kwiv´ ə lənt) *n.* something that is equal

esophagus (i sof´ ə gəs) *n.* the muscular tube through which food moves from the throat to the stomach

except (ek sept´) *prep.* not including

exertions (ig´ zûr´ shənz) *n.* plural form of **exertion:** physical or mental effort

experimental (ek sper´ ə ment´ əl) *adj.* from or relating to experiments

faint (fānt) *adj.* not clear or strong; weak

farewell (fâr´ wel´) *n.* goodbye and good luck

favored (fā´ vûrd) *v.* past tense of **favor:** to approve of; believe in; support

federal (fe´ dər əl) *adj.* having to do with the central government of the United States, thought of as separate from the government of each state

feeble (fē´ bəl) *adj.* not strong; weak

fees (fēz) *n.* plural form of **fee:** money requested or paid for some service or right

felt the jitters (felt thə ji´ tûrz) *v. phrase* past tense of **feel the jitters:** to be nervous

ferocious (fə rō´ shəs) *adj.* savage; fierce

fertile (fûr´ təl) *adj.* able to produce crops and plants easily and plentifully

figure (fig´ yər) *n.* a form or outline; shape

flattered (fla´ tûrd) *v.* past tense of **flatter:** to praise too much or insincerely

flee (flē) *v.* to run away

fleeting (flē´ ting) *adj.* passing very quickly; very brief

free (frē) *v.* to release from captivity or confinement

funding (fund´ ing) *n.* money provided for a specific purpose

furious (fūr´ ē əs) *adj.* very angry

gala (gā´ lə) *n.* a festive occasion; celebration

galleries (gal´ ə rēz) *n.* plural form of **gallery:** a room or building where works of art are shown or sold

generations (jen´ ə rā´ shənz) *n.* plural form of **generation:** one step in the line of descent from a common ancestor

genes (jēnz) *n.* plural form of **gene:** one of the tiny units of a cell that determines the characteristics that an offspring inherits from its parent or parents

germinate (jûr´ mə nāt) *v.* to begin growing from a seed; to sprout

glanced (glanst) *v.* past tense of **glance:** to take a quick look

gland (gland) *n.* a part inside the body that takes certain substances from the blood and changes them into chemicals that the body uses or gives off

gleam (glēm) *n.* a faint or short appearance or sign

glimpse (glimps) *n.* a quick look; glance

glistened (glis´ ənd) *v.* past tense of **glisten:** to shine with reflected light

gorgeous (gôr´ jəs) *adj.* very pleasing to look at; beautiful

grazing (grāz´ ing) *v.* form of **graze:** to feed on growing grass

griddle (grid´ əl) *n.* a heavy, flat metal pan with a handle, used for cooking pancakes and other food

grievance (grēv´ əns) *n.* a reason for complaining or being unhappy with a situation

grove (grōv) *n.* a group of trees standing together

guilt (gilt) *n.* a feeling of having done something wrong; shame

gullible (gəl´ ə bəl) *adj.* believing or trusting in almost anything

hailed (hāld) *v.* past tense of **hail:** to greet or attract the attention of by calling or shouting

halo (hā´ lō) *n.* a circle of light

harmony (här´ mə nē) *n.* friendly agreement or cooperation

harnesses (har´ nes əz´) *n.* form of **harness:** a set of straps and other gear used to connect a person to something

hatch (hach) *n.* an opening in the deck of a ship

herculean (hûr kyə lē´ ən) *adj.* having enormous strength, courage, or size

hoarse (hors) *adj.* having a rough or harsh, deep sound

honor (on´ ûr) *v.* to show or feel great respect for a person or thing

honorable (ä´ nûr ə bəl) *adj.* deserving honor; worthy of respect

huddle (hud´ əl) *v.* to gather close together

humbly (hum´ blē) *adv.* in a quiet and mild-mannered way

identity (ī den´ tə tē) *n.* who a person is or what a thing is

illusion (i lōo´ zhən) *n.* a false impression or belief; misleading idea

immense (i mens´) *adj.* of great size; very large; huge

immigrant (im `i grənt) *n.* a person who comes to live in a country in which he or she was not born

impact (im´ pakt) *n.* the force of one object striking against another

impetuous (im pech´ ōo əs) *adj.* acting or done too quickly; without planning or thought

in partnership with *prep. phrase* (in pärt´ nər ship´ with) together with

increase (in krēs´) *v.* to make or become larger in size or number

indignantly (in dig´ nənt´ lē) *adv.* showing anger about something unfair, wrong, or bad

individual (in´ də vij´ ōo əl) *adj.* single; separate

infant (in´ fənt) *n.* a child during the earliest period of life; baby

inspections (in spek´ shənz) *n.* plural form of **inspection:** the act of looking at something closely and carefully in order to learn more about it

institute (in´ sti tūt´) *n.* a school or other organization that is set up for a particular purpose

insulating (in´ sə lāt´ ing) *adj.* covering or surrounding with a material that slows or stops the flow of electricity, heat, or sound

interpreters (in tûr´ prə tûrz) *n.* plural form of **interpreter:** someone who changes the language of a message without changing the message´s meaning

item (ī´ təm) *n.* a single thing in a group or list

jostled (jo´ səld) *v.* past tense of **jostle:** to bump or push roughly

judge (juj) *v.* to find something wrong with

lack (lak) *n.* the condition of needing something

landscape (lan´ scāp´) *n.* the stretch of land that can be seen from a place; view

lead (led) *n.* a heavy, soft, gray metal that is easy to bend and melt

league (lēg) *n.* a number of people, groups, or countries joined together for a common purpose

lens (lenz) *n.* a piece of glass or other clear material curved to make light rays move apart or come together

lever (lev´ ər) *n.* a rod or bar attached to a machine, used to work or control it

levying (lev´ ē ing) *v.* form of **levy:** to impose or collect by lawful actions or force

limit (lim´ it) *v.* to keep within a bound or bounds; restrict

longed (lôngd) *v.* past tense of **long:** to want very much; yearn

loyal (loi´ əl) *adj.* having or showing strong and lasting affection and support for someone or something

lumberjack (lum´ bər jak´) *n.* a person who cuts down trees and gets logs ready for the sawmill

luminous (lōō´ mə nəs) *adj.* of or relating to a steady, glowing light

mainland (mān´ land´) *n.* the chief land mass of a country or continent, as distinguished from an island

majesty (ma´ jəs tē) *n.* a title used in speaking to or about a king, queen, or other royal ruler

makeshift (māk´ shift) *adj.* used for a time in place of the correct or usual thing

malfunction (mal fungk´ shən) *n.* a failure to function or work correctly

manner (ma´ nûr) *n.* the way in which something is done

mark (märk) *v.* to take note of

marveling (mär´ vəl ing) *v.* form of **marvel:** to feel wonder and astonishment

mast (mast) *n.* a tall pole on a sailing ship that supports the sails and rigging

match (mach) *n.* something or someone who can compete as an equal

material (mə tîr´ ē əl) *n.* what something is made of or used for

meandering (mē an´ dûr ing) *adj.* going along in a winding way

media (mē´ dē ə) *n.* plural form of **medium:** a substance or means through which something acts or is done

meet (mēt) *n.* a gathering for the purpose of competing in sporting events or other contests

mental (men´ təl) *adj.* done or having to do with the mind

merge (mûrj) *v.* to join and become one; come together

mill (mil) *n.* a building where machines make raw materials into finished products

millet (mil´ ət) *n.* a type of grass that is grown for its seeds, which are used as food

mint (mint) *n.* a place where coins are made

mission (mi´ shən) *n.* a special job or task

module (mä´ jōōl) *n.* a part of a spacecraft that has a special use and can be separated from the rest of the craft

molecules (mol´ ə kūlz) *n.* plural form of **molecule:** the smallest particle into which a substance can be divided without changing chemically

monarch (mo´ nərk) *n.* a large orange and black butterfly found in North America

monument (mon´ yə mənt) *n.* a building, statue, or other object made to honor a person or event

mortal (môr´ təl) *adj.* human

mournfully (môrn´ fəl ē) *adv.* with sorrow or grief

mucus (mū´ kəs) *n.* a slimy fluid that coats and protects the inside of the mouth, nose, throat, and other parts of the body

murmured (mûr´ mûrd) *v.* past tense of **murmur:** to speak in a low, soft voice

mused (mūzd) *v.* past tense of **muse:** to think long and quietly

newly (nōō´ lē) *adv.* lately; recently

nimble (nim´ bəl) *adj.* light and quick in movement

nocturnal (nok tûr´ nəl) *adj.* active at night

nourishment (nûr´ ish mənt) *n.* something needed for life and growth

obedient (ō bē´ dē ənt) *adj.* tending or willing to obey

obliged (ə blījd´) *v.* past tense of **oblige:** to give in to a request or a demand; to do a favor

oblivious (ə bli´ vē əs) *adj.* not conscious or aware of someone or something

observe (əb zûrv´) *v.* to make a careful study of

of her life (uv hûr līf) *prep. phrase* pertaining to the lifetime of someone

omens (ō´ mənz) *n.* plural form of **omen:** something that is supposed to be a sign of good or bad luck to come

operations (o´ pə rā shənz´) *n.* plural form of **operation:** the act or way of working or directing

opportunities (o´ pər tū´ ni tēz) *n.* plural form of **opportunity:** a good chance; favorable time

opposite (o´ pə zit) *adj.* on the other side of or across from another person or thing; facing

orbit (ôr´ bit) *n.* the path an object follows as it moves around another object

overcome (ō´ vûr kum´) *v.* to cause to lose physical ability or emotional control

P

pamphlet (pam´ flit) *n.* a small book that has a paper cover

papers (pā´ pûrz) *n.* documents issued by a government proving citizenship or granting permission to do something

parchment (pärch´ mənt) *n.* the skin of sheep, goats, or other animals prepared so that it can be written on

patch (pach) *n.* a small piece of ground where something grows

patent (pa´ tənt) *n.* a piece of paper issued to a person or company by the government that gives them the right to be the only one to make, use, or sell a new invention for a certain number of years

patrol (pə trōl´) *n.* a group of people or vehicles that guard an area or make sure everything is all right

pep (pep) *n.* a lively, vital quality; spirit

peril (per´ əl) *n.* a chance or risk of harm; danger

permitted (pûr mit´ id) *v.* past tense of **permit:** to allow or let

persuade (pûr swād´) *v.* to cause to do or believe something by pleading or giving reasons; convince

petition (pə ti´ shən) *v.* to make a formal request to

phantom (fan´ təm) *n.* something that appears to be real but is not

plantation (plan tā´ shən) *n.* a large estate or farm worked by laborers who live there

platoon (plə tōon´) *n.* a military unit that includes two or more squads

plump (plump) *adj.* full and round; nicely fat

poke (pōk) *n.* something moving slow or lazily

pollinate (po´ lə nāt´) *v.* to transfer pollen from the stamen to the pistil of the same flower or another flower

port (pôrt) *n.* a place where boats or ships can dock or anchor safely; harbor

posed (pōzd) *v.* past tense of **pose:** to be perceived as a risk or danger

posh (posh) *adj.* elegant; fashionable

prairie dogs (prâr´ ē dôgz) *n.* plural form of **prairie dog:** an animal that is related to the squirrel, living in underground dens in the prairies of the western United States

precise (pri sīs´) *adj.* definite; exact

predators (pre´ də tûrz) *n.* plural form of **predator:** an animal that lives by hunting other animals for food

prejudice (pre´ jə dis) *n.* hatred or unfair feelings about a particular group, such as members of a race or religion

preoccupied (prē ok´ yə pīd´) *adj.* to be concerned with a situation

presentation (pre´ zən tā´ shən) *n.* the act of putting something before an audience

preserve (pri zûrv´) *v.* to keep from being lost, damaged, or decayed; protected

prey (prā) *n.* an animal that is hunted by another animal for food

prick (prik) *v.* to make a small hole with a sharp point

procedure (prə sē´ jûr) *n.* a proper way of doing something, usually by a series of steps

professional (prə fe´ shə nəl) *adj.* having to do with an occupation that requires special education or training

protrude (prō trōōd´) *v.* to stick out

prowling (proul´ ing) *adj.* moving or roaming quietly or secretly

pry (prī) *v.* to move or raise by force

pulsating (pul´ sāt ing) *adj.* possessing a regular, rhythmic beat

quarters (kwôr´ tûrz) *n.* a place to live or stay

quenches (kwench´ es) *v.* form of **quench:** to make something stop burning; put out; extinguish

quest (kwest) *n.* a search or pursuit

radiation (rā´ dē ā´ shən) *n.* energy given off in the form of waves or very tiny particles; radiant energy

rallies (ra´ lēz) *n.* plural form of **rally:** a meeting for a purpose

range (rānj) *n.* a variety of choices within a scale

rank (rangk) *n.* a position or grade

rare (râr) *adj.* not often happening, seen, or found

react (rē akt´) *v.* to act because something has happened; respond

reassured (rē´ ə shurd´) *v.* past tense of **reassure:** to restore confidence or courage in

rebellion (ri bel´ yən) *n.* an armed fight against one's government

recent (rē´ sənt) *adj.* done, made, or happening not long ago

recruits (ri krōōts´) *n.* plural form of **recruit:** a newly enlisted soldier or sailor

regiment (re´ jə mənt) *n.* a military unit made up of several battalions

reinforcement (rē´ in fôrs´ mənt) *n.* additional support, encouragement

relieve (ri lēv´) *v.* to free from discomfort or pain

represented (rep´ ri zent´ id) *v.* past tense of **represent:** to be a symbol of; to stand for

republic (ri pub´ lik) *n.* a form of government in which the power belongs to the people and in which the people elect representatives to manage the government

reputation (rep´ yə tā´ shən) *n.* what most people think of a person or thing

reserve (ri zûrv´) *v.* to arrange to have something kept for someone of something

resist (ri zist´) *v.* to overcome the effect or action of

retreat (ri trēt´) *v.* to draw or move back

rich (rich) *adj.* able to produce much; fertile

ripple (ri´ pəl) *n.* a very small wave

roost (rōōst) *v.* to rest or sleep on a perch as a bird does

S

sagged (sagd´) *v.* past tense of **sag:** to sink or hang down

saguaros (sə gwar´ ōz) *n.* a tall cactus that is native to Arizona, Mexico, and California

saunter (sôn´ tûr) *v.* to walk in a slow or relaxed manner

scramble (skram´ bəl) *v.* to move or climb quickly

scurry (scûr´ ē) *v.* to go or move in a hurry

secretary (sek´ rə ter´ ē) *n.* a person who is the head of a government department

secreting (si krēt´ ing) *v.* form of **secrete:** to produce and release a chemical substance

secure (si kyur´) *v.* to make safe

seek (sēk) *v.* to try to find

sense (sens) *n.* feeling

sensor (sen´ sôr) *n.* a device or structure that detects or senses heat, light, sound, motion, or pressure and then reacts to it in a particular way

sentinel (sen´ tə nəl) *n.* a person stationed to keep watch and warn others of danger; guard

separate (se´ pə rit) *adj.* set apart; not joined

severity (sə vâr´ ə tē) *n.* seriousness; harshness

shears (shirz) *n.* a cutting instrument like scissors

sheer (shir) *adj.* steep

shudder (shu´dûr) *v.* a tremble or shake caused by a strong force

signal (sig´ nəl) *n.* something that warns, directs, or informs

sites (sīts) *n.* plural form of **site:** position or location of something

skirt (skûrt) *v.* to move or lie along the border or edge of

sly (slī) *adj.* clever and shrewd; crafty

soar (sôr) *v.* to fly high in the air

solemnly (so´ ləm lē) *adv.* done in a serious and sorrowful manner

sought (sôt) *v.* past tense of **seek:** to try to find; go in search of

spacecraft (spās´ kraft) *n.* a vehicle used for flight in outer space

spanned (spand) *v.* past tense of **span:** to extend across or over

specifically (spi sif´ ik´ lē) *adv.* clearly described in a manner leaving no doubt

specimens (spes´ ə mənz) *n.* plural form of **specimen:** a single item that shows what the whole group is like; sample

spectacular (spek tak´ yə lûr) *adj.* very unusual or impressive

spewed (spūd d) *v.* past tense of **spew:** to expel

spies (spīz) *n.* plural form of **spy:** a person who watches others secretly

spring (spring) *v.* to more forward or jump up quickly

stance (stans) *n.* a position or opinion

station (stā´ shən) *n.* a building or place used by a business or other organization

stealthy (stel´ thē) *adj.* slow, deliberate, and secret in action or character

steerage (stir´ ij) *n.* a section in a passenger ship where passengers with the cheapest tickets would stay

sternly (stûrn´ lē) *adv.* in a strict or hard manner

stock (stok) *n.* a supply of things kept to be sold or used

strategy (strat´ i jē) *n.* the planning and directing of actions used to win a competition or achieve a goal

stretch (strech) *v.* to reach; extend

sturdy (stûr´ dē) *adj.* strong; hardy

substance (sub´ stəns) *n.* material of a certain kind

subway (sub´ wā) *n.* an electric railroad that runs underground in a city

sulkily (sulk´ ə lē) *adv.* done in an angry and silent manner

sum (sum) *n.* an amount of money

superstition (soo´pûr sti´ shən) *n.* a belief based on ignorance and fear

surface (sûr´ fis) *n.* the outside of a thing

suspiciously (sə spi´ shəs´ lē) *adv.* having or showing a feeling that something is wrong

sweet (swēt) *adj.* pleasing to the ear or eye

swiftly (swif´ lē) *adv.* in a quick manner

tactics (tak´ tiks) *n.* plural form of **tactic:** a method planned and used to win a competition or achieve a goal

target (tär´ git) *n.* a mark or object that is aimed at

technique (tek nēk´) *n.* a method or way of bringing about a desired result in a science, art, sport, or profession

temper (tem´ pûr) *n.* a tendency to become angry or irritated

tension (ten´ shən) *n.* the force that affects objects that are pulled or stretched

textile (teks´ tīl) *n.* a fabric that is made by weaving or knitting

texture (teks´ chûr) *n.* the look and feel of something

theory (thēr´ ē) *n.* an idea about the way things are or work

thick (thik) *adj.* growing or being close together; dense

tide (tīd) *n.* the regular rise and fall of the water level of the oceans and other large bodies of water that is caused by the pull of the moon and sun on Earth

> **Pronunciation Key:** **a**t; l**ā**te; c**â**re; f**ä**ther; s**e**t; m**ē**; **i**t; k**ī**te; **o**x; r**ō**se; **ô** in b**ou**ght; c**oi**n; b**oo**k; t**oo**; f**or**m; **ou**t; **u**p; **ū**se; t**û**rn; **ə** sound in **a**bout, chick**e**n, penc**i**l, cann**o**n, circ**u**s; **ch**air; ri**ng**; **sh**op; **th**in; **th**ere; **zh** in trea**s**ure.

tidings (tī´ dingz) *n.* plural form of **tiding:** news or information

tinkering (ting´ kûr´ ing) *v.* form of **tinker:** to try to repair or improve something by making small changes

titanic (tī tan´ ik) *adj.* enormous in size, strength, or power

tittered (ti´ tûrd) *v.* past tense of **titter:** to laugh in a quiet or nervous way

ton (tun) *n.* a measure of weight equal to 2,000 pounds (in the United States and Canada)

took shape (took shāp) *v. phrase* formed

topple (top´ əl) *v.* to fall or make fall forward

towering (tou´ ər ing) *adj.* very tall

track and field (trak ən fēld) *n.* a group of sporting events that includes running, jumping, and throwing contests

tranquil (trang´ kwəl) *adj.* free from noise or disturbance; calm, peaceful

transmission (tranz mi´ shən) *n.* the broadcasting of radio or television waves

transparent (trans pâr´ ənt) *adj.* allowing light to pass through so that things on the other side can be clearly seen

transplant (trans´ plant´) *n.* an event in which something is taken from one place and put into another

treacle (trē´ kəl) *n.* molasses; a sweet, thick, yellowish brown syrup made from sugarcane

tread (tred) *n.* the way or sound of walking

trench (trench) *n.* a long narrow ditch

trial (trī´ əl) *n.* a trying or testing of something

trickle (trik´ əl) *n.* a small flow or thin stream

tricksters (trik´ stûrz) *n.* plural form of **trickster:** someone who tricks or deceives people in order to get something

tuned in (toond in) *v. phrase* past tense of **tune in:** to listen to or view a radio or television program

ultimately (əl´ tə mət´ lē) *adv.* in the end

underground (un´ dûr ground´) *adv.* done in secret or while in hiding

unless (un les´) *conj.* except on the condition that

unraveling (un rav´ əl ing) *v.* form of **unravel:** to separate the threads of something knitted, woven, or tangled

uphold (up hōld´) *v.* to support or defend

urge (ûrj) *n.* a strong desire or impulse

uttered (ə´ tûrd) *v.* past tense of **utter:** to give voice to; express out loud

version (vûr´ zhən) *n.* a form of something that is different in some way from other forms

vertical (vûr´ ti kəl) *adj.* straight up and down; upright

veterans (vet´ ûr ənz) *n.* plural form of **veteran:** a person who has been in the armed forces

vicious (vi´ shəs) *adj.* fierce or dangerous

vital (vī´ təl) *adj.* necessary to or supporting life

warrant (wär´ ənt) *v.* to declare the truth of

wealth (welth) *n.* a great amount of money or valuable things; riches

wearily (wîr´ ə lē) *adv.* in a tired way

weep (wēp) *v.* to show sorrow, joy, or other strong emotion by crying

welfare (wel´ fâr) *n.* the condition of being happy and healthy; well-being

whittled (wit´ əld) *v.* past tense of **whittle:** to cut small bits or pieces from wood with a knife

wicked (wik´ id) *adj.* evil, mean, and very bad

wise (wīz) *adj.* having or showing good judgment and intelligence

wistfully (wist´ fə lē) *adv.* done in a way full of longing and some sadness

withered (wi´ thûrd) *adj.* dried up or shriveled

without further ado (with out´ fûr´ thûr ə dōō´) *prep. phrase* right away

worked (wûrkt) *v.* to shape, as by pressing and rolling

woven (wō´ vən) *adj.* made by passing strands or lengths of material over and under one another

wretched (re´ chid) *adj.* very bad or evil

yield (yēld) *v.* to stop fighting or disagreeing

Reading Resources

Reading Comprehension

Comprehension Strategies will help you understand what you are reading.

Asking and Answering Questions

As you read, ask yourself the following questions:

1. What do I already know about this topic?

2. What else would I like to know about this topic?

3. What questions do I think the author will answer as I read this selection?

4. How does this information connect to what I already know about the topic?

5. How does this information connect to the unit theme?

6. What is not making sense in this selection?

7. What is interfering with my understanding?

8. How does this information answer my question?

9. Does this information completely answer my question?

10. Do I have more questions after finding some of my answers?

11. Can I skim the text in order to find an answer to my question?

Clarifying

As you read, ask yourself the following questions:

1. What does not make sense? If it is a word, how can I figure it out? Do I use context clues, word analysis, or apposition, or do I need to ask someone or look it up in the dictionary or glossary?

2. If a sentence is complicated, have I reread it as well as the sentences around it to see if the meaning is clarified? Have I read the sentence part by part to see exactly what is confusing? Have I tried to restate the sentence in my own words?

3. The paragraph is long and full of details. What can I do to understand it? How much will I need to slow down to make sure I understand the text? Do I need to back up and reread part of the text to understand it?

4. Do I need to take notes or discuss what I have just read in order to understand it?

5. What is the main idea of what I just read?

6. Can I put what I just read into my own words?

Making Connections

As you read, ask yourself the following questions:

1. What does this remind me of? What else have I read like this?

2. How does this connect with something in my own life?

3. How does this connect with other selections I have read?

4. How does this connect with what is going on in the world today?

5. How does this relate to other events or topics I have studied in social studies or science?

Predicting

As you read, ask yourself the following questions:

1. What clues in the text can help me predict what will happen next?

2. What clues in the text tell me what probably will not happen next?

Revising/Confirming Predictions

As you read, ask yourself the following questions:

1. How was my prediction confirmed?

2. Why was my prediction *not* confirmed?

3. What clues did I miss that would have helped me make a better prediction?

Summarizing

As you read, ask yourself the following questions:

1. What is this selection about?

2. What are the big ideas the writer is trying to get at?

3. Have I said the same thing more than once in my summary?

4. What can I delete from my summary? What is not important?

5. How can I put what I have just read into my own words?

Visualizing

As you read, ask yourself the following questions:

1. What picture do the words create in my mind? What specific words help create feelings, actions, and settings in my mind?

2. What can I see, hear, smell, taste, and/or feel in my mind?

3. How does this picture help me understand what I am reading?

4. How does my mental picture extend beyond the words in the text?

Accessing Complex Text Skills will help you understand the purpose and organization of a selection.

Cause and Effect

Cause-and-effect relationships help you understand connections between events or ideas. The cause is why something happens. The effect is what happens as a result. A cause produces an effect.

Classify and Categorize

An author often includes many details. Putting the like things together, or classifying those like things into categories, helps you see how actions, events, or characters are related.

Compare and Contrast

To compare means to tell how things, events, or characters are alike. To contrast means to tell how things, events, or characters are different. Writers compare and contrast to make an idea clearer or to make a story more interesting.

Fact and Opinion

Writers often use facts and opinions in their writing to make their writing more believable, to explain things, or to persuade readers. A fact is a statement that can be proven true. An opinion is something a person or group believes is true, although others may disagree.

Main Idea and Details

The main idea is what the story or paragraph is mostly about. Writers use details to tell more about or explain the main idea.

Making Inferences

You make inferences when you take information in the selection about a character or an event and add this information to what you already know. You can use this combination of information to make a statement or conclusion about that character or event.

Sequence

Sequence is the order in which things happen. The more you know about the sequence of events, the better you will understand the story or information. Writers use time and order words such as *first, then, finally, tonight,* and *yesterday* to tell the order of events.

Writer's Craft

Author's Purpose

Everything is written for a purpose. That purpose may be to entertain, to persuade, or to inform. Knowing why a piece is written—what purpose the author had for writing the piece—gives the reader an idea of what to expect and perhaps some prior idea of what the author is going to say. It is possible for an author to have more than one purpose.

Character

A character is a person or creature that interacts with others within a story. There are different kinds of characters in stories, and different ways to describe them. Readers learn to identify the different characteristics of the characters (physical features, character types such as heroes or villains, personality types, feelings, and motivations), and the ways the author describes the characters, such as with descriptive details, dialogue, and illustrations.

Genre Knowledge

Readers learn to recognize the differences between fiction and nonfiction. Subgenres of fiction include realistic fiction, fantasy, fairy tales, folktales, plays, and poems. Subgenres of nonfiction include informational texts, biographies, and reference books. Readers determine which features are used for these different subgenres.

Language Use

Readers learn to recognize the ways authors communicate important details and events in a story. Language use may include rhyme, repetition, sentence structures (simple, compound, declarative, interrogative, imperative, and exclamatory), alliteration, simile, metaphor, exaggeration, onomatopoeia, personification, sensory details, descriptive words, effective adjectives and adverbs, dialogue, and formal vs. informal language.

Plot

Readers learn to recognize the overall structure, or plot, of a story. A plot usually includes a beginning, a problem that must be solved, the climax or highest point of the story, a resolution of the problem, and an ending. Authors may use sequence, cause and effect, details, and dialogue to build the plot.

Point of View (Narrative/Fiction)

Point of view in a narrative involves identifying who is telling the story. If a character in a narrative is telling the story, that character describes the action in the story and tells about the other characters. This is called first-person point of view. If the narrative is told in third-person point of view, someone outside the story who is aware of all the characters' thoughts, feelings, and actions is relating them to the reader.

Point of View (Informational or Persuasive Text)

The author's point of view in an informational text is the position or perspective the author takes on the subject he or she is writing about. The author may arrange topics in a certain sequence, or the author might present facts in such a way as to inform or to persuade his or her audience.

Setting

The setting of a story is composed of three pieces: the place where the story occurs, the timeframe or when the story takes place, and the amount of time that passes within the story from the beginning to the end.

Text Features

Text features are usually used in informational texts, and they help readers make sense of what they are reading. Text features may include headings, illustrations, photos, captions, diagrams, charts, maps, punctuation, font size or color, and numbered or bulleted lists.

Vocabulary Strategies

Apposition

Sometimes the word is defined within the text. In apposition, the word is followed by the definition, which is set off by commas.

Context Clues

When you come to an unfamiliar word in your reading, look for clues in the sentence or in the surrounding sentences. These clues might help you understand the meaning of the word.

Word Analysis

Examining the parts of a word can help you figure out the word's meaning. For example, the word *unfriendly* can be broken down into word parts: the prefix *un-*, the base word *friend,* and the suffix *-ly.* Knowing the meaning of each part will help you come up with the definition "not friendly."

Comprehension Discussion Strategies

Asking and Answering Questions

1. What if . . .
2. How do we know . . .
3. I wonder what would happen if . . .
4. What do we know about . . .
5. I wonder why the author chose to . . .
6. I found I could skim the material because . . .

Clarifying

1. I have a question about . . .
2. I am still confused about . . .
3. Does anyone know . . .
4. Could we clarify . . .
5. I figured out that . . .
6. I had difficulty understanding _____ because . . .
7. I still do not understand . . .
8. What did the author mean when he or she wrote _____?
9. Who can help me clarify _____ ?

10. Why did the author _____?
11. I decided to read this more slowly because . . .

Making Connections

1. This made me think . . .
2. I was reminded of . . .
3. This selection reminds me of what we read in _____ because . . .
4. This selection connects to the unit theme because . . .
5. I would like to make a connection to . . .
6. I found _____ interesting because . . .
7. This author's writing reminds me of . . .

Predicting

1. I expect . . .
2. I predict . . .
3. Based on _____, I predict . . .
4. I can support my prediction by/ with . . .
5. I would like to change my prediction because . . .
6. My prediction was confirmed when/by . . .
7. My prediction was not confirmed because . . .

Summarizing

1. I think the main idea is . . .

2. I think an important supporting detail is . . .

3. I think the best evidence to support the main idea is . . .

4. To summarize . . .

5. I learned . . .

6. I can conclude . . .

Visualizing

1. When I read _____, I visualized . . .

2. The author's words _____ helped me visualize . . .

3. Visualizing helped me understand . . .

4. The author made the story really come alive by . . .

Collaborative Conversation Starters

Personal Response

1. I did not know that . . .

2. I liked the part where . . .

3. I agree with _____ because . . .

4. I disagree with _____ because . . .

5. The reason I think _____ is . . .

6. I was surprised to find out . . .

7. I like the way the author developed the character by . . .

Agreeing with a Response

1. I agree because . . .

2. I see what you mean because . . .

Disagreeing with a Response

1. I disagree because . . .

Rules for Collaborative Conversation

Speaking Rules

☐ Speak clearly.

☐ Speak at an appropriate pace.

☐ Stay on topic.

☐ Use appropriate language for the setting.

☐ Make eye contact with the audience.

Listening Rules

☐ Look at the person who is speaking.

☐ Respect speakers by listening attentively.

☐ Keep your hands still and in your lap when someone is speaking.

☐ Do not talk when someone else is speaking.

☐ When you want to say something, raise your hand and wait to be called on.

☐ Ask a question if you do not understand something you heard.

Discussion Rules

☐ Listen carefully as others speak.

☐ Do not interrupt a speaker.

☐ Raise your hand when you want to speak.

☐ Ask questions to get more information from a speaker.

☐ Keep quiet as others speak.

☐ Take turns speaking.

☐ Respond to questions that others have asked you.

☐ Keep your questions and responses focused on the item being discussed.

Text Credits

Getting Started

Carroll, Lewis. *Alice's Adventures in Wonderland.* (2009). Urbana, Illinois: Project Gutenberg. Retrieved January 19, 2017, from www.gutenberg.org/ebooks/28885

Unit 1 Making a Difference

Excerpt adapted from *Ava and Pip* ©2014 by Carol Weston, published by Sourcebooks Jabberwocky, an imprint of Sourcebooks, Inc. www.sourcebooks.com. Used with permission, all rights reserved. AVA & PIP by Carol Weston. Copyright © 2014 by Carol Weston. Used with permission from the author and Writers House LLC.

Charlotte's Web. Copyright 1952 by E.B. White. Text copyright renewed 1980 by E.B. White. Used by permission of HarperCollins Publishers; Charlotte's Web [1980] by E.B. White. Used by Permission of ICM Partners. All rights reserved.

SEEDS OF CHANGE by Jen Cullerton Johnson, illustrated by Sonia Lynn Sadler. Text Copyright © 2010 by Jen Cullerton Johnson. Illustrations Copyright © 2010 by Sonia Lynn Sadler. Permission arranged with LEE & LOW BOOKS, Inc., New York, NY 10016. All rights not specifically granted herein are reserved.

Nelson Mandela. Copyright © 2013 by Kadir Nelson. Used by permission of HarperCollins Publishers.

"The Statesman" From *When Thunder Comes: Poems for Civil Rights Leaders* © 2012 by J. Patrick Lewis. Used with permission of Chronicle Books LLC. San Francisco. Visit ChronicleBooks.com

"Swim, Girl, Swim." Creative Editions is an imprint of The Creative Company, Mankato, MN 56001 USA

Unit 2 Science Fair

From RUBY GOLDBERG'S BRIGHT IDEA by Anna Humphrey. Text copyright © 2014 by Anna Humphrey and Simon & Schuster, Inc. Reprinted with the permission of Simon & Schuster Books for Young Readers, an imprint of Simon & Schuster Children's Publishing Division. All rights reserved.

"Michael Built a Bicycle." TEXT COPYRIGHT © 1984 by JACK PRELUTSKY. ILLUSTRATIONS COPYRIGHT © 1984 BY JAMES STEVENSON. Used by permission of HarperCollins Publishers.

From *My Brothers' Flying Machine: Orville, Wilbur, and Me* text by Jane Yolen, paintings by Jim Burke. Text copyright © 2003 by Jane Yolen. Illustrations copyright © 2003 by Jim Burke. By permission of Little Brown Books for Young Readers.

Wright, Orville and Wilbur. *Wilbur and Orville Wright Papers.* Library of Congress. Diaries and Notebooks: 1903, Orville Wright, Wilbur Wright and Orville Wright Papers, 1809 to 1979, Library of Congress, http://hdl.loc.gov/loc.mss/mwright.01007

"Crazy Boys" by Beverly McLoughland from HAND IN HAND © 1994. Reprinted by permission of the author.

GODSPEED, JOHN GLENN, written and illustrated by Richard Hilliard. Copyright ©2006 by Richard Hilliard. Published by Boyds Mills Press. Used by Permission.

To Space & Back. COPYRIGHT © 1986 BY SUSAN OKIE AND SALLY RIDE. Used by permission of HarperCollins Publishers. To Space and Back [1986] by Sally Ride with Susan Okie Used by Permission. All rights reserved.

Unit 3 Our Heritage, Our History

The Unbreakable Code by Sara Hoagland Hunter, illustrated by Julia Miner. Copyright © 1996 by Sara Hoagland Hunter. Illustration copyright © 1996 by Julia Miner. Used with permission of Rowman & Littlefield Publishing Group.

From *Ben and the Emancipation Proclamation* by Pat Sherman, illustrated by Floyd Cooper. Text copyright © 2010 by Pat Sherman. Illustrations copyright © 2010 by Floyd Cooper. Used with permission of Eerdmans Books for Young Readers, an imprint of Wm. B. Eerdmans Publishing Co.

"The Emancipation Proclamation," National Archives, accessed March 17, 2017, https://www.archives.gov/exhibits/featured-documents/emancipation-proclamation/transcript.html.

"Follow the Drinking Gourd," *Strange Fruit,* directed by Joel Katz (Oniera Films LLC, 2002), Lee Hays to Pete Seeger, Undated, Lee Hays Collection, Smithsonian Center for Folklife & Cultural Heritage.

From FIONA'S LACE by Patricia Polacco. Copyright © 2014 by Patricia Polacco. Reprinted with the permission of Simon & Schuster Books for Young Readers, an imprint of Simon & Schuster Children's Publishing Division. All rights reserved.

Hope and Tears by Gwenyth Swain. Copyright © 2012 by Gwenyth Swain. Published by Calkins Creek, an imprint of Boyds Mills Press. Used by permission.

MY DIARY FROM HERE TO THERE by Amada Irma Perez, illustrated by Maya Christina Gonzalez. Text Copyright © 2013 by Amada Irma Perez. Illustrations Copyright © 2013 by Maya Christina Gonzalez. Permission arranged with LEE & LOW BOOKS, Inc., New York, NY 10016. All rights not specifically granted herein are reserved.

FISH FOR JIMMY text and illustrations copyright © 2013 by Katie Yamasaki. All rights reserved. The illustrations have been abridged and adapted from the original work. Used by permission of Holiday House Publishing, Inc.

"Shaped by Words." From LION TREASURES: Cuba's Warrior of Words by Margarita Engle. Copyright © 2016 by Margarita Engle. Reprinted with the permission of Atheneum Books for Young Readers, an imprint of Simon & Schuster Children's Publishing Division. All rights reserved. Reproduced with permission by Margarita Engle/Martha Kaplan Agency.

Unit 4 Adaptations in Action

"Why Bat Flies Alone at Night," "How Owl Got His Feathers," "Why Ants Are Found Everywhere," "How Brazilian Beetles Got Their Gorgeous Coats," "Rabbit Counts the Crocodiles," and "Why Bear Has a Stumpy Tail." From HOW & WHY STORIES World Tales Kids Can Read & Tell by Martha Hamilton & Mitch Weiss. Copyright © 1999 by Martha Hamilton & Mitch Weiss. All Rights Renewed and Reserved. Published by August House, Inc. and reprinted by permission of Marian Reiner on their behalf.

"Animal Defense Academy" by Nicole Gill; Ask Magazine, February 2016. Copyright © by Carus Publishing Company. Reproduced with permission. All Cricket Media material is copyrighted by Carus Publishing Company, d/b/a Cricket Media, and/or various authors and illustrators. Any commercial use or distribution of material without permission is strictly prohibited. Please visit http://www.cricketmedia.com/info/licensing2 for licensing and http://www.cricketmedia.com for subscriptions.

"Ghost Crab." *Now You See Them, Now You Don't: Poems About Creatures That Hide,* Text copyright © 2016 by David L. Harrison, Illustrations copyright © 2016 by Giles Laroche. Used with permission by Charlesbridge Publishing, Inc., 85 Main Street, Watertown, MA 02472, (617) 926–0329, www.charlesbridge.com. All rights reserved.

Survival at 40 Below. Text Copyright © 2010 Debbie S. Miller. Illustrations Copyright © by Jon Van Zyle. Published by Bloomsbury Children's Books.

Survival at 120 Above. Text Copyright © 2012 Debbie S. Miller. Illustrations Copyright © by Jon Van Zyle. Published by Bloomsbury Children's Books.

Unit 5 National Treasures

Longfellow, Henry Wadsworth. "Paul Revere's Ride." *The Atlantic Monthly 7, no. 39* (January, 1861): 27–29. Boston: Ticknor and Fields, 1861.

GIVE ME LIBERTY. Text Copyright © 2000 by Russell Freedman. All rights reserved. Reproduced from GIVE ME LIBERTY! by permission of Holiday House Publishing, Inc.

The Declaration of Independence (1776).

U.S. Const. preamble.

LADY LIBERTY. Text copyright © 2008 Doreen Rappaport. Illustrations copyright © 2008 Matt Tavares. Reproduced by permission of the publisher, Candlewick Press, Somerville, MA.

Lazarus, Emma. 1883. "The New Colossus." Catalogue of the Pedestal Fund Art Loan Exhibition. New York: National Academy of Design.

Charles P. Daly quote. *Appleton's Annual Cyclopædia and Register of Important Events of the Year 1879.* New York: D. Appleton and Company, 1886.

Unit 6 Literature Meets Arts

Laughead, W.B. *The Marvelous Exploits of Paul Bunyan.* Minneapolis, Westwood, Cal., Chicago, Los Angeles, San Francsico: The Red River Lumber Company, 1922.

Table 1: South Korean Yearly Average Consumption of Rice. "World Rice Statistics Online Query Facility," International Rice Research Institute and the Food and Agriculture Organization of the United Nations, accessed March 9, 2017, http://ricestat.irri.org:8080/wrsv3/entrypoint.htm.

"Sleeping Beauty" from *The Fairytale Princess: Seven Classic Stories from the Enchanted Forest,* published by Thames & Hudson, London and New York, 2012. Paper sculptures © 2012 Su Blackwell, www.sublackwell.co.uk, words by Wendy Jones, photography by Tim Clinch.

Image Credits

17 (tl)Digital image courtesy of the Getty's Open Content Program, (tr)Rawpixel.com/Shutterstock.com, (c)PNC/Brand X Pictures/Getty Images; **18–19** (bkgd)youngvet/E+/Getty Images; **19** (l)Wavebreak Media/Getty Images, (tr)Blend Images/Image Source, (br) wavebreakmedia/Shutterstock.com; **35** Comstock Images/Alamy Stock Photo; **49** (b)McGraw-Hill Education; **63** (l)Simon Murrell/ Alamy Stock Photo, (r)Thomas Males/iStockphoto/Getty Images; **90** Louise Gubb/Corbis Historical/Getty Images; **91** Chris Willig; **92** MonkeyApple/Alamy Stock Photo; **93** Arab/Shutterstock.com; **100–101** (bkgd)McGraw-Hill Education; **101** (l)Library of Congress Prints and Photographs Division [LC-DIG-hec-13257], (r)C Squared Studios/Photodisc/Getty Images; **102** Library of Congress Prints & Photographs Division [LC-USZ62-27663]; **102–103** (bkgd) McGraw-Hill Education; **103** Bettmann/Getty Images; **104** (t)U.S. National Archives and Records Administration [6802718], (b) Image Source/Getty Images; **104–105** (bkgd)McGraw-Hill Education; **105** Bettmann/Getty Images; **106** Bettmann/Getty Images; **106–107** Comstock Images/Alamy Stock Photo, (bkgd) McGraw-Hill Education; **108** Library of Congress Prints and Photographs Division [LC-USZ62-114745]; **108–109** DNY59/E+/ Getty Images, (bkgd)McGraw-Hill Education; **109** Library of Congress Prints and Photographs Division [LC-DIGggbain-30939]; **112** (tl)Image Source/Getty Images, (br)Bettmann/Getty Images; **113** DNY59/E+/Getty Images; **115** Library of Congress Prints and Photographs Division [LC-DIG-ggbain-31219]; **116–117** (bkgd)Paolo De Santis/123RF; **117** (l)LightField Studios/Shutterstock, (tr)Estrada Anton/Shutterstock, (br)Steve Debenport/E+/Getty Images; **133** Library of Congress Prints and Photographs Division [LC-DIG-hec-47244]; **164** (l)Ingram Publishing, (r)Library of Congress Prints & Photographs Division [LC-DIG-ppprs-00626]; **164–165** (bkgd)Wilbur and Orville Wright Papers, Manuscript Division, Library of Congress; **165** (t)U.S. Air Force photo, (b)Wilbur and Orville Wright Papers, Manuscript Division, Library of Congress; **166–167** (bkgd)National Park Service; **167** Michelle Malven/ iStock/Getty Images; **173** Library of Congress Prints and Photographs Division [LC-DIG-ppprs-00603]; **194** NASA; **196** NASA; **197** NASA; **198** NASA; **199** NASA; **200** Purestock/ SuperStock; **201** Human Space Flight/Johnson Space Center/ NASA; **202** NASA; **203** NASA; **204** NASA; **207** NASA; **208–209** NASA/MSFC; **210** NASA; **211** NASA; **212** NASA; **213** NASA; **215** NASA; **217** NASA/Bill Ingalls; **218** NASA; **221** NASA/Joel Kowsky; **222–223** (bkgd)Jongcheol Park/EyeEm/Getty Images; **223** (l) The George F. Landegger Collection of Alabama Photographs in Carol M. Highsmith's America, LOC Prints and Photographs Division, (tr)R_Litewriter/iStock/Getty Images, (br)Andrew Bret Wallis/Digital Vision/Getty Images; **239** Courtesy of The United States Mint; **256** U.S. National Archives and Records Administration [299998]; **258** Dan Thornberg/iStockphoto/Getty Images; **259** (t)Library of Congress Prints and Photographs Division [LC-DIG-pga-08284], (b)Francis Miller/The LIFE Picture Collection/Getty Images; **283** Courtesy National Gallery of Art, Washington - Patrons' Permanent Fund; **284** Catholic University of America: Terence Vincent Powderly Photographic Prints Collection, The American Catholic History Research Center and University Archives, Washington, D.C.; **285** (l)Library of Congress, Prints & Photographs Division, LC-USZ62-20622, (r) Library of Congress, Prints & Photographs Division, LC-DIG-ggbain-01561; **287** Courtesy of National Park Service: Statue of Liberty National Monument; **289** Library of Congress, Prints & Photographs Division, LC-USZ62-95431; **291** Library of Congress, Prints & Photographs Division, LC-USZ62-40103; **293** Library of Congress, Prints & Photographs Division, LC-USZ62-68281; **294** Courtesy of National Park Service: Statue of Liberty National Monument; **296** Gwenyth Swain; **298** Courtesy of National Park Service: Statue of Liberty National Monument; **301** Library of Congress, Prints and Photographs Division [LC-USZ62-116221].; **323** Library of Congress Prints and Photographs Division [LC-U9-37548-29/29A]; **341** (l)Andrezej Wojcicki/Mopic/Alamy Stock Photo, (c)Alchemy/Alamy Stock Photo, (r)NPS photo; **342–343** (bkgd)Ingram Publishing; **343** (l)